£1

Penguin Education x59

Public Enterprise

Penguin Modern Economic Readings

General Editor
B. J. McCormick

Advisory Board
K. J. W. Alexander
R. W. Clower
J. Spraos
H. Townsend

D0928411

Public Enterprise

Selected Readings

Edited by R. Turvey

Penguin Books

Penguin Books Ltd, Harmondsworth,
Middlesex, England
Penguin Books Inc., 7110 Ambassador Court,
Baltimore, Md 21207, U.S.A.
Penguin Books Australia Ltd, Ringwood,
Victoria, Australia

First published 1968

Made and printed in Great Britain by
Richard Clay (The Chaucer Press), Ltd.,
Bungay, Suffolk
Set in Monotype Times

Contents

Introduction

Since the economics of public enterprise is studied both for its own sake and as an exercise in the application of economic theory, the readings collected in this book have been chosen to suit both purposes and also to be of international interest. For this reason, material which is purely descriptive has been omitted, as have writings which are relevant only to a particular country.

The aim, then, is to provide some good examples of the application of economic analysis to problems of public enterprise. Most of these examples involve a mixture of welfare economics and operational research, since they are largely concerned with what to maximize (or minimize) and how to maximize it. Because it is public, what interests us about public enterprise is how it ought to behave. Thus we are not so much concerned with understanding its behaviour and making predictions as with criticizing and making recommendations. For this reason, some of the arguments presented in this book may arouse dissent, particularly the emphasis on marginal cost pricing which is not balanced by the presence of an attack upon it.

This has been done for the simple reason that the choice of items has been dictated more by a search for interest and quality than by an attempt at balance. A completely balanced selection would presumably require a classification of the subject into a set of topics and the allocation to each topic of a space proportioned to some notion of its intrinsic importance. The result would be boring and very uneven in quality, since some of the spaces could be filled only with second-rate or mainly descriptive material.

Perhaps the two main topics which are under-represented are the efficiency of public enterprises and their political and social objectives. It may well be that competent administration, good labour relations, and technical brillance on the part of public enterprise contribute more to economic growth than do the niceties of economic calculation. This book concentrates on the latter, however, an area in which economists have far more to say. Similarly, fiscal, regional, balance of payments, and social considerations may weigh more in policy-making than economic efficiency in the technical sense, but they arise in particular contexts and any general discussions of them are therefore fairly inconclusive. Two other topics which have been omitted are demand-forecasting, because there is nothing to differentiate it from forecasting undertaken by private enterprise, and the problem of public transport enterprises, since there is a separate volume in this series devoted to the economics of transport.

One of the readings in this book is by a non-economist. Economists seldom realize how much good work is done in their field by engineers and operational researchers. Many of the most interesting economic problems of public enterprises relate to operational and investment decisions. Economists tend to think of these as trivial and to subsume their solution in given cost or production functions, leading to oversimplification and disregard of a large body of knowledge. Econometric attempts to ascertain the presence and extent of economies of scale in electricity generation, for instance, have been a complete waste of time. However, planning engineers are directly concerned with this issue in so far as it is relevant to action, for their job lies in optimizing the expansion of an interconnected system. Thus an attempt to infer technology from *ex post* data, even if it were adequately sophisticated and even if it gave a clear result, would merely furnish out-of-date information about what was already known.

In preparing these readings I have been very much helped by the authors, several of whom have introduced necessary amendments to the original versions of their work.

Part One Principles of Optimal Pricing and Investment

All four articles in this section deal with general issues in theoretical terms and do not refer to individual problems of particular enterprises except by way of illustration. Mrs Ruggles' classic survey article, which comes first, was written nearly twenty years ago and naturally a good deal has appeared since then, particularly the theory of the second-best and the complications of peak-load pricing. Farrell's and Williamson's papers are self-contained expositions on these topics which build on the contributions of a number of other writers. Finally, Henderson's paper provides an up-to-date survey of recent extensive literature on investment criteria.

1 Nancy Ruggles

Recent Developments in the Theory of Marginal Cost Pricing

Nancy Ruggles, 'Recent developments in the theory of marginal cost pricing', *Review of Economic Studies*, vol. 17 (1949–50), pp. 107–26.

This paper is concerned with recent formulations of the marginal cost pricing principle, the controversy surrounding it, and an evaluation of the general argument in terms of its welfare basis.

Hotelling's statement of the marginal cost pricing principle

Most of the present-day discussions of marginal cost pricing take for their basis the work of Harold Hotelling.[1] His presentation consists of both a mathematical treatment of the problem and a detailed explanation of the implications of the principle. It is directed both toward those who understand an argument based on a rigorous mathematical proof and toward those who must be shown the common-sense applications. The following summary of Hotelling's view on marginal cost pricing will serve as a basis for the discussion of the marginal cost controversy which it evoked, and also as a starting point for the last section of this paper, the general evaluation of the marginal cost pricing thesis within the framework of the new welfare economics.

Hotelling did not refer at all to the development of the marginal cost pricing principle in the period just prior to that in which he wrote. Instead, he chose to go back to the work of an engineer, Jules Dupuit, who wrote on the subject of utility in about the year 1844, in connection with an analysis of such public works as roads and bridges.[2] Dupuit defined the total benefit of a public

1. Harold Hotelling, 'The general welfare in relation to problems of taxation and of railway and utility rates', *Econometrica*, vol. 6 (1938), pp. 242–69.

2. Collected and reprinted with comments by Mario di Bernardi & Luigi Einaudi: 'De l'utilité et de sa mèsure', *La Riforma Soziale*, Turin, 1932.

work such as a road or a bridge as the aggregate of the maximum prices which a perfectly discriminating monopolist could charge, equal to the costs of the best alternatives to its use. Applying this definition to the search for a method of maximizing the total benefit, he reasoned that charging a toll, however small, would cause some individuals to do without these services. The services of an already existing road or bridge have no real cost, so that any diminution in its use would represent a net loss of benefits. The greatest benefit would be obtained from a bridge if its services were free, and the higher the toll which was charged the greater would be the damage done. Dupuit's argument was based upon a concept of measurable utility and free interpersonal comparison, but Hotelling maintained that by virtue of the analysis made possible by modern mathematical methods the essence of Dupuit's propositions could be substantiated without any necessity for such dependence.

As a start on his modernization of Dupuit, Hotelling postulated an economy in which products are priced at marginal cost, and the difference between this amount and total cost is made up by taxation. He then derived algebraically the fundamental theorem that 'if a person must pay a certain sum of money in taxes, his satisfaction will be greater if the levy is made directly on him as a fixed amount than if it is made through a system of excise taxes which he can to some extent avoid by rearranging his production and consumption'. The truth of this theorem is evident, both from the mathematical proof and from an analysis of indifference curves. Hotelling then extended the analysis from one individual to the whole community, postulating that 'if government revenue is produced by any system of excise taxes, there exists a possible distribution of personal levies among the individuals of the community such that the abolition of the excise taxes and their replacement by these levies will yield the same revenue while leaving each person in a state more satisfactory to himself than before'. On this basis, he recommended a system of pricing at marginal cost. The deficits which would occur in decreasing cost industries should be made up out of the public treasury, he said, with the requisite funds collected by means of lump-sum taxes.

Hotelling next considered what sources of revenue are of the nature of lump-sum taxes, and whether such sources of revenue would be adequate to cover the deficits which would be incurred by decreasing cost industries as a result of the marginal cost pricing system. He recommended income taxes, taxes on inheritances, and taxes on the site value of land, since all of these, he said, are lump-sum taxes which do not affect the price of any commodity. There is also, he pointed out, one other source of revenue available to the State which would not impair the marginal conditions; this is to be found in the price of commodities available in limited quantity. Such a scarce commodity is space on trains during holiday periods. If the total demand for rail travel during the year is not sufficient to provide enough cars to accommodate all who wish to travel during holiday periods, the limited space in existing cars will acquire a rental value similar to that of land. The appropriate way to handle this situation is to set the price high enough to limit demand to the amount of space available. This solution, Hotelling said, would be more satisfactory than either permitting overcrowding or selling tickets at marginal cost only to those who happen to be first in line. Using these sources of revenue, Hotelling thought that it would always be possible to obtain enough revenue to finance the marginal cost pricing system. He recognized that for reasons of political expediency it may not be feasible to raise all of the revenue from these sources, so that excise taxes may have to be resorted to; in this event the excise taxes should be so distributed as to minimize the resulting loss. With an appropriate system of compensations and collections, Hotelling thus argued, a change from an average cost pricing system to the marginal cost pricing system can increase everyone's satisfaction.

Hotelling recognized that the 'system of collections and compensations' is an essential element if the change to marginal cost pricing is to increase everyone's satisfaction, but in practice he thought it probably would not be feasible to carry through all of the collections and compensations. The general well-being would have to be purchased at the expense of sacrifices by some. For example, it might be that the introduction of cheap electricity into a region would raise the level of its economic existence so much that the benefits received by the individuals in the region would far exceed the money cost of the development. Yet it might not be possible to devise a system of lump-sum taxes on the

13

inhabitants of the region which would cover total costs. Rather than forgo the investment, Hotelling argued, it would be better to sell the electricity at its marginal cost and make up the difference from revenues derived from other parts of the country – a procedure which, of course, involves a shift in the distribution of income. Hotelling defended his recommendation on the grounds that, in the first place, the benefits from such regional development are not confined to the area most immediately affected, and in the second place, considering many projects together the benefits of all of them may be so widespread that most persons in all parts of the country would be better off as a result of the programme as a whole. Hotelling believed that the latter condition would probably in general be met by a system of marginal cost pricing, although he recognized that at least two groups of persons – those in the highest income groups and landowners – could be expected on balance to suffer a loss.

In order to illustrate the application of marginal cost pricing, Hotelling considered two cases, one relating to tolls on bridges and the other to railway rates. With respect to bridges, for the use of which marginal cost is zero, Hotelling pointed out, as Dupuit originally had, that the bridge will be used more if there are no tolls and the cost is paid by taxes on the site value of land and on incomes and inheritances. If the bridge services are not sold at marginal cost, i.e. if tolls are charged, the total amount of benefit will be decreased by the decreased use. The returns to society will be greater if the bridge is financed by either land or income taxes, for then only the distribution of income will be affected, not its total amount. It is sometimes argued, Hotelling said, that if tolls are not charged the benefits will go to people who do not pay for them, whereas those whose taxes do pay for the bridge do not necessarily benefit from it, and furthermore that payment for the bridge by tolls would injure no one since everyone who uses the bridge does so willingly and is better off thereby. But, he replied, the surrounding landowners may also have benefited from the increase in land values occasioned by the bridge, and the bridge would get very much more use if it were free. The attempt to make such projects self-liquidating, he maintained, will greatly reduce the total benefit.

The railroad rate case is similar. The current running costs of railroads are only a small fraction of their total costs, and the actual extra costs of marginal use are even smaller. In a rational economic system, Hotelling said, rates should be set in such a fashion that they would even out the traffic over the year, ensuring full utilization of capacity at all times. In practice, he argued, the exact opposite is true, and furthermore both freight and passenger rates are extremely complex and remote from marginal cost. The present rate structures are presumably based on the estimated elasticity of the different demands, but it cannot be assumed, Hotelling maintained, that the rate differentials have been determined accurately even for the purpose of maximizing revenue, much less for that of maximizing utility. And from the point of view of the users of the railroads the very complexity of the rates is an impediment to the accurate distribution of budgets so as to maximize satisfactions.

Hotelling admitted that a number of problems would arise in an actual application of marginal cost pricing. Aside from the purely technical problems of determining costs (which it is assumed could be solved) problems of interpretation would also exist. For instance, when a train is completely full the marginal cost of carrying an additional passenger is equal to the cost of running another train, but in the more normal situation when a train is not full the extra cost of carrying an extra passenger is very small. A sharp increase in rates to the unlucky first passenger on each train can be avoided by an averaging of rates according to the probability of having to run another train. If it is not feasible to run another train, a fare should be charged (as was pointed out above) which is of sufficient magnitude to distinguish between the purchasers, enabling those who are willing to pay the most to ride.

A second special problem arising with respect to expenditures which are not for consumption. The usual criterion for private investment is whether or not it will pay for itself, but this criterion obviously becomes inapplicable with marginal cost pricing. Hotelling offered instead the criterion that the investment should be undertaken if some distribution of the burden is possible such that everyone concerned would be better off than without the new investment. He stressed that it is not necessary that any such distribution of the burden be practicable, but did agree that compensation should be paid to those who are injured by the new investment when the failure to compensate would cause undue hardship. Anticipating the objection that the overhead of an industry must be met in order to determine whether the investment was a wise policy, Hotelling maintained that such a method of testing is absurd. The question of whether it was wise to build the Union Pacific Railroad is an interesting historical problem, but the attempt to solve it now by charging rates high above marginal cost is too costly, since it may in the process ruin the territory the Union Pacific was designed to serve. Furthermore, it would probably give the wrong answer, since what a perfectly discriminating monopolist would charge and what the Union Pacific can charge are two entirely different matters. It would be far better, he said, to operate the railroads for the benefit of the present-day population, and let dead men and dead investments lie in their graves. It may well be that under present conditions no distribution of the burden exists which would make the investment in a particular railroad worth while, but this does not mean that it would be wise to let the investment, which has already been made, go unutilized.

This is Hotelling's presentation of the marginal cost pricing principle, with the reasoning which supports it. As such, it constitutes the credo of those who advocate marginal cost pricing on the grounds of the new welfare economics. Hotelling's position actually represents one of the more conservative statements of the principle, and he took care to protect himself on a number of issues regarding which some of his followers have not been as careful. Few, if any, of the advocates of the marginal cost pricing principle have taken a less extreme position on the issue than has Hotelling, and for this reason its fate may legitimately be identified with the fate of his presentation of it.

The marginal cost pricing controversy

Up to 1938, the development of the marginal cost pricing principle had for the most part been on a highly theoretical plane concerned with the basic welfare principles, with some attention to the problems of designing an optimum price system for a socialist state. At about this time, the emphasis of the discussion shifted to more concrete considerations of pricing systems. This shift was to a large extent due to Hotelling, since much of the later work in the field was stimulated by his article.

Almost simultaneously with the appearance of Hotelling's article, however, at least one other writer was advocating that marginal cost pricing be applied in specific situations. R. H. Montgomery, in two articles on government ownership and operation of railroads and electric utilities,[3] independently reached almost the same conclusions as Hotelling, although the basis of his reasoning was essentially the welfare economics of Marshall and Pigou rather than the 'new' welfare economics. On the basis of his analysis, he recommended that both of the industries he discussed charge only incremental costs (i.e. price at marginal cost), without attempting to maximize profits.

One of the earliest comments specifically directed at Hotelling's article was Frisch's.[4] He raised four objections. In the first place, he undertook to demonstrate that it was not necessary for prices actually to equal marginal cost provided they were proportional to it. Hotelling, in his reply to Frisch,[5] agreed that proportionality is all that would be necessary. But, as a number of people, including Lerner[6] and Samuelson,[7] have since pointed out, Frisch and Hotelling were both wrong on this point. Exact equality really is necessary for consistency in the system as a whole, taking account of the prices of the factors of production. It is apparent that if the prices of consumers' goods were not equal to marginal cost, but factor payments were maintained equal to the marginal products of the factors, the relationship between work and leisure would be altered and the marginal conditions throughout the system would not be met. On the other hand, if prices of factors

3. R. H. Montgomery, 'Government ownership and operation of Railroads', *The Annals of the American Academy of Political and Social Science*, vol. 201 (1939), pp. 137–45; and 'Government ownership and operation of the electric industry', ibid., pp. 43–9.

4. Ragnar Frisch, 'The Dupuit taxation theorem', *Econometrica*, vol. 7 (1939), pp. 145–50; and 'A further note on the Dupuit taxation theorem', ibid., pp. 156–7.

5. H. Hotelling, 'The relation of prices to marginal costs in an optimum system', *Econometrica*, vol. 7 (1939), pp. 151–5.

6. A. P. Lerner, *The economics of control*, New York, 1944, pp. 102–4.

7. P. A. Samuelson, *The foundations of economic analysis*, Cambridge, 1947, p. 240.

as well as finished goods were all raised proportionally, nothing would be accomplished; it would still be found that prices were *equal* to marginal costs. In his reply to Frisch, Hotelling did recognize in connection with another point that an income tax is an excise tax on a factor of production, but he never fully integrated this point into the proof that *equality* of price to marginal cost is necessary.

The second objection which Frisch raised related to Hotelling's criterion of the welfare of the country as a whole. Hotelling advocated marginal cost pricing on the ground that it would increase the general welfare, even though he admitted that some classes would lose by it. Frisch correctly drew attention to the fact that this conclusion is at variance with Hotelling's original definition of welfare, which had been taken over from Pareto and was designed to avoid the need for interpersonal comparisons. Frisch pointed out that in the analysis of any change which would make the welfare indicators of different individuals move in different directions (which Hotelling admitted would happen as a result of the introduction of marginal cost pricing), no general indicator of welfare can be used without dependence upon interpersonal comparisons. For this reason, Frisch claimed that Hotelling's conclusions with regard to the desirability of marginal cost pricing do not follow from the mathematical propositions he had proved. In his first reply to Frisch, Hotelling did not answer this charge, and Frisch did not repeat it in his second note.

In addition to these two points, Frisch raised two more objections which Hotelling did effectively refute. First, Frisch maintained that there was nothing in the actual mathematics which related in any way to marginal cost. A non-proportional change in prices (i.e. by an excise tax), he said, would diminish satisfactions irrespective of whether or not marginal cost pricing was in effect before the imposition of the taxes. Hotelling showed in his second rejoinder [8] that the mathematical proof requires either that the original prices be set at marginal cost or that the quantities taken be completely unaffected by the change in price, and he considered the second alternative trivial. Secondly, Frisch argued that the gain in utility resulting from the government's spending the tax revenue should be taken into account, as well as the loss in

8. H. Hotelling, 'A final note', *Econometrica*, vol. 7 (1939), pp. 158–60

utility resulting from the tax itself. Hotelling rightly replied to this objection that his argument was concerned not with the question of whether the collection of any tax at all would increase welfare, but rather with the question of whether, once the amount to be collected had been determined on some other basis, welfare would be greater if it is collected by an income or an excise tax.

Unfortunately, not all of the other points which were made in the marginal cost controversy were as brief or as clear-cut as Frisch's. For instance, H. W. Robinson[9] entered the fray with great vigour, but the issue which he brought up was almost an irrelevant one. He was concerned about the fact that income taxes were collected at the end of the year, so that the consumer might have great difficulty in arranging his budget so as to maximize his satisfactions and still be able to meet the income tax at the end of the year. This difficulty, Robinson claimed, might more than offset the increase in welfare which would otherwise be expected to result from the substitution of income for excise taxes. The pertinence of this point is reduced, however, with the introduction of current payment income tax plans, and in any case it does not bear upon any of Hotelling's basic issues.

Not only negative reactions were stimulated by Hotelling's work; among writers in the field of public control and public utility economics, there were positive reactions as well.[10] No less an authority in the field than Bonbright hailed Hotelling's work as 'one of the most distinguished contributions to rate-making theory in the entire literature of economics'. Unfortunately, after this laudatory comment, Bonbright showed that he did not fully grasp the relation of Hotelling's marginal cost pricing principle to utility rate-making. He indicated that the striking discrepancies between marginal and average costs of public utilities are not due

9. H. W. Robinson, 'Consumer's surplus and taxation: Ex-ante or ex-post?', *South African Journal of Economics*, vol, 7 (1939), pp. 270–80.

10. J. C. Bonbright, 'Major controversies as to the criteria of reasonable public utility rates', *Papers and Proceedings of the American Economic Association*, vol. 30 (1940), pp. 379–89.

Donald Wallace, 'Kinds of public control to replace or supplement anti-trust laws', *Papers and Proceedings of the American Economic Association*, vol. 29 (1939), pp. 194–212; and Temporary National Economic Committee, *Economic Standards of Government Price Control* (Monograph no. 32, Senate Committee Print, 76th Congress, 3rd Session, 1941), esp. pp. 414–15.

primarily to long-run increasing costs, but rather to the temporary or chronic presence of excess plant capacity. Thus, according to Bonbright, it is not the difference between long-run average and marginal cost which makes average cost pricing unsatisfactory, but rather the existence of off-peak periods in the short-run. Bonbright did not seem to realize that Hotelling's marginal cost pricing thesis does not necessarily imply the use of the same rate for both peak and off-peak periods. Hotelling's system adequately allowed for short-run problems of this nature by the use of commodity rents. He had recommended adjusting prices in such a way as to even out peak loads, by charging a rent in addition to marginal cost whenever the demand at marginal cost would exceed the available supply. Bonbright's misinterpretation of Hotelling's thesis again resulted from the misunderstanding of long- and short-run marginal cost.

This prevalent confusion between long- and short-run marginal cost was pointed out by E. W. Clemens,[11] in an article on the subject of price discrimination in decreasing cost industries. He showed that Montgomery had misunderstood the nature of marginal costs when he laid down the principle that the extension of capacity should continue 'as long as the output which would be taken at incremental cost can be produced at lower average cost'.[12] Clemens showed that since the lowest point on the long-run average cost curve coincides with both the long- and short-run marginal cost curves, only the single criterion of marginal cost is needed, and the condition that average cost be a minimum is superfluous. However, Clemens vigorously dissented from both Montgomery's and Hotelling's conclusions that pricing at marginal cost is the only satisfactory solution. He maintained that this solution is necessary only if a one-price system is postulated, but that a system of price discrimination could also arrive at the point of ideal output. He had no adequate discussion of what he meant by price discrimination, however; apparently he believed that the use of a block system of rates could achieve the ideal solution. This argument is not necessarily valid, since the use of block rates for different customers could violate the marginal

11. E. W. Clemens, 'Price discrimination in decreasing cost industries', *American Economic Review*, vol. 31 (1941), pp. 794–802.

12. R. H. Montgomery, loc. cit., p. 143.

conditions for some of the customers. Hotelling had recognized that perfect price discrimination would satisfy the marginal conditions, but rejected it on the basis of its impossibility in actual practice. To be consistent, Clemens would have had either to advocate perfect price discrimination or to maintain that discontinuities in demand exist such that the use of block rates will not lessen the total amount bought by each consumer below that which would be bought at marginal cost.

Further exploration of price discrimination as an alternative to marginal cost pricing was undertaken by W. A. Lewis.[13] The conclusions Lewis reached are similar to those Clemens had arrived at. In addition, he went on to point out that the issue between the marginal cost pricing system and price discrimination is one of social justice, not economics – but he did not explain what he meant by this statement. He also said that in peak periods the proper rate should not be determined by the previous level of marginal cost, but rather by whatever can be obtained maintaining capacity operation, thus agreeing with Hotelling's commodity rent principle.

The final contribution of the public utility economists to the controversy was an exchange between Emery Troxel and D. F. Pegrum.[14] Pegrum pointed out that 'the equating of gains to consumers against the losses of those called upon to bear the fixed costs would not represent any problem if the consumers and taxpayers were identical and if their incomes were the same or inequalities a matter of indifference'. This is, of course, the same objection to marginal cost pricing as that raised by Frisch in mathematical terms. Troxel's answer on this point was that he recognized that 'the public authorities cannot always accept dispassionate reasoning when they want to stay alive politically'. In other words, Troxel refused to admit that the conclusions of

13. W. A. Lewis, 'The two-part tariff', and 'The two-part tariff: A reply', *Economica*, N.S. vol. 8 (1941), pp. 249–70 and 399–408.

14. E. Troxel, 'Incremental cost determination of utility prices', *Journal of Land and Public Utility Economics*, vol. 18 (1942), pp. 458–67; vol. 19 (1943), pp. 28–39, 292–9.

D. F. Pegrum, 'Incremental cost pricing: A comment', *Journal of Land and Public Utility Economics*, vol. 20 (1944), pp. 58–60.

E. Troxel, 'Incremental cost pricing: A further comment', *Journal of Land and Public Utility Economics*, vol. 20 (1944), pp. 60–63.

the marginal cost pricing system involve any logical problem of interpersonal comparison.

It was not only the public utility economists who took part in the controversy on marginal cost pricing in this period. An examination of some of the budgetary implications of the marginal cost pricing principle was carried out by J. E. Meade, along with the development of a criterion of price and output policy for state enterprise.[15] Meade stated that it is entirely possible for the operation of socialized industries at marginal cost to involve losses commensurate with the total income earned on property in the rest of the economy. At this point Meade recognized what Hotelling had ignored: that if the amount of funds which must be raised is substantial, the necessary income tax might have to be high enough to interfere seriously with the achievement of the best balance between work and leisure. This point is an important qualification to Hotelling's thesis that income taxes are superior in all instances to divergence from the marginal cost conditions elsewhere in the economy. For this reason, Meade felt that the operation of decreasing cost industries at marginal cost should be accompanied by some measure of public ownership of property.

In answer to Meade's proposals for public ownership, J. M. Fleming brought up several points, some of which are valid and some are not.[16] First, he pointed out that increasing cost industries which operate to capacity will cover their overhead and in addition may yield competitive rents; for this reason it is not true that all of the overhead in the economy will have to be subsidized. Meade, in his reply, recognized this point as valid, and admitted that he had not considered the possibility of marginal cost curves becoming discontinuous at capacity. A second point made by Fleming, one which is much less well taken, was that a general indirect tax on all output would have no net effects on incentive or income distribution since it is only necessary for price to be proportional to marginal cost, not equal to it. Meade, in his reply, agreed, but, as has been pointed out above, the point is not valid. The Fleming proposition of a general indirect tax on output is in

15. J. E. Meade, 'Price and output policy of state enterprise', *Economic Journal*, vol. 54 (1944), pp. 321–28; 'Rejoinder', pp. 337–9.

16. J. M. Fleming, 'Price and output policy of state enterprise: A comment', *Economic Journal*, vol. 54 (1944), pp. 328–37.

effect an expenditures tax; it not only has the defects outlined in the discussion of Frisch, but in addition would violate the marginal conditions between spending and saving.

A. P. Lerner, in *The economics of control*,[17] developed the theory of marginal cost pricing in a more general form than had until then been done. He recognized the necessity for meeting all of the marginal conditions, including those of work and leisure – but then, having recognized it, he proceeded to erect a structure which does not meet it. As Samuelson has pointed out, it is not easy to devise a tax or subsidy which will not affect the marginal conditions, so that it is extremely difficult to change the distribution of income from that which a pricing system automatically yields without violating the marginal conditions. Taxes cannot be related to actual performance, since this will alter the relation between work and leisure;[18] instead they would have to be adjusted to an individual's capabilities or potentialities, and as Lerner himself seems to realize, this would be an impossible task. But Lerner was not willing to accept the income distribution which would necessarily result from his system as socially right or desirable; in Chapter 3 he advocated equality of income among individuals. Whether he intended to achieve this equality of income by departing from marginal productivity as the criterion of wage payments or by superimposing a system of income taxes and subsidies is not made clear, but in either case the end result would be the same. The marginal conditions relating to the factors of production would not be met – and the failure in this case would be great enough so that it would certainly affect the supply of the factors. In Lerner's system, therefore, the allocation mechanism for labour (as well as for the other factors) would tend to break down, since no means would be available to lure labour from one occupation to another. If, as Lerner advocated, all money incomes were equal, people would choose the work they preferred, or for that matter no work at all, and there would be a scarcity of labour for unpleasant or tedious jobs. Thus for Lerner, as for the other advocates of marginal cost pricing, the problem of obtaining the desired income distribution

17. pp. 174–240.
18. A somewhat similar point is made by J. E. Meade, in his review of Lerner's book, *Economic Journal*, vol. 55, pp. 47–69.

would interfere with satisfying the marginal conditions of work and leisure.

A practical question concerning the workability of marginal cost pricing was brought up at about this time by T. Wilson.[19] He raised the objection that in making investment decisions under the marginal cost pricing system there would be no test of the accuracy of the forecast. Hotelling, of course, covered this question from a theoretical point of view when he said that there is little interest in the wisdom of making an investment after it has been made, since then the question is purely academic. But as Wilson pointed out, it is true that past experience can provide a guide for the laying of future plans. A successful enterprise of one type encourages duplication, whereas one that is a failure serves as a warning. Requiring an investment to pay for itself is undoubtedly over-conservative, but where estimation of the outcome is difficult Wilson felt that some such criterion is necessary.

Another dissent from the view of Meade, Fleming, and Lerner was expressed by R. H. Coase.[20] Coase did not disagree with the thesis that price should equal marginal cost, but argued that total cost would also have to be covered if there was not to be a redistribution of income in favour of the consumers of products in which fixed costs form a high proportion of total costs. He was in effect again pointing out that marginal cost pricing without compensation leads to a change in the income distribution, so its result cannot be compared in welfare terms with that of average cost pricing. The method of exposition is different, but the argument is essentially the same as that set forth by Frisch and Pegrum. Correct price discrimination, Coase said, would permit both the marginal and the total conditions to be met – but the advocates of marginal cost pricing would probably reply to this that in practice price discrimination could not be correctly adjusted to meet the marginal conditions and that, therefore, its abolition in favour of marginal cost pricing would increase welfare.

19. T. Wilson, 'Price and output policy of state enterprise: A comment' *Economic Journal*, vol. 50 (1945), pp. 454–61.

20. R. H. Coase, 'Price and output policy of state enterprise: A comment' *Economic Journal*, vol. 55 (1945), pp. 112–13.

Coase further extended his arguments against marginal cost pricing in a later article.[21] In this article, he developed an example of a situation in which average costs are different from marginal costs, yet all costs are directly assignable to specific consumers. The example is that of purchases from a centrally located store by customers located in a radial pattern, so that delivery to each customer must be made individually. The cost of supplying goods to any customer would then be the store cost of the goods plus the cost of delivery. Together these make up total cost. The charge, he argued, should be a delivery fee plus the store cost of the goods. This device Coase referred to as multi-part pricing. He maintained that Hotelling and Lerner had overlooked this possibility in favour of a system in which all delivery charges would be paid by the public at large through taxation. The adoption of the marginal cost pricing system, he said, would involve a redistribution in favour of those to whom the cost of delivery was greatest – i.e. those who lived farthest away.

Two fundamental conditions for an optimum pricing system were laid down in this article. In the first place, Coase said, for each individual consumer the same factor should have the same price wherever it is employed or else the price system will misallocate resources, i.e. the usual marginal conditions of production and exchange must be satisfied. In the second place, Coase said that the price of a factor should be the same for all consumers, since otherwise one consumer would be obtaining more for the same amount of money than another consumer. This is the first instance in which the criterion of price uniformity had been held up as a welfare principle. Coase used it because of his concept of the distribution of income; he stipulated uniform prices to different consumers so that the distribution of money income would be equivalent to the distribution of income in terms of the factors of production. (In no place has he recognized that the question of the utility of the income is also relevant.) But this stipulation of uniform prices is inconsistent with Coase's own earlier statement that correct price discrimination would meet both the marginal and the total conditions. Multi-part pricing, Coase maintained, would satisfy both the marginal conditions

21. R. H. Coase, 'The marginal cost controversy', *Economica*, N.S. vol. 13 (1946), pp. 169–82.

and the criterion of uniform factor pricing, and Hotelling and Lerner, by considering only average and marginal cost pricing, omitted the one satisfactory solution.

With respect to the alternative merits of marginal and average cost pricing, Coase emphasised that both systems have advantages and disadvantages. He recognized that if consumers are not allowed to buy additional units at marginal cost there will be a maldistribution of the factors of production, and he also admitted that production which is worth undertaking can sometimes be carried out with marginal cost pricing when it could not with average cost pricing. The disadvantages of marginal cost pricing lie, according to him, in the fact that the income taxes which must be levied to subsidize the decreasing cost industries impose a tax on effort and on waiting, and in the fact that taxing some individuals to provide factors of production for the use of other individuals involves a redistribution of income which cannot be avoided in any way except by levying excise taxes on the products of decreasing cost industries – a self-defeating measure, since it would only result in a return to average cost pricing. With reference to investment, Coase repeated the objections originally raised by Wilson that the market test is necessary as a guide, even if it is more conservative than might be wished. Finally, Coase claimed that the marginal cost pricing principle destroys the guide to policy, making it exceedingly easy to make errors.

Considerable controversy was stirred up by this article of Coase's. Both G. F. Thirlby[22] and H. Norris[23] criticized the multi-part pricing solution on the ground of its limited applicability. Thirlby suggested that Coase discuss certain elements which are inherent in the multi-part pricing model, for instance, the costs of administration and credit, which create problems if such costs are to be included as a part of charges made to individual purchasers. Norris also pointed out that it is the common or joint costs which cause the trouble. J. A. Nordin,[24] in another reply to Coase, suggested again that it was not necessary to have prices equal to

22. G. F. Thirlby, 'The marginal cost controversy: A note on Mr Coase's model', *Economica*, N.S. vol. 14 (1947), pp. 48–53.

23. H. Norris, 'State enterprise and output policy and the problem of cost imputation', *Economica*, N.S. vol. 14 (1947), pp. 54–62.

24. J. A. Nordin, 'The marginal cost controversy: A reply', *Economica*, N.S. vol. 14 (1947), pp. 134–49.

marginal cost, provided they were proportional to it. Coase[25] rightly criticized Nordin for this statement, and in addition pointed out that such a price system would still alter the distribution of income in favour of those consuming the products of decreasing cost industries.

Most of the participants in the discussion on the general merits of marginal cost pricing implicitly agreed with Hotelling that the income tax provided the best method of raising revenue to finance the marginal cost pricing system. One or two people – Meade, for example – had realized that if the amounts in question were large the departure from the marginal conditions on the factor side occasioned by the use of the income tax might be serious, but in general very little attention was paid to this aspect of the problem. At the same time, however, a parallel discussion was going on which was not concerned with the issue of marginal cost pricing at all, but dealt solely with the problem of the alternative merits of the income and excise tax.[26] Hotelling, in agreement with the whole classical theory of taxation, had assumed that an income tax would in welfare terms be exactly the same as a lump-sum tax. It was now shown by a number of writers that under certain circumstances excise taxes are not more burdensome to the individual than are income taxes. H. P. Wald's demonstration of the question is perhaps the clearest. He pointed out again that, unlike a lump-sum tax, an income tax is an excise tax on work. In cases where a commodity excise tax does not affect the amount which is purchased, such a commodity excise tax will therefore be superior to an income tax. An excise tax upon a commodity whose demand is inelastic with respect to both price and income would fulfil this condition, and would therefore be less burdensome than an income tax which produced an economic effect by

25. R. H. Coase, 'The marginal cost controversy: Some further comments', *Economica*, N.S. vol. 14 (1947), pp. 150–53.

26. H. P. Wald, 'The classical indictment of indirect taxation', *Quarterly Journal of Economics*, vol. 59 (1945), pp. 577–96. Wald examines the conventional treatment of this subject given by J. R. Hicks (*Value and Capital*, pp. 40–41); Ursula Hicks (*The finance of British government*, 1920–36, p. 254); and M. W. F. Joseph ('The excess burden of indirect taxation', *Review of Economic Studies*, vol. 6 (1939), pp. 226–31). He points out that all of these analyses neglect the effect of the income tax upon the marginal conditions of work and leisure.

altering the marginal conditions between work and leisure. Hotelling's implicit assumption that what he had proved mathematically for a lump-sum tax would also hold for income taxes is therefore untenable; following Wald's analysis, there may exist a number of types of excise taxes which are superior to general income taxes in terms of welfare.

One of the most complete discussions of marginal cost pricing, aside from Lerner's, is to be found in Melvin Reder's book on welfare economics.[27] There is, however, an implicit contradiction in Reder's work. First, as has been pointed out earlier, he maintained that the existence of the possibility of paying compensation to those harmed by a given class of reorganization is not sufficient; this compensation must actually be paid if the economist is to be able to advocate policies on welfare grounds. The economist's entire argument for the policy, he said, may be formally incorrect if compensation is not paid.[28] But, on the other hand, in his discussion of monopoly he indicated several times that the introduction of marginal cost pricing will increase welfare, since compensation *could* be paid.[29] He did not anywhere in this section indicate that the compensation must be paid before any judgment can be made about the change in welfare. Yet, if a new product priced at marginal cost and requiring subsidization were brought on to the market, people who were taxed but did not consume the product would suffer. According to Reder's compensation principle, it would seem that the taxes should be borne only by those who consume the product – but, as Coase has pointed out, an excise tax on these commodities would only result in raising the price back to average cost. Reder got out of this dilemma by using a partial analysis which failed to consider the source of the funds with which to subsidize the decreasing cost industries.

One of the most recent contributions to the literature of this field is an article by William Vickrey.[30] This article considered a number of diverse objections to marginal cost pricing, in the end

27. M. W. Reder, *Studies in the theory of welfare economics*, New York, 1947.

28. p. 97.

29. pp. 51, 52, 54.

30. William Vickrey, 'Some objections to marginal cost pricing', *Journal of Political Economy*, vol. 56 (1948).

disposing of all of them. One of these related to the problem of making investment decisions under a marginal cost pricing system. This problem arises, he said, not because of the use of marginal cost pricing, but because of the existence of decreasing cost industries. In these industries, average cost pricing does not provide an adequate guide for investment decisions either, since average cost pricing would prevent many worth while projects from being undertaken. Vickrey also considered price discrimination as an alternative means of reaching an optimum, but concluded that although price discrimination would represent an improvement over average cost pricing, it still would result in a failure to meet the marginal conditions for some people, and therefore would not achieve a proper allocation of resources. Finally, Vickrey argued that marginal cost is in most cases no more elusive as a basis for pricing than average cost – a point which is probably well taken. In this article again, marginal cost pricing was advocated without any examination of the source or nature of the subsidies it would require, even though there is an implicit assumption that whatever method is used to obtain the subsidies will meet the marginal conditions. The use of the concept of consumers' surplus was an important part of Vickrey's discussion; in fact, his treatment was much closer to that of Pigou than it was to the later welfare economists.

Such is the history of the marginal cost controversy. It is apparent that not all of the contributors to it have had an adequate appreciation of the previous development of welfare economics in general or the marginal cost pricing principle in particular. For the most part the contributions of the mathematical economists have not been integrated with those of the non-mathematical economists, and those in the special field of public utilities have not been completely aware of the theoretical framework within which the discussion was set by the other writers. More than anyone else, Samuelson has adequately covered all of the major points at issue. These points appear in scattered form throughout Samuelson's discussion of welfare economics, but they are not integrated into a form which would show their relevance to questions of pricing policy. To the casual observer, the whole controversy may seem to have lacked any common ground, or to have failed to reach any accepted

29

conclusion. Yet as a result of it, the advocates of marginal cost pricing have gained a large following – larger, in all probability, than that of their opponents. The following section will bring together the threads of the story, and will attempt to evaluate its contribution to the theory of the operation of different pricing systems as mechanisms for resource allocation.

Summary and Evaluation

The advocates of marginal cost pricing maintain that in any situation in which all prices are not equal to marginal cost the general welfare can be increased by setting these prices equal to marginal cost. Furthermore, they say that this conclusion can be reached without requiring any judgments comparing the utilities of different persons. This claim for the superiority of marginal cost pricing is based on the argument that it meets the marginal conditions for maximizing welfare, and that for this reason it represents an optimum. In evaluating marginal cost pricing, it is therefore necessary to consider three questions: (*a*) Is meeting these marginal conditions a sufficient basis for recommending a pricing system? (*b*) Does the marginal cost pricing system meet these marginal conditions? (*c*) Does the marginal cost pricing system, in fact, avoid any necessity for interpersonal comparisons? This paper has surveyed the literature dealing with these questions; it will now be useful to summarize briefly the findings of this literature.

Summary

The use of marginal analysis for reaching a maximum is, of course, a fundamental part of the methodology of economic analysis. In one form or another it has been applied to the specific field of welfare economics from almost the earliest writers in this field onward. Pigou and Wicksell, on the one hand, and Pareto and Barone on the other, firmly established marginal analysis as a tool for finding a maximum of the social welfare. The marginal conditions in relation to welfare have by now been developed to a great degree of refinement by a number of the mathematical economists. Bergson, Lange, Samuelson, and Arrow have all contributed to this development. As is true with any marginal analysis, however, it must be remembered that the marginal conditions provide a mechanism for finding a relative maximum, but not an absolute maximum. Within this limitation, the literature which has been discussed in the preceding part of this paper adequately demonstrates that, other things being equal, a pricing system which meets the marginal conditions will yield greater welfare than a pricing system which fails to meet the marginal conditions.

Marginal cost pricing is supported on the ground that it would meet these marginal conditions, and so would yield a maximum of welfare. This is the argument that has been put forth throughout the development of the marginal cost pricing principle, from its first appearance in Dickinson's article through the work of Lerner, Meade, and Lange, to Hotelling, and on through Troxel, Reder, and finally Vickrey. To the extent that prices are actually set equal to marginal cost, it is obvious that marginal cost pricing will meet the marginal conditions. But, although the argument has sometimes been left at this point, the question is not so simple. Marginal cost pricing would, of course, make necessary the payment of subsidies to producers with decreasing costs, since otherwise they could not cover their total costs. Before the system can be considered complete, some consideration must be given to the method of financing these subsidies. Many of the supporters of marginal cost pricing have failed to consider this question. Lerner and Meade among the earlier writers, Troxel among the public utility economists, and more recently Reder and Vickrey, all fall into this group. All of their arguments are partial, since they do not provide any mechanism in their systems for supplying the revenue necessary to finance the subsidies. A number of writers have considered this necessity for financing the system, however, and a number of suggestions have been made.

In the first place, it has been suggested that the need for subsidies can be avoided altogether, by making prices proportional to rather than equal to marginal cost. The marginal conditions of exchange will be just as well satisfied, it is argued, and at the same time it will be possible to cover total cost. This view was put forth by Frisch in his reply to Hotelling, and agreed to by the latter. It was again proposed by Fleming in answer to Meade, and Meade agreed. Finally, it was suggested by Nordin in reply to Coase. But the fallacy of the argument has also repeatedly been pointed out, among others, by Lerner, Samuelson, and Coase. Unless the prices paid to the factors of production, as well as the prices paid for consumers' goods, are included in the set which is raised proportionally to marginal cost, the marginal conditions with respect to the factors of production will be violated. If factor prices as well as commodity prices are included, nothing will be accomplished by the proportional increase; it will be found that marginal costs will have risen in the same proportion and that prices will still be equal to marginal costs.

Hotelling's original presentation of the marginal cost pricing thesis included the provision that the necessary revenue be raised by taxes on inheritances, rent of land, and incomes, since, he argued, all of these are lump-sum taxes and therefore would not interfere with the marginal conditions. A true lump-sum tax is by definition one which falls on either producers' or consumers' surplus, and therefore does not violate the marginal conditions. Taxes on inheritances and taxes on the rent of land in all probability do fall into this category, and should the revenue derivable from them be sufficient to meet the subsidies, Hotelling's system would meet the marginal conditions. But even Hotelling does not expect this to be true, and income taxes are a different matter. As Meade and Samuelson have pointed out, income taxes are in effect excise taxes on the supply of certain factors of production, and if they are at all substantial they will prevent the marginal conditions of production from being met. Coase has also pointed out that income taxes are, as he put it, taxes on effort and on waiting. Finally, Wald has demonstrated not only that the income tax will violate the marginal conditions, but furthermore that in certain instances excise taxes on specific commodities would diminish the welfare of the individual paying the tax less than would a generalized income tax.

Finally, because of this difficulty in raising the revenue required to finance the subsidies, pricing systems which would in themselves meet total costs have been proposed as alternatives to marginal cost pricing. Price discrimination, for instance, was suggested by Clemens, Lewis, and Coase. Coase also offered multipart pricing, but it was quickly pointed out that the latter covered only a very special case. All such proposals, of course, represent departures from marginal cost pricing. For the most part, they have been rejected by the advocates of marginal cost pricing on the grounds of complexity and impossibility of actual operation. It thus becomes apparent that none of the variants of the marginal cost pricing system which have as yet been proposed actually do meet all of the marginal conditions for maximizing welfare. And, furthermore, it has been shown by some writers that it is not necessarily more important, from the point of view of increasing welfare, to meet the marginal conditions relating to the pricing of consumers' goods than it is to meet those conditions relating to payments to the factors of production.

The question which remains to be considered is that of whether or not the marginal cost pricing principle can be supported without reliance on interpersonal comparisons of utility. The interpretation of this question has given rise to considerable difference of opinion. The early writers who set out to establish a welfare system which was independent of interpersonal judgments – Pareto and Barone – defined such a system as one in which decisions about specific measures could only be made if everyone who would lose as a result of each measure were fully compensated for his loss. It would not be sufficient, they said, to consider what the results of such compensation would be if it were made; it must actually be made. This view of the meaning of the compensation principle was maintained later by Harrod and Robbins. Kaldor and Hicks, on the other hand, suggested that it was not necessary actually to pay compensation to determine whether or not a given measure would be beneficial. If the measure would increase welfare with compensation paid, they said, it would also increase welfare even if the compensation were not paid, and requiring the payment of the compensation would constitute an undue sanctification of the *status quo*. Since the economist cannot decide without making interpersonal comparisons whether the income distribution which preceded the change or that which would result from it would be preferable, he cannot say that it would be better to pay the compensation, so returning to the initial distribution of income. This concept of the compensation principle was further refined and extended by Scitovszky, who, by introducing a double criterion of increased welfare, removed a certain degree of ambiguity from it. Since then, however, it has been effectively demonstrated by, among others, Samuelson, Reder, and Arrow that compensation must actually be paid if interpersonal comparisons are to be avoided. It is true that no choice can be made between the income distribution existing before a proposed change and that which would result afterward, but it is for this very reason that no opinion can be offered on the desirability of the change, unless the compensation necessary to return to the original income distribution is actually paid. As Samuelson has said, the economist cannot say that the change *should* be made and the compensation paid; he can only say that the change *could* be made and the compensation could be paid with an increase in welfare. He cannot say that it is better to pay the compensation than not to; he simply cannot say anything at all about the case in which compensation is not paid.

The advocates of marginal cost pricing have in general not explicitly discussed the question of interpersonal comparisons – except to the extent of stating that marginal cost pricing would not require them – and they have, therefore, never specified whether their arguments depend upon the looser or the stricter forms of compensation principle. But it is apparent that implicit in the arguments of virtually all of the proponents of marginal cost pricing (for instance, Meade, Lange, Hotelling, Reder, and Lerner) is the idea that it is only necessary that compensation be possible, not that it be paid, in order to be able to say that a change to the marginal cost pricing system is desirable. Hotelling came the closest to an explicit consideration of the matter, in his statement that certain groups in the economy would probably suffer as a result of the introduction of marginal cost pricing – namely, landowners and those in the upper income groups – but that the general well-being would have to be purchased at the cost of sacrifices by some. That the general well-being cannot be purchased at the cost of sacrifices by some without requiring the interpersonal judgment that the loss in utility by those who sacrifice is less than the gain in utility by those who gain was immediately pointed out by Frisch, and was again brought up by Pegrum and Coase. Even if it were possible, therefore, to finance the necessary subsidies entirely by means of lump-sum taxes, the arguments in favour of the marginal cost pricing system would still be dependent upon interpersonal comparisons of utility.

From this summary of the literature, it is evident that the Hotelling version of the marginal cost pricing principle is formally inconsistent on at least two points. Because it is proposed to finance the necessary subsidies by means of revenue derived from an income tax, the system fails to meet the marginal conditions relating to the factors of production. And, because the tax is not necessarily collected from the people who receive the benefit of the subsidies, support of the marginal cost pricing principle must be based on interpersonal comparisons of utility. The Reder–Lerner version of the principle, which fails to specify how the subsidies would be financed, is also inconsistent on two counts. It still requires interpersonal comparisons, in that it favours those who consume the products of decreasing cost industries over those who do not. And, secondly, the failure to consider the method of financing does not avoid the necessity for raising the revenue in some way or other. The system in this form is partial, and would break down if made general. The following section will consider the practical importance of these points: whether because of these inconsistencies the whole idea must be rejected, or whether in spite of them marginal cost pricing still would be advantageous.

Evaluation

Since the marginal cost pricing system does not meet the standard its advocates claim for it, an evaluation of the proposal must consider the significance of this failure. As a first step in this direction, it will be useful to determine what changes would be needed to make the marginal cost pricing system conform to that standard, and also exactly what conditions and assumptions are involved in the system as it stands.

In order to make the marginal cost pricing system fulfil the requirements claimed for it, a method of financing would have to be provided that would meet the marginal conditions, and the compensation that has been omitted from the plan would have to be introduced. Introducing the compensation would in effect mean that the revenue for subsidizing any given product would have to be derived from the people who consumed that product, and not from anyone else. To do this without violating the marginal conditions, the tax would have to fall on the consumers' surplus derived by the purchasers from the consumption of that specific product. It could not bear upon the marginal unit purchased by any consumer, so any form of per-unit tax would be inadmissible. A tax that must fall upon the consumption of a specific product, but not upon the marginal unit, would of necessity yield a form of price discrimination. The marginal units to each consumer would have to be sold at marginal cost, with the difference between marginal cost and average cost made up by charging more than average cost on pre-marginal units. In order, therefore, to reach a pricing system which does actually meet the conditions which the advocates of marginal cost pricing claim their system meets, it would be necessary to abandon marginal cost pricing altogether, and adopt in its stead a special form of price discrimination. The proponents of marginal cost pricing have argued that price discrimination which is properly designed to meet the marginal conditions would be impossible to achieve in practice. If this objection should be well founded, it would then have to be concluded that this line of analysis yields no one consistent and feasible system of pricing which will meet the marginal conditions and at the same time avoid any necessity for interpersonal comparisons of utility.

The assumptions upon which the marginal cost pricing system actually is based are easily derived. With respect to interpersonal comparisons, marginal cost pricing involves a redistribution of income from those who do not consume the products of decreasing cost industries to those who do. If this redistribution is to be either a matter of indifference or a net contribution to total utility, one of two conditions must be met: either the distribution of income, whatever it be, must be a matter of indifference, or this particular redistribution of income must not lessen welfare. To meet the first of these conditions, the original Pigovian assumption is necessary – the utility of income must be the same to all individuals, and therefore, for all practical purposes, constant. If the marginal utility of money is the same for all people, marginal transfers of income among individuals become a matter of indifference. The total utility of the community would not then be altered by a change in the distribution of income, even though the distribution of that total utility would be different. The manner in which the burden of financing the necessary subsidies is distributed would be a matter of indifference, and on this score marginal cost pricing would be acceptable. As for the second condition (that this particular redistribution be acceptable even though others might not be), the redistribution in question would not be systematic with respect to income so that the only assumptions about the utility of income which would meet this condition are trivial. It thus becomes apparent that with regard to interpersonal comparisons of utility marginal cost pricing depends upon the same assumption that the old welfare economics of Marshall and Pigou did. Like Pigou, it of necessity defines an increase in welfare as an increase in total output, somehow determined, and it does not even make the elementary restrictions with regard to distribution that Pigou did. If this definition of welfare is accepted, marginal cost pricing will not on this count interfere with the reaching of a maximum. In any other case it will.

The second implicit assumption made by the advocates of marginal cost pricing is to be found in the consideration of the marginal conditions. The financing of the Hotelling version of marginal cost pricing is based upon the income tax, and for this reason involves a violation of the marginal conditions relating to the factors of production. This violation of the marginal conditions would have no effect upon the allocation of resources, however, if it did not change the supply of the factors of production. It is therefore necessary, if the marginal cost pricing system is to meet all of the marginal conditions, to assume that the supply of the factors of production is fixed. The price received by the factors of production would then be a matter of indifference from the point of view of resource allocation, since it would have no effect upon their utilization, and the marginal conditions of production would be met regardless of what the net return to the factors might be. In other words, the income tax would be the same as a true lump-sum tax if it did not alter the supply of any of the factors of production.

These, then, are the assumptions which are implicit in the marginal cost pricing system: that, in the first place, the marginal utility of income is constant, and, in the second place, the supply of the factors of production is fixed. The reasonableness of these particular assumptions is of prime importance in assessing the practical merits of marginal cost pricing. Obviously, no unique decision can be made about the reasonableness of a set of assumptions; the question is one of personal opinion, and each person is entitled to base his recommendations regarding the pricing system upon whatever assumptions seem to him to be most acceptable. It should be recognized, however, that advocacy of marginal cost pricing does involve these two particular assumptions, and that it does not rest upon the assumptions its champions maintain that it does.

In these circumstances, there are certain additional comments which seem relevant to the question of the desirability of marginal cost pricing. In the first place, it would seem to be true, as has been pointed out above, that it is not possible to design a pricing system upon the basis of some criterion of efficiency, and then to alter the income distribution in any desired way without affecting the efficiency of the pricing system. No such separation of the problem is possible. Every pricing system results in some sort of income distribution, and no substantial redistribution of income is possible without changing that pricing system. For this reason, it is imperative that the question of interpersonal valuations be taken specifically into account. It is because of the failure to recognize this necessity, in maintaining that no interpersonal comparisons are involved, that objections can be raised to the marginal cost pricing thesis. Had the specific set of interpersonal valuations which is implicit in marginal cost pricing been chosen deliberately, one would have been entitled to differ with the choice but one could not have accused the thesis of inconsistency. In choosing a pricing system, it thus becomes necessary to make specific assumptions about interpersonal comparisons of utility, and then to judge the pricing system in relation to these assumptions as well as in relation to the marginal conditions.

In practice, for the design of a specific pricing system with interpersonal comparisons taken into account, the framework of marginal cost pricing would in many instances be found too restrictive. For example, assuming that a redistribution of income from the wealthy to the poor is desirable – as would be implied by the use of the income tax to finance marginal cost pricing – it is not always true that the income tax is the most efficient means of accomplishing this purpose and at the same time achieving an efficient allocation of resources. In certain situations, it has been demonstrated in the literature that excise taxes are more efficient in raising revenue than equivalent income taxes. The necessary conditions for this to be true are in all probability met by many luxury goods. Excise taxes on such luxury goods would therefore constitute an important source of revenue, which in cases of products for which the demand is inelastic could be obtained without significant violation of the marginal conditions. Reliance solely upon the income tax, insisting that the prices of all consumers' goods be set at marginal cost, thus neglects a device which would help to provide necessary revenue in a manner which would tend to alter the income distribution in the desired direction. The practical significance of such alternative sources of revenue becomes greater if the objective is not primarily that of achieving a certain specified distribution of income by lowering those at the top but rather that of raising the level of the lower groups so that no one falls below some minimum. If a system of income taxes on income above a certain level is used to collect revenue to redistribute to persons with incomes below that level, there will, of course, be some limit to the amount that can be collected. A high tax rate will eventually restrict the supply of the factors of production offered by the group which is taxed – but excise taxes of equivalent amount might have no such restrictive effect. The total amount of revenue which could be collected (and so the total amount of productive factors freed for redistribution), might, therefore, be greater with excise taxes than with income taxes alone. With such an objective, a system which included excise taxes might produce greater general welfare than would income taxes alone even if it did not add to the welfare of the taxpayers themselves.

A second problem, in addition to that of integrating specific interpersonal comparisons into the pricing system, relates to the practical problems to which any proposed pricing system would give rise. It was, in fact, upon this very basis that the advocates of marginal cost pricing rejected perfect price discrimination in favour of a system of constant pricing at marginal cost. Perfect price discrimination, they argued, would be too complex and too difficult to apply in practice, and marginal cost pricing would be much simpler. On this same basis it is evident that marginal cost pricing would also raise difficulties; there are a number of sectors of the economy in which for technological reasons marginal cost pricing would be unsatisfactory. This is particularly true of the distributive trades. By their very nature, distributive firms operate with marginal costs considerably below average cost. Operation of all retailing and wholesaling units with marginal cost pricing would pose almost insoluble problems with regard to entry, and therefore with regard to the correct operation of the whole distributive industry. Marginal cost pricing, in other words, does not satisfactorily solve many of the problems which are now disturbing the economy, and there is reason to believe that the adoption of marginal cost pricing might make some of the existing flaws even more troublesome. In many such instances, other methods – price discrimination itself, for instance – would prove far more workable. And if these alternatives should not prove adequate, it is frequently a moot question whether violating the marginal conditions by raising price slightly above marginal cost would diminish welfare any more than would the necessity for coping with the technological problems involved in marginal cost pricing.

Furthermore, it is quite likely that in certain sectors of the economy, price discrimination which would meet the marginal conditions would not be difficult to arrive at, despite the protestations to the contrary of the proponents of marginal cost pricing. Demand curves are not smooth and continuous and single-valued; they contain many discontinuities, and there are many products for which demand is almost perfectly inelastic within the relevant range. Taking advantage of such discontinuities and inelasticities, the construction of workable systems of price discrimination which will not violate the marginal conditions is quite feasible. For example, it is probably true that the use of block systems of rates for electricity does not appreciably interfere with the meeting of the marginal conditions, since it is to be doubted whether house-holders greatly reduce their consumption of electricity because they cannot obtain additional amounts at the industrial rate. Similarly, with respect to many large items of consumers' expenditures – household appliances, for example – many consumers are quite willing to pay average cost for one unit, and the fact that they cannot buy a second unit at marginal cost has no effect upon their purchases, since they would not buy an additional unit even if it were priced at marginal cost. And whether or not they buy the first unit may be primarily a question of the distribution of income, rather than of pricing alone. Such discontinuities make it possible to meet total costs in many decreasing cost industries without violating the marginal conditions appreciably. In other instances, inelasticities perform the same function. Price discrimination between different lines of a product produced by one firm, for instance, is a device to cover total costs by charging more than average cost on some lines and less than average cost on others. Examples of such price discrimination are to be found in the pricing of consumers' durables – radios, for instance. Some consumers are willing to pay more for a radio in a fancy case, but no consumer who can pay even marginal cost will go without one, since a low-priced line in a plain case is also available. The consumer who buys the more expensive radio will pay a price which is greater by far more than the actual difference in marginal cost of the two radios – in other words, the low-priced line may be sold at very nearly marginal cost, and most of the overhead recovered on the high-priced line. Such devices for covering total costs and at the same time approaching the marginal conditions are prevalent in the economy today, and especially so in those industries which would technologically lend themselves best to marginal cost pricing. The abolition of all presently existing price discrimination in favour of constant marginal cost pricing would therefore not necessarily represent a net gain. The existence of high or inelastic demand may even limit the application of the marginal cost pricing principle in the specific case most often used as an example by the advocates of marginal cost pricing, that of tolls on bridges. Hotelling himself would recognize that if the traffic is greater than the capacity of the bridge a rental charge may properly be made, in order to assure that the privilege of utilizing the existing capacity will go to those who most desire it. On this basis, the tolls on the Hudson River bridges and tunnels (to which Hotelling so vigorously objects) may not be so objectionable after all, at least at certain periods of the day. Furthermore, if the toll is small in comparison with the other costs incurred by the individuals making use of the service, demand may be sufficiently inelastic so that the toll will have little or no effect upon use. Such, for instance, may be the case with respect to the tolls on the New York parkway system. Gasoline costs and the difference in time saved in comparison with the size of the toll may make for considerable inelasticity in demand over the relevant range. The social cost (reduction in use) involved in allocating the cost of the highway to those who make use of it thus may be very small in relation to the total revenue involved.

Finally, it should be pointed out that there is a whole set of arguments advanced by the advocates of marginal cost pricing which can equally well be used to support pricing at other than marginal cost levels. Hotelling, for instance, supported the pricing of power projects at marginal cost on the ground that others besides those directly involved would benefit. This is a very good argument for pricing many commodities below, rather than at, marginal cost. Milk for children, subway transportation in large cities, and many other commodities and services might better be so priced. The nation has a stake in healthy children, and the benefits accrue to others besides the children and those upon whom they are dependent for support. Similarly, it can be argued that the subways benefit landowners, automobile drivers, and employers in large cities. There is therefore no necessary reason why the price charged to those who ride the subways should be equal to marginal cost – some part of that marginal cost might well be borne by the others who benefit from each person's riding, or, if the benefit is widespread, by general taxation.

It thus appears that, since the distribution of income must be taken into account, there is no one general pricing system which will be more efficient than all others for all sectors of the economy. Different pricing principles are economic tools which find applicability in different circumstances. The task of the economist in designing price systems is not so much one of finding a general panacea, but rather one of the systematic analysis of the special problems which arise in different sectors of the economy. Marginal cost pricing may very well increase welfare in certain specific situations. The fact that it is not applicable as a general system does not mean that it should be disregarded altogether. Certain railway and utility rates do provide an area in which marginal cost pricing would increase welfare. Hotelling was undoubtedly right in pointing out that the gain enjoyed by those who benefit from the lower price is frequently greater than the loss borne by those helping to subsidize the industry, and the attempt to assess the burden carefully may lead to greater diseconomy than allocating it incorrectly (even though in so stating he contradicted his original assumptions).

In summary, then, the design of a pricing system must take into account the conditions which do exist in the economy. The various sectors of the economy differ from one another in the restrictions which they impose on the pricing system, and what is appropriate for one sector may be completely inappropriate for another. No one formula can be established which will be valid as a general principle. But one statement can be made: the search for a panacea, for a single simple rule by which to guide all conduct, is, because of the technological requirements of the different parts of the economy and because of the problems of redistribution, a vain search and even a foolish one. A set of tools is available with which to accomplish a complicated job. A better job can be done if each tool is used where it is appropriate, instead of throwing away all but one and expecting it to serve all purposes.

2 M. J. Farrell

In Defence of Public-Utility Price Theory

M. J. Farrell, 'In defence of public-utility price theory', *Oxford Economic Papers*, new series vol. 10 (1958), pp. 109–23. Amended by the author.[1]

The purpose of this paper is to defend the principle that a public utility should relate its price to its marginal cost of production.[2] The importance of this defence is twofold. As a matter of practical economic policy, the adoption of the principle is of the first importance, but, in addition, it may be regarded as an important test case for the whole class of general principles of economic policy. Many of the arguments that have been advanced against marginal cost pricing by public utilities represent attacks, more or less explicit, on the use of rules derived from economic theory to determine *any* prices, and in some cases, on the use of any *general* policy rules whatever. As it is impossible to give a comprehensive defence of so wide a class of principles against a variety of detailed objections in the space of one short article – it would involve reviewing the greater part of established economic theory – the argument is confined to the public utility rule; but

1. I am indebted to A. D. Bain, M. R. Fisher, J. E. Meade and T. Wilson for comments on various versions or portions of this paper.
2. The principle had, by the end of the forties, generated an extensive controversy of which the interested reader will probably find Nancy Ruggles's survey articles, 'The welfare basis of the marginal cost pricing principle' and 'Recent developments in the theory of marginal cost pricing', paper 1 in this edition, together with A. M. Henderson's classic 'The pricing of public utility undertakings', *The Manchester School* (1947), a sufficient sample; but an abundance of further references can be found in these articles. However, in 1957 J. de V. Graaff, *Theoretical welfare economics*, Cambridge (especially chap. 10), provided an elegant and sustained attack, with which we shall be much concerned (page references to Graaff are to this work). At about the same time, R. G. Lipsey & R. K. Lancaster, in 'The general theory of the second best', *Review of Economic Studies*, vol. 24, no. 1, introduced a new and powerful argument, which we shall consider in section 2 below.

the reader will notice that most of the arguments apply much more widely.

1. Increasing or Decreasing Average Cost

Early discussions were based on the rule that, for a welfare optimum, the price of every commodity should equal its marginal cost, and the assumption that public utilities operate under conditions of decreasing average cost, so that marginal cost is less than average cost. In this case, the rule implies a price less than average cost, and is open to the following objections:

1. It will usually be only in the short run that average cost exceeds marginal, and in this case the magnitude of marginal cost depends on the (arbitrary) definition of the length of the 'short run'.

2. A price less than average cost implies a deficit, which has somehow to be covered. The various suggested methods of raising the necessary money – taxation, multi-part tariffs, and price discrimination – are all open to objection.

3. Criteria of efficient administration are more difficult to apply in an organization that does not attempt to cover its costs.

4. Since a public utility necessarily raises its capital on gilt-edged terms, its costs will include no element corresponding to the risk-margin of venture capital used in private enterprise, and to this extent marginal cost would represent too low a price.

5. A welfare optimum requires *all* goods to be priced at marginal cost, so that to the extent that monopolistic conditions or taxation lead to prices above marginal cost in the rest of the economy, the best price under the circumstances for the public utility may be greater than marginal cost. (The implicit assumption, that a higher than optimal price for some goods raises rather than lowers the optimal price for all other goods will be discussed in the next section, but will be retained for the present.)

These objections to a public utility's setting its price equal to marginal cost (where average cost is decreasing) are formidable, but we need only note that they constitute no reason for its setting its price *below* marginal cost.

However, decreasing average cost is not the usual, let alone the invariable, situation of what are thought of as public utilities.

45

Some roads, bridges, railway lines, and telephone trunk lines are indeed under-utilized, but examples of congestion are increasingly common in all these cases. Electricity generation shows economies of scale to the individual plant, but scarcity of suitable sites probably produces increasing average costs for the industry as a whole, at least in the more densely populated areas. Coal-mining is straightforwardly an increasing average cost industry. And so on. When we ask how the objections of the previous paragraph apply to marginal cost pricing under conditions of increasing average cost, we find that the first three objections vanish: there is no arbitrary exclusion of costs that is not escapable in the 'short run', while spending a surplus involves none of the problems of financing a deficit. Objections (4) and (5) remain, but again, they imply a price *above* rather than *below* marginal cost.

Thus, the optimal price is greater than or equal to marginal cost. Where decreasing returns prevail, average cost is less than marginal, so that the latter is always[3] closer than the former to the optimal price. In times of high marginal rates of tax, the possibility of using the economic rent earned by the public utility to improve the allocation of resources elsewhere in the economy by reducing these rates is a positive argument in favour of the marginal rule. Thus the rule that 'a public utility should never set its price below marginal cost' has much to commend it.

It may be desirable to introduce here a word or two on the relationship between necessary and sufficient conditions. A necessary condition for an optimum must be fulfilled at the optimal point, but may also be fulfilled elsewhere. A sufficient condition can only be satisfied at the optimum, but may not be even there. Clearly, what is ideally wanted is a condition (or set of conditions) that is both necessary and sufficient – that must be satisfied at the optimal point and can be satisfied nowhere else. But this does not mean that a necessary condition that is not sufficient should be ignored. Thus 'price not less than marginal cost' is a necessary but not a sufficient condition for an optimum.[4] It does not tell us what the best price is, but it does tell us

3. But see the discussion in section 2 below.
4. So far as the arguments of this section go. This statement, and others in this paragraph, are subject to the qualifications discussed in the remaining sections of the paper.

that it is not less than marginal cost, so that we can rule out all prices less than marginal cost as non-optimal. It is thus a valuable piece of information, as is any necessary condition, whether or not it is sufficient. However, the arguments of the present section go farther than this, for they show that a price equal to marginal cost is better than any lower price, which is sufficient to justify the recommendation 'if your price is less than marginal cost, raise it till it equals marginal cost'. It may be desirable to raise it still farther, but the limited increase is bound in itself to be an improvement.

2. The Second Best

It was implicitly assumed in the previous section, as indeed it was generally assumed in early discussions of the subject, that taxation or monopolistic conditions elsewhere in the economy raise rather than lower the optimal price for a public utility. More generally, suppose the economy contains n commodities, and one wishes to determine the optimal price for one of these (say commodity i) taking the ratio[5] k_j of price to marginal cost for each of the other $n - 1$ commodities as given. Then, if k is the least and K the greatest of these fixed ratios, it is intuitively plausible that the optimal ratio $\hat{k_i}$ for commodity i should be neither greater than K nor less than k; and this was generally assumed to be so, prior to the pioneering article by Lipsey and Lancaster.[6]

It was one of their most important contributions in this paper, to dispute this assumption; but since they did not make entirely clear the details of their argument or the assumptions on which it was based, their conclusion was debatable. However, McManus, in an important clarificatory article[7] established that the argument

5. That taxation and monopolistic pricing imply a fixed ratio of price to marginal cost is, of course, a rather special assumption. In general, the ratio kj will depend on all the other prices in the economy, including that of commodity i, which generates some interesting problems for the economic theorist; however, we shall not go into these, as they seem rather fine points from the point of view of practical policy.

6. Op. cit. But see also J. E. Meade, *Trade and welfare*, London, 1955.

7. M. McManus, 'Comments on the general theory of second best', *Review of Economic Studies*, June 1959.

was valid and its assumptions realistic. *In general*, $\hat{k}_i$ may be either less than k or greater than K; and indeed, it may lie arbitrarily far outside these limits. Thus, *in general*, economic theory would seem incapable of giving any guidance as to the optimal price to be charged by a public utility (even before considering the points discussed in later sections of this paper).

Fortunately, however, Professor Green has carried the matter farther by examining the conditions in which these surprising results can obtain.[8] In the situation described above, he shows (section 4(*b*)) that $\hat{k}_i$ is a weighted sum of the fixed ratios, with the weight w_{ij} attached to k_j positive if commodities i and j are substitutes and negative if they are complements. Thus, so long as i is a substitute for each of the other commodities, the intuitive proposition described in the first paragraph of this section will be true; and it will remain true even in the presence of complementarity, unless the negative terms corresponding to complementary commodities 'outweigh' the positive terms corresponding to substitutes.

More precisely, we shall find $\hat{k}_i$ less than k only if $\sum\limits_{j \neq i} w_{ij}(k_j - k)$ is negative; and the non-zero terms in this sum are positive or negative as j is a substitute or a complement for i. Turning to our public utility, if k is not less than unity (that is, none of the fixed prices is below marginal cost), its optimal price will be less than marginal cost if taxes on or monopolistic pricing of commodities complementary to it produce negative terms in the above sum greater in magnitude than all the positive terms arising from taxes on or monopolistic pricing of substitutes. Thus the paradox that *in general* taxes or monopolistic conditions elsewhere in the economy can reduce the optimal price for a public utility below its marginal cost turns out, on inspection, to be no more than the quite reasonable statement that this can happen if, in a *particular* case, these phenomena are heavily concentrated on goods complementary to the public utility.[9]

8. H. A. J. Green, 'The social optimum in the presence of monopoly and taxation', *Review of Economic Studies*, October 1961.

9. As this paper is concerned with the dictum that a public utility's price should not be set below its marginal cost, the case where $\hat{k}_i$ is greater than K is not directly relevant, since it would imply a price set even more above marginal cost than is the case for any other commodity. It is, however,

However, we must note that this analysis assumes that k is not less than unity – an assumption which is patently false since the commodities whose k_js are taken as given include other public utilities. Strictly, for $\hat{k}_i$ to be less than unity (in the absence of complementarity) we need not only that k_j should be less than unity for some commodities, but also that these commodities should be sufficiently close substitutes for l for the corresponding terms to outweigh those corresponding to substitutes for which k_j is greater than unity. Unfortunately, this combination of circumstances is all too likely to occur.[10]

Fortunately, Professor Green has also studied the more general problem of determining the optimal prices for a number of commodities, the k_j s for the remaining commodities being fixed. We can apply this analysis to the problem of determining simultaneously the optimal prices for all public utilities (that is, for all commodities whose prices are determined as a matter of public policy), taking the k_j s for the products of private industry as given. We may now assume k to be not less than unity since businessmen, whatever their other shortcomings, do not usually sell below marginal cost.[11] Green (section 4(d)) shows that, so long as each public utility's output is a substitute for each of the other commodities, the optimal ratios $\hat{k}_i$ for all the public utilities must be at least k and at most K. Thus, once again, the optimal price for a public utility will be below marginal cost only as a result of complementarity. In this case, unfortunately, it is more difficult to see precisely how much complementarity is needed to invalidate the rule, and in particular, the effects of complementarity between two public utilities seem difficult to assess.

----

worth noting for the sake of completeness that the analysis is essentially symmetrical: the case would arise if the complements of the public utility had very low values of k_j and the substitutes high ones, on a scale sufficient for the terms associated with the former to outweigh those associated with the latter.

10. Road and rail transport, and gas and electricity are obvious pairs of public utilities whose products are close substitutes.

11. k_j might, of course, be less than unity because the government subsidized commodity j; but it would be decidedly odd to set the price of a public utility below marginal cost in order to offset the effects of a subsidy which the government itself was giving.

Supposing the latter sort of complementarity to be absent, a high value of k_j for a privately produced commodity complementary to one of the public utility products will tend to lower $\hat{k}_i$ for each of the public utilities; however, we again need close complementarity and high values of k_j for this effect to outweigh the terms corresponding to substitutes.

In sum, the practical implications of the 'second-best' analysis for our rule, that the optimal price for a public utility should not be less than its marginal cost, is that this rule may be invalid if the incidence of taxation and monopolistic pricing is sufficiently heavily concentrated on close complements for this or other public utilities.

3. Redistribution of Income

There is an important problem associated with the optimal distribution of income, but it is important to be clear as to its nature. The Pareto conditions are necessary but not sufficient: for an optimum one must choose from among all those positions satisfying the Pareto conditions that which has the 'best' distribution of income. This in itself constitutes no objection to the Pareto conditions, nor does the fact that even in principle it is impossible to find taxes and subsidies that will not change supply and demand curves. Since any redistribution of income will change the Pareto conditions, it must be accompanied by a change in prices, not in breach of the Pareto conditions, but so as to maintain them Neither of these *theoretical* complications raises an important problem.

There is, however, a serious problem connected with the *practical* difficulties of redistributing income. Dr Graaff points out (p. 78) that it presupposes a system of taxes based not on earnings but on potential earning capacity, and that the consequent problems of assessment are in practice insoluble. Thus it may be that the optimum is not in practice attainable, and that society must be content with some 'second best' solution. In such a solution not all the necessary conditions for an optimum can be fulfilled, and it may be that none is. Thus the Pareto conditions may well not be necessary for the 'second-best optimum' – another argument that might seem at first sight to remove the whole justification for the marginal cost rule. Happily, a closer look will reassure us that this is far from being the case.

In the first place, the arguments given in the Appendix give grounds for rejecting Dr Graaff's assertion 'that tinkering with the price mechanism is one of the more feasible and generally satisfactory ways of securing whatever distribution of wealth is desired' (p. 171). However, not even this is essential to the argument of the present paper, for it will be shown that, even granting, for the sake of argument, the desirability of Dr Graaff's tinkering, there is still no case for a public utility's charging less than marginal cost.

There are two ways in which the redistribution of income may involve subsidizing a commodity. It may do so directly, as a means of raising those incomes judged to be too low, or indirectly, by applying such taxes and subsidies to other commodities that the conditions for a second-best optimum demand a subsidy. But subsidies to the consumption of commodities are a particularly inefficient way of redistributing income – their justification lies rather in the paternalistic argument that people 'don't know what's good for them'.[12] The best way of making a particular individual better off is to give him an appropriate sum of money. To do so by subsidizing the consumption of one or more commodities involves raising the incomes of all the other consumers of those commodities and raising a correspondingly larger amount of money by taxation (thus violating the Pareto conditions indirectly as well as directly). Nor is the problem of assessment so difficult for subsidies as it is for taxes, for childhood, widowhood, infirmity, sickness, and the like furnish objective criteria of need. Thus, commodity subsidies are unlikely to be involved in optimal methods of income redistribution, so that the only way in which distribution considerations can lead to optimal prices below marginal cost is through the indirect effect of taxation. That is to say, redistribution must involve such a set of taxes that the effect of these on the commodity's complements outweighs that of those on its substitutes.

Redistributive taxes can be roughly divided into those on the earnings of factors of production and those on the consumption

12. Or, possibly, in the argument that social costs are less than private costs.

of commodities. So far as the latter are concerned, to tax a commodity and then subsidize its close complement is to take away with one hand and give back with the other. The taxation of earnings is a more complex matter. If the commodity is a consumption good, it is necessary that the effect of taxation of factors via the prices of its close complements should outweigh the effect via the prices of its substitutes – a most unlikely occurrence. If the commodity enters into production, it is necessary that the effect of taxation of those factors that are complementary to it should outweigh that of taxation of its substitutes. This again seems unlikely, although it is possible to conceive rates of tax upon the different factors of production that might produce such a result.

It is thus unlikely that consideration of the distribution of income should lead to an optimal price below marginal cost for any commodity. This is true in particular of public utilities, but it is perhaps worth noting that most public utilities (e.g. fuel, power, transport) sell a large proportion of their product as an intermediate rather than a final commodity. This reinforces the argument against the direct use of subsidies on public utility products to redistribute income, but makes it important to emphasize the possible exception due to the taxation of complementary factors of production. Thus, if capital were subject to much heavier taxation than other factors of production, and were, *over the economy as a whole*, a close complement of fuel, then it might be desirable to subsidize the use of fuel. The latter condition is not very likely to be fulfilled, and it seems unlikely that a very high marginal rate of tax on the earnings of capital would be a good way of redistributing income. Thus, with one possible but unlikely exception, the optimal price for a public utility is unlikely to be less than its marginal cost, even on the assumption that 'tinkering with the price mechanism' is desirable – and tinkering on any but the smallest scale is itself unlikely to be desirable.

4. Some Further Points

We shall now consider briefly a number of other objections raised by Dr Graaff to the optimality of the Pareto conditions. Some of the objections are quite trivial, while others, although they involve problems of considerable technical difficulty, are not directly relevant to our present thesis. In the former category comes the point that the Pareto conditions are also necessary for a position of minimum welfare or for a local maximum. This is just another instance of necessary conditions that are not sufficient – but remain necessary.

There is the argument[13] that the Pareto conditions should be abandoned in favour of discriminatory pricing designed to turn the terms of trade in favour of a particular country. But while discriminatory pricing (including as a special case the 'optimum tariff') can be very profitable to a country if it alone practises it, such a state of affairs is not likely to last long. Other countries will retaliate, and in Dr Graaff's own words, 'the progressive disruption of the allocative efficiency of the world economy as more and more countries resort to protection will [more probably] lead to all being worse off than under free trade'.[14]

The Pareto conditions presume that the efficiency of factors of production is independent of their consumption patterns. There are cases in which this is not true – for instance, under-nourishment or over-indulgence in alcohol may reduce the efficiency of labour, and it may then be desirable to subsidize food or to tax gin. These exceptions may be important, particularly in a very poor country, but they are sufficiently rare and recognizable to be dealt with *ad hoc*.

Then there is the dilemma apparently faced whenever short-run marginal cost exceeds long-run marginal cost.[15] If price is equated to the latter, a position of excess demand will be set up, and the price mechanism will cease to fulfil its short-period allocative function. On the other hand, if price is equated to short-run marginal cost, purchasers will make extensive adjustments, including long-run investments, to a high price that is purely temporary. Fortunately, the second horn is a mere stage property, for so long as producers are aware of the temporary nature of the high price, there is no reason to expect them to make more

13. Graaff, p. 146.

14. Ibid., p. 138.

15. There is, of course, a whole spectrum of 'short-run marginal costs', corresponding to the possible definitions of the short run. It is however convenient to talk as though there were only one.

than temporary adjustments to it. Indeed, if they are accurately informed about future price-movements, there is every reason to expect their adjustments to be optimal. Thus, 'marginal cost' must be interpreted to mean the greater of short- and long-run marginal cost.

The Pareto conditions also presume perfect divisibility of all commodities. The full treatment of indivisibilities is a technical problem which cannot be treated here for reasons of space, but we may point out that most indivisibilities can be removed by averaging over time. Thus, it is not a practical proposition to see three-quarters of a play and one-quarter of a film each week; but three plays and one film per month present no difficulties.[16]

External economies of scale are often thought to invalidate the Pareto conditions, but this is a product of confused thinking. It is true that the presence of external economies can prevent a competitive system from attaining the Pareto conditions,[17] but this is a very different matter. Unexploited external economies in an industry mean that it is charging a price greater than marginal social cost for its product, and the effect of this is usually (as in sections 2 and 3) to raise the optimal price for any other commodity. Thus, unexploited external economies elsewhere in the economy do not affect our rule for the price of a public utility.

Since the public utility is a monopoly, it cannot be subject to the kind of external economies discussed by Adams and Wheeler, i.e. those that are external to the firm but internal to the industry. There are, however, two ways in which it can be subject to external economies. It may, first of all, be faced by a falling supply curve for one or more of its factors of production. If so, this fact should be reflected in its calculation of marginal cost – but this will happen anyway if marginal cost is correctly calculated according to the ordinary definition.

The second possibility is that an increase in the utility's scale of operation will lower the cost curves of firms elsewhere in the economy, other than by making its product available more cheaply. This will only happen if it has some sort of by-product

16. Graaff makes this point (p. 108) in respect of production goods, but fails to apply his own argument to consumption goods two pages later.

17. See R. W. Adams and J. T. Wheeler, 'External economies and the falling supply curve', *Review of Economic Studies*, 1952–3.

which is socially useful but not marketable. Such a by-product will lead the marginal social cost of expanding the utility to be less than the marginal private cost, and the optimal price must, of course, be based on the former. Here again, a complete treatment of external economies is beyond our present scope, but it is not unreasonable to suggest that they should be treated *ad hoc* as particular exceptions to the public utility rule.

There remain the inter-related problems of time-discount and risk-discount, which may be thought of in terms of a two-dimensional array of rates of interest. (It is a useful piece of shorthand to refer to this array as 'the rate of interest'.) One cannot, of course, claim to have reached the welfare optimum unless one uses the optimal rate of interest in computing one's prices, and determining the optimal rate is a very difficult problem. However, in any particular situation a rate will rule in the rest of the economy, and it seems most unlikely that the constrained optimum, taking this *de facto* rate as given, will involve applying a different rate to public utilities.

Each of these last three problems (and particularly that of the rate of interest) deserves a much fuller discussion, which I hope to give elsewhere. I think, however, that I have said enough to suggest that none of them is likely to invalidate our public utility pricing rule.

5. The Practical Importance of the Rule

It was the thesis of the foregoing sections that it is a necessary condition for a welfare optimum that no public utility (except in certain recognizable exceptional cases) set its price below marginal cost, and further, that a price equal to marginal cost is better than any lower price. (The latter and stronger proposition is the more useful in practice.) Apart from the problem of economies of scale, the only exceptions to this rule that are at all likely in practice occur when it is desirable to subsidize the utility's product, in order to increase the efficiency of the labour force, or for paternalistic reasons, or because social costs fall short of private costs. In the present section we shall (with these qualifications) take the thesis as established and consider some examples of its practical importance.

It must be emphasized that the exact calculation of marginal cost often involves considerable difficulties, both mathematical and empirical; but that these difficulties are no bar to seeing the magnitude of the possible gains from observance of the rule, nor, indeed, any reason why, in the absence of such exact calculations, the greater part of such gains should not be obtained by using an approximate estimate of marginal cost.[18] It is in principle advisable to use a conservative estimate, for if the present price is too low, any price between it and marginal cost must be better, while some prices in excess of marginal cost may be worse than the original price. Bearing in mind that the optimal price is at least as great as, and on the arguments of section 1 will usually be greater than marginal cost, and that present prices in the cases discussed below are a good deal less than marginal cost, it is clear that only a gross overestimate of marginal cost could lead to such a situation; but it remains true that it is safer to err on the conservative side.

The point may be illustrated by the case of coal, an apparently very simple commodity which yet has a two-dimensional array of optimal prices, depending on the grade of coal and its geographical location. The former can be handled fairly easily, but the latter involves a very difficult programming problem. This problem has yet to be solved exactly,[19] but nonetheless it can be seen that a great improvement can be obtained by an approximate solution. For it is not difficult to obtain a solution to the locational–variation problem, such that deviations from optimal price are of the same order of magnitude as differences in transport costs to a market, between pits which might reasonably be expected to serve that market – which are, in Britain, likely to be pretty small differences. [. . .]

A network of roads is obviously a much more complex commodity than coal, and computing the relevant marginal cost is correspondingly more difficult.[20] Again, however, a conservative

18. Indeed, the costs of making the exact calculations may be so high that the optimal procedure is to use the approximate estimate.

19. For a treatment of a greatly simplified version of the problem, see A. Land, 'An application of linear programming to the transport of coking coal', *Journal of the Royal Statistical Society* (Series A), 1957.

20. For some first steps towards solving this probem, see M. Beckman, C. B. McGuire, and C. B. Winsten, *Studies in the economics of transportation*.

estimate can be made, and it is of the greatest importance that it should be, for in a road-system that is extensively congested there are the twin dangers, that society will engage in a cripplingly expensive programme of road construction, and that it will suffer great losses from the congestion. It will succumb to either of these dangers (and perhaps to both) through a failure to make each vehicle bear the marginal social cost of its use of the congested roads. It is perhaps worth saying a word about the ways in which these conservatively estimated charges should be levied. Tolls are, of course, the ideal method in theory, but in practice their collection involves such heavy costs to both state and road-user that they will be the best method only in very exceptional cases. A tax on the fuel used by road vehicles is an easy method in practice of making a charge roughly proportional to road-use in vehicle-miles, but is open to the objection that it does not distinguish between the use of congested and uncongested roads or reflect the differing construction costs of roads used. A tax on parking-space is likely to be a very useful method, for the congestion is worst and the cost of road construction highest in the centres of large towns. In such cases the congestion is often overwhelmingly due to vehicles using central parking-space, so that a tax on parking becomes a convenient way of levying the abnormally high charge appropriate to the use of these central roads. This tax is, of course, over and above charging at marginal cost for the use of the parking-space, i.e. making the charges for street-parking equivalent to those for expensive off-street parking in those areas where the latter has to be provided.

Council housing is another public utility where there is a serious danger of over-investment. It must, of course, be recognized that there is a relatively strong paternalistic argument for subsidizing housing. Paternalistic arguments are generally repugnant to most people – there is a well-founded distaste for the sort of man who tries to make people consume what he feels they ought to like in face of their obvious preference for some other commodity. But this distaste is neither so strong, nor so well-founded, in the case of children's consumption, as this is in any case paternally determined. Thus, while few people would deny a man's right to decide his own relative consumption of, say, beer and housing, many might question his increasing his own consumption of the former at the expense of his children's consumption of the latter. It may thus be optimal to subsidize the consumption of housing by some or all families; but if so, the size of the subsidy should be determined explicitly, as a value judgement based upon accurate knowledge of the situation. In fact, the pricing principle suggests that, in addition to the overt subsidies by the central and local governments, there is a large concealed subsidy represented by the uncollected economic rent. Indeed, some authorities talk quite openly of 'averaging' the rents of new and older houses, without apparently being aware of the economic implications of this process. This non-optimal price can be regarded either as a simple example of charging average cost in an increasing cost industry, thus dissipating the economic rent, or as a result of a faulty accounting procedure which fails to take (adequate) account of the appreciation in money value of the older (and especially pre-war) houses. However, accounting methods are a notably intricate field of argument, and the former method has the great advantage of direct analogy with other public utilities. It also gives a clear and simple answer to the question, 'What is the unsubsidized price of a council house?' It is the cost of providing an equivalent marginal house.

These examples, together with electricity, where it would be foolish to try to improve upon Professor Houthakker's classic analysis[21] of the optimal price structure, show that the price policy of public utilities is no academic matter. The observance of the rule would make a considerable contribution to the welfare of the nation, and conversely its violation is costing it dear in terms of unnecessary poverty. The word 'unnecessary' must be stressed, because here for once the economist can genuinely offer something for nothing. There is no need to work harder or to spend less – merely to substitute a rational price structure for an irrational one.

6. The Nature of Rules for Economic Policy

The foregoing discussion can be used to illustrate two fundamental misconceptions of the nature of rules for economic policy

21. H. S. Houthakker, 'Electricity tariffs in theory and practice', *Economic Journal*, 1951.

– misconceptions which I believe to be responsible for the recent ill-founded attacks not merely on the public utility rule, but on policy rules in general. The first misconception – generally associated with the term 'welfare economics' – is that policy rules should hold with logical certainty. Human psychopathology being what it is, it is in fact impossible to obtain any universally accepted value judgement on which to base one's deductions. But more important is the fact that, if the policy rule is to apply in the real world, it must be based on empirical generalizations – which naturally do not hold with logical certainty. Moreover, since economies are complex, the generalizations will have in practice to be quite broad; and the only game easier than thinking up possible exceptions to broad empirical generalizations is thinking up perverse value judgements! Thus, to set out to derive policy rules with logical certainty is to invite the sort of facile 'de-bunking' that has recently been applied to welfare economics.

> Ah, what a dusty answer gets the soul
> When hot for certainties in this our life!

This is illustrated by our finding, in the case of the public utility rule, that several of the objections consisted merely in 'possible' exceptions which were likely to occur, if at all, only so rarely that they could conveniently be dealt with *ad hoc*. But we also found that some objections, while quite valid in that they suggested reasons why the optimal price should deviate regularly from marginal cost, held *a fortiori* against the currently used rule of setting price equal to average cost. Thus, the marginal cost rule was not optimal, but was a good deal better than its only apparent rival, the average cost rule.

This illustrates the second misconception – that policy rules should be tested against the purely theoretical criterion of whether they give optimal results, and rejected if they do not. On the contrary, they should be tested against the available alternative rules, and the best rule accepted, even if it is clearly a long way from optimality. This is so because decisions must be taken according to some rule, even if, in default of a better, it is the rule that each decision is taken arbitrarily by some arbitrary individual. It is important to emphasize that such attractive-sounding proposals as 'considering each utility individually' or 'making available the positive knowledge on the basis of which laymen can pass judgement' are tantamount to the 'arbitrary decision by default' rule. For the time taken in considering or passing judgement is quite long – twenty years up to now in the case of the nationalized industries – and in the meantime prices have perforce been set at some level. This sort of thing would be harmful in a static economy, in a dynamic and rapidly changing one it can be catastrophic.

A set of simple, specific policy rules is, then, essential; and in each case we must choose the best of those available. The adoption of a simple rule does not, of course, mean that one should not consider what deviations from its observance are desirable in particular cases; but this is a very different matter from doing without the rule. A good analogy is provided by the fact that, since clocks and watches are subject to error, it is desirable to check them by astronomical observations; it is not a good idea to dispense with clocks and watches, and take astronomical observations whenever one wants to know the time.

Appendix

Although the arguments of this paper would be quite unaffected if Dr Graaff's assertion 'that tinkering with the price mechanism is one of the more feasible and generally satisfactory ways of securing whatever distribution of wealth is desired' were accepted, one cannot allow such a wild assertion to pass unchallenged. In fact, although it is difficult to argue conclusively about such a broad generalization, all the arguments suggest that it is the direct opposite of the truth.

The arguments that follow assume that to give everyone more of every commodity represents an improvement. This will doubtless seem to the reader, as it does to me, a very mild value judgement with which any normal person would agree. However, it has been suggested[22] that people may be so eaten through with envy that if some people get (in some sense) a smaller rise than others, they will not regard it as an improvement. For my part, I think sufficiently well of my fellow-men to believe that such people are extremely rare; but in any case, for an economist to

22. See Graaff, pp. 51 and 61.

consider them in his prescriptions represents an unwarranted excursion into psychopathology.

Sir Dennis Robertson has put the matter very well:[23] 'How much better, merely to assert as a plain matter of fact that *economic* welfare undoubtedly *will* be increased in this event; and *then* to call in the Archbishop of Canterbury to smack people over the head if they are stupid enough to allow the increased happiness which might be derived from this plain fact to be eroded by the gnawings of the green-eyed monster!'

We may agree with Dr Graaff that the Pareto conditions and the optimal income distribution are not simultaneously attainable: but it does not follow that the former should be ignored in pursuit of the latter. Indeed, there are reasons for believing that the second best optimum lies much nearer to the opposite extreme, where only such redistributions of income are attempted as do not violate the Pareto conditions. Let us consider this solution, which it will be convenient to call the 'best Pareto' position. It is reached by starting from a position where the Pareto conditions are fulfilled and changing the distribution of income by lump-sum taxes and subsidies until it is the best that is consistent with maintaining the Pareto conditions.[24]

Any further redistribution will involve violating the Pareto conditions through taxation at the margin. This will reduce the national product by diverting factors of production from more to less productive occupations. The extreme case of a less productive occupation is usually thought to be leisure, but leisure is at least desirable in itself. A much more serious loss to the community occurs when the effect of a tax is to divert factors of production into attempts to circumvent it – and this happens, to a greater or lesser extent, with any tax. Smuggling is the classic example, and avoidance of direct taxation the topical one, but the phenomenon is quite general, and indeed extends beyond taxes to all sorts of controls and restrictions. Just as the human body devotes all its strength to healing a wound or fighting an infection, so the economy mobilizes all its resources to overcome any obstacle to its natural working. It is insufficiently appreciated that ill-considered

23. 'Utility and all what?', *Economic Journal*, 1954, p. 677.
24. Of course, as was pointed out in section 3, the Pareto conditions themselves change as the distribution of income alters.

interference with the economy contributed to Britain's poor post-war recovery not merely directly through the inefficiency it produced, but also indirectly by drawing off so much entre-preneurial ability into black market operations. But whether the factors are diverted to tax-avoidance, to leisure, or merely to less useful production, the result is the same – a substantial reduction in the national product. Moreover, this reduction will be cumulative if the factors diverted include those (e.g. capital, enterprise, and management) that affect the rate of growth, rather than the level, of production. Thus redistribution carried beyond the best Pareto position will have, even in a static economy, to be bought at the expense of a considerable reduction in the general level of incomes, while in a growing one the price will be the far higher one of a reduction in the rate of growth – and the arithmetic of growth is such that a small difference in rates of growth rapidly produces a large difference in income levels. Moreover, the lower the general level of incomes, the more likely is it, *ceteris paribus*, that people will be preoccupied with redistribution, so that a 'vicious spiral' is likely to appear, excessive redistribution leading to poverty, and poverty to demands for further redistribution. Great Britain affords an instructive example of this process, and may be compared with the United States to show what a greater respect for the Pareto conditions might have produced.[25]

These arguments suggest that the second best optimum must be near to the best Pareto position, and in an economy where all economic decisions were in the hands of an absolute dictator, it might be proper to engage in nice calculations as to just how near – as to just how much redistribution it was worth buying at the

25. It must be noted that Britain's greater violation of the Pareto condi-tions is not limited to redistributive taxes – price controls, rationing, trades union restrictive practices, and many other forms of violation have also been more extensive. Thus the difference in income levels measures the cost of violation in general, and not merely of redistributive violation.

It may be argued that part of the difference is due to differences in natural resources. This is true, but a glance at the performance of manu-facturing industry in the two countries will show how unimportant it is. In any case, the United States, although nearer than Britain, is still some way from the best Pareto position (witness her heavily subsidized and pro-tected agriculture) so that on balance the difference between the two countries is likely to underestimate rather than overestimate Britain's loss through violation of the Pareto conditions.

cost of general poverty. But in a state where economic decisions are taken in part politically and in part by collective bargaining, this is hardly true. The cost to an economy of industrial strife on the one hand, and of economic decisions designed to buy votes on the other, may well be immense. Both these sources of loss would be largely eliminated if the exact fulfilment of the Pareto conditions were regarded as above dispute. This suggests that the second best optimum will actually coincide with the best Pareto position, so that the Pareto conditions remain necessary.

3 Oliver E. Williamson

Peak-Load Pricing

Oliver E. Williamson, 'Peak-load pricing and optimal capacity under indivisibility constraints', *American Economic Review*, vol. 56 (1966), pp. 810–27.

The problem of peak-load pricing has been 'solved' at least four times in the post-war literature (by Marcel Boiteux [1], Hendrik Houthakker [6], Peter Steiner [10], and Jack Hirshleifer [5]), and thus an additional treatment of this subject requires some justification.[1] Ours is threefold. First, the welfare motivation of these analyses has been generally lacking,[2] and it is therefore difficult to evaluate the results obtained. Second, the geometric techniques that have been provided are awkward and unconventional, require that costs be redefined for each change in the number of subperiods, and cannot easily be generalized to handle the case of unequal-duration-subperiod loads. We attempt to remedy each of these deficiencies and, in addition, extend the analysis of peak-load pricing by replacing the usual assumption of fully divisible

1. A valuable summary of the post-war French literature on marginal cost pricing (including peak-load pricing) has recently been provided by Jacques Drèze [3, pp. 8–35]. The problem of peak-load pricing has also been treated recently by Arnold Harberger and N. Andreatta [4]. Their paper appears to be an application of the previous literature to the electricity-supply problems in India, with special attention to the question of optimal use of thermal and hydro capacity. Since they make no references to the earlier literature, their paper may represent still another 'solution'.

2. Steiner sketches the welfare objective in a footnote [10, p. 587, n. 6] but fails to integrate the argument with the text beyond calling for a price-equal-marginal-cost result. Houthakker supplies a more comprehensive welfare motivation for his analysis, but he is concerned only with conditions that prevailed in Great Britain in the early 1950s. Since these conditions appear to be somewhat special, the applicability of the results is correspondingly circumscribed (which he explicitly points out [6, p. 1]). Our analysis, like those of Boiteux, Steiner, and Hirshleifer, is concerned with the general problem rather than with a particular set of time-place conditions. Our reference to 'earlier treatments' in subsequent parts of this paper will therefore be restricted to these latter writers unless otherwise indicated.

plant by one in which investment opportunities are discrete. This latter may be of little practical importance,[3] but it helps shed additional insights on the welfare attributes of the problem.

The welfare motivation for the analysis is supplied in section 1. Optimal pricing and the optimal adjustment of capacity to changes in demand, given a single uniform class of demands but indivisible plant, are investigated in section 2. The principal part of the paper is section 3, where a perfectly general geometric technique for combining periodic loads, given that costs are linear and subperiod demands are independent, is provided. Once costs are correctly specified, we show that the problem of optimally adjusting capacity in a periodic-load situation can always be solved by use of our 'effective demand for capacity' construction. Criteria for optimal pricing to peak and off-peak loads are also derived. As contrasted with the optimal capacity problem, optimal pricing to periodic demands is not a weighting problem but involves efficient use of existing capacity to service each demand class taken separately.

The Social Welfare Function

We simplify our analysis by assuming that all of the optimum conditions of production and exchange are satisfied elsewhere in the economy. This is a strong assumption and may vitiate the analysis in the minds of some. However, some such assumption is necessary if we are to avoid 'second best' digressions, and implicitly this assumption underlies the analyses of Boiteux, Steiner, and Hirshleifer. We are therefore merely making explicit what has previously been implicit in the peak-load-pricing literature. Moreover, since this assumption supplies us with conditions which permit us to employ the theoretical apparatus of partial

3. Houthakker claims that indivisibilities are unimportant in Great Britain since they operate in a fully interconnected system [6, p. 9]. Regions where interconnections are less extensive and economic generating units represent a nontrivial fraction of market size are presumably ones where indivisibilities could be significant. One caveat is, however, essential: although the presence of indivisibilities implies lumpiness in certain inputs, the lumps cannot be so large as to produce changes in relative outputs and prices over the whole economy. If this were the case, our partial equilibrium approach would have to be replaced by a general equilibrium analysis.

welfare economics *to derive benchmark relations* if nothing else, and as there is no well-specified alternative (the claim that our assumptions are not obviously satisfied needs to be articulated before it becomes useful), we will proceed on this basis.[4]

Social benefit will therefore be given by total revenue plus consumers' surplus, and social cost (treated as opportunity cost and assuming no technological externalities) will be separable into total pecuniary cost less intramarginal rent. Assuming that all factors are available to the enterprise in completely elastic supply, intramarginal rents will be zero and the net welfare gain is:

$$W = SB - SC$$
$$= TR + S - TC \tag{1}$$

where W = net welfare gain, SB = social benefit, SC = social cost, TR = total revenue, S = consumers' surplus, and TC = total cost.

Differentiating this expression with respect to output, we obtain as necessary[5] and sufficient conditions for a maximum the familiar relations:

$$\frac{dW}{dQ} = \frac{d}{dQ}(TR + S) - \frac{d}{dQ}(TC) = 0 \tag{2}$$

4. That assumptions of this sort are enormously helpful in producing insights on complex economic questions is illustrated by the remarkably insightful treatment of the fishery regulation problem by Ralph Turvey [11]. The reason we believe he was able to get so far with the fishery problem is precisely because he was willing to make simplifying assumptions and thereby provide a fundamental welfare motivation for his analysis.

5. That the derivative of the total revenue plus consumers' surplus term $(TR + S)$ with respect to quantity is simply price can be seen from the fact that

$$TR + S = \int_0^Q P(Q')dQ',$$

where $P(Q')$ is the demand curve. Differentiating this expression with respect to Q yields

$$\frac{d}{dQ}(TR + S) = \frac{d}{dQ}\int_0^Q P(Q')dQ'$$
$$= P(Q).$$

As pointed out below, we treat $P(Q')$ as the uncompensated demand curve and thus consumers' surplus is given by the Marshallian triangle. It is not necessary, however, to define consumers' surplus in this way to show that the welfare gain is maximized by equating price to marginal cost. But clearly this specification leads to the $P = MC$ result, which is all that we require in order to support the argument in the text.

whence $P - MC = 0$

$$\frac{d^2W}{dQ^2} = \frac{dP}{dQ} - \frac{d^2}{dQ^2}(TC) < 0. \tag{3}$$

Assuming that we have completely divisible plant, that capacity costs (defined more precisely in section 2) are β per unit per period, and that operating costs are b per unit per period, we have:

$$TC = (b + \beta)Q, \tag{4}$$

so that by (2) the optimal scale (for a given uniform class of demands) will be that value of Q for which $P = b + \beta$.

If the physical plant is taken as given and the only decision is one of pricing optimally within the capacity constraint ($\bar{Q}$), we have:

$$\text{max. } W = (TR + S) - bQ \tag{5}$$
$$\text{s.t. } Q \leqslant \bar{Q}.$$

Setting this up as a Lagrangian

$$\text{max. } L(Q, \lambda) = (TR + S) - bQ - \lambda(Q - \bar{Q}), \tag{6}$$

and differentiating partially with respect to Q and λ and equating to zero, we have:

$$P = b + \lambda \tag{7}$$
$$Q \leqslant \bar{Q}. \tag{8}$$

By the Kuhn–Tucker Theorem [9], if the constraint is not binding and equation (8) is satisfied as an inequality, λ is zero, and the optimal price is where output equates price to short-run marginal cost, namely b. When the capacity constraint is reached, however, the value of λ becomes positive, and the resulting price necessarily exceeds b. If $b + \lambda > b + \beta$ (and demand is expected to continue at this level), an expansion of plant is signalled, whereas if $b + \lambda < b + \beta$, plant should be retired.[6]

The above are the principal optimality rules for a system in

6. If $b + \lambda > b + \beta$, clearly $\lambda > \beta$ and the shadow price of the constraint exceeds the cost of installing an additional unit of capacity. Hence plant expansion is indicated. Where $b + \lambda < b + \beta$, so that $\lambda < \beta$, plant should be retired rather than renewed until an equality between λ and β is restored.

which plant is fully divisible and a single uniform class of demands exists. We turn now to consider the effects of relaxing these two assumptions. First, however, two characteristics of our welfare function not explicitly stated above are noted: (1) benefits and costs are weighted equally 'to whomsoever they may accrue', and thus society is indifferent to the income redistribution effects under this formulation; (2) the welfare function can be re-arranged in a form more convenient for the subsequent exposition by expressing it as

$$W = S + (TR - TC) \qquad (1')$$

where the first term is the consumers' surplus and the second term the producers' net revenue. For purposes of symmetry (although contrary to the standard usage, where the expression applies only to rents to intramarginal factors) we will refer to this net revenue term as 'producers' surplus'.

Uniform Load and Indivisible Plant

As already indicated, we distinguish between operating costs and capacity costs. Operating costs are mainly the energy costs of generation and transmission. Marginal operating costs (short-run marginal costs) are assumed to be constant, at a rate of b per unit per period, so long as output is less than capacity. When capacity is reached, however, marginal operating costs become effectively infinite. Thus a sharp kink develops at the existing capacity level.

Plant can be efficiently supplied only in integer multiples of output units of size E and cost Γ. The foregone alternative is an equivalent risk annuity which pays an amount γ per period over the useful life of the plant. Average capacity costs per period of a fully utilized efficiency unit of size E are thus γ/E plus the average maintenance cost per period, the sum of which we will call β. Subject to these indivisibility conditions, constant returns to scale prevail and long-run marginal costs are given by $b + \beta$.

We assume that the enterprise is initially in a fully adjusted equilibrium position in which short-run marginal costs, long-run marginal costs, and price are all equal. This is shown in Figure 1 where the demand curve is D_1 and the output $Q_1{}^* = nE$, where n is a positive integer. Price in these circumstances will be $b + \beta$

so that total revenue equals total cost. Producers' surplus is therefore zero and the net gain, W, is given by the consumers' surplus region UNG (assuming constant marginal utility of money over the relevant range).[7]

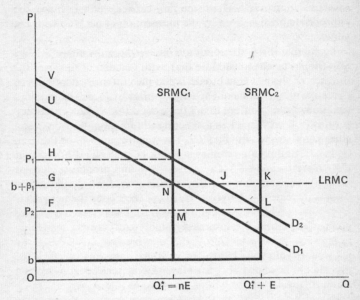

Figure 1

Assume now we have a once-for-all shift in demand to D_2. Under what conditions does it become optimal to add a new capacity unit? Clearly if D_2 were to pass through K so that at a price of $b + \beta$ the quantity demanded would be $Q_1^* + E$, a new efficiency unit would be warranted. But what if D_2 passes through some intermediate position between N and K such as J? Is there

7. This is another simplifying assumption, but one which, we suspect, is not likely to be seriously violated. See Alfred Marshall [6, pp. 132, 334–5, 842] for a similar view that the inaccuracy involved in employing this assumption is usually negligible. D. M. Winch has recently argued that, even where the marginal utility of money is not constant, the Marshallian triangle continues to be an accurate measure of what he refers to as 'consumers' gain' so long as income distribution is a matter of indifference [12, pp. 395–407, 422].

any justification for adding a new efficiency unit under these circumstances, and if so what price should be charged? Given our welfare function, the answer is clearly affirmative and the condition under which it becomes desirable is when the area IJN just exceeds the area JKL. With the new capacity unit in place, the appropriate price is given by the intersection of $SRMC_2$ with D_2, namely P_2.

To see that this is the condition under which the new efficiency unit should be added suppose that, with demand at the level D_2, the area IJN is just equal to JKL and the enterprise continues to operate with $Q_1{}^*$ units of capacity. A price of P_1 will be required to ration capacity output under these conditions. Thus producers' surplus (total revenue less total cost) will be given by $HING$ and consumers' surplus will be VIH. The welfare gain will be the sum, or $VING$. Should a new efficiency unit be added and price set at OF (where D_2 and $SRMC_2$ intersect), we find producers' surplus reduced in the amount $HING + GJLF + JKL$ while consumers' surplus increases by $HING + GJLF + IJN$. Thus the net gain is $IJN - JKL$, which by assumption is zero. Hence, from a welfare point of view, one is presumably indifferent between remaining at $Q_1{}^*$ and moving to $Q_1{}^* + E$. But whenever $IJN > JKL$ the net welfare gain will be positive, in which case the new efficiency unit should be added and, for all positions intermediate between J and K, the enterprise will be operated at a loss.

Indeed we see that, in this system with indivisible plant, the fully adjusted long-run static equilibrium can be one in which either positive or negative net profits are realized despite (discontinuously) constant returns to scale. Only accidentally [8] will the enterprise earn zero profits at the welfare maximum.

If the assumption that the shift from D_1 to D_2 is a once-for-all change is replaced by one in which D_2 is merely a transitory position in a system where demand is continuously increasing, does our criterion for installation of the additional capacity require modification? In some superficial sense it might appear that these dynamic conditions would warrant installation prior to the time at which the static criterion is satisfied. It is obvious, however, that if the new capacity is added before the area $IJN \geqslant JKL$,

8. This will occur with probability zero if demand is a random variable with continuous distribution function.

the welfare gain is less in those periods when $IJN < JKL$ than it otherwise would be, and no type of discounting procedure that expresses future gains in terms of present values will alter this result. Thus the criterion for installation remains the same: add the new capacity when IJN first exceeds JKL, but not before.[9]

The introduction of uncertainty requires that the analysis be adapted accordingly. In circumstances such as these where we are prescribing optimal social policy and the risk of *system* ruin due to the failure of any particular *enterprise* is negligible, and where we are assuming that the mix of projects is suitably diversified so as to secure the advantages of pooling, special allowance for risk would appear unnecessary. Instead, simple conversion to expected values would seem appropriate so that the counterpart of our previous criterion is to add capacity whenever $E(IJN) \geqslant E(JKL)$, where $E(\cdot)$ denotes expectation.

Peak and Off-Peak Loads

The analysis of periodic loads requires that costs and demands be specified with more than ordinary care. Specifications that conveniently solve a special case (such as the principal case examined

9. If there is an installation lag, of course, it will be necessary to anticipate demands in order for capacity to be operative at the desired time. With a positive rate of interest, the capacity should be timed to come into operation after $IJN > JKL$. This correction is trivial, however, and also applies if there is an installation lag under once-for-all changes in demand.

If the assumption of continuously increasing demand is replaced by one of secularly increasing demand with cyclical variation about the trend, the criterion still remains largely intact. Thus, installation lags aside, installation never precedes but is always made subject to the condition that $IJN \geqslant JKL$. However, whereas this was the necessary and sufficient condition for adding capacity under our welfare criterion given the static or continuously increasing demand conditions, it is only a necessary condition when cyclical variation is present. Whether the installation should be made at the time that demand first satisfies this relation, or be deferred to the second or nth time that the inequality $IJN < JKL$ is reversed, depends on the phase and frequency of cyclical variation. More specifically, our objective is to time the installation so as to maximize the discounted value of net benefits, and this need not coincide with the first switch-over from $IJN < JKL$ to $IJN \geqslant JKL$. Thus if, for example, the first switch-over occurred at the very peak of a cycle, installation at the time of the switch-over would be quite without purpose for the downturn would set in immediately and the additional capacity would exceed optimal ($IJN < JKL$).

71

by Boiteux, Steiner, and Hirshleifer in which there are two loads, each of identical length) may be difficult or awkward to generalize. Even more serious, the 'apparent' generalization may lead to error. We therefore take *the entire demand cycle* as the natural unit against which to express costs. Assuming that the 'period' referred to in sections 1 and 2 is the same length as an entire cycle (typically a day), the specification of costs used previously applies directly to our analysis of peak-load pricing. Thus under our formulation there is no difference between the conventional costing practices used in the analysis of uniform loads and those used to study the periodic-load problem, whereas this is not true in each of the papers referred to above. We therefore define short-run marginal costs as the operating costs of supplying the incremental unit of output (at levels of operation less than capacity) over an entire cycle, namely b per unit per cycle. Since incremental capacity costs continue at the rate of β per unit per cycle, long-run marginal costs are $b + \beta$ per unit per cycle.

In order for this specification of costs to be 'appropriate' to the problem of peak-load pricing, it is also necessary that demands be specified in a consistent way. In particular, it is necessary to weight each demand by the fraction of the cycle over which it prevails. Thus, demand is expressed as $D_i^{(w_i)}$, where i refers to the subperiod in question and superscript (w_i) to the fraction of the cycle during which the demand in question prevails, with each demand curve showing the amount of output per cycle which would be demanded at every price were the demand in question to prevail over the entire cycle. This permits us to handle subperiods of unequal duration, whereas equal-length subperiods are all that are explicitly dealt with (and appear to be implicit where the length of period is not stated) in earlier analyses. Thus our formulation is more general in this respect than those which have been developed previously. In order to simplify the analysis we make the conventional assumption that each periodic demand is independent. Whether or not this is a reasonable assumption is, of course, an empirical question. In circumstances where time patterns of consumption are relatively inflexible, the independence assumption is presumably a close approximation.[10]

10. The independent demand assumption has been examined again recently by Jora Minasian. As he points out, and as indeed is reasonably

We assume divisible plant initially and consider the two-period case with an off-peak load of length 8 hours and a peak load of 16 hours, so that demand is expressed as $D_1^{(1/3)}$ and $D_2^{(2/3)}$, respectively. These demand conditions, together with the cost relations specified above, are shown in Figure 2.

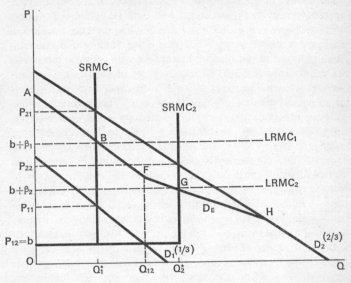

Figure 2

Solving for the optimum plant size geometrically requires that we develop a technique for combining the individual periodic-load curves to obtain an over-all 'effective demand for capacity' relation. For this purpose we note that, taking each periodic

---

evident, uniqueness is no longer assured when interdependent demand conditions prevail [9, pp. 360–62]. The general form of the solution to the interdependent demand problem is sketched out by Drèze [3, pp. 16–17].

Minasian also makes the interesting point that if a single uniform price is charged, and if plant capacity falls short of peak-load demands at this uniform price, the pattern of demand will be redistributed to reflect the waiting time associated with peak-load uses. Thus the implicit waiting time charge produces an effective set of differential prices despite a uniform pecuniary charge [9, pp. 356–7].

load by itself and assuming that the plant is operated only for the one load and is shut down during the remainder of the cycle, the price charged in the interval during which the plant is operated must be $b + \beta/w_i$ (where w_i is the fraction of the cycle during which load i prevails) in order that enterprise net revenue be zero. That is, under the conditions described, total revenue from operations will be $P_iQ_iw_i$, total costs will be $bQ_iw_i + \beta Q_i$, and only if $P_i = b + \beta/w_i$ will total revenue less total costs yield the zero net revenue result. Since this latter condition necessarily holds in long-run equilibrium in a system with constant returns to scale and divisible plant, clearly the price of $b + \beta/w_i$ is correct. We want now to construct a demand-for-capacity curve for each periodic-load curve which has the property that it intersects the long-run marginal cost curve at the capacity level Q_i corresponding to the price $b + \beta/w_i$. If such a curve can be obtained by a simple transformation of the periodic-load curve, the appropriate capacity (and consequently price) can be found directly rather than through the indirect process described above.

A curve with these properties can be constructed by taking the vertical difference between the periodic-load curve and short-run marginal costs (b), multiplying this difference by the fraction (w_i) of the cycle during which the periodic load in question prevails, and adding vertically this weighted demand-for-capacity curve to the short-run marginal cost curve. The resulting curve intersects $b + \beta$ at precisely the value of Q_i for which $P_i = b + \beta/w_i$ on the corresponding periodic-load curve. Extending the analysis so as to obtain an over-all demand-for-capacity curve requires that we combine the contributions to capacity made in every subperiod. This is accomplished by adding vertically to the short-run marginal cost curve the vertical summation of the individual weighted demand-for-capacity curves (obtained according to the procedure described above). The resulting effective demand-for-capacity curve for $D_1^{(1/3)}$ and $D_2^{(2/3)}$ is shown as D_E in Figure 2. It will be noted that D_E is kinked at F, which corresponds to output level Q_{12}, since for outputs that exceed Q_{12} the demand price along the off-peak-load curve is everywhere below $SRMC$. That this construction is correct and leads to a set of results that parallel those obtained for the uniform-load analysis in section 2 can be seen by considering the solutions that obtain under two different values of capacity cost (β_1 and β_2) in Figure 2.

For $\beta = \beta_1$ the $LRMC_1$ intersects the demand-for-capacity curve D_E at B, so that the optimum scale is Q_1^*. $SRMC_1$ is horizontal at level b from O to Q_1^* and is vertical thereafter. Thus the appropriate output in each subperiod is Q_1^*, with the price being P_{11} in the off-peak-load period and P_{21} at peak load. Total revenue is given by $P_{11}Q_1^*(\frac{1}{3}) + P_{21}(Q_1^*)(\frac{2}{3})$ while total cost is $(b + \beta_1)Q_1^*$. That these must be equal is seen by observing that for any value of β_1 for which the corresponding $LRMC$ curve intersects D_E anywhere in the range AF, and assuming that capacity is optimally adjusted and that P_{11} and P_{21} are chosen so as to equate $SRMC_1$ and demand price, the following relation will hold: $(b + \beta_1) - P_{11} = 2[P_{21} - (b + \beta_1)]$. Thus, the amount by which revenues in the off-peak-load period fail to cover pro rata total costs is precisely offset by revenues in the peak-load period in excess of pro rata total costs. Put differently, net revenue is identically zero in this system with completely divisible plant so long as (1) the intersection of the demand-for-capacity curve and the long-run marginal cost curve is used to define plant capacity and (2) prices in each period are set at the level at which the short-run marginal cost curve intersects the respective periodic-load demand curve. Our construction of D_E guarantees this result.

Consider now a capacity cost of β_2 per unit per period. $LRMC_2$ now intersects D_E at G, so that the optimum scale is Q_2^*. $SRMC_2$ is horizontal at level b from O to Q_2^* and then moves vertically upward. The appropriate prices and outputs, therefore, are $P_{12}(=b)$ and Q_{12} in the off-peak period, and P_{22}, Q_2^* during peak load. The revenues and operating costs during the off-peak load are equal. Thus revenues during peak load must be sufficient to cover both operating costs and the entire capital charge if zero net revenues are to be realized. Again, our construction of the effective demand-for-capacity curve, D_E, assures this result. To see this, we observe that, by virtue of this construction, P_{22} necessarily equals $b + (3/2) \beta_2$ at Q_2^*. Therefore revenue during peak load is $[b + (3/2)\beta_2]Q_2^* (2/3)$, or $(2/3)bQ_2^* + \beta Q_2^*$. Operating cost during peak load is $(2/3)(bQ_2^*)$. Hence the excess of revenue over operating cost during peak load is $\beta_2 Q_2^*$, which is the capacity cost per cycle, and zero net revenue results.

That positions B and G are optimal as claimed can also be seen by considering the effect on welfare of an incremental change in Q_1^* and Q_2^*, respectively. An increase in scale leads to a decrease in producers' surplus that exceeds the gain in consumers' surplus; a decrease in scale yields an increase in producers' surplus that is less than the loss of consumers' surplus. This can be judged by reference to either the D_E curve or the individual load curves taken separately.[11]

The problem can also be formulated algebraically and identical results obtained. Using subscripts 1 and 2 to refer to off-peak and peak-load demands, respectively, and w_1 and w_2 as the corresponding fraction of a cycle accounted for by each (and $w_1 + w_2 \leq 1$, with the equality holding unless there is a third period in the cycle during which plant is shut down altogether), we have as our periodic-load counterpart of (1)

$$W = (TR_1 + S_1)w_1 + (TR_2 + S_2)w_2 \\ - bQ_1w_1 - bQ_2w_2 - \beta Q_2. \quad (9)$$

The objective is to find the pricing rule in each subperiod and the optimum capacity, Q_2. If, as in case 1 described above, plant is utilized to capacity during both off-peak and peak-load periods, we have $Q_1 = Q_2$. Letting $Q = Q_1 = Q_2$, optimum plant size is obtained by differentiating

$$W = (TR_1 + S_1)w_1 + (TR_2 + S_2)w_2 - \\ bQ(w_1 + w_2) - \beta_1 Q \quad (9')$$

11. James Buchanan makes the point that if the marginal price is made to vary with the quantity demanded, and if income effects are at all important, the uniqueness of the solution is no longer assured despite independent demands [2]. While formally correct, the variations in marginal price that he employs rest, as he puts it, 'on the decision-maker's evaluation of different distributions of net consumers' surplus among separate periods' demanders' [2, p. 466]. Lacking specific reasons for holding otherwise, a neutral preference would seem usual, in which case the uniformity of marginal price over quantity is restored. Moreover, since even under his price variation scheme the price to any user never falls below b, the significance of the income effect that he discusses is strictly limited.

with respect to Q. Thus we obtain:

$$\frac{\partial W}{\partial Q} = P_{11}w_1 + P_{12}w_2 - b(w_1 + w_2) - \beta_1 = 0 \quad (10)$$

or

$$P_{11}w_1 + P_{12}w_2 = b(w_1 + w_2) + \beta_1.$$

Letting $w_1 = 1/3$ and $w_2 = 2/3$, this is precisely the result obtained from our geometry in Figure 2 for the case where $\beta = \beta_1$.

If instead plant is utilized to capacity only under peak-load demands, we have by differentiating (9) partially with respect to Q_1 and Q_2:

$$\frac{\partial W}{\partial Q_1} = P_{21}w_1 - bw_1 = 0 \quad (11)$$

or

$$P_{21} = b$$

$$\frac{\partial W}{\partial Q_2} = P_{22}w_2 - bw_2 - \beta_2 = 0 \quad (12)$$

or

$$P_{22} - b = \frac{\beta_2}{w_2}.$$

These are precisely the results obtained from our analysis of Figure 2 for $\beta = \beta_2$. Thus price in the off-peak interval is set equal to short-run marginal cost. The price during peak load is set at incremental operating cost (b) plus incremental capacity cost (β_2) divided by the fraction of cycle time accounted for by peak load (w_2).[12]

12. If, as in section 2, we take capacity as given by the constraint $\bar{Q}$ and formulate the welfare maximization problem as a Lagrangian, the parallel results to those obtained in equation (7) are:

(i) if $Q_1 = Q_2$ (the case where $\beta = \beta_1$)

$$P_{11}w_1 + P_{12}w_2 = b + \lambda_1,$$

(ii) if $Q_1 + Q_2$ (the case where $\beta + \beta_2$)

$$P_{12} = b$$

$$P_{22} = b + \frac{\lambda_2}{w_2}.$$

Again λ_i is the shadow price associated with the constraint, and if $\lambda_i > \beta_i$ an expansion is signalled whereas if $\lambda_i < \beta_i$ a contraction is indicated.

The multiperiod generalization of equations (9)–(12) is both easy and obvious. The welfare function in this instance becomes

$$W = \sum_{i=1}^{n} (TR_i + S_i)w_i - \sum_{i=1}^{n} bQ_iw_i - \beta Q^*,$$

where Q^* refers to optimum system capacity. Optimality requires that $P_i = b$ in those periods when plant is not utilized to capacity and, letting I be the subset of periods when capacity is fully utilized,

$$\sum_{i \in I} (P_i - b)w_i = \beta$$

By way of summarizing the argument, we have as basic principles for dealing with periodic demands (assuming that costs and demands are defined as suggested above):

A. Optimal plant size (assuming fully divisible plant) is given by the intersection of the $LRMC$ curve and the effective demand-for-capacity curve.
B. Optimal price in every subperiod is given by the intersection of the $SRMC$ curve and the subperiod demand curve.
C. In a fully adjusted, continuously utilized system with only two periodic loads:
   (a) Peak-load price always exceeds $LRMC$.
   (b) Off-peak-load price is always below $LRMC$.
   (c) Only when the off-peak load fails to use plant to capacity when priced at $SRMC$ does the peak load bear the entire burden of the capacity costs.

Before extending the analysis to deal with indivisible plant, we consider first how our approach differs from those of Boiteux, Steiner, and Hirshleifer. With respect to Boiteux, the principal difference is that he uses only equal-length subperiods (both in his geometry and [apparently] in the appendix) and hence there is a lack of generality in his results. Although he solves the optimum pricing problem for the two-period case both geometrically and analytically, he lacks a device for aggregating periodic loads geometrically and thus solves the optimum capacity problem only analytically (and only for the special case of equal-length-subperiod loads).

Steiner and Hirshleifer each employs a geometric technique that correctly handles the peak-load capacity and pricing problem for the case of two equal-length-subperiod loads. Instead of using a weighted average of subperiod demands to obtain an effective demand-for-capacity curve in the way we have done, they sum the periodic loads vertically. This technique, together with the way in which they define their costs in order to support the technique, suggests that the periodic-load problem requires rather unconventional apparatus for its solution. It thus appears that the solution to the periodic-load problem is something other than a simple generalization of the usual uniform-load results. In addition, both Steiner's geometric treatment of the three-period case [7, pp. 590–91] and Hirshleifer's verbal generalization to the $n-$ (equal length) period case [3, pp. 456–7] require that capacity costs be redefined for each condition. It is obvious, however, that capacity costs *per cycle* are independent of the number of subperiods included, and expressing costs in terms of the cycle, as we have, rather than for the subperiod, as they do, avoids this respecification problem. Moreover, since neither explicitly indicates the necessity for this respecification, uncritical implementation of their results easily leads to error.[13]

13. Consider, for example, what seems to us the 'natural' interpretation of Hirshleifer's argument. For the two-period case he observes that 'If the demand price . . . for a single period alone did exceed $b + \beta$, an increase in capacity is obviously called for' [5, p. 456]. Generalizing to the n-period case he states that 'more capacity should be added if . . . [in any of the n-periods] the demand [price] for *any* single period alone . . . exceeds $b + \beta$' [5, p. 457 (italics added)]. In the absence of explicit instructions to the contrary, the standard presumption is that the specification of β in both citations is identical. But, assuming that both statements are correct, this is clearly impossible. Thus suppose that demand price exceeded $b + \beta$ in only one of the subperiods in both the two-period and n-period cases and that during the remainder of the cycle capacity is never reached, so that service is supplied at the short-run marginal cost price of b. Thus the only contribution to capacity costs in each case occurs during the one subperiod when price exceeds b. Letting capacity be Q^*, the [net revenue over operation costs is $\beta Q^* (1/2)$ for the two-period case and $\beta Q^* (1/n)$ for the n-period case, assuming that each of the n periodic loads is of equal length. Obviously if capacity costs are covered for the two-period problem they can not be for the n-period case. Hence the presumption that β is the same in both the two-period and n-period cases must be replaced by one in which, if β_2 is the capacity cost in the two-period case and β_n in the n-period case,

Consider now the extension of our analysis to deal with indivisible plant. Replacing the assumption of fully divisible plant by one in which indivisibilities are present is made easy by our construction of an effective demand-for-capacity curve. Using this device, our analysis in section 2 applies directly. Thus the criterion for shifting from Q_1^* to $Q_i^* + E$ is identical to that shown in Figure 1: whenever the triangular area defined by Q_1^*, the effective demand-for-capacity curve, and the $LRMC$ exceeds the area within $Q_1^* + E$, the D_E curve, and $LRMC$, the additional efficiency unit should be installed. The conditions under which one would be just indifferent between adding the capacity or not are shown in Figure 3.

Again we assume that the off-peak load prevails for 1/3 of the cycle and the peak load for 2/3, D_E being the weighted sum of $D_1^{(1/3)}$ and $D_2^{(2/3)}$. By construction, $IJN = JKL$, so that the benefits of installing the additional efficiency unit are just offset by the costs. In terms of the individual demand curves, the following relation holds: $2/3(NFG) - 2/3(GKH) - 1/3(MNKO) = 0$, where $2/3(NFG - GKH)$ is the amount by which the increase in consumers' surplus that is realized by adding the new capacity exceeds the loss in producers' surplus during peak-load operations (assuming that demand is supplied at $SRMC$ prices both before and after), and $1/3\ MNKO$ is the amount by which the additional consumers' surplus falls short of the loss in producers' surplus during off-peak operations.

All of the implications that were developed in section 2 concerning the effects of indivisibilities, including those that were obtained in connection with variable demand, likewise apply to the analysis of periodic demand. One additional comment, however, might be useful.

It will be noted that peak-load price in Figure 3 after installation of the new efficiency unit is less than $LRMC$. This appears to contradict our proposition C(a) given earlier. Actually, however, there is no inconsistency; the circumstances are different be-

---

$\beta_n = n/2\beta_2$. Given this respecification, Hirshleifer's optimality rules are correct, but not otherwise. Since both he and Steiner fail to indicate that such a respecification is necessary, the possibility that their prescriptions would lead to error can hardly be dismissed.

tween Figures 2 and 3 – the difference of course is that fully divisible plant is no longer assumed, whereas it was previously. Optimally adjusted plant under the assumptions of constant returns to scale and complete divisibility leads to zero profits and, necessarily, peak-load price will exceed *LRMC*. The optimally

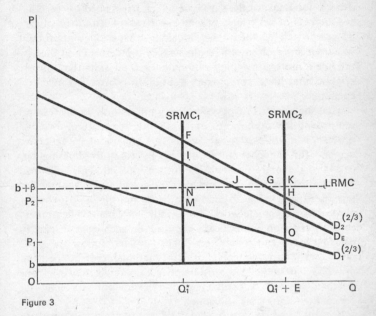

Figure 3

adjusted plant when indivisibilities are present, however, will only accidentally lead to zero profits. Thus, if demand is $D_E + \epsilon$, the optimal plant size is $Q_1^* + E$, and although P_2 may exceed *LRMC*, it need not (and indeed does not in the circumstances shown in Figure 3).

Conclusions

Although we have hardly disposed of all of the interesting questions that relate to the optimal pricing of periodic loads, we believe that the approach employed tends to clarify the issues in a useful way and readily lends itself both to specific application and to possible extensions. By explicitly introducing a social welfare function at the outset we attempt to emphasize that the choice of optimal size plant and the pricing of services from plant of given capacity are not special problems at all but are merely particular applications of a perfectly general welfare formulation. Thus a good deal of the mystique which has tended to surround the analysis of peak-load pricing can be dispelled at the outset. This approach has the further advantage that we can interpret in welfare terms each of our results as they are derived and thereby provide a more convincing rationale for the results than merely arguing that they come from 'straightforward maximization techniques'.

That the analysis of periodic loads differs only in degree and not in kind from the more commonly investigated uniform-load problem is made particularly evident by our use of the 'effective demand for capacity curve' device. By carefully defining our cost and demand relationships in advance, any periodic-load problem can be reduced to a demand-for-capacity analysis for purposes of selecting optimal plant size, and this holds whether we deal with completely divisible or indivisible plant. The optimal capacity criterion is identically the same in each case. Pricing to periodic loads and to uniform loads similarly follow the same pricing criterion: equate short-run marginal cost to demand price. Each periodic load must be priced separately, however; our weighted average demand curve is relevant only for long-run optimality (plant size) adjustments.

Possible extensions of our analysis would presumably include relaxing the assumption that demands in each period are independent. It is unlikely, however, that a useful geometry can be devised to deal with this more general case. Likewise it may be desirable to qualify the proposition that continuously equating short-run marginal cost to demand price is optimal. As Boiteux has pointed out, it may be useful for customer planning purposes to follow a more stable pricing policy [1, pp. 70–2]. However, Boiteux's proposal that 'Whatever the capacity of existing plant, *the need to keep prices steady* generally leads prices to be fixed as if the plant were of optimum size' [1, p. 72] itself appears to be sub-optimal. Rather, optimality requires that the benefits of pricing according to short-run marginal cost (the pricing rule that ob-

tains under our welfare formulation) be weighed against the benefits of Boiteux's stable price proposal and an appropriate balance
struck. For this purpose, a more broadly conceived social welfare
function that makes explicit the gains to be secured through price
stability is required. The trade-off between the short-run benefits
of price flexibility and the long-run benefits of stability can then,
presumably, be optimally arranged.

Generalizing the analysis to deal with nonlinear costs might
also seem useful. This is easily accomplished analytically, but our
geometry fails to apply in this instance. Under the assumption
of long-run constant returns to scale, so that the *LRMC* curve
remains horizontal and only the short-run cost curves display
curvature, the nonlinear case yields results qualitatively similar to
those obtained above.[14] Since the analysis of unequal-length
periodic loads with nonlinear costs is somewhat more involved,
does not lend itself to treatment geometrically, and fails to produce insights that differ appreciably from those obtained from
the linear model, there are obvious advantages, for purposes of
explicating the peak-load problem, in using the simpler linear
form.

The relevance of the analysis to problems other than electricity

14. The nonlinear cost problem can be formulated as: maximize,

$$W = \sum_{i=1}^{n} (TR_i + S_i)w_i - \sum_{i=1}^{n} (TVC_i)w_i - \beta Q^*.$$

Differentiating partially with respect to Q_i, we obtain n equations of the
form

$$P_i = SRMC|_{Q_i},$$

and differentiating with respect to Q^*, we have

$$\beta = -\sum_{i=1}^{n} \frac{\delta}{\delta Q^*} (TVC_i)w_i.$$

Thus price in every period is set equal to short-run marginal cost, and
capacity is extended until the weighted average marginal change in operating
costs is equal to the marginal capacity cost, β.

It should be noted that Hirshleifer solves geometrically the case of nonlinear costs with constant returns to scale for the problem of iden-
tical-length-subperiod load by employing Steiner's vertical summation
procedure [5, pp. 452–7). We also point out that, as anyone familiar with
the Hirshleifer–Steiner dispute over the interpretation of marginal costs as
they apply to the economics of peak-load pricing will recognize, we agree
with Hirshleifer that the solution does not involve discriminatory prices.

generation might also be indicated. The optimality principles derived above regarding capacity and pricing of electricity apply to any public service which our welfare formulation and cost and demand specifications properly embrace. This would presumably include the investment in and operation of transportation facilities (airports, public surface transportation, bridges, etc.), recreation facilities, natural gas transmission, etc. Since the bridge problem is one of such long-standing interest, yet remains the source of continuing confusion, an application of the analysis to this question might be particularly useful. The major cause for misunderstanding here is the failure to distinguish between circumstances where capacity is a parameter from those in which it is a variable. Optimal pricing for a facility of *specified* capacity is given by the rules shown in equation (7) and footnote 10. As is obvious from inspection of these relations, if (for whatever reason) an oversized bridge is 'inherited', so that the value of λ_i in these expressions is zero or negligible, and if operating costs are also so small that they can be disregarded, a zero use charge will be optimal. If, however, capacity is a variable rather than a parameter so that facility size can be adjusted (and indivisibility constraints aside), optimal pricing and optimal plant size are given by the relations shown in Figure 2 and equations (10)–(12). Even with zero operating costs, a positive use charge will be required here since, with capacity correctly selected, a positive price will be needed to ration capacity between those activities for which marginal benefits are high and those for which it is low. Assuming constant returns to scale, optimal pricing to this fully adjusted facility will yield precisely zero net revenues, and the bridge in these circumstances will be self-supporting. This latter, however, has no special normative significance. If there are indivisibilities, if increasing or decreasing returns to scale exist, or if capacity is given rather than subject to determination, optimal pricing will yield the zero net revenue result only accidentally if at all.

References
1. MARCEL BOITEUX, 'La tarification des demandes en pointe: application de la théorie de la vente au coût marginal', *Revue Générale de l'Electricité* (August 1949), *58*, 321–40; translated as 'Peak-load pricing', *Jour. Business*, April 1960, *33*, 157–79; reprinted in James R. Nelson (ed.) *Marginal cost pricing in practice*, Englewood Cliffs, N.J. 1964, pp. 59–90.
2. J. M. BUCHANAN, 'Peak loads and efficient pricing: Comment', *Quart. Jour. Econ.*, August 1966, *80*, 463–71.
3. J. H. DRÈZE, 'Some postwar contributions of French economists to theory and public policy', *Amer. Econ. Rev.*, supplement, June 1964, *54*, 1–64.
4. A. HARBERGER & N. ANDREATTA, 'A note on the economic principles of electricity pricing', *Applied Econ. Papers*, March 1963, *3*, 37–54.
5. JACK HIRSHLEIFER, 'Peak loads and efficient pricing: Comment' *Quart. Jour. Econ.*, August 1958, *72*, 451–62.
6. H. S. HOUTHAKKER, 'Electricity tariffs in theory and practice', *Econ. Jour.*, March 1951, *61*, 1–25.
7. H. W. KUHN & A. W. TUCKER, 'Nonlinear programming', in J. Neyman (ed.), *Proceedings of the Second Berkeley Symposium on Mathematical Statistics and Probability*, Berkeley, Calif., 1951, pp. 481–92.
8. ALFRED MARSHALL, *Principles of economics*, 8th edn, New York, 1948.
9. J. R. MINASIAN, 'Ambiguities in theory of peak-load pricing and application of theory of queues', *Land Economics*, August 1966, *42*, 355–62.
10. P. O. STEINER, 'Peak loads and efficient pricing', *Quart. Jour. Econ.* November 1957, *71*, 585–610.
11. RALPH TURVEY, 'Optimization and suboptimization in fishery regulation', *Amer. Econ. Rev.*, March 1964, *54*, 64–76.
12. D. M. WINCH, 'Consumer's surplus and the compensation principle', *Amer. Econ. Rev.*, June 1965, *55*, 395–423.

4 P. D. Henderson

Investment Criteria for Public Enterprises

P. D. Henderson, 'Notes on public investment criteria in the United Kingdom', *Bulletin of the Oxford University Institute of Economics and Statistics*, vol. 27 (1965), pp. 55–89. Amended by the author.

A. Introduction

1. This paper reviews in broad terms some problems of devising suitable rules and procedures for guiding the investment decisions of public enterprises. It outlines some of the main issues of policy which have arisen in recent discussions of public investment criteria, and considers briefly, with special reference to the United Kingdom, some alternative ways of resolving these issues.

2. The paper has a number of limitations which must be mentioned at the outset. First, no reference is made to the special problems of project evaluation in developing countries. The analysis relates to public enterprises which are operating in an advanced economy in which full employment – using this term in a rather broad sense – can be assumed to be the normal state of affairs. Second, the main purpose of the paper is expository, so that it contains little that can be claimed as original. At the same time, a good deal of discretion has necessarily been exercised in the selection and treatment both of the issues that arise and of the sources that have been used, and personal judgements have not been excluded. Third, the analysis is by no means comprehensive. Some loss of rigour and thoroughness has been consciously incurred, in the interests of brevity and simplicity; and it is to be feared that further sacrifices of the same kind have been unwittingly made, for less defensible reasons. Thus the list of references appended, though fairly extensive, is far from complete, and some problems to which other authors have given considerable attention have been neglected here. In short, this is a partial and introductory survey.

3. In one respect the scope of the discussion is wider than might appear from the title of the paper, since the same issues

may arise in considering public investment projects which are undertaken by central or local government authorities, rather than by public enterprises. The main difference between the two is that public enterprises typically produce goods or services for sale, whereas with some forms of government investment – for example, in roads or health services or education – this may not be the case. In these latter situations special problems arise of estimating the prospective benefits from investment, problems which are less commonly encountered in the case of public enterprises and which are not considered in this paper.[1] With this reservation, however, the argument is applicable to investment in the public sector as a whole.

4. One can indeed go farther than this. If investment is defined more broadly, to include all outlays which are currently undertaken in the expectation of returns which will accrue mainly or entirely in future accounting periods, then the objects of such expenditure are clearly not confined, as in the usual national accounts classification, to new fixed assets and increases in stocks. A substantial though unknown proportion of public authorities' current expenditure on education, training, research and development, health services, and defence should in that case be included; and though the problems of measurement and identification which arise here may often be more serious than is the case with investment as conventionally defined, some of the broad issues which this paper tries to discuss are in principle equally relevant.

5. In the section which immediately follows we consider the choice of an appropriate decision formula for evaluating investment projects under certain restrictive assumptions. From this the familiar conclusion emerges that a rate of interest must be chosen for purposes of discounting future costs and benefits, and in section C the problem of deciding on such a rate is examined. In the next three sections the main initial restrictive assumptions are successively relaxed, and the implications of doing this are discussed. Section D deals with some questions concerning the definition of benefits; section E with problems posed by the existence of risk and uncertainty; and section F with

1. On these, the reader is referred to Dorfman [9], and to Prest and Turvey [46] and the references given there.

constraints, particularly with those that relate to the amount of capital expenditure that can be undertaken in a given period. Finally, section G contains some general concluding remarks. There are also two appendices. Appendix I sets out a simple arithmetical example, in order to illustrate different possible methods of evaluating and ranking investment projects, while Appendix II contains some necessary acknowledgements and disclaimers.

B. Investment Decision Formulae

6. It is convenient to begin with some preliminary definitions and assumptions.

7. First, the heroic but useful assumption is made that all the costs and returns associated with an investment project, or an investment choice, are measurable and known with certainty. We thus abstract from the problems presented by the definition and measurement of costs and benefits, and by the existence of risk and uncertainty. Consideration of these problems is deferred to sections D and E, though in fact it is not possible to ignore them completely until then, since as will be seen the choice of interest rate, and the ranking of projects with an agreed interest rate for discounting, may be affected by the treatment of uncertainty and the way in which costs and benefits are defined.

8. Although this assumption makes it unnecessary to define costs and benefits at all rigorously at this stage, it should be said that both are conceived in comprehensive terms, and should not be identified with the financial returns accruing to the investing agency. By the *net benefits* associated with a project in any period we mean the difference between the value of the benefits or returns arising in that period and the costs attributable to it; thus net benefits in a given period may be negative. (The illustrative figures presented in Table 1 of Appendix I are of net benefits in this sense.) The use of the term 'net' here has nothing whatever to do with deducting depreciation, which has no place in calculations of this kind since all capital expenditures are accounted for in full at the time when they are incurred. Both for this reason and because costs and benefits are defined comprehensively, net benefits need bear no particular relation to net profits.

9. In many instances, the evaluation or choice of a project does not involve the computation of benefits. This is the case where a particular objective can be taken as given, such as the production of a specified amount of electric power, and the problem is to minimize the cost of achieving this objective.

10. A second simplifying assumption which it is convenient to make for the time being is that capital rationing is absent – i.e. that there is no predetermined allocation of permitted investment expenditure to particular enterprises or agencies or sectors of the economy. In this case any investment project can be undertaken which satisfies some agreed criterion, and the problem is to specify the criterion. Where, however, a constraint is imposed, for example in the form of a limited capital budget, then the problem is to choose the best set of projects that is consistent with observing the constraint. Consideration of this, and of other problems associated with the existence of constraints, is deferred until section F.

11. Whether or not there is capital rationing, it is necessary to have some means of evaluating investment projects, and of ranking them in order of merit in cases of possible incompatibility, that is, where the choice of one project either will or may preclude the choice of another. It is often suggested or implied that this can be done by calculating in each case the rate of return on the project. There are, however, two reasons why this method of approach may be unsatisfactory. First, as will be seen below, the rate of return – even when it is correctly defined and meaningful – is not a reliable criterion for ranking projects: it is not the case that a project with a higher rate of return is necessarily to be preferred to one with a lower rate. Second, different concepts of what is meant by the rate of return are in use, and these may lead to widely differing results.

12. There are various ways in which it is possible to calculate, from the same set of net benefit figures, something which can be called a 'rate of return'. A number of these are illustrated in Appendix I, from which it can be seen that not only the absolute values for the rate of return on a given project, but also the ranking of projects in relation to one another, may depend critically on the method of calculation that is used. What seem to be the most popular rule of thumb methods of evaluation – namely the

average rate of return (in some sense) and the payoff period – share the basic defect that they fail to take proper account of the timing of costs and returns. Both this and other possible weaknesses – such as dependence of the calculations on the particular depreciation formula that happens to be in use – can be avoided by the use of *discounted net benefits*, or to use a more familiar term, discounted cash flows.[2] This involves setting out the prospective costs and returns associated with an investment for each year over the life of the project, and discounting them according to the period in which they accrue. By doing so, it is possible to calculate a rate of return that takes account of the two dimensions that any investment possesses, namely the amount of prospective net benefits and their timing.

13. Despite this crucial advantage, the use of the discounted cash flows method of appraisal sometimes meets with resistance. Three grounds of opposition are commonly encountered.

14. First, the method is sometimes alleged to be difficult and esoteric. This objection is hard to take seriously: an acquaintance with the basic principles of compound interest is not an unreasonably exacting demand to make of top management and senior civil servants, and of those who prepare submissions for them.[3] Moreover, use of the method may well simplify understanding of the issues. For example, it would certainly have made it possible to avoid the sort of confusion that was generated a few years ago in the minds of two government departments, and of the House of Commons Select Committee on the Nationalized Industries, when confronted with the various methods that had been used to evaluate the rate of return on a big railway electrification scheme.[4]

2. As we have noted in paragraph 7 above, net benefits are defined in comprehensive terms, and are thus not identical with the net cash inflows to the investing agency. The case where cash flows can be taken as measures of net benefits is a special one, though possibly fairly common with public enterprises.

3. Good expositions of the method may be found in several sources, including Hirshleifer [23], Merrett and Sykes [38], Grant and Ireson [21], and N.E.D.O. [41]. A lucid exposition of the mathematics involved is given in chapter 6 of Kemeny [26]. Sets of tables for discounted cash flow and related calculations are given, together with explanatory notes and examples, in Lawson and Windle [28].

4. House of Commons Select Committee [25], pp. *i–lii*, and references given there to the minutes of evidence taken by the Committee.

15. Second, it may be argued that so many other factors will affect the success or failure of an investment project that the choice of formula to estimate the rate of return is a comparatively small matter. In particular, the argument has been used that where the degree of uncertainty is great the extra refinement of setting out annual expected cash flows, rather than using cruder short-cut methods, may be pointless. This again seems wrong. It is not the case that the choice of formula is a minor matter, since different formulae can lead to widely different evaluations and sets of rankings. Further, the recognition of uncertainty is a poor reason for not making explicit forecasts of magnitudes which ought in principle to affect the decisions that are made. Uncertainty is difficult to deal with, but oversimplification of this kind is not a sensible method of trying to allow for it.

16. A third argument is that many types of investment decisions do not lend themselves to analysis in terms of prospective cash flows. For example, it may be thought impossible or unnecessary to apply such a test to what are regarded as 'routine' replacements, or to investment which is not undertaken for straightforward commercial reasons, such as expenditure on prestige advertising or welfare facilities. There is something in this argument, since some investments do not yield a predictable cash return. On the other hand, the argument is sometimes applied to situations in which it is invalid. For example, discounting can and should be applied to replacement outlays, and possibly to some other forms of investment where at first sight it might appear inapplicable. This can be done by making use of the 'with and without' principle – that is, by comparing the anticipated cash flows in the case where the project is undertaken with those where it is not, and by discounting the net cash flows or differences. Further, as was noted in paragraph 9 above, the method of discounting can be used to select the least-cost means of realizing a given objective. In such cases there is no need to quantify returns.

17. It may be concluded that wherever possible the method of discounted net benefits should be used in the appraisal of investment projects in the public sector. It is clear that the advantages of the method have become increasingly recognized in the

United Kingdom during recent years, both in public enterprises and in the government departments concerned, and that its use is now becoming general. Nevertheless, it may still be the case that the formal and universal adoption of this method of appraisal, to the exclusion of a variety of inferior decision formulae, would be a significant step forward.

18. Granted that discounting is to be used, a choice then arises between two different ways of applying it. The issue here is a technical one, and in many instances the two alternatives, properly interpreted, will give the same results; but arguments have been advanced on both sides for preferring one to the other. These two alternatives are the *present value* rule and the *internal rate of return* rule.

19. The present value of an investment is arrived at by discounting all prospective net benefits back to the present, using a predetermined rate of interest. If there is no capital rationing, the correct course is to undertake all those projects which have a positive present value of discounted net benefits.

20. The internal rate of return on an investment is that rate of interest for which the present value of discounted net benefits is zero. With this decision formula, and again on the assumption that there is no capital rationing, the correct course is to undertake all projects which have an internal rate of return higher than a predetermined rate of interest. It can be seen that with a given rate of interest this will lead to precisely the same results as the present value rule.

21. The rules as just stated fail to cover one important – perhaps typical – form of decision, namely that between incompatible projects, where the choice of one precludes the choice of another. Topical examples of this in the public sector are the choice between nuclear and thermal power stations, and between diesel and electric traction on the railways. A special and frequent case of incompatibility is the choice between undertaking a project now and undertaking it at some later date;[5] decisions about the timing of replacement expenditure fall into this cate-

5. The problems which arise in connexion with this choice have been extensively analysed in Marglin [36]. A summary treatment is provided by the same author in chapter 4 of Maass [31].

gory. Where incompatible projects are being compared, use of the present value rule implies choosing the project which has the largest present value. Use of the internal rate of return rule implies taking the stream of differences between the net benefits of the two projects, and calculating the internal rate of return on these. This rate is then compared with the predetermined rate of interest. Once again, for a given rate of interest, the two rules will yield identical results, at any rate provided that a unique internal rate of return exists.[6]

22. It is clear that if there are two incompatible projects, it is not necessarily correct with either rule to choose the one with a higher internal rate of return.[7] A simple numerical example will illustrate this point. Suppose that project A involves a present outlay of 1,000 and will yield a constant annual stream of net benefits of 200 for ten years; and that an alternative project B involves an immediate outlay of 2,000 and will yield a constant annual stream of net benefits of 360, also for ten years. The internal rate of return on A is about 15 per cent, while for B it is rather over 12 per cent; but it does not follow that A is to be preferred. Suppose that the rate of interest that has been laid down as appropriate for discounting purposes is 8 per cent. This should be compared with the internal rate of return on the stream of differences between the net benefits of the two projects. If B is undertaken rather than A, this implies an immediate outlay of 1,000 together with annual net benefits of 160 for ten years. The internal rate of return on this 'project' is over 9 per cent, and in these circumstances B is therefore preferable. (The present value rule with the same rate of interest would lead to the same result: discounting at 8 per cent, the present value of A is 342 and that of B is 416.)

23. So far the argument has given no reason for choosing one rule rather than the other. Some of the main reasons that have

6. The significance of this qualification is made clear in paragraph 26 below.

7. Some authors, for example Turvey [49], seem to regard this as constituting the essential difference between the two rules – i.e. acceptance of the internal rate of return rule is taken to imply choosing an investment with a higher rate of return in preference to one with a lower. But it is possible to restate the rule in a more acceptable way, as is done here.

been advanced on both sides are briefly summarized in the remainder of this section.[8]

24. An advantage of using the internal rate of return is that it is stated in a much more familiar form, since people are used to thinking in terms of rates of return on capital.

25. It is further claimed on behalf of this rule that it permits a clearer and more straightforward presentation of the different possibilities in two situations which are prevalent in business enterprises: first, where the cost of capital to the enterprise, which may be taken as the appropriate minimum rate of interest, is hard to determine; and second, where risk is present. In each case use of the internal rate of return will normally give a single figure for the rate, which can then be directly compared with alternative estimates of the cost of capital, or with the rates that may be laid down as the minimum required in the case of risky projects.[9] With the present value rule, on the other hand, it is necessary to compute the present value of the projects for different rates of interest, and to present therefore a range of values corresponding to these rates. It can be argued that this is more complicated and time-consuming.

26. On the other hand, use of the internal rate of return rule has the disadvantage that there may be no unique value for the rate. In what may be regarded as the normal case, an investment project is associated with two phases: an initial period of negative net benefits is followed by a phase in which the stream of net benefits is positive. Thus the sign of the values of net benefits changes once only, from negative to positive. In this case there is a single unique solution for the internal rate of return, which is also the highest rate of interest for which the project is acceptable. If, however, there is more than one change of sign, so that the period of the life of the investment falls into more than two phases, there will be more than one value for the internal rate of return; in fact, it is easy to invent examples in which the values of the rate will not even be real numbers. While such examples

8. The discussion here draws mainly on Hirshleifer [23], chapter 7; Merrett and Sykes [38], chapter 5; Wright [54, 55]; and Feldstein and Flemming [19].

9. This is not meant to imply that risk should necessarily be taken into account by fixing a higher minimum acceptable rate of interest or rate of return, a question which is discussed below, in section E.

often bear little relation to any conceivable investment project, the possibility of multiple solutions has to be taken seriously. For example, there are investments which involve significant terminal costs for damage, disposal or restitution: mine shafts which lead to subsidence, nuclear power stations, and iron-ore workings are cases in point. Again, where incompatible projects are being compared, so that what have to be discounted are the differences between net benefit streams, changes of sign are possibly more likely to occur than where separate projects are being considered on their own.

27. The possibility of non-uniqueness has sometimes been regarded as a fatal objection to the generalized use of the internal rate of return rule; and it is certainly a disadvantage, from which the present value rule is free. On the other hand, one could argue that in the usual case, where a unique solution exists, the internal rate of return should be used. Further, it has been persuasively argued that multiplicity of solutions is not a decisive objection to using the internal rate of return.[10]

28. A second argument in favour of the present value rule is that it admits of the possibility of varying the rate of interest, and thus the discounting factor, over the life of the project, whereas with the internal rate of return formula the discounting factor is a uniform one for all periods. This is certainly a formal advantage, but it is doubtful whether it has much practical significance, since there is no generally acceptable rule for adjusting discounting factors over time.

10. Cf. Wright [55]. The argument can be roughly summarized as follows. The only case that need be taken seriously as a practical possibility is the three-phase one, where the stream of net benefits is first negative, then positive, and then negative again. Here there are two solutions for the rate of return. There are thus three possibilities: no real solution; one real solution (within the meaningful range of discounting factors); and two real solutions (possibly coincident). Which of these is the case may easily be determined in advance by inspection of the undiscounted cash (net benefit) flows. Where there is no real solution, the project is obviously unacceptable. Where there is one real solution, this is the relevant one, and is (as in the two-phase case) the highest rate of interest for which the project would be acceptable. Where there are two real solutions, these determine the limiting values of the rate of interest within which the project is acceptable; for values outside this range, whether higher *or lower*, the project would have a negative present value.

29. In the absence of capital rationing, the arguments in favour of choosing one formula rather than the other do not seem decisive. At the present stage of evolution of British practice, it is probably more important to stress the advantages of the discounting procedure in evaluating public investments, rather than the superiority of one particular way of applying it. Properly interpreted, both rules should lead to the same results, and the choice becomes largely one of convenience. It may be concluded that there should be an understanding of, and a readiness to use, each of the rules.

30. The possibility of capital rationing, however, introduces a further consideration. It has been argued that in this situation the present value rule is superior on formal grounds and in convenience of operation.[11] The choice here, however, depends largely on the criterion that is adopted for ranking investment projects, in a situation where some projects that would be acceptable in the absence of capital rationing must be abandoned or postponed because of it. The choice of a criterion for ranking in turn depends on the basis that is adopted for arriving at a particular interest rate, for purposes of discounting net benefits. The latter question is discussed in the section which follows, while capital rationing is treated in section F below. In the meantime, we may note that the choice between the present value rule and the internal rate of return rule may be affected by a judgement on the prevalence of capital rationing, and on the best way of selecting projects in this situation.

31. Whether present value or the internal rate of return is used, the same basic issue arises. In the former case, a predetermined rate of interest has to be used in discounting net benefits. In the latter case, it is necessary to specify a minimum acceptable rate of return which projects must reach in order to qualify for approval. The section which follows considers in outline the problem of arriving at an appropriate rate of interest for discounting.

C. The Choice of an Interest Rate

32. The problem of choice here is inescapable, and a decision on the question can only be taken centrally, by the government.

11. Cf. Feldstein and Flemming [19] and Turvey [49].

Unfortunately, there is no unique or agreed way of arriving at an answer. So far in this paper it has been fairly easy to reach conclusions of a sort; but from now on it is only possible to do so on the basis of arguments and assumptions that are clearly open to dispute.

33. We may distinguish at least four ways of deriving a rate of interest for use in the evaluation of public investments. (Strictly, the second method can be regarded as a variant of the fourth, but the order of exposition adopted here is convenient.) They do not lead to the same result, nor indeed does any of them except the first lead to a unique result. Each of them will be outlined in turn.

34. The *first* possibility is to use the rate of interest on long-term government securities. This rate has the useful characteristics that it exists and is known precisely. Unfortunately, it also has obvious demerits, the nature of which can most easily be made clear in reviewing the alternatives. Choice of the government bond rate may be regarded as a last resort, the outcome of despair of the possibility of reaching a result by another route.

35. The *second* possible method is to use a *social time preference rate* for discounting, which reflects the government's judgement about the relative value which the community as a whole is believed to assign, or which the government feels that it ought to assign, to present as opposed to future consumption at the margin. It is occasionally argued either that the government bond rate already represents such a social time preference rate, or that an object of government policy should be to ensure that it does. Neither of these arguments is convincing. It is clear that existing gilt-edged rates reflect a number of factors – such as the market's assessment of the likelihood of future increases in the price level, or of the chances of fluctuations in bond prices – which are unconnected with the community's marginal rate of substitution between present and future consumption. It is hard to see how government policy could guarantee to change this state of affairs; and in any case monetary policies will rightly be influenced by other considerations, such as the pressure of demand, the current state of the balance of payments, and the monetary policies pursued by other countries.

36. Moreover, even in the absence of such influences, the

connexion between market-determined rates of interest and social time preference would be open to question. A number of authors have argued that public decisions concerning the allocation of resources over time should be taken on the basis of a politically determined social time preference rate, rather than the rate that would exist even in a perfect capital market. One reason for holding this view is the belief that individuals may discount future benefits at too high a rate, because of what Pigou termed a 'defective telescopic faculty'.[12] Another and perhaps more persuasive argument is that the time preference of individuals may be different with respect to public (and thus collective) investment decisions: each person may be willing to make greater sacrifices than he would in his private capacity, and to place a lower premium on current as opposed to future consumption, when he knows that the sacrifice is shared by the community as a whole. But this collective willingness to provide for future generations is not reflected in market rates of interest, which therefore provide no guidance as to how people would wish the government to act. Thus market rates of interest have no normative significance for public investment decisions.[13] It is thus incorrect to state, as some economists have done, that in choosing a rate of interest for discounting in the public sector the government long-term borrowing rate can be taken as a minimum.[14] On the contrary, if the arguments of this and the previous paragraph have any force at all, the presumption must be that the marginal social time preference rate is below the bond rate.

37. However, it is easier to arrive at this negative conclusion, that the market rate is unacceptable, than to reach agreement on a suitable value for a social time preference rate.[15] Some economists have argued that there is no valid reason to discount

12. Pigou [44], p. 25. A cynic might remark that of all human entities it is governments which exhibit the most obvious signs of such a defect.

13. Cf. Marglin [34]. The limitations of market rates are well summarized, with a lot of useful references, in Feldstein [16].

14. For example, Day [7], p. 40.

15. There is, of course, a very considerable body of writings on this subject, to which the summary treatment here does not pretend to do justice. Recent discussions, which contain extensive references to earlier work, are to be found in Eckstein [11], Feldstein [16, 17], Marglin [34], and Berman [3].

future benefits merely because they will occur later in time.[16] There are, however, three main lines of argument from which it is possible to derive a positive rate.

38. The first of these is that expected future consumption is subject to risk and uncertainty. Strictly, this is ruled out for the moment by our assumption that risk is to be ignored. But even if we accept the view that different investments should be subject to higher or lower rates for discounting, according to the degree of risk that seems to be involved, it is not clear that the least risky should be discounted at a positive rate.

39. The second line of argument regards time preference as being rationally implied by the inevitability of death. If I have an assurance of £100 in twenty years time, it is not rational of me to regard this as equivalent to £100 now, since although it is certain that I shall receive the money if I survive, it is not certain that I shall survive. Thus the sum should be multiplied by the probability of my receiving it in order to determine its present value; and this is equivalent to discounting it at a positive rate. Such a rate could be determined for a community (ruling out the possibility of a major war) from a knowledge of the age distribution and the actuarial probabilities of survival at each age. For a country such as the United Kingdom, the resulting rate would be very low, probably of the order of 1 per cent.[17] It is debatable, however, whether this argument for a positive time preference rate is one which governments ought to be ready to accept.[18]

40. The third argument for a positive rate is based on the assumption that as the level of real consumption per head of a community increases, each absolute addition to it will yield successively smaller increases in economic welfare – i.e. that the marginal utility of consumption is falling for each individual. In so far as it can be expected that real consumption per head will rise over time, it follows that a given future increase in consumption

16. A recent example is Bhagwati [4], p. 108: 'A system of time-discount is popular with economists, but seems to have little justification: after all, the very purpose of prior calculation is to avoid the kind of myopia that the use of time-discount rate implies.'

17. Cf. Eckstein [11], pp. 456–60.

18. One reason for rejecting it is that if only the welfare of those who are at present alive is taken into account, all benefits which would accrue more than a century or so ahead must be totally ignored.

per head is worth less than an equal present increase; for even if we discount future utility at a zero rate – thus rejecting the idea of pure time preference based on uncertainty or death – the same increase in consumption per head will yield a smaller increase in utility in the future. By making explicit assumptions about the utility-consumption function, and about the future rate of growth of consumption per head, it is possible to derive a corresponding rate of time preference.

41. The problem here is, of course, to choose the right set of assumptions. In particular, some value has to be assigned to the elasticity of the marginal utility function with respect to changes in consumption, and this is one of the economist's conspicuously empty boxes. Projections of the rate of growth of consumption are more firmly based, but even here there is scope for disagreement.[19] Further, the rate of time preference derived will also be affected by two other factors:[20] first, how far the government is concerned to maximize consumption per head, as opposed to total consumption; and second, whether it is thought desirable to incorporate some element of pure time preference, say because of the fact of mortality or the existence of uncertainty.

42. Thus it is not possible to do more than compute the range of possible rates which can be derived from different sets of assumptions; and since the range is quite wide, and any set of assumptions must be based on a combination of value judgements and assertions of fact which are alike disputable, this does not necessarily lead to a generally acceptable result.

43. For illustrative purposes only, the results of a specimen calculation may be given. Let us assume (i) that the concern of policy is with consumption per head, rather than consumption; and (ii) that pure time preference is ruled out. With respect to the other parameters, assume (a) that the rate of population growth is 1 per cent per annum; (b) that consumption per head will grow at 2 per cent per annum; and (c) that the utility function is of the Bernoulli form, so that individual utility is proportional to

19. Strictly, the rate of growth of *per capita* income and consumption will tself depend on the rate of time preference chosen, since this will affect the ratio of investment to final expenditure. (Cf. paragraph 46 below.)

20. The analysis here is based on Feldstein [17], from which the specimen calculations of paragraph 43 are also taken.

the logarithm of consumption, and the marginal utility function
has a constant elasticity of -1. This set of assumptions yields a
social time preference rate of 3 per cent per annum. If, however,
we change the value of the elasticity to -2, and incorporate the
positive pure time preference rate of 1 per cent derived in paragraph 39 above, the figure rises to over 6 per cent per annum.
These are not, of course, meant to be taken as extreme or limiting
values.

44. In each case it was here assumed that the elasticity of the
marginal utility function is constant. This itself is questionable,
not only because we do not actually know the shape of the function, but for a more specific reason. It is arguable that in the case
where consumption per head falls below the level previously
achieved the elasticity will assume higher values. Thus if my
income has increased from £900 to £1,000, and then falls again to
£900, I may feel worse off in the final situation than in the initial
one. If there is anything in this argument, then the social time
preference rate should be adjusted upwards in situations where
investment is rising rapidly enough to cause consumption per
head to fall.[21]

45. The difficulty of deriving a unique and acceptable rate in
this way has led one group of economists at least to propose an
alternative method of approach to the problem. In a recent
consultants' report to the U.S. Bureau of the Budget [52], it is
suggested that the government's chosen rate of time preference
can be inferred from other policy decisions that have been taken.
Suppose that a particular target rate of growth has been adopted,
and that the rate of investment required to achieve it – and therefore the sacrifice of present consumption, by comparison with
what would have been required with a lower growth target – can
be estimated. In this case a definite and calculable rate of time
preference is implied.

46. This method is open to an obvious objection, namely that
the target rate of growth ought to be derived from the social time

21. Rather than varying the rate used, it would be possible to impose as
a constraint on government policy that consumption per head should not
be allowed to fall, or alternatively (and more generally) that its rate of
increase should not be allowed to fall below a figure greater than or equal
to zero.

preference rate, and not vice versa. The objection is not too serious, however, since the choice has to be made between different related combinations of growth rate, investment rate, and time preference rate.[22] A more damaging objection is that the relation between the rate of investment and the rate of growth is not known at all precisely. The report in fact suggests a possible range of social time preference rates of between 2·5 per cent and 4 per cent; but it is not clear why the authors should feel so confident that these are limiting values.

47. The outcome of this discussion is twofold. First, the determination of a social time preference rate is an uncertain and speculative matter. Arguments can be found to defend the choice of particular rates lying between extreme values which may be disturbingly wide. Second, a rate which might be roughly appropriate to British conditions, and consistent with the value judgements of present-day British governments, could reasonably be taken to be of the order of 3–4 per cent, which is well below the current and recent level of the long-term rate of interest.

48. It may be felt that this second conclusion is evidence that it is a waste of time to try to arrive at a rate of interest for use in public investment decisions by the second method – that is, by making use of a social time preference rate. At present, in both the public and the private sectors, any investment project with a prospective rate of return of no more than 4 per cent, even after allowing for risk and uncertainty, would normally be ruled out.[23] To adopt (say) 4 per cent as the rate of interest for discounting in the public sector might seem to involve a drastic change, not necessarily for the better. Further, if all public sector projects which passed this test – i.e. which promised a positive present value when net benefits were discounted at 4 per cent – were to be sanctioned, this might imply a substantial rise in investment above current levels. Such an increase might be impossible to achieve over a period, because of physical constraints; and even if feasible it might involve a sacrifice in terms of current consump-

22. Cf. Marglin [34], pp. 110–11.
23. The qualifying adverb is needed to take account of the exceptional projects which appear to be sponsored without any serious expectation of a rate of return even as high as this.

tion which the electorate would strongly disapprove of.[24] In either case, it would be impossible to apply the 4 per cent rule. Some way would have to be found of limiting investment demands below the level which the rule would imply; and it might be argued that the obvious way of doing this would be to discard 4 per cent and use a much higher rate.

49. Thus it may appear that the government would do better to choose directly a higher rate, with the existing long-term rate of interest as a minimum; and in making its choice, to disregard the futile arguments of futile economists about what an appropriate social time preference rate might be if it were possible to find one. As will be seen, such a conclusion may be too sweeping. For the moment, however, it can be concluded that the second possible approach to the choice of a rate of interest for use in the public sector has not yielded a solution to the problem.

50. The *third* possible method is to make use of an *opportunity cost rate* of interest. The opportunity cost of undertaking a particular public investment project may be defined as the value to society of the use to which the resources employed in the project would otherwise have been put – in other words, the value to society of whatever it is that the project precludes. By expressing the opportunity cost as an equivalent rate of return it is possible to derive an opportunity cost rate of interest for discounting.

51. The case for using this approach, and a particular procedure for applying it, have been developed in Hirshleifer [23].[25] It is there argued that any public investment project must be regarded as displacing an equivalent amount of investment in the private sector; that the marginal rate of return (i.e. the minimum acceptable rate of return) in the most closely comparable part of the private sector in the United States might be put, at the time of writing, at around 9 per cent; and that 10 per cent would therefore be a suitable rate of interest to use in evaluating water

24. The argument of paragraph 44 above may be relevant here.

25. A similar argument has been advanced by Stockfisch [48], though he derives a different and higher opportunity cost rate. The same procedure is recommended for the United Kingdom in Merrett and Sykes [38], p. 170, and in Munby [39], but neither of these sources contains any extended discussion of it.

resource projects in the United States, allowing for what is alleged to be the greater element of risk in public investments.[26]

52. In order to arrive at a result of this kind, it is necessary to overstep the bounds of our initial assumptions, for the estimated marginal rate of return in the private sector is not a riskless rate. It is affected by the bond rate, which itself is by no means risk-free; and it presumably embodies a further risk premium, which arises from uncertainty about the yields that will be achieved on private investments. Thus the figure of 9 per cent quoted in the previous paragraph is not comparable to the illustrative figures given earlier, of a possible social time preference rate.

53. This third approach, at any rate in the particular form outlined, has the merit of producing a determinate and apparently reasonable result by a fairly straightforward set of arguments. Also, it may appear as a merit rather than a defect that the (possibly metaphysical) problem of determining a riskless rate can be by-passed, and that the rate of interest chosen in this way is likely to exceed rather than fall short of the government borrowing rate. Nevertheless the method is open to a number of objections.

54. One difficulty is that the marginal rate of return on comparable private investments is not known at all precisely. A minimum required rate of 15 per cent is sometimes quoted as being standard practice in private industry, but such a figure should probably not be taken at face value. Rates of return are often calculated on the basis of unsatisfactory conventional formulae, which may give misleadingly high figures.[27] Again, it may be that a high figure such as 15 per cent is designed to cover specific risks and contingencies not explicitly allowed for in project estimates. Even where firms do not add a risk premium as a matter of policy, it may be convenient to do so in practice. It is more polite to tell the sponsor of a project that its rate of return just fails to measure up to the exacting standards of a progressive

26. If public investments were thought to be less risky than private, a corresponding downward adjustment could be made. This is suggested in Day [7] in relation to investment in the road system in Britain. Either adjustment – positive or negative – should be made only if it is held that degrees of risk should be reflected in the rate of interest used for discounting.

27. Some interesting recent evidence on this point is given in Neild [42].

enterprise, than to tell him that his estimates of costs and returns are grossly optimistic. Finally, the enforcement of a minimum rate of return which is significantly higher than the marginal cost of capital to the enterprise is justified only in the case where there are immediate constraints – human or organizational – which restrict the rate of growth of the enterprise. A well-publicized insistence on high rates of return seems occasionally to be regarded as a symbol of corporate virility, but may equally well be evidence of failure to maximize profits.

55. What is required in order to arrive at an opportunity cost rate is the estimated marginal cost of long-term capital to large private businesses. Unfortunately, this involves problems both of theory and of measurement which have not been fully resolved.[28] As a result, different estimates made for a given country at a given time would not necessarily coincide; and in point of fact quite widely different figures have been suggested as the appropriate opportunity cost rate of interest.[29]

56. Apart from the difficulty of measuring this opportunity cost rate, a number of arguments have been adduced against the view that such a rate is the correct one to adopt for discounting the net benefits of public investments.

57. First, it has been argued that the benefit that will accrue to society from private investment will generally exceed the private return to investors, which is more correctly measured by the marginal output–capital ratio.[30] On this view, a higher opportunity cost rate would be required if the third method were used. Consideration of this argument is postponed to section D below, where the problem of defining benefits is discussed. Fortunately the postponement does not affect the issue under consideration

28. An introduction to these problems can be found in Dryden [10], where further references are given. Cf. also Merrett and Sykes [38], chapters 3 and 4.

29. Thus Stockfisch [48] argues for a rate of 15 per cent, in which no element of risk premium is embodied. He presents evidence to suggest that this is the average rate of return to private investment in the United States, and that the marginal rate may not be significantly below the average. The point is made by Enke [13] that in evaluating systems which offer future savings in operating costs at the expense of higher initial cost the U.S. Department of Defense has used a criterion which seems to imply a rate of interest for discounting of about 15 per cent.

30. Cf. Feldstein [16], p. 364, and references there cited.

here – namely, the choice of a rate of interest for discounting – since those who have argued that the social rate of return on private investment exceeds the return to the firm have also rejected the use of an opportunity cost rate of interest, for one or both of the reasons that follow. Thus no one has in fact suggested using a rate of interest in the public sector which is higher than what is believed to be the marginal (private) rate of return on comparable investments in the private sector.

58. Second, it has been argued that it is a mistake to suppose that any single rate can be found which will measure the opportunity cost of public investments. In evaluating these, the opportunity cost should be separately calculated, using an independently determined social time preference rate in doing so. This is in fact the fourth method of approach, which is considered in paragraphs 61–88 below.

59. The third objection is in effect subsumed under the second, but may conveniently be stated separately. It may be asked what reason there is to assume that public investment projects will displace at the margin private investment, rather than private consumption or government current expenditure on goods and services. The advocates of an opportunity cost rate based on this assumption have argued that the composition of investment, as between the public and the private sectors, must be treated as an entirely distinct problem from that of deciding the total amount. If the government has reason to think that private investment projects which would be in the social interest are not being undertaken because they are thought by businesses to be insufficiently profitable, it can take appropriate measures – for example, by bringing down interest rates, or through fiscal concessions – in order to remedy the situation. In the United Kingdom at present, the system of investment grants and capital allowances can be regarded as a means to this end. Thus the government should try to ensure that all investment projects, whether public or private, are undertaken only if they meet certain standards which it can itself determine and which are common to both sectors. It should not apply a dual standard, as between the two sectors, which can only lead to a misallocation of resources.

60. On the other side, it has been held that this argument overestimates the capacity of the government to ensure that the level

of private investment is optimal. Such a difference of opinion is clearly not easy to resolve. But it is evident that the government's knowledge of the plans of private investors, of the likely effects of these plans, and the quantitative result of any given policy measure designed to influence them, is in each case very limited. In so far as this is the case, the notion of a single standard for both the private and the public sectors, and therefore a discounting factor for public investment based on the estimated marginal rate of return in the private sector, becomes questionable. The application of dual standards, as between the private and public sectors, can be defended as both difficult to avoid and not necessarily harmful. The danger that low-yielding public investments may displace high-yielding private ones cannot be ignored. On the other hand, the use of the opportunity cost rate described above carries with it the danger that socially desirable projects in the public sector will not be undertaken.

61. We turn now to the *fourth* method of tackling the problem. This combines the use of a social time preference rate with a calculation of the social opportunity cost of public investments.[31]

62. This method differs from the second one, outlined in paragraphs 35–46 above, in that it incorporates into cost–benefit calculations an estimate of the opportunity cost, as distinct from the money cost, of a given project. It is thus more general, since the situation in which the money cost and the opportunity cost coincide may be thought of as a special case. On the other hand, this gain in generality has to be paid for, both in additional complexity and through the introduction of further grounds for disagreement about the best procedure to follow. These problems are of course superimposed on those of determining a social time preference rate, which have already been outlined above.

63. The fourth method also differs from the opportunity cost approach that has just been discussed, in two respects. First, it rejects the assumption that public investment should be regarded as displacing at the margin an equivalent amount of private

31. The summary treatment here is largely based on Eckstein [11], the consultants' report to the U.S. Bureau of the Budget [52], and Feldstein [15, 18]. Other important references under this heading include Krutilla and Eckstein [27], Steiner [47], Marglin in chapter 4 of Maass [31] and Marglin [35].

investment. In this respect also it can be regarded as more general, and less simple. Second, it makes use of a previously determined social time preference rate both in evaluating the opportunity cost of a project, and also in computing the present value of the net benefits it is expected to produce after completion. In contrast, the third method compares the money cost of a project with the present value of prospective net benefits after completion, the latter being discounted at the estimated marginal rate of return on comparable private investments.

64. The difference between these two methods may be illustrated by a simple numerical example. Consider the case of project X of which the initial capital cost is 1,000, which produces constant annual net benefits of 160 for ten years after completion. If these net benefits after completion are discounted at a positive opportunity cost rate of 9 per cent, their present value is 1,027. The present value of the project as a whole is thus positive at 27 (i.e. 1,027 *less* the capital cost of 1,000), and (in the absence of capital rationing) the project is admissible. With a 10 per cent interest rate the present value of the net benefits after completion is only 983. The project then has a negative present value and becomes inadmissible.

65. In appraising the same project by the fourth method, the net benefits after completion must be discounted at whatever is taken to be the social time preference rate. Suppose that this is 3 per cent. In that case the present value of these net benefits is 1,365. This figure must now be compared with the opportunity cost of the project, which may well exceed 1,000, and the estimation of which is considered below, in paragraphs 73–86. The project is admissible if and only if the opportunity cost is below 1,365.

66. The same argument can be put in a slightly different form using the notion of *benefit–cost ratios*. This notion can be given a variety of interpretations, according to the way in which costs and benefits are treated in computing it. Because of this ambiguity, and since the use of such ratios as a method of ranking investment projects can easily give mistaken results,[32] it is necessary to give an explicit definition of what is meant by the term in this context.

32. There is a good discussion of the varieties and limitations of benefit–cost ratios in McKean [33], chapter 7.

The benefit–cost ratio is defined here as the ratio of the present (discounted) value of all net benefits, apart from the initial capital costs, to those capital costs. The capital costs are to be measured in *money* terms – i.e. they are the actual costs that are anticipated. For brevity, though not strictly correctly, we term this the ratio of net benefits after completion to capital costs.[33] In our example of project X, and using the 3 per cent rate of interest for discounting net benefits after completion, the value of the benefit–cost ratio, thus defined, is 1·365. Using the fourth method of project appraisal, the project should be undertaken only if this ratio is higher than a predetermined minimum or cut-off value, which is given by the estimated ratio of the opportunity cost of public investment projects to their actual capital cost.

67. Thus in our example the project becomes a borderline one (*a*) using the third method of arriving at a rate of interest for discounting, if the chosen rate is about 9·6 per cent; and (*b*), using the fourth method with a social time preference rate of 3 per cent, if the minimum benefit–cost ratio is 1·365. In this particular instance, therefore, the use of a 3 per cent interest rate together with this cut-off benefit–cost ratio is equivalent to discounting at a rate of 9·6 per cent, with a cut-off benefit–cost ratio of unity.

68. A similar equivalence can be established for any project: a particular combination of a social time preference rate for discounting and a minimum benefit–cost ratio can be shown in each case to yield the same result as discounting by a 'synthetic' rate of interest which differs from the social time preference rate. If the cut-off ratio exceeds unity – i.e. if the opportunity cost of projects exceeds the money costs – the equivalent synthetic rate will exceed the social time preference rate, as in the case of our illustration; if the cut-off ratio is below unity, because the opportunity cost is thought to be less than the money cost of a project, then the converse is true.

69. It does not follow, however, that the fourth method is simply a rather more elaborate method of deriving a single opportunity cost rate which can be generally applied. If we

33. This formulation does not cover the case in which a project begins to yield positive net benefits before final completion, even when the remaining capital costs are taken into account in computing net benefits.

consider two different investments, each of which is evaluated in accordance with this method, the corresponding synthetic rates will in general be different: they will only coincide if the time profile and duration of net benefits are the same for each project.

70. The difference may easily be illustrated by taking another numerical example. Suppose that project Y, like our earlier project X, also involves an outlay of 1,000, but that it yields net benefits in only one instalment of 2,150 ten years after completion. The present value of these net benefits discounted at 9·5 per cent – a rate at which the net benefits after completion of project X just exceed its capital cost of 1,000 – is only 868. Judged in this way, Y is clearly inferior to X; only at rates of interest below 8 per cent would it have a positive present value. On the other hand, the present value of 2,150 in ten years time, discounted at an assumed social time preference rate of 3 per cent, is 1,600, whereas the present value of the prospective net benefits after completion of project X is only 1,365. With a cut-off benefit–cost ratio of say 1·5, Y would be accepted and X rejected by this criterion. The use of a lower rate of interest for discounting has had the effect of giving a greater relative weight to more distant benefits, and thus of changing the order of merit of projects.

71. From this it can be seen that the fourth method is not simply a more elaborate method of arriving at an opportunity cost rate of interest. As was foreseen in paragraph 58 above, the use of any single opportunity cost rate is inconsistent with the method. On grounds of simplicity, this is a disadvantage.

72. The main objections to the fourth method, however, arise from the difficulty of determining the opportunity cost of a project. There are four distinct problems here, which will be outlined in turn.

73. (a) First, it is necessary to decide whether a public investment project, or set of projects, should be treated as displacing an equivalent amount of some other category or categories of final expenditure. The decision will depend on what is assumed or believed about the current level of final demand and the desired level, and about the effectiveness of government policies to bring the two together. On the one hand, it can be argued that the correct assumption to make is that the level of demand should be taken as given and appropriate, so that any public investment

under consideration must be regarded as precluding other final expenditures by an exactly equivalent amount. In this case the opportunity cost will in general be at least equal to the nominal or money cost. On the other hand, if it could be shown that a project would make use of resources that would otherwise remain unused – for example, by absorbing unemployed labour in a depressed region then the opportunity cost would be below the money cost, since to the extent that such resources were used expenditure on the project would not be at the expense of some other component of demand.

74. This is not at all an easy question. It cannot be answered simply by saying that either we have (or must be assumed to have) full employment, in which case public investment must displace *pro tanto* other expenditures, or we do not have full employment, in which case it displaces none or some small amount.

75. Consider first the assumption that there is full employment. There are two reasons why this may be too facile. First, what is relevant is not merely the existing pressure of demand and level of output, but the prospective values of these over the period in which the investments under review will actually be undertaken. Second and more important, genuinely full employment of resources is in practice seldom if ever realized. Even in the periods of very high pressure of demand in the United Kingdom in recent years, there have been low participation rates and involuntary unemployment in particular areas.[34] Further, at any given time, and again even with very high levels of demand, it is usually possible to find plants, firms or even whole industries where excess capacity exists, so that the firms involved could argue that the marginal social cost of meeting an increase in demand would be small. Thus the assumption of full employment fails to do justice to the complexity of real life. In fact, it is best regarded not as an attempt to describe reality, but rather as a way of stating a particular convention or decision rule, namely that an increase in one form of final demand is to be treated as precluding an equivalent amount of some other form. The reason for advocating such a convention is clear: so far as possible, questions of allocation, and of the composition of final demand, should be kept separate from questions of stabilization policy.

34. Cf. N.E.D.O., [40], chapter C.

But the fact that there are almost always some unemployed or underemployed resources means that it is not sensible to adopt such a convention uncritically, and to insist on its observance in all situations.

76. On the other hand, it is not the case that the opportunity cost of using unemployed resources is necessarily zero or negligible. Once again, the point is not merely whether they are unemployed at present, but whether in the absence of the investment projects concerned they would remain so. More important, the use of unemployed resources in a particular region or industry may prevent or delay a transfer to more socially productive forms of activity, in which case there will be a positive opportunity cost to society from employing them in this way. The doctrine that a low or zero shadow price should be assigned to unemployed resources may extend an open invitation to a potentially long list of regional or industrial pressure-groups, with harmful effects on efficiency and growth over any but a short period.

77. Thus one can only conclude that the extent to which any given public investment project will preclude other final expenditure, and should be reckoned as doing so, will vary according to circumstances.[35] This is a matter on which even well-informed and disinterested observers are likely to disagree; and most participants in public investment decisions are (reasonably enough) by no means disinterested.

78. (b) We come now to the second problem. Once it has been decided that an investment project should be regarded as displacing a given amount of other final expenditure, it is necessary to decide how this amount will be distributed between private consumption, private investment, and public authorities' current expenditure on goods and services.[36] Two ways of handling this problem have been suggested. First, it has been argued that this is something over which the government itself has full control; thus no difficulties of estimation arise.[37] Second, it is possible to

35. This problem seems to have received less attention from economists than it deserves. An honourable exception is McKean [33], chapter 9.

36. In the case where some form of constraint applies to total public expenditure, or to the total of public investment done, the displaced expenditure can be presumed to fall within these categories.

37. Cf. Berman [3], p. 21.

make alternative assumptions about the particular means which the government will adopt in order to reduce other forms of demand by the required amount, and to estimate the effects of these on the various components of final demand.[38] The first view is something of an oversimplification: the authorities can decide (for example) that all the displaced expenditure shall be personal consumption, and there is of course a variety of measures which they can take to try to ensure that this is what happens; but they can never be quite sure how far they have succeeded in their aim. Moreover, there may be constraints which limit their freedom to choose between different possible sets of measures. Thus there is a genuine problem here, which the second approach sets out to meet. But since we cannot be certain about either the kind of measures that would be adopted by the government or about their effects on the composition of demand, the results of using this approach can be no more than an educated guess, about which there is unlikely to be unanimity.

79. (c) The third problem is an extension of the second. A strict measure of the opportunity cost of adopting a project will be affected not only by the present value of what it displaces now, but also by its effects in later periods. As an illustration, the choice between nuclear and conventional power stations may be taken. In so far as nuclear stations are chosen, current investment requirements will be higher, and the opportunity cost of this difference must be computed. But in future periods the choice of nuclear power, since it involves lower currently incurred running costs, will enable final expenditure in the economy as a whole to be greater than would have been the case if thermal stations had been chosen. The present value of these future gains may exceed their nominal amount, and this should properly be taken into account in reckoning the opportunity cost of the extra investment now required in the nuclear case.[39] Although formal methods can be developed to handle this sort of problem, this can only be done at the cost of increasing the complexity of calculations and

38. Cf. the consultants' report to the Bureau of the Budget [52], pp. 16–20.

39. This point is quite distinct from the argument that benefits arising from the reinvestment of surpluses should be taken into account, which is considered in section D below.

widening the potential area of disagreement that surrounds them.

80. (d) The fourth and last problem is perhaps the most serious. Suppose that we have decided that a public investment project costing x will displace other final expenditure to the value of αx $(0 \leqslant \alpha \leqslant 1)$, and that the amount αx has been distributed in some reasonably convincing way between personal consumption, private investment, and public authorities' current expenditure on goods and services. We now have to determine the present value of the displaced expenditure in each of these categories, so as to arrive at the opportunity cost of the initial capital cost of x.

81. There is no generally accepted formula for doing this, and the methods that have been suggested may easily lead to very different results.

82. Let us consider first consumption, whether public or private. Two principal ways of deriving the present value of such expenditures have been put forward. The first proceeds by calculating where the reductions will fall, classifying consumers by income group, and then arrives at an aggregate rate of marginal (private) time preference for consumers on the basis of information about the rates at which the members of the groups have actually borrowed or lent.[40] The estimated marginal time preference rate is then regarded as a perpetual yield on the consumption expenditures foregone, the present value of which can be found by discounting at the social time preference rate. Thus suppose that private consumption is expected to fall by an amount k; that the marginal private time preference rate is put at 5 per cent; and the marginal social time preference rate is taken as 3 per cent. The social opportunity cost of the consumption foregone is then $0 \cdot 5k/0 \cdot 3$, or $1 \cdot 6k$.

83. This method has been criticized on three grounds: first, that the borrowing and lending rates used in the calculation may not be genuinely marginal rates; second, that they are far from riskless; and third, that private time preference rates are not relevant, for reasons that have mentioned in paragraphs 35–6

40. This is an inadequate summary of a complex calculation, which is described in full in Krutilla and Eckstein [27]. It is well summarized and criticized in Feldstein [18].

above. These objections could be simultaneously met by sub-stituting the marginal social time preference rate for any private rates that might be derived in the way just described. This yields the straightforward result that the opportunity cost of £1's worth of consumption is £1.

84. This seems to be a better as well as a simpler procedure. However, there is one practical difficulty in applying it, which is that both private and public consumption as defined in national income accounts contain a considerable element of expenditures that will yield benefits beyond the current accounting period. The present value of these (net) benefits should in principle be found by discounting them at the social time preference rate; and this would require an estimate of the amount of these expendi-tures and of the net benefits they are expected to produce over time.

85. We now consider private investment. The method of deal-ing with this is to take the estimated marginal rate of return on investment in the private sector as a perpetual yield, and to dis-count it at the social time preference rate. Thus suppose that private investment is expected to fall by an amount m, and that the marginal rate of return is taken to be 9 per cent and the social time preference rate 3 per cent. The social opportunity cost of the investment foregone is then $0.9m/0.3$, or $3m$. This raises the difficulty that was referred to in paragraph 55 above, of arriving at an agreed estimate for the marginal rate of return on private investment; and the difficulty is increased if it is held that the rate used should be a riskless one, since actual market yields are affected by risks of various kinds.

86. Apart from this difficulty, it has been argued – as we noted in paragraph 57 above – that the marginal private rate of return on private investment will differ from the social return, for which a better measure would be the marginal output–capital ratio. Rates of return defined in this way could be expected to be considerably higher than marginal rates of profit, so that the opportunity cost of private investment foregone would be corre-spondingly greater. This again is a question on which agree-ment is lacking.[41]

41. The case for measuring the social returns on investment by the marginal output–capital ratio is discussed in paragraphs 95–8 below.

87. We have now considered the four main problems which arise in estimating the opportunity cost of the funds employed in a public investment project, and it is clear that in relation to each of them there is considerable scope for disagreement, both on formal and on empirical matters. Thus it would be quite possible for two estimates of the opportunity cost of a project, arrived at independently by disinterested and well-informed observers, to differ by a factor of two or more. Since as we have noted such estimates are usually made by people who are far from disinterested, wide divergences may be regarded as predictable and even normal.

88. This objection to the fourth method becomes more serious when it is considered in conjunction with another property of the method, namely its total lack of familiarity at present to non-economists. Thus there may be a real danger that it would prove difficult or impossible to operate in practice. The officials or executives who are sponsoring a particular project may accept, even if grudgingly, a negative verdict which is based on the argument that the project fails to promise a sufficiently high rate of return on the actual capital expenditure. They are much less likely to acquiesce in a rejection derived from a calculation that the opportunity cost of the project is (say) 1·75 times its nominal cost. Even if they understand and are prepared to accept this way of looking at the problem, they will be fully aware that any particular estimate of opportunity cost is open to dispute, on a variety of possible grounds, in each individual case.

89. The outcome of this lengthy (but by no means exhaustive) summary is inconclusive and therefore unsatisfactory, since it appears that none of the four methods of deriving a rate of interest for use in the public sector is free from substantial objections. This outcome is the more disturbing in that the choice of a rate is not just a matter of philosophical interest, but may have a considerable influence on public investment programmes. The higher the rate chosen, the greater the bias in favour of investments with relatively low initial expenditure, and with benefits that accrue earlier rather than later. Thus wherever there are alternative systems, which differ in the time profiles of their respective net benefits, the rate of interest that is used for discounting may affect the order in which they are ranked. It might,

for instance, determine the choice between nuclear and thermal power stations; the extent to which railway electrification is undertaken; and the size of the road investment programme, the choice of projects within it, and the details of system design – for example, whether motorways should be initially constructed with four or six lanes. Two other areas of decision where the choice of rate might have important consequences are standard-ization – since conversion to standard systems typically involves initial capital expenditure which yields benefits into the distant future – and housing and town planning, where such issues as whether to modernize existing dwellings or to replace them by new ones may be affected by the valuation placed on time.

90. The total amount of public investment undertaken may also be affected, as well as the composition of a given amount. It is not necessarily true that the choice of a lower rate will imply a larger total: even apart from the possibility of capital rationing, this will depend on the way in which the opportunity cost of public investments is reckoned. But it is a reasonable presumption that the volume of public investment will be inversely related to the chosen rate of interest.

91. Precisely because the choice of a rate is important, it is desirable for the government to make up its mind despite the difficulties of doing so. Failure to specify a rate may open the door to inferior methods of project appraisal, in which proper account is not taken of the timing of prospective net benefits; and it will permit the use of a wide variety of rates, which will not necessarily be explicit or consciously chosen, in different public sector projects. The French example, where the use of discounting procedures in public enterprises has been combined with a centrally determined rate of 7 per cent, shows at any rate that a decision can be reached on this question.[42]

92. However, such a decision may be affected not only by the considerations that have been raised in this section, but also by

42. Though the reasons why 7 per cent has been thought to be a suitable rate do not seem to be clear. On this point, there is a reference in P.E.P. [45]. Further, there is evidence that higher rates than 7 per cent have been used as a rationing device, since not all projects with a positive present value at 7 per cent could be sanctioned.

factors which have been largely excluded up to now by our initial restrictive assumptions. Questions that arise in connexion with the reckoning of net benefits, the existence of risk and uncertainty, and the prevalence of financial constraints, may have a bearing on the choice of a rate of interest, in addition to raising separate problems of their own. In the three following sections we consider some aspects of each of these.

D. The Concept of Net Benefits

93. As was noted in paragraph 3 above, the problem of estimating net benefits is often much more straightforward in the case of public enterprises than with many other forms of public investment, since these enterprises are producing goods and services for sale on the market. Thus the amount that purchasers are expected actually to pay for these goods and services may give a reasonable approximation to the prospective values of gross benefits, without the need for resorting to indirect methods of estimation. Subtracting from these values in each period the anticipated costs of providing the benefits gives a stream of net benefits over time, which can be discounted. In the limiting case, where the gross benefits are taken to be the receipts that will accrue to the enterprise as a result of undertaking the investment, and the costs are reckoned as those that will actually be paid out by the enterprise as a result of it, the evaluation of the investment becomes a matter of estimating its profitability. We then have the situation referred to in paragraph 12 above, in which discounted net benefits are taken to be identical with discounted cash flows to the enterprise.

94. In so far as net cash flows can be taken as the measure or indicator of net benefits, the evaluation of projects is greatly simplified. There is also the advantage that the method of appraisal which should be used is broadly familiar to managers of public enterprises and consistent with an accepted standard – namely profitability – for assessing managerial performance. Unfortunately, the profitability measure of net benefits is not necessarily reliable, and a number of reasons can be given for qualifying or rejecting it. Some of these have already been encountered in the previous section: the argument that the oppor-

tunity cost of a public investment may differ from its nominal or money cost is an example. We now consider the issue in more general terms. The argument is set out in five brief sub-sections, each of which refers to a different aspect of the same basic problem.

95. *(a) The social profitability of investment*

We have already had occasion, in paragraphs 57 and 86 above, to mention the view that the social profitability of an investment is measured not by its profitability to the enterprise which undertakes it but by its output–capital ratio, and that this ratio should therefore be used in estimating social benefits. This view has not received much attention in writings on cost–benefit analysis;[43] but since it has been endorsed by a number of economists, and since its adoption would make a very considerable difference to the evaluation and ranking of public investment projects, by comparison with the more usual present value or rate of return calculations, it deserves to be considered. Indeed, it is a rather sad commentary on the state of economics that different sets of authors should be advocating such widely divergent criteria for measuring benefits, with little apparent meeting of minds, simply because they happen to have approached the question from a different direction.

96. We define the output–capital ratio of an investment as the ratio of the value added that will be generated by the investment, in a typical year after its completion, to its initial capital cost. It is perhaps surprising that this measure of benefits should have gained support, since its use is open to two serious objections.

97. First, when defined in this way as a single figure, the ratio has the defect that it fails to take proper account of either the amount or the timing of prospective value added. Even if we suppose that the ratio is constant over time, society is clearly not indifferent between two projects which offer the same ratio, but of which one generates a stream of value added for ten years while the other does so for twenty. Moreover, the assumption of a constant ratio is highly unrealistic. Projects may take very different lengths of time to reach maturity, and to yield their full

43. As we have seen above, a notable exception is Feldstein [16].

benefits. So long as a positive rate of interest is used for discounting, this property should be taken into account by the method of evaluation that is used; but the use of a single output–capital ratio is not consistent with this. Again, there are many cases where the annual rate of value added will change over time; and two time-streams, even if they have the same duration and the same average annual ratio, need not be equivalent when discounted at a positive rate. In both these respects – that is, in the neglect both of the duration of benefits and of their possible variation over time – the use of the output–capital ratio is open to precisely the same objections as the use of the average rate of profit on an investment, which is described and illustrated in Appendix I.

98. This point could be met by dispensing with the concept of a single ratio, and reformulating the criterion so as to take account of timing and duration. In this case what is suggested is a present value or rate of return calculation, but with value added, rather than the difference between currently accruing receipts and costs, taken as the measure or as a principal constituent of net benefits. But even in this modified form the suggested criterion is open to the second objection, which is that it is wrong to assume that the wage and salary costs which form part of value added should not be treated as costs to society. According to the criterion, society should be indifferent between two projects, each of which has the same prospective figure for the (discounted) present value of value added, but of which one has consistently higher wage and salary costs than the other because greater quantities of labour are involved. This can be justified only if the extra labour employed in the first project has no alternative use at any time during the life of the project, and thus no opportunity cost, so that it can properly be assigned a shadow price of zero. As a universal assumption with respect to an advanced economy, for all projects and in all future periods, this does not make sense.[44]

44. It might seem that the output–capital ratio would be a suitable criterion in a developing country with widespread unemployment and under-utilization of labour. However, the point is made by Little [30] that a zero shadow price for labour is a necessary condition for the criterion to be valid, but not a sufficient one.

99. *(b) The reinvestment of surpluses*

A second reason that has been advanced for departing from
profitability as a measure of net benefits is that the surpluses that
arise from an investment – i.e. the differences between currently
accruing receipts and costs – may be reinvested to yield a positive
return, and thus give rise to extra benefits which should be
allowed for. The argument can be illustrated by taking the arithmetical example already used in paragraphs 64–70 above. Projects X and Y each have an initial capital cost of 1,000. X will
produce constant annual net benefits of 160 for ten years, while Y
yields net benefits in only one instalment of 2,150, ten years after
completion. It was seen that if these two streams of net benefits
are discounted with a rate of interest of 3 per cent, their respective
present values are 1,365 and 1,600, so that by this test Y is
superior. Let us now suppose that the annual net benefits from X
can be reinvested as they accrue to yield 8 per cent. In this case
the total of cumulated benefits, including those that arise from
reinvestment, amounts to approximately 2,320 at the end of ten
years, which exceeds the 2,150 which will be yielded at that date
by Y. By taking into account the assumed reinvestment of surpluses, X has been changed from being an inferior project – at a
rate of interest of 3 per cent – to a dominant system: even with a
zero rate of interest it is now superior to Y.

100. It can be seen that if reinvestment is allowed for in this
way, the estimation of benefits becomes a more complicated
matter. In addition to calculating future prospective surpluses
arising, we have to estimate the extent to which they will be reinvested and the rate of return that will be earned when this is
done. Moreover, the possibility of reinvestment may affect estimates of the opportunity cost of public investment; for in so far
as private investment is displaced we must take into account the
present value not only of the expected returns from such investment, but also of the returns from the reinvestment of these.[45]

101. Whether reinvestment of surpluses should be taken into
account seems to be a less straightforward issue than is often

45. The returns from reinvesting the surpluses that arise from a public
investment could also be treated, not as part of the benefits arising, but as a
reason why the opportunity cost might be lower than the money cost.
This convention is suggested by Marglin in chapter 4 of Maass [31].

assumed. Some writers fail to mention the subject, and it seems doubtful whether explicit allowance for reinvestment has yet been made in the evaluation of any real-life project. On the other hand, those who have referred to reinvestment appear to be unanimous that in principle at least the benefits arising from it should be allowed for and evaluated; but this also may be too simple a view.

102. The crucial question here is not merely whether (and to what extent) the surpluses arising from an investment will be saved rather than consumed, but whether if they are saved the aggregate rate of investment will be correspondingly higher. This is not necessarily the case. Even if we consider the situation where the surpluses arising from a public investment project will accrue entirely to the enterprise which carries out the investment, and will be used for financing further investment, it does not follow that this further investment would not have been undertaken without them, since some alternative means of financing might be used. More generally, if we consider the economy as a whole, it is not the case that the total volume of investment in any period must be affected by the size of the surpluses currently arising from some past investment project. By making use of its powers of taxation, the government can influence, and within limits determine, the aggregate rate of saving and investment, which therefore need not depend on the current profitability of particular projects.

103. If this is correct, then the fact that surpluses may in part be saved, or even that they will predictably be used for financing specific investments by public enterprises, does not necessarily imply that the level of investment will be higher than would otherwise have been the case. It follows that it is a mistake to assume that estimated benefits from reinvestment must always be taken into account in evaluating and ranking public investment projects. There are some circumstances in which this would be justified, and others in which it would not.[46] The correct procedure must therefore depend on what assumptions are thought

46. One set of circumstances in which reinvestment should be allowed for is described in Little [30], where public sector investment choices are considered in relation to the Indian economy. We could also associate surpluses with higher investment in the case where they accrued to a public enterprise which was subject to a rigid borrowing constraint.

to be realistic and reasonable.[47] Because of the complications that
arise from taking account of reinvestment, there is something to
be said for adopting a convention that it should be ignored unless
there are obvious and peculiar reasons for associating surpluses
with investment that would not occur without them.[48]

104. *(c) Other external effects*

In the two preceding sub-sections, we referred to particular
reasons that have been given for believing that the benefits and
costs generated by a public investment will not necessarily be
reflected in the accounts of the enterprise that undertakes it. We
now consider some further aspects of the matter, and the problem
which it raises for the conduct and terms of reference of public
enterprises.

105. *(i) Pricing policy and benefits.*

An important case is that in
which benefits are not charged for, or in which their value is only
partially recovered by the enterprise concerned through some
conventional system of charges which does not relate to the
amounts that beneficiaries would be willing to pay. This situation
may arise for a number of reasons. First, it may be impracticable
to charge people according to benefits received. This may be the
case with investment in transport facilities, where the main benefits are savings in time, and possibly fuel, to consumers of
transport services. A good recent example in Britain is the
construction of the new Victoria line by London Transport. A
substantial part of the benefits from this project is expected to
accrue to users of other transport modes, rather than those using
London Transport facilities. Moreover, in so far as the gains to
users of London Transport facilities arise from shorter journeys,
they will result in an actual loss of revenue to the enterprise with a
system of charging in accordance with distance travelled. Thus the
social gain from constructing the line could not be measured by

47. The distinction is significant, and we shall return to it later in section
F. Thus for example it may be realistic to assume that the government at
present imposes certain constraints or means of control which have harmful
effects, but unreasonable to assume that this will continue to be the case.

48. If surpluses are to be taken into account, this may be regarded as an
argument for discounting net benefits at the marginal rate of return on
reinvested funds. This point is taken up below, in paragraphs 158–9 below.

an ordinary calculation of profitability.[49] Second, it may be decided on distributional grounds that certain services should be provided free or at a charge which leaves consumers very substantially better off. This seems to be a frequent practice with irrigation schemes. Third, a system of charges which attempts to recover total costs, or to maximize profits for the investing agency, may be inconsistent with maximizing the present value of net benefits. This will be true where marginal cost is below average cost, and price discrimination is ruled out;[50] and there may be other situations in which the value of benefits is sensitive to the means adopted for financing the investment.[51]

106. In each of these situations the profitability criterion breaks down, and it becomes necessary to specify the nature and prospective amount of the benefits that are expected to arise, and then to attribute a value to them. A similar principle applies to costs, which may be thought of as negative benefits. The very considerable practical problems that may be posed fall outside the scope of this paper.

107. *(ii) Intangibles.* In some cases, there may be external effects of which the nature is known, and the amount might possibly be estimated or guessed, but where there seems to be no basis for assigning unit values so as to derive a monetary measure of benefit or cost. A good example is the effect of an investment project on landscape or on buildings of architectural value. Although it is not easy to take account of such effects, this is no excuse for neglecting them altogether.

108. *(iii) Secondary benefits and windfall gains and losses.* Up to now we have been concerned with what have been termed the *efficiency benefits* of an investment. We regard any investment as giving rise to certain flows of goods and services over a period, which can be dated and (with the reservation made in the pre-

49. Cf. Foster and Beesley [20].

50. This case has, of course, been the subject of very extensive analysis, starting with the classical paper of Dupuit.

51. The Victoria line seems to be a good illustration of this. Beesley and Foster [2] have argued that if the investment is financed by higher charges on the London Transport system, a substantial proportion of the potential benefits will be lost.

vious paragraph) valued in terms of willingness to pay. Given this information about prospective changes in outputs and inputs, we can choose, if we wish, to maximize net efficiency benefits defined as the present value of the positive flows (benefits) less the present value of the negative flows (costs). But there may be other effects of the investment, not taken into account by valuing these physical flows, which some people would be willing to pay to obtain or to avoid. This is partly because efficiency gains and costs may be unequally distributed, as between persons or (more particularly) regions. But there is also the point that gains and losses will arise because of the effects on existing prices – of outputs, factors, and assets – which would not be taken into account in a measure of net efficiency benefits defined, as above, in real terms.

109. It is possible to define net benefits in such a way that some of these further effects are taken into account. Thus it has been a common practice in certain types of project, such as irrigation and land reclamation, for indirect or secondary benefits of a project to be counted, where these may include derived increases in the income of local producers who sell to, or buy from, the farmers who are the direct beneficiaries from the project, and also local increases in the land value of residential property.[52] This practice has been strongly criticized by economists on two principal grounds, both of which seem to be valid. First, the inclusion of higher profits or earnings in local related activities, in addition to the value of the prospective increases in output that will directly result from a project, will almost certainly give rise to double counting of efficiency benefits.[53] Second, it is improper to include windfall gains from the appreciation in value of already existing assets, since even if such gains are not offset by losses (or benefits foregone) elsewhere in the economy they represent a monetary gain to individuals rather than a real gain to society as a whole. Thus in evaluating projects it is necessary to distinguish clearly between the net efficiency benefits that may be generated

52. Cf. the analysis of procedures used by the U.S. Bureau of Reclamation in McKean [33], chapter 9. U.S. agency rules are of interest not only in themselves, but also because they have sometimes been followed in other countries.

53. Secondary benefits mainly consist of some part of the local multiplier effects of the higher output and income that will be directly generated by a project.

and the other possible effects.[54] It does not, however, follow that these other effects should be ignored, since the prospective efficiency benefits of an investment may not be the only aspect of it that we wish to take into account. This point is taken up in sub-section (d) below.

110. *(iv) External effects and the conduct of public enterprises*. The question arises of whether and to what extent public enterprises should take account of prospective external effects in reckoning the efficiency benefits of an investment, and in evaluating alternative projects, rather than leaving this to the government which can amend the calculations made by the enterprises so as to allow for these effects. There is no simple answer to this. It has sometimes been suggested that the only clear and satisfactory procedure is for public enterprises to act according to strict 'commercial' principles, as though they were private corporations, and thus to maximize profits subject to certain rules, constraints or instructions which are laid down by the government. This principle has the merit of recognizing the need for a reasonably clear division of responsibility between public enterprises and the government, but apart from this there is little to be said for it. The analogy with private enterprise is not particularly helpful, since it is not the case that the notion of acting in accordance with commercial criteria is both unambiguous and necessarily acceptable to large private firms.[55] Further, it is unrealistic to suppose that public enterprises will be disposed to ignore external effects. They will generally recognize them, and even tend to exaggerate them, whenever the implications of doing so appear to be consistent with their own interests, which they will rarely define in exclusively financial terms.[56] There is no way of preventing this. Indeed it would be undesirable to prevent it, since the specialized

54. The same distinction has been made in different terms, using the concept of 'technological spillovers' to refer to those external effects which are associated with the provision of efficiency benefits, and that of 'pecuniary spillovers' to describe those which are not. There is a good discussion in McKean [33], chapter 8. McKean points out that secondary benefits are not the same thing as pecuniary spillovers; but in our terminology they are alike in that both should be excluded from a measure of efficiency benefits.

55. Cf. Henderson in Worswick and Ady [53], chapter 10.

56. It would have been astonishing if London Transport had opposed the construction of the Victoria line, or refused to consider it seriously.

knowledge and experience which the enterprises possess will usually be needed if informed estimates of the size of external effects are to be made: this is a task which cannot be left entirely to government departments. There is of course a danger that public enterprises will choose to ignore or underestimate external effects when the results of allowing for them would be to make their investment proposals look worse rather than better. But it is more sensible to deal with this by trying to induce the enterprises to take a wider view, rather than by maintaining a pretence that their only proper concern is with the financial consequences to themselves of their actions.

111. *(d) Efficiency benefits and other criteria*

We have noted, in paragraphs 108 and 109 above, that the effects of an investment are not fully described by taking into account net efficiency benefits alone. In particular, the effects on the distribution of income between social groups or geographical areas do not appear, although these may be matters of concern to the community. It has been seen that in some cases public agencies have wrongly included certain local or regional gains arising from their investments under the heading of efficiency benefits, thus overestimating the size of these. Some commentators have ascribed this to mere confusion of thought, or to a natural but culpable tendency of public enterprises to exaggerate the benefits of their activities, in order to increase their own size and prestige. A more charitable view is that the inclusion of so-called secondary benefits may be interpreted as an attempt to recognize and allow for the fact that the efficiency benefits of an investment are not its only significant property.[57] Society has other objectives than economic efficiency, and these may properly be taken into account in the design and evaluation of public investments.

112. This again is an issue on which there is disagreement. A case can be made out for adopting the convention that only efficiency benefits should count. If the government wishes to change the distribution of income between persons or regions, it can do so by other means than through the choice and design of public investment projects, and these may involve a smaller

57. This view has recently been advanced by Maass [32].

sacrifice in terms of efficiency benefits foregone. Thus for example regional development should be promoted by general measures rather than by exercising bias in the selection of particular types of project.[58] In the long run, the choice of less efficient rather than more efficient projects will mean a lower national product, and may lead to a situation in which every one is worse off than need have been the case, including even the people whom it was intended to benefit by the choice of the inefficient projects. Further, the introduction of factors other than efficiency benefits will at best make the problem of choice and design more complex, and at worst may open the door to bogus calculations and various undesirable forms of local or sectional lobbying. Thus it can be argued that not only should efficiency benefits and other features of an investment be kept distinct – about which there might be general agreement – but that the only way to ensure this, and to avoid otherwise predictable social losses, is to rank projects according to efficiency criteria alone.[59]

113. A less extreme and perhaps more widely held view would acknowledge, if only as a concession to human frailty and the sordid realities of political life, that factors other than efficiency will inevitably be taken into account, but would hold that projects and programmes should be designed, and in the first instance ranked, in accordance with efficiency. It would then be a matter for the government to decide, in the light of the efficiency ranking and information relating to the other factors which might be thought relevant, to make the final choice.

114. As against the view that efficiency benefits alone should count, it has been pointed out by Marglin that the community may be justified in wishing to make use of public investment

58. A good instance of this view is provided in the report of the Plowden committee on the United Kingdom aircraft industry [51], with reference to the special problem of the Short Bros. and Harland plant in Northern Ireland. The committee's view was that 'if the Government were to conclude that special assistance was justified to help employment in Northern Ireland, we believe this should be given by measures for promoting general economic development, rather than to the aircraft industries of Shorts' (report, paragraph 449).

59. There seems to be an analogy here with the convention referred to above, in paragraph 75, that public investment should be regarded as always displacing an equivalent amount of some other ingredient of final expenditure.

projects as a means of affecting the distribution of income. There are two reasons why this is so. First, there may be limits on the extent to which other means of redistribution can be used. Second, the community may not be indifferent as to the means by which a given amount of redistribution is achieved: it may well have a positive preference for helping poorer groups or regions through the choice and design of projects, thus generating income for them, rather than through fiscal transfers which redistribute income already earned. Thus 'the size of the economic pie and its division may not be the only factors of concern to the community – the method of slicing the pie may also be relevant';[60] and the government may therefore be ready to sacrifice efficiency benefits, not only in the interests of a fairer distribution of income, but also in order to effect a more acceptable means of bringing about a fairer distribution. Once the force of these arguments is admitted,[61] it is only possible to defend the view that efficiency benefits alone should count in the cases – which may however be quite numerous – where questions of distribution seem to be of minor significance. Moreover, even the less extreme view, that considerations other than efficiency will inevitably have weight but should not initially be taken into account in project design, may cease to be tenable. Maass has argued persuasively that

Where government programmes are intended for complex objectives they should be designed, where this is possible, for such objectives, not designed for one objective, which may not be the most important, and subsequently modified in an attempt to account for others.[62]

60. Marglin in chapter 2 of Maass [31], p. 63.
61. It becomes more evident if we consider the case of international redistribution, from richer to poorer countries. One might argue that poor countries could be best helped by concentrating investment in the areas where it would bring the highest return, so as to maximize the income of the world as a whole, and then by redistributing income within this higher total in the form of unilateral transfers. But quite apart from the argument that the poorer countries may succeed in getting a greater total amount of aid if it comes to them in a variety of ways, it is obvious that the problem of raising income levels in these countries cannot and should not be treated as one of organizing an effective system of poor relief. Similar considerations apply, often with very little diminished force, to the problem of rich and poor regions within national boundaries.
62. Maass [32], p. 220.

Where multiplicity of objectives has not been openly recognized, and consequently little has been done to establish the trade-off ratios between conflicting objectives, it is likely that the final selection will exhibit the worst features of political bargaining. Paradoxically, the loss of efficiency may be reduced if the existence of objectives other than efficiency is recognized at the outset, and is explicitly taken into account in project design.[63]

115. Efficiency and distributive fairness may not be the only objectives which have to be considered. Thus, for example, a public enterprise which is concerned with the construction of new towns or housing projects may wish (or be instructed) to promote racial or social integration. This might affect the choice of system design, and cause it to differ from what would have been preferred if efficiency benefits alone had counted. Again, the construction of a U.S. supersonic civil transport has been advocated on the grounds that it is necessary in order to maintain American aviation supremacy, a goal which for some people has value aside from considerations of efficiency. In these and other cases it seems best to recognize explicitly that there may be more than one objective, and to try to establish the relevant trade-offs between them. Although this is no easy task, it is better attempted than shirked.

116. As in the case of external efficiency gains and losses, to which allusion was made in paragraph 110 above, the existence of multiple objectives raises a problem concerning the conduct and terms of reference of public enterprises. In the United Kingdom at any rate, these enterprises have often been ready to acknowledge that distributive considerations should be taken into account, and in some cases – as, for example, with cross-subsidization in public transport – they have been explicitly instructed to do this. In recent years there has been a strong reaction against this state of affairs. Various inquiries – in particular those of the appropriate select committee of the House of Commons – have revealed an unsuspected wealth of instances in which enterprises have adopted unprofitable policies in accordance with what they believed to be the national interest, or accepted so-called social obligations because they regarded this as

63. The problem of designing projects to meet distributional as well as efficiency objectives is analysed by Marglin in chapter 2 of Maass [31]. We refer to this analysis again below, in paragraph 149.

part of their function. Many of these instances appeared to be questionable, and some even ridiculous. There was accordingly a natural and justified reaction, which led to two principal recommendations. First, the duties and terms of reference of public enterprises should be more clearly defined by the government. Second, in so far as profitability was to be subordinated to other social or national objectives, this should be decided by the government rather than by the enterprises themselves, and set out clearly in the form of direct instructions to them.

117. These recommendations were broadly justified. It is not the business of public enterprises to decide on their own responsibility which objectives should be pursued, and which trade-offs it is appropriate to fix. At the same time, the critics of past mistakes have sometimes gone too far in asserting that the sole concern of these enterprises should be with profitability – or more broadly, with efficiency – objectives. The managers concerned must be expected to be aware of the possibility that objectives may conflict, and to have views of their own on how such conflicts might be resolved: it would be foolish to confine the choice of senior appointments to those who are prepared to deny themselves this freedom. Again, the specialized knowledge that exists within enterprises may be useful or necessary in order to estimate trade-offs between objectives. In short, these issues should not be left to public enterprises to decide for themselves; but the enterprises are entitled to have opinions about them, and these opinions may deserve to be taken into account.

118. *(e) Deviations from the optimum and shadow pricing*

It has been seen that profitability tests for public investments are subject to serious limitations. These arise from what we have termed external effects, which may cause profitability to be an unreliable measure of economic efficiency, and because efficiency may not be the only objective with which the community and the government are concerned. The fact that it may be hard to arrive at a satisfactory and agreed measure of efficiency benefits is disturbing not only in itself, but because in the absence of such a measure it may be impossible to estimate trade-off ratios at the margin between efficiency and other possible goals.

119. In summary terms, the problem of defining net efficiency

benefits arises because of the limitations of the market mechanism. Existing prices are not equal to marginal social costs and benefits; and in some cases the market fails to establish a price for services or disservices that are created.[64] The economic theory of public enterprises has tried to deal with this situation along two distinct though related lines. First, attempts have been made to formulate rules for determining the prices of the outputs sold by the enterprises, so as to ensure that these prices bear some appropriate relation to costs. Second, the use of shadow prices, rather than the actual market prices with which enterprises will be confronted, has been recommended in computing the value of net efficiency benefits.

120. In so far as the object of different pricing policies or of shadow pricing is to bring prices more closely into line with marginal social cost, both these ways of correcting or improving existing market valuations fall into the category of 'second-best' strategies. They are thus open to the possible objection that, in so far as widespread and varying divergences between price and marginal cost exist in the economy as a whole, an apparent improvement in practice within one particular sector of it may decrease rather than increase aggregate efficiency and welfare.[65] It has been argued that this may not be especially worrying, since in so far as such divergences persist they are evidence that efficiency is not a very important social objective; for if it were important, the government would have taken measures to correct prices in the economy as a whole.[66] But this is clearly very

64. These are cases of external economies and diseconomies, in the usual sense of these terms. We have been using the notion of 'external effects' in a rather different sense, to refer to the costs and benefits arising from a public investment project which are not reflected in the accounts of the enterprise which undertakes it.

65. Cf. Lipsey and Lancaster [29].

66. This is suggested by Marglin in chapter 2 of Maass [31], p. 54, though the argument is explicitly confined to economically advanced countries. Marglin also remarks (ibid., p. 59) that economies such as the United States, 'approximately fulfil' the condition that prices are equal to marginal cost, which if true would be a further ground for cheerfulness. Presumably this statement is intended to apply only to the prices of currently produced goods and services, since Marglin advocates the use of shadow (opportunity cost) pricing for the funds used for financing public investments, and of a social time preference rate of interest which itself is a shadow price.

debatable: it is easy to think of reasons why a concern for efficiency would not necessarily cause a government to act in such a way.[67] Thus the difficulties of identifying a genuine second-best solution may be very real, and a cause for concern. At present economists usually advocate what seem to be improvements in particular pricing rules, because some rules have to be adopted and the current ones look very much worse; but private reservations may be hard to dispel. We shall refer in paragraph 123 below to a case in which the definition of a second-best objective seems to give rise to difficulties. Moreover, even if such doubts are set aside there are problems in arriving at an agreed set of rules, as we have had occasion to note already in relation to certain questions of shadow pricing.

121. Issues of pricing policy fall outside the scope of this paper. But it has been noted, in paragraph 105 above, that the net efficiency benefits of an investment may be sensitive to the pricing rules that are in force. It was also seen there that shadow pricing may be used for outputs, as in the case where no market price exists, or where charges are fixed according to some conventional principles.[68]

122. As to other forms of shadow pricing, for costs rather than benefits, a number of possible instances have already been encountered. These include the use of a zero or low notional wage rate where a project makes use of unemployed labour, of a social time preference rate – or indeed any form of 'riskless' rate – rather than existing market rates of interest, and of higher than nominal values for the funds used in a public investment project, in so far as this is expected to displace private investment at the margin. Shadow pricing has also been advocated for current purchases other than labour services, when the prices of the goods and services concerned are thought to differ markedly from

67. One such reason is that the arguments for equating price to marginal cost are familiar to economists alone, while a belief in the practicability and potential benefits of equating them is not shared even by all economists. It is hardly surprising that such an esoteric doctrine, advocated with varying degrees of reservation and lukewarmness among the limited number of economists whose opinions have ever gained attention in official circles, has never been embraced by a government.

68. The possible significance of pricing policies is also noted in a rather different context in the footnote to paragraph 156 below.

marginal cost, and for foreign exchange – whether saved or earned – in the case of balance of payments difficulties. It has been seen that there may be disagreement both about the need for using shadow prices, on the grounds that market values are already satisfactory or could easily be made so, and also about the values that should be assigned to shadow prices even when the case for them has in principle been accepted. Further, they may be awkward things to administer, since they are not a familiar notion and their use in any given case is likely to be – or at least to appear to be – contrary to some particular interest. This may be taken as a reason for not adopting them even when other objections do not arise.

123. A good illustration of the difficulties of choice is that of a shadow price for foreign exchange. Various reasons may be advanced for introducing this within the public sector, and the appropriate shadow rate of exchange will vary, within what may be very wide limits, according to which is thought to be applicable.[69] Even granted agreement on these things, doubts may arise about the wisdom of applying a shadow price to public sector decisions alone, when the private sector is unaffected. Such qualms about second-best strategy may well be reinforced if, as is very likely to be the case, the extent to which the agreed shadow price can be adopted for public sector calculations is limited by the government's adherence to existing international agreements or conventions which rule out such practices, so that the dangers arising from loss of goodwill or active retaliation have to be considered. In this case the shadow premium that can be used within the public sector may vary from zero to some quite high figure. It may require a certain robust optimism to believe that the use of such a family of rates within the public sector alone can be justi-

69. There has been surprisingly little discussion of the possible justification of shadow rates of exchange in a country such as the United Kingdom. The problem is referred to briefly in chapter 15 of the Plowden report on the United Kingdom aircraft industry [51]. One argument for shadow pricing is rejected, but the conclusion is reached that some margin of protection for the industry is justified as a temporary measure, since at present a pound spent abroad has a higher real cost to the economy than a pound spent at home. The fact that the appropriate shadow price depends crucially on the assumptions made, and may vary within very wide limits indeed, has been brought out in an unpublished paper by Mr M. FG. Scott.

fied on allocative grounds. If to these difficulties is added that of resistance to the principle of shadow pricing by the enterprises or agencies who actually make the purchases – on the grounds that their efficiency will be impaired, their financial performance made to look worse, and their freedom of action unreasonably curtailed – it can be seen that this apparently straightforward device may lose much of its charm and simplicity on closer examination.

124. Two broad conclusions seem to emerge from our discussion of this problem. The first is that the use of shadow prices may often appear justified. Almost every economist who has written about these problems has in fact recommended some resort to this device, because of what seems to be a clear objection to taking existing market values without adjustment or correction.[70] The second conclusion is that though shadow prices may be useful and even necessary, they may also be difficult to determine and to operate in practice. This is not a very helpful result, but its unhelpfulness arises from the complexities of the real world.

E. The Treatment of Risk and Uncertainty

125. Uncertainty is not only pervasive but very hard to deal with. The problems that may arise have been the subject of extensive and often highly technical discussion, which is not adequately summarized below.[71] In this section we attempt only to raise some of the more obvious practical aspects of the problem, and to consider briefly some of the ways of handling it that have been used or advocated.

126. Possibly the most important single point to make is that uncertainty should not be ignored. This may seem so obvious

70. Thus, for example, Eckstein [12], reviewing the book by Hirshleifer and his colleagues [23], remarks that 'Water resource economists can be ranked according to the extent of their belief in the price mechanism. . . . The authors of this study are fundamentalists.' But in the study thus described there is an explicit acknowledgement (pp. 142–3) that existing market rates of interest, in so far as they are affected by the expectation that the price level will rise over time, are not appropriate for use in discounting and may need to be adjusted. It is hard to find a true fundamentalist.

71. Good short reviews of the subject can be found in Eckstein [11], Dryden [10], in the analysis of Dorfman in chapter 3 of Maass [31], and in Baumol [1], chapters 19 and 23.

a recommendation as to be unnecessary. But it is remarkable how often project analyses present single values for prospective costs and benefits, with little indication that the outcomes depicted may not be realized, and with no consideration of the likelihood and characteristics of other possible outcomes. Where uncertainty is present it should be brought explicitly into the analysis. Although this can be done most simply by means of verbal qualifications, it is preferable to introduce numerical values also. If only single-valued estimates are presented in key tables, it is difficult for those who have to assess project analyses not to treat these figures as the only ones that matter.

127. The design of presentations which take account of uncertainty is a difficult and highly skilled task. It is necessary to describe and evaluate a more or less complex set of outcomes with their associated probabilities, without overloading the analysis with detail.[72] One method of treatment that is often useful is *sensitivity analysis*. Here attention is concentrated on a few key factors or assumptions, to which the measure of costs or net benefits seems to be highly sensitive, and on the implications of varying these. In the U.S. Department of Defense it has apparently been found useful to try to present possible outcomes in terms of three sets of figures. These comprise an 'optimistic' estimate, a 'pessimistic' one, and a 'best' estimate which is the one thought to have the highest probability of being realized.[73] This method of handling the problems of analysis and presentation may have advantages in other situations.

128. Given that uncertainty has been explicitly recognized and depicted in a satisfactory way, the problem arises of how to allow for it in evaluating investments. Are projects which appear subject to greater degrees of risk or uncertainty less attractive on that account, and in what way should the prospective present value of net benefits be adjusted for these factors?

129. A certain amount of confusion surrounds this subject

72. It has to be remembered that the complications produced by uncertainty are additional to those that may arise from the existence of external effects, the possible need for shadow pricing, and multiplicity of objectives.

73. Cf. Enthoven [14], where it is remarked that 'These terms are not very rigorous. A subjective judgment is required. But it is surprising how often reasonable men studying the same evidence can agree on three numbers where they cannot agree on one.'

because of the different senses in which the terms 'risk' and 'uncertainty' can be used. In one sense, which is quite commonly met with but which is not very relevant to the question now under discussion, risk is used to refer to the strong probability that the net benefits of an investment have been overestimated. A risky investment in this sense is one for which more or less extravagant claims have been made, and to allow for this a 'risk premium' is added in some way.

130. One reason for extravagant claims is poor estimating, whether deliberate or unconscious. Thus prospective costs may be put at what proves or is suspected to be an unrealistically low figure, and prospective benefits at an unrealistically high one. Such overoptimism is a notoriously common feature of project estimates.[74] But it is best dealt with, not through an adjustment for risk, but by substituting for the original project estimates what are believed to be more realistic values. Contingency allowances are a standard method of trying to accomplish this, and are then best regarded as a means of improving projections rather than as an allowance for risk. They can serve a useful purpose, though they may often be little more than a sort of co-efficient of mistrust.[75] The problem of making realistic projections of costs and benefits is a basic and universal one. It may be doubted whether many public enterprises – or for that matter, many private firms or government departments – assign to it more than a small fraction of the resources that could be profitably employed in tackling it. But it is probably best regarded as a distinct problem from that of allowing for risk and uncertainty.

131. A second reason why net benefits may be overestimated, even with what are thought to be good projections, is that the probability distribution of benefits may be negatively skewed, so that the modal outcome – the single most likely one – will exceed the mean or expected value.[76] This again may be quite a

74. It is often found in conjunction with unacceptably large or optimistic claims with respect to the non-efficiency benefits or the foreign exchange proceeds of a project.

75. In which case the knowledge that they will be imposed may give a further inducement to those preparing initial estimates to underestimate costs and overestimate gains.

76. In the case of costs alone, the skewness will be positive, so that the mean value will exceed the mode.

common occurrence. The realization of the modal value may depend on the occurrence of a number of events; and while each of these individually has a high probability of occurrence, so that it is treated as virtually certain, the compound probability that all of them will occur may be small. In this case it is possible to take the expected value of costs or net benefits, rather than the mode, as the 'best' single estimate. This again is not strictly an adjustment for risk and uncertainty.

132. Even if we set aside the sense of risk in which it is roughly equivalent to overoptimism, some issues of terminology remain. Economic theory makes a distinction between risk and uncertainty. Risk is defined as a situation in which the outcome is uncertain, but the probability distribution of outcomes is known with certainty. This may be called pure *actuarial risk*. At the other extreme, where nothing whatever is known about the probability distribution, we have the case of *pure uncertainty*. Although most actual situations fall strictly under neither heading, they may quite often approximate more or less closely to one or the other, and be treated accordingly. The intermediate cases which are not close to one extreme or the other can be described as situations of *uncertainty*, with no qualifying adjective. The *degree* of actuarial risk may be represented by the variance or the standard deviation of the probability distribution. We shall call this *variability risk*. It arises not only in the situation of pure actuarial risk, but also in the more general case of incomplete knowledge, or uncertainty. While there is no corresponding measure of the degree of uncertainty, it is often possible to characterize situations as more or less uncertain.[77]

133. In addition, the term risk is also used to describe the degree of seriousness of the consequences of an unfavourable outcome.[78] Thus if I gamble for high stakes, the degree of actuarial risk is no greater than if the stakes are low, but the degree of risk in this second sense may be considerably greater. This may be termed the *risk of disaster*.

134. We may start with the case of pure actuarial risk. An

77. We return to this notion of the degree of uncertainty in paragraph 139 below.

78. Cf. the discussion of uncertainty and risk in relation to military procurement, in chapter 2 of Peck and Scherer [43].

adjustment for this would ensure that two projects with the same expected value of net benefits would not be ranked as equivalent if the variance of the benefits differed. In this case we might think of the discounting process as being applied to 'certainty-equivalent' net benefits: the government or the community is thought of as being ready to trade off a certain amount of net benefit at the margin in exchange for a given reduction in the degree of actuarial risk. This notion that actuarial risk is undesirable is sometimes defended with reference to the widespread practice of insurance by individuals, who thus exhibit a willingness to sacrifice some expected income for a greater degree of assurance of a given income. But this is not necessarily a helpful analogy. There are two good reasons why individuals may have an aversion to actuarial risk. One is that the marginal utility of income may be falling, and the second is that risk of disaster may be involved. Neither of these factors need apply in the case of public investments. Many investment projects, perhaps the great majority, will have no significant effect on the aggregate income per head of the community as a whole, or of any well-defined group within it; and (though this may be a matter of judgement) the risk of disaster is usually absent. Thus there seems to be no good reason in the general case for making any adjustment for actuarial risk.

135. The exception will arise if a project is sufficiently large and localized for it to have a considerable effect on the average income of a specified group, or if disaster risk is present. Water resource projects which provide for flood control seem to be a good example of this. The greater the likelihood of a given degree of flooding, the greater will be the variance of expected income. If allowance is made for diminishing marginal utility of income, so that the measure of net benefits is converted into a measure of the utilities which these will provide, this will cause a shift in the direction of designs which incorporate a greater degree of flood protection, at the cost of some sacrifice in prospective net benefits as measured in terms of increases in incomes. Admittedly, as we had occasion to note in section C above, there is little evidence to go on when we try to specify the utility function; but since some assumption about this is implicit in any actual system for ranking project designs, it is an advantage that particular assumptions

should be made explicit. Again, it may be decided that a given degree of insurance should be provided against some specified disaster risk. This again will lead to some sacrifice of expected net benefit in exchange for a reduction in the risk of disaster; and since this risk will be greater the greater the dispersion of expected outcomes, it has also the effect of adjusting for the degree of variability risk. The difficulty here is that there may be no clear basis either for specifying the nature of the disaster risk which it is hoped to guard against, or for deciding the degree of insurance which it is desirable to provide.[79]

136. The analysis of the last two paragraphs has been concerned with the rather unusual situation of pure actuarial risk. But it is equally applicable to the more typical case, where something is known about the probability distribution of expected outcomes but this knowledge is less than complete – i.e. the general case of uncertainty, as distinct from pure risk or pure uncertainty. As in the situation of complete knowledge, variability risk may be measured by the variance of the probability distribution; and it may be desirable to adjust expected values of benefits for this, either because of falling marginal utility of income, or else because risk of disaster exists and the probability of disaster is an increasing function of variability risk. But in many public investment projects these factors may not be present, and in these cases there seems to be no good reason to regard investments that are subject to a greater degree of variability risk as less desirable on this ground alone.[80] In this respect the situations of pure risk and (partial) uncertainty are alike, and an attempt to distinguish between them is unhelpful.

79. The situations referred to in this paragraph are both discussed in the relevant section of Eckstein [11], with illustrations of the argument.

80. Dorfman has suggested (in chapter 3 of Maass [31], pp. 144–5) that even apart from these factors there may be a cost attached to variability risk as such, since it means that people have less assurance about the size of future income and therefore find it more difficult to make plans. (He describes this as a 'cost of uncertainty *per se*', but his use of the term uncertainty corresponds to what is called here variability risk.) Although this may be so, it is doubtful whether many public investment projects will create significant risks of this kind. They may do so if they are large and their effects are localized, but as has been seen these are precisely the conditions in which it may in any case be desirable to allow for variability risk.

137. There is no simple and agreed method of allowing for variability risk, even though its degree can be measured or at least estimated. The most promising line of attack on the problem seems to be that of decision theory, in which a scale of utilities is defined in such a way that any given combination of uncertain outcomes can be ranked according to the utility it yields. The scale, and thus the ranking system, can in principle be determined by ascertaining the response of those concerned to hypothetical choice situations. Thus the expected value of net (monetary) benefits can be translated into utilities, and the expected value of utility is then to be maximized. However, the applicability of this procedure to public investment decisions seems to be very much in doubt. As Dorfman has remarked, 'decision theory does not so much solve the difficulties as shift their locale. It makes deciding among alternatives easy at the cost of requiring us to determine a scale of utilities in a particular way.' [81] This is in fact one instance of the difficulty that was noted in paragraph 135 above, of specifying utility functions so that an allowance for variability risk can be made in some non-arbitrary way.

138. One device that is often suggested as a means of allowing for this form of risk is the addition of a 'risk premium' to the rate of interest that is used for discounting. This is sometimes defended on the grounds that variability is likely to increase over time. However, even if this is the case it does not enable us to determine the appropriate size of the risk premium, so that any given figure is no more than a guess. Moreover, the use of a higher interest rate in order to rank alternative projects has logically nothing to do with time. If two investments offer the same time stream of expected net benefits, but one has a greater variability risk throughout, then this latter project is discounted at a higher rate of interest *in each period* – i.e. when no difference in timing arises. Thus the use of a higher interest rate as an allowance for variability risk is a very crude expedient, which can be defended only on the grounds that some adjustment has to be made and other methods are impracticable. But it has been seen that an adjustment may not necessarily be appropriate; and where it is, there may be a case for at least exploring less arbitrary ways of making it.

81. Chapter 3 of Maass [31], p. 144.

139. We turn now from variability risk to uncertainty. The distinction between these is significant, though not always clearly made. While variability risk can be represented by the dispersion of the probability distribution of expected outcomes, the extent of uncertainty, in the sense in which we are here using the term, is given by *the degree of ignorance concerning the probability distribution*. These are clearly two quite different things. We may know from very good evidence that the dispersion of expected outcomes is wide: here there is no uncertainty in our sense, but considerable variability risk.[82] On the other hand, we may have rather poor evidence about probabilities, which however suggests that the dispersion of possible outcomes is narrow. Here there is considerable uncertainty in our sense, but some indication that variability risk is not great.

140. Not only is the degree of uncertainty (in this sense) quite distinct from variability risk, but the problems raised and the ways of adjusting to it are different. It has been seen above that in the case of many public investments there may be no strong reason to regard variability risk as a disadvantage. But *uncertainty arising from ignorance is always a disadvantage*. This is because whatever it is that we wish to try to maximize, a better knowledge of the probability distribution of expected outcomes will improve the chances of achieving the objective, or approximating it more closely. Uncertainty therefore gives rise to costs in the form of loss of utility, and it is always worth incurring some cost if by doing so the degree of uncertainty can be significantly reduced. Thus if two investments have the same expected present value of net benefits and the same variability risk, but our

82. There is, of course, another sense of the term in which uncertainty is associated with dispersion of outcomes, since the greater the dispersion the less certain we are about what the actual outcome will be. Many (perhaps most) writers have used uncertainty in this sense. There are in fact two dimensions of uncertainty. The important thing is to distinguish between them, and it is possibly unfortunate to reserve the term 'uncertainty', as we do here, for one dimension alone. However, this usage has the advantage that it fits into the well-known classification of cases into those of pure risk at one extreme and total uncertainty at the other. In our sense, the degree of uncertainty increases as we move along this scale. This seems to have a close affinity with the approach adopted by Peck and Scherer, who define uncertainty as 'the relative unpredictability of the outcome of a contemplated action' [43], p. 17.

knowledge of the probability distribution of the outcomes is significantly greater in the first case than in the second, the first is preferable on this account.

141. Allowance for uncertainty is therefore desirable. But no simple way of making it can be found. The addition of an 'uncertainty premium' to the rate of interest used for discounting has been defended on the grounds that uncertainty increases with time; but it is open to the objections raised in paragraph 138 above, where the same procedure was considered as a way of allowing for variability risk. The information that we would ideally like to have seems clear enough. In comparing two similar investments with different degrees of uncertainty, we need to know how much it would be worth paying in order to reduce the degree of uncertainty of the more uncertain project to that of the less uncertain one. But it is clear that this may be very difficult to determine even approximately.

142. If, however, the problem is posed in this way, attention is directed to what is perhaps the most important practical question that arises from the existence of uncertainty, which is to find effective ways of reducing it that appear to have a positive present value. These may include research designed to throw light on particular areas of uncertainty; [83] the use of prototypes and pilot plants for small-scale experiments to acquire knowledge which can be taken into account in determining the final choice of project or system design; and the use of duplication in research and development, to guard against the possibility that what seems to be the most fruitful approach may prove to be inferior or worthless. In addition, it may be desirable to choose among system designs, or among particular ways of phasing and executing projects, in such a way as to ensure both versatility and flexibility. By versatility is meant the property of performing well in a variety of contingencies. By flexibility is meant that the system lends itself to adaptation at various stages as new and better information becomes available. [84] Thus where considerable

83. This should cover market research and research into the factors that determine the costs of projects, both of which are often seriously neglected in comparison with research of a technical kind.

84. Building these properties into a project or system or programme may seem advisable, not only as a way of allowing for uncertainty, but also to provide some degree of insurance against particular forms of disaster risk.

uncertainty exists and is allowed for, a new dimension of choices appears: it becomes desirable to explore systematically various possible ways of hedging our bets on the future. A strategy which fails to incorporate hedging will turn out to be right only by a more or less fortunate accident. This underlines the point which was stressed at the beginning of this section, that where risk or uncertainty are significant they should be explicitly taken into account.[85]

143. There remains for consideration the case of pure or total uncertainty, where nothing whatever is known about the probability distribution of expected outcomes. But this situation seems likely to be extremely rare in relation to the investment decisions of public enterprises. It is hard to imagine a case in which we know nothing whatever about the likelihood of possible outcomes, and can do nothing to reduce the extent of our ignorance. However, a brief and very elementary illustration of some of the rules that have been suggested for decision-making under complete uncertainty is given in the final section of Appendix I.

F. Constraints and Investment Criteria

144. Investment decisions are always subject to constraints of one kind or another. These can be usefully classified into a number of categories, though the border line between different categories is not always clearly defined, and different forms of constraint may sometimes be interrelated. Thus *physical* constraints restrict choices to what is regarded as technically feasible; *legal* constraints impose restrictions on what can be done without a change in the law; *administrative* constraints may preclude the adoption of certain courses of action which involve excessive complication or too drastic a change in existing practice; *political* constraints may affect the freedom of choice of governments; and *financial* constraints may set limits to the amounts that can be spent by public enterprises or agencies over some specified period.[86] In

85. There is a very clear and illuminating treatment of the points raised in this paragraph in Hitch and McKean [24], chapter 11.
86. This is the classification suggested by Eckstein [11]. Eckstein expresses a doubt as to whether the recognition of political constraints is wise, but the concept seems a useful if not a necessary one. A form of political

this section we shall first consider some general aspects and properties of constraints, and then proceed to look more closely at the particular case of financial constraints.

145. *(a) Some general points*[87]

Constraints have two related properties which confer on them an often dangerous attractiveness. First, they greatly simplify the problem of choice, by ruling out *ab initio* options which might otherwise have had to be given serious consideration. Second, they can be represented as more or less unalterable, so that acceptance of them can be made to appear as recognition of necessity, or at least as statesmanlike acknowledgement of the bounds of what is practicable. The advantages which arise from the first property often lead to an unwarranted exploitation of the second. Thus the danger arises that in the interests of making life simpler, which in itself is admittedly a virtue, promising or even demonstrably superior courses of action will be excluded from consideration. A very good illustration of this point has been provided by Maass, in the context of water resource planning in the United States.

In the past water-planners and engineers, in search of constraints to simplify their task of system design, have found it convenient to read inflexibility into government institutions and to treat them as immutable, if irrational, restrictions. On the contrary, there is and should be considerable flexibility in legal and administrative forms, which are quite adaptable in the face of demonstrated economic, technologic, social or political need.[88]

A good recent British example of the introduction of a dubious though superficially appealing constraint can be found in the Buchanan report on *Traffic in towns*, where the assertion is made at an early stage that

although persuasive arguments can be adduced in favour of urban dispersal, this island is not big enough for large-scale dispersal if a sensible

---

constraint with which British government officials are extremely familiar arises from a need for new legislation if a proposed course of action is to be undertaken.

87. This sub-section draws on a number of arguments advanced in Henderson [22].

88. Maass in chapter 15 of Maass [31], p. 565.

relationship is to be maintained between developed area and open country.[89]

This assumption conveniently simplifies analysis by ruling out a particular line of policy. It also obscures the point that what constitutes a 'sensible relationship' in this connexion depends on the estimated costs and gains associated with different possible combinations of measures, including varying degrees of urban dispersal.

146. The moral of this is twofold. First, constraints should not be taken for granted or casually imposed, despite the temptations, and often incentives, to do this. On the contrary, they should be scrutinized and criticized; and one of the criteria for appraising the official machinery and procedures for decision-making is the extent to which this occurs.[90] Even when constraints have been decided after considerable thought, it may be best to regard them as provisional only, and subject to revision as new evidence comes to light.[91] Second, so far as possible constraints should be made fully explicit.[92] This helps to ensure widespread awareness of what is being done, and thus a greater disposition to question it and to consider alternative courses of action.

147. It is also desirable that the objectives of policy, and the constraints which may bear on the realization of these objectives, should be determined at an appropriately high political level. Thus in the case of public investments, the choice and design of constraints is not a matter which ought to be left by default to the managements of the enterprises concerned. As was noted in paragraph 116 above, the inquiries of the House of Commons

89. Buchanan [5], paragraph 60.

90. It may be noted that in so far as clear and scrupulously observed responsibilities and spheres of influence are assigned to different organizations, or to particular forms of expertise – a state of affairs much beloved by British public administrators – the likelihood that constraints will be uncritically accepted is increased.

91. Thus Marglin has made the point, in relation to choice of system design, that 'Rather than being the end of the planning process, design on the basis of initial constraints may be virtually the beginning' (chapter 2 of Maass [31], p. 78).

92. This is not the same as to say that they should be widely publicized, a question which raises further issues.

Select Committee on the Nationalized Industries have disclosed a rich selection of cautionary examples.[93]

148. So far we have been concerned with the negative consequences that may follow from the adoption of constraints. It is this aspect of them that has been chiefly emphasised by economists, both because examples of dubious constraints have not been difficult to find, and also because the defining characteristic of a constraint has been perceived as consisting in the fact that it precludes the attainment of some ideal. Although this emphasis is understandable, and up to a point quite justified, it is also one-sided. Constraints may have the positive function of furthering the realization of social or economic objectives.

149. This point is effectively illustrated in Marglin's treatment of the problem of system design in a situation where income redistribution, as well as efficiency, is an objective in choosing and planning public investment projects. Here it may be useful to express the problem as one of maximizing efficiency gains subject to a specified redistribution constraint, or of maximizing a particular redistributive effect subject to a requirement that efficiency gains reach a specified level.[94] In these formulations the constraints appear as ways of ensuring that suitable weight is given to different objectives which are in some degree conflicting. They serve the useful purpose of formalizing the problem so that better-informed choices can be made. Whenever multiple objectives are recognized, this positive function of constraints comes into play. Indeed, it has been pointed out by Dorfman that in this situation the distinction between constraints and objectives may not be easy to define.[95]

150. A distrust of constraints often arises from the view, which was considered in paragraphs 111–15 above, that the only criterion which should be taken into account in choosing public investments, or at any rate in the initial design of projects, is that of prospective efficiency gains. The argument of the previous paragraph then ceases to apply. Reasons have been given for not

93. The point made in this paragraph is admirably developed by Maass in chapter 15 of Maass [31].

94. Cf. chapter 2 of Maass [31].

95. Dorfman [8], p. 61, where a very useful working distinction is in fact suggested.

accepting this view. But even when efficiency gains alone are in question, it may not be correct to assume that constraints can never be anything but regrettable pseudo-necessities. There are cases where constraints are imposed partly or wholly with the object of increasing efficiency, and their potential usefulness is therefore not necessarily restricted to the situation in which it is explicitly recognized that more than one objective is in question.

151. *(b) Financial constraints*

Up to this point the assumption has been made that all public investment projects which have a positive present value at some agreed rate of interest can be undertaken:[96] there is no problem of choosing between them, except in so far as some may be incompatible with others for technical reasons. If, however, financial constraints are in force it may not be possible to undertake all projects which are in principle desirable. In this case it is necessary to establish some method of ranking that can be used to determine the best set of projects that is consistent with observing the constraint. Some of the issues that were considered in section C above are therefore raised again in a new context. In particular, the question of how to assess the opportunity cost of public investments, and the choice of a rate of interest for discounting, have to be reconsidered.

152. Constraints may be applied to public expenditure at different levels and with varying degrees of restrictiveness. In the United Kingdom it has become the practice of governments to prepare and publish surveys of public expenditure covering a period of five years ahead. In the most recent of these, a maximum permitted rate of increase in total public expenditure was laid down, which had been determined at Cabinet level in relation to the expected increase in output over the period concerned. A general constraint was thus imposed on the total; and within it, the planned changes in particular broad categories of expenditure were also specified.[97] This system has the merit of ensuring that

96. Strictly speaking, the test of present value becomes only a partial one in the case where objectives other than economic efficiency are recognized. Although this is an important qualification, we shall ignore it in this section.

97. Cf. the 1966 White Paper [50].

projections of expenditure are explicitly made and brought together, and that they are considered in the context of a general economic model which embodies some projection of the rate of growth in the economy as a whole.

153. The effects of such a system on the investment programmes of public enterprises will partly depend on the definition of public expenditure that is used. This in turn should logically be related to the purpose of imposing a constraint on the total. One reason for limiting aggregate public expenditure may be a belief that existing rates of taxation are too high.[98] In this case a comprehensive definition of public expenditure is appropriate, which should include the investment undertaken by public enterprises in so far as this is subject to government authorization and control. In the earlier British public expenditure surveys, the investment of the nationalized industries was in fact included within the total to which a limit was assigned, but more recently it has been placed in a separate category. This may be evidence that the underlying reason for imposing the constraint has changed over time.

154. In so far as a broad limit is set for public expenditure as a whole, in which the investment programmes of public enterprises are included, it becomes reasonable to assume that the opportunity cost of public investments should be defined in terms of other items of public expenditure foregone. Which items will be affected will depend on the form of the constraints imposed, and may not be easy to determine. Thus if a more specific constraint is applied to the total of public investment, then the expenditure displaced must be treated as falling within this total. If constraints of a still more detailed kind are imposed, so that fixed investment budgets are prescribed for public agencies or enterprises, then the situation is one of capital rationing, in which a project should be regarded as displacing some other investment that might have been undertaken by the enterprise concerned.

155. Some controversy has occurred among economists as to whether or not it is reasonable to assume that capital rationing in

98. In so far as this belief arises from a judgement that high rates of taxation have a bad effect on the rate of economic growth, we have an instance of the situation referred to in paragraph 150 above, where a constraint is imposed with the object of improving economic efficiency.

this sense is prevalent. One view is that such an irrational practice cannot be treated as being of much importance in the real world.[99] The opposing view, which seems to have a comfortable majority of those whose votes have been recorded, is that rightly or wrongly governments make a practice of assigning limited investment budgets to public agencies or enterprises, so that it is worth while to devise decision rules for ensuring that these funds are put to the best possible use. Since the dispute concerns a matter of fact, it is perhaps surprising that little serious research seems to have been undertaken into the subject of the financial constraints that actual public enterprises appear to be subject to.[100] This may not always be clear, and will probably vary from case to case.

156. It is possible that the situation of many public enterprises is not correctly described by either of these assumptions. This is because a common criterion for the investment of these enterprises is whether or not it seems to be necessary in order to meet demand. In so far as this can be shown, the test of prospective present value may not be imposed, and the notion of assigning a fixed investment budget has no meaning. In order to cover this situation, it may be useful to define the concept of capital rationing in terms of observed effects, rather than the supposed existence of a known limit on capital expenditure over a specified period. Thus it may be said that capital rationing exists if investment projects which have a positive present value at the agreed rate of interest are precluded on grounds of financial stringency. This definition is applicable to the situation in which investment is justified mainly with reference to the need to meet expected increases in demand,[101] since a given expansion in capacity can often be carried out in more or less capital-intensive ways. Thus rationing is thought of as affecting what may be called the

99. Cf. Hirshleifer [23], p. 170.

100. An uncharitable person might say that this is not at all surprising, given that the parties to the dispute are economists.

101. This is not meant to imply that the criterion of meeting demand is one that can be accepted without question. This depends on how the demand has been estimated, particularly in the case where there is competition between public enterprises. Moreover, the criterion is only admissible if the pricing policies which are assumed in estimating demand are regarded as satisfactory. This is another instance of a constraint which should not be accepted without question.

discretionary element in the investment programme of an enterprise.

157. In so far as capital rationing exists, two alternative ranking systems have been proposed for investments. The first makes use of the rate of interest as a rationing device, which is equivalent to discounting net benefits at the internal rate of return of the marginal project. The second ranks projects according to benefit cost ratios, discounting at an agreed social time preference rate. Where the constraint applies strictly to capital expenditure only, the benefit–cost ratios are defined as in section C above – that is, they measure the ratio of net benefits after completion to initial capital cost. If, however, the constraint applies not only to initial capital cost but to future operating expenditures also, then the form of the ratio used will change accordingly: the denominator is in each case the amount of the constrained resource that will be used.

158. A choice between these methods of ranking is likely to depend on whether or not the general case for using a social time preference rate of interest in the public sector is accepted – that is, on arguments which have already been summarized in sections B and C above. It has, however, been suggested that if funds are constrained the choice may depend on whether or not it can be assumed that surpluses will be reinvested at the marginal internal rate of return, since if so this is the correct rate to use for discounting, rather than the social time preference rate.[102] But it is possible in this situation to use a social time preference rate, and to allow for reinvestment, when comparing particular pairs of projects, by counting the reinvestment benefits foregone as part of the opportunity cost of the investment which is inferior in this respect.

159. This point may be illustrated with reference to the arithmetical example which was used in paragraph 99 above. It was seen there that an imaginary project X, which cost 1,000 and yielded constant annual net benefits of 160 for ten years after completion, would be ranked as inferior to an alternative project Y, which also cost 1,000 and yielded net benefits of 2,150 in a single instalment ten years after completion, if these net benefits were discounted at an assumed social time preference rate of

102. Cf. McKean [33], chapter 5, and Little [30].

3 per cent and reinvestment was ignored. In this case the respective benefit–cost ratios would be 1·365 for X and 1·600 for Y. If, however, it was assumed that the surpluses arising from X would be reinvested at 8 per cent, then X would be superior to Y. Discounting at 8 per cent, the respective benefit–cost ratios are in this case 1·075 for X and 0·996 for Y. But if X and Y are alternatives the opportunity cost of Y is the benefits foregone by not choosing X, and this will exceed the nominal cost of 1,000 by the amount of reinvestment benefits that are lost. If these are taken into account, the opportunity cost of Y becomes approximately 1,267;[103] and the respective benefit–cost ratios, using the 3 per cent rate, now become 1·365 for X and 1·263 for Y. Not only is X now correctly ranked above Y, but the margin of superiority is the same as when an 8 per cent rate is used for discounting.

160. Whether reinvestment should be taken into account is a debatable matter, for the reasons already stated in paragraphs 101–3 above. It will depend on the nature of the budgetary constraints and their expected duration. Any assumption about how long a particular constraint will remain in force, and with what degree of severity, is likely to be very much a matter of judgement. In particular, it may be necessary to form a view about what is practical politics within the machinery of decision-making. If a constraint seems to have little rational justification, it may be more reasonable and more beneficial to anticipate its disappearance than to advocate the use of decision rules which are valid only if it can be expected to last. These writers who have argued against allowing for financial constraints may be open to the charge of taking a utopian view of institutions, as well as of neglecting the possibility that such constraints may in some instances fulfil a useful function. On the other hand, those who try to make allowance for constraints in formulating decision rules may fall into the opposite error, of taking as given, practices that could and should be changed.[104] Thus difficulties of choice

103. That is, $160 \times (0·08/0·03)$ *plus* 840.

104. In some cases, the implied degree of pessimism about institutions may verge on the self-contradictory, since a government machine that was intelligent enough to understand and approve the decision rules proposed, and resourceful enough to get them adopted, might reasonably be regarded as capable of eliminating arbitrary or irrational constraints which give rise to the need for them.

arise under budgetary constraints because the best course of action will depend on what is assumed about the constraints that are in force in later periods, and there is considerable scope for disagreement about what assumptions it is reasonable to make.[105]

161. Apart from this thorny issue, the presence of budgetary constraints complicates the problem of determining the optimal time-sequence of investments in the case where the benefits are affected by the date at which a project is undertaken.[106] The task of selecting the best set of projects that is compatible with observance of the constraint may also be made more difficult because there is interdependence between projects, so that the prospective net benefits arising from any particular one may depend on what is decided about others. Again, the fact that projects often have long construction periods creates problems of phasing and programming, which have to be allowed for in the design and operation of financial constraints. However, there is not much that can usefully be said about these matters in general terms. The two main conclusions that arise from this discussion have already been anticipated in the previous subsection, in which other constraints were also considered. Where financial constraints are in force, both the form which they assume and the underlying reasons for imposing them should be made explicit; and they should not be taken for granted or accepted without question.

G. Concluding Remarks

162. It is clear from what has been said that the main issues which arise in formulating investment criteria for public enterprises are far from settled. Thus there is no agreed code of practice which is available for general adoption, no manual of instruction which can be taken as an authoritative guide by governments and by public enterprises themselves. In part, this results from inevitable differences of opinion about what is practicable or

105. This point is well made in McKean [33], p. 88, and illustrated on page 485 of Eckstein [11], where the author describes the differences between McKean's treatment of the issue and his own, in relation to U.S. water resource investments.

106. Cf. Marglin [36] and the shorter treatment of these questions by the same author in chapter 4 of Maass [31].

tactically wise. When it comes to translating broad objectives into decision rules and operating procedures, what appears to be the most suitable course of action is bound to depend on judgements about how much can be done in given circumstances, and about the extent to which existing practices or institutional arrangements can be altered within a specified period of time. It is not surprising that economists and practical men should disagree about such matters, both with each other and among themselves. A good example of this is the question, which was considered in section C above, of whether the use of a social time preference rate of interest for discounting, in conjunction with calculations of the opportunity costs of particular public investments, is likely to prove workable and acceptable.

163. What is perhaps more disturbing is the extent of disagreement among economists about more fundamental questions concerning criteria, questions which fall largely within their province. It is true that here also differences of opinion may sometimes arise from largely practical considerations. Thus as has been seen it is possible to hold the view that efficiency benefits alone should count in evaluating investments, despite awareness that society may have other objectives than economic efficiency, because it is believed that the non-efficiency benefits that may arise from public investments are not only rarely significant but usually much exaggerated, so that it is best to advocate the use of a convention which treats them as non-existent. Again, disagreement may often arise over questions of fact rather than analytical points;[107] and though it is unfortunate that we know so little about the working and properties of actual economic systems, it is not very strange or discreditable. But though it may be easy enough to account for disagreements, and to take a reasonably tolerant view of them, the fact remains that the basic issues which were considered in sections C to E above, and with which economists are particularly concerned, are still subjects of dispute. Since the amount and composition of public investment may be very substantially affected by the way in which these issues are resolved in practice, this is an unsatisfactory state of affairs.

107. In any given case, however, it may not be easy to make this distinction with precision.

164. Despite these limitations, however, cost–benefit analysis may sometimes be of considerable value in helping to improve the quality of investment decisions in the public sector. Without in any way underrating the extent or significance of the disagreements that have been referred to, it is possible to derive at least a certain degree of reassurance from three closely related considerations.

165. First, where complexities and grounds for disagreement exist it is better to make them explicit, and to subject them to analysis, rather than to act as though oversimplified decision rules and criteria could be accepted without question. The world would be a simpler place if the timing of costs and benefits were a matter of indifference, or its precise significance were obvious; if risk and uncertainty were always negligible; if profitability could always be taken as an adequate measure of efficiency gains; if economic efficiency, or any other single criterion, were the only objective to be considered in relation to any given decision;[108] and if all existing constraints could either be dispensed with or treated as immutable. But since none of these things is the case, the use of investment criteria which depend (whether consciously or not) on their acceptance may lead to unfortunate results. It is preferable to face the complications of the real world, and to bring out by means of sensitivity analysis the implications of different possible ways of treating the contentious issues.

166. Second, it is clear that actual investment decisions are often taken on the basis of criteria, and methods of analysis, which are more or less seriously inadequate. Thus it is common if not typical for project studies and submissions to ignore matters of timing, or to allow for them in very crude ways; to pay insufficient regard to uncertainty; to fail to consider relevant alternative choices; to use extremely questionable concepts of costs and gains; to exaggerate uncritically the significance of

108. A common weakness in British administration is to treat issues of policy as one-dimensional, so that a given question is labelled from the outset as either political or economic. This not only fails to recognize that multiplicity of objectives is almost always present, but means that no attempt is made to establish trade-off ratios between them. This way of thinking is often associated with a bad linguistic practice, by which the term 'economic' is used as a synonym for cheaper, more profitable, or simply more desirable.

particular forms of benefit arising; to omit serious research into the factors determining costs and benefits; and to impose or accept constraints which are very much open to question. Since these are defects which largely arise from ignorance of the underlying problems, often amounting to a total lack of awareness that they exist, it is possible to find every single defect, together with some elementary maltreatment of statistical evidence, in the same appreciation. Moreover, such studies are often subject to bias for one reason or another; and this is not necessarily avoided by the use of outside consultants.[109] It is therefore often possible to improve the quality of decisions by straightforward improvements in criteria and methods of analysis, none of which take us beyond the point at which the kind of disagreements that have been considered in this paper must arise.[110] In this respect cost–benefit analysis may have a clear and useful therapeutic function.

167. Third, an advantage of trying to formulate investment criteria explicitly, and without resort to convenient oversimplification, is that attention is directed to the need for evidence of particular kinds, and to gaps in the information that is currently available. This in turn gives a useful stimulus to those concerned, both in government departments and in public enterprises, to improve the quality of the data at their disposal.[111] Such improvements may often be very much needed. It is possible for investment decisions to be taken on quite unnecessarily poor evidence, simply because no one concerned is aware that something much

109. The following shrewd observation of Lauchlin Currie, made in the context of Latin America, may well have wider applicability. 'It is quite common to turn to engineering firms for preliminary feasibility studies and I know of only one case where such a firm made an adverse report. In the private sector a client usually wants the best advice he can get from technicians. In the public sector the client usually wants a favorable finding from the technician' (Currie [6], p. 201).

110. Excellent illustrations of this are given in Hitch and McKean [24].

111. The situation with respect to cost–benefit analysis is in this respect very much the same as that described by Dorfman in relation to operations research. 'Much of the work of the practising analyst is the work of filling gaps in substantive knowledge, just as much of the value of the model-building approach resides in disclosing and defining those gaps. There is much testimony to indicate that the most valuable results of operations research are by-products' (Dorfman [8], p. 66).

better could be done. Good cost–benefit analysis can help to create a more educated awareness of the scope for improvement.

168. It is unfortunate that the practice has developed, at any rate in Britain, of referring to cost–benefit analysis as a 'technique'. Not only is this inaccurate, but it serves to create the misleading impression among executives and administrators that what is involved is substantially the mixture as before, but with the addition when appropriate of compound interest and discounting, or of regard to so-called 'social' benefits. This misses the main point. Improvements in the investment criteria that are used in the public sector, and in the extent to which given social or economic objectives are realized through public investments, may be effected in different ways. Probably the most important means are better analytical formulation of issues, better data together with greater concern for evidence, and better organization or administrative machinery. These different aspects of the problem can be treated separately, and useful changes can often be made with respect to any one of them in isolation.[112] But in the general case all three are involved, with a more or less close degree of interrelationship, and often substantial progress can only be made if this is recognized from the start and the problem is tackled as a whole.[113] A characteristic feature and merit of good cost–benefit analysis is that it tries to do this; the role of any particular technique is purely instrumental, and generally of subordinate interest. Because of this synoptic quality, as well as for the reasons that were given in the three preceding paragraphs, economic analysis has been able to bring about some useful improvements in a variety of sometimes unexpected places, despite the difficulties and limitations which it has been necessary to emphasize in this paper.

112. However, it is a common practice within the British government machine to give disproportionate emphasis to the third factor, and to form unrealistic estimates of the benefits that are likely to ensue from organizational and administrative changes alone.

113. A very good illustration of this point, and of its possibly revolutionary implications, is the set of reforms that has been introduced within the U.S. Department of Defense since Mr McNamara became Secretary of State. The view is sometimes expressed that these changes can be adequately summarized as consisting in the introduction of the 'techniques' of cost–effectiveness analysis. This reveals a total lack of understanding of what has taken place.

Appendix I

Rates of Return and Ranking Methods: Some Illustrative Examples

1. In this Appendix some very simple arithmetical illustrations are given, in order to clarify or amplify points that are made in the main text. In the first section some different ways of computing rates of return, and of ranking projects, are shown. In the second section the same basic numerical example is used to illustrate some of the decision rules that have been suggested for dealing with the problem of choice under conditions of pure uncertainty.

(a) *Rates of return and ranking methods*

2. Table 1 presents figures of six imaginary and highly simplified investment projects, designated A to F. Each of these is assumed to involve an initial expenditure of 100, incurred at time zero, and to produce zero or positive net returns accruing at the end of each of five subsequent periods.

Table 1

Project Costs and Returns

Project	0	1	2	3	4	5	Net (periods 1–5)	Net returns (periods 0–5)
A	—100	100	10	—	—	—	110	10
B	—100	50	50	10	10	—	120	20
C	—100	40	30	30	20	10	130	30
D	—100	28	28	28	28	28	140	40
E	—100	10	20	30	40	50	150	50
F	—100	—	—	—	40	120	160	60

The penultimate column shows total net benefits after completion, and the final column the net benefits after allowing for construction cost, in each case undiscounted. All figures are supposed to be known with certainty, and no account is taken of the possibility of reinvesting net benefits as they arise.

3. The rate of return on each project can be computed in various ways. The main variants that appear to be used are:

  (i) Average rate of return

    (a) 'gross' return on initial investment
    (b) 'net' return on initial investment
    (c) 'net' return on average book value

  (ii) Payoff period rate of return
  (iii) Internal rate of return

Each of these will be considered in turn.[114]

4. First, there is the *average rate of return* in its various forms. For each of the projects in Table 1, the average 'gross' return on investment is calculated by taking the figure shown in the penultimate column, that is, undiscounted net benefits after completion, dividing by the number of periods (in this case five) to get the average value for each period, and expressing this as a percentage of the initial capital expenditure. Thus the rate of return on project A is 22 per cent, that on project B 24 per cent, and so on. These and other rates of return are shown in Table 2. It will be seen that by this criterion the six projects will be ranked in reverse alphabetical order. The complete set of rankings that we get from different criteria, including present value as well as rate of return methods, are set out in Table 4.

5. In order to compute the average 'net' return on investment, the figure in the final (rather than the penultimate) column of Table 1 is divided by five and expressed as a percentage of the initial capital expenditure. This of course yields lower absolute figures for the rate of return in each case, but the same ranking.

6. The same numerator – that is, the average for net benefits in each period, subtracting initial capital expenditure – is used in computing the 'net' return on average book value, but a different denominator. Instead of the amount of initial capital expenditure, an average is taken of the book value of the investment

114. Different forms of rate of return calculation are considered more fully in Grant and Ireson [21], chapters 10 and 19, and Merrett and Sykes [38], chapter 7. Meek [37] makes the interesting point that the use of crude methods of assessment, such as the average rate of return or payoff period, may impart a bias against the choice of more capital intensive techniques.

in each of the time periods involved. This value will depend on taxation law, and on the accounting conventions that are used for depreciating fixed assets. For the sake of example, we make here the simplest possible assumption, of straight line depreciation with zero salvage value. In this case the average book value of the initial capital expenditure in our example is fifty, and the net return on average book value is exactly double the net return on investment. Once again, the ranking remains unaffected.

7. The *payoff period* rate of return is calculated by taking in each case the length of time that is expected to elapse before the cumulative sum of net benefits equals the initial capital expenditure, expressing this in terms of number of periods, and dividing it into 100 to obtain a percentage. Thus in the case of project A in Table 1 the whole of initial expenditure is recovered after one period, so that the payoff period rate of return is 100 per cent, while for project B two periods are required, so that the rate of return is 50 per cent. The rates thus derived for all six projects are shown in Table 2. It will be seen that the ranking of projects by this method is precisely the opposite of that yielded by the use of the average rate of return: the order of merit, as shown in the second column of Table 4, now becomes alphabetical.

8. Each of these methods of computing rates of return is seriously defective. The average rate of return calculation, in all its forms, takes no account of the timing or duration of net benefits; it considers only their average annual amount. The payoff period calculation allows for timing, but neglects altogether all returns that may accrue after the date at which the initial outlay has been recovered.

9. As was noted in paragraph 12 of the paper, the use of the *internal rate of return* permits allowance to be made simultaneously for both the absolute amounts and the timing of costs and benefits. The internal rate of return – defined as the rate of interest at which the present discounted value of all costs and returns will be zero – is shown for each of the six imaginary projects in the final column of Table 2. The corresponding ranking of projects is given in the third column of Table 4.

10. It was seen in paragraph 22 of the paper that in the case of incompatible projects it is not necessarily correct to prefer one with a higher internal rate of return to one with a lower rate.

Given that a rate of interest for discounting net benefits has been chosen, a better criterion is to rank projects in accordance with present value at that rate. In order to illustrate the effect of

Table 2

Project Rates of Return

(Figures in percentages)

Project	Average rate of return			Pay off period rate of return	Internal rate of return
	(i) Gross return on investment	(ii) Net return on investment	(iii) Net return on average book value		
A	22	2	4	100	9·1
B	24	4	8	50	10·7
C	26	6	12	$33\frac{1}{3}$	11·8
D	28	8	16	28	12·4
E	30	10	20	25	12·0
F	32	12	24	$22\frac{2}{9}$	10·4

choosing different rates of interest, and since the choice of a rate may be a matter of contention, the present value of the six projects is shown in Table 3 for three widely spaced values of the rate, $2\frac{1}{2}$ per cent, 8 per cent, and 15 per cent.

Table 3

Project Present Values at Different Interest Rates

Project	$2\frac{1}{2}\%$	8%	15%
A	7·1	1·2	—5·4
B	14·8	4·5	—6·4
C	22·4	8·0	—6·4
D	30·1	11·8	—6·2
E	37·1	13·6	—8·7
F	42·3	11·1	—17·4

It will be seen that all six projects have a positive present value when costs and returns are discounted at a rate of $2\frac{1}{2}$ per cent or 8 per cent, and have a negative present value when 15 per cent is used for discounting. This follows from the internal rates of

161

return which are tabulated in the last column of Table 2, since all six projects have internal rates of return that lie between 8 and 15 per cent.

11. As one would expect when the time-pattern of net returns is so different, the ranking of projects is considerably affected by the choice of interest rate. With a rate of $2\frac{1}{2}$ per cent the ordering is reverse alphabetical, with project F the best. With 15 per cent F becomes easily the least attractive project and A the best, though the ordering is not precisely alphabetical. It may be noted that with none of the three rates of interest chosen here does D, the project with the highest internal rate of return, appear to be the best.

12. The complete set of project rankings, for each of the methods that have been outlined above, is set out in Table 4.

Table 4

Project Ranking by Alternative Criteria

Rank	Average rate of return	Payoff period	Internal rate of return	Present value at		
				$2\frac{1}{2}\%$	8%	15%
1	F	A	D	F	E	A
2	E	B	E	E	D	D
3	D	C	C	D	F	B
4	C	D	B	C	C	C
5	B	E	F	B	B	E
6	A	F	A	A	A	F

(b) *The problem of choice under uncertainty*[115]

13. The same illustrative numerical values that are set out in Table 3, for the present value of projects at different rates of interest, can be used to outline some of the decision rules that have been suggested for dealing with the case of pure uncertainty. For this purpose we consider only the three projects F, E, and A, which rank first at the three interest rates that were taken, and the choice between these. We may suppose that the respective

115. This sub-section is no more than a brief sketch. A fuller summary treatment can be found in Baumol [1], chapter 23; Dorfman in chapter 3 of Maass [31]; and Dryden [10].

present value of these three projects, as shown in the appropriate rows of Table 3, are the values that can be associated with three possible outcomes, where one of these outcomes will certainly occur but nothing whatever is known about the likelihood of their occurrence. We might, for example, assume that one of the three projects must be selected now, when the appropriate rate of interest is undecided. In the meantime a committee of economists has been appointed to choose a rate, which will report only after the choice of project has been made, which has been given the three rates of interest to choose from – so that no other outcome is possible – and about whose final decision total uncertainty prevails.

14. We can then set out the present value for each of the three projects, for each of the three outcomes, in the form of a *payoff matrix*. This is shown in Table 5 below. The column headings correspond to the three rates of interest used in Table 3.

Table 5

Payoff Matrix Derived from Table 3

Project	Outcome		
	I	II	III
A	7·1	1·2	—5·4
E	37·1	13·6	—8·7
F	42·3	11·1	—17·4

The problem now is to choose the best project given this information.

15. One rule or strategy that has been suggested is that of *maximin*, which implies the choice of the course of action which will lead to the most favourable result in the worst possible case. In the situation depicted in Table 5, the worst possible case for all projects is outcome III, and the best choice then becomes A, which in this case yields a better result than E or F. The strategy thus requires the choice of the highest row minimum.

16. This rule has been criticized on the grounds that in many situations of uncertainty it may not be reasonable to assume that only the worst result that can ensue from the choice of a particular strategy should be taken into account. In the case of games

or conflict it may be rational to assume that one's opponent will adopt a strategy that will be unfavourable to oneself; but the situation in which a choice of projects or operating procedures has to be made is a different one. With no guidance whatever as to the likelihood of different outcomes, it becomes questionable whether only a few of the possibilities shown in the payoff matrix – namely the row minima – should be taken into account to the exclusion of all others. This strategy may therefore appear too conservative, as it does in our illustration where the choice of A precludes the possibility of realizing much higher gains from E or F if either of the first two outcomes materializes.

17. A second criterion that has been suggested is to *minimax regret*. In order to illustrate this criterion we construct a second payoff matrix, in which each element shows the difference that would result from a given choice and a given outcome, as compared with the choice that would have been best under that outcome. Thus, for example, if A is chosen and outcome I materializes, the gain realized is only 7·1, as compared with 42·3 if F had been chosen. The measure of 'regret' thus assigned to this element in the payoff matrix is therefore 35·2, the difference between the two results. The full regret matrix derived from Table 5 is set out in Table 6.

Table 6

Regret Matrix Derived from Table 5

Project	Outcome		
	I	II	III
A	35·2	12·4	0
E	5·2	0	3·3
F	0	2·5	12·0

The criterion of minimaxing regret implies the choice of the strategy which has the lowest maximum value for regret, that is, the lowest of the row maxima. In our case this leads to the choice of E.

18. This principle, like that of maximin, has been criticized on the grounds that only the row maxima are taken into account in the final choice. It has also been shown that both it and the

P. D. Henderson

criterion of maximin returns are open to the objection that the ranking of projects in accordance with them may be affected by the introduction of what appear to be logically irrelevant factors.[116]

19. Other rules have been put forward for making choices under uncertainty, which resemble the two that have been outlined in that no assumption is made about the respective likelihood of the various possible outcomes. But since none of them has escaped objection, it can be argued that resort to assumptions about probabilities may lead to better results. This of course poses the problem of how to assign probabilities to possible outcomes, when by definition there is no evidence about these. One rule for this situation is to assume that all possible outcomes should be regarded as equally probable. In our illustration, we should then assign a probability of one-third to each of the outcomes, the results of which are shown in Table 5. Another procedure that has been suggested is to assign subjective probabilities, which represent the best guess of those involved in the decision. Thus if we go back to our rather frivolous notion of paragraph 13 above, of the committee of economists meeting to choose one of three rates of interest, we might hazard the guess that a compromise solution was more likely than either extreme, and thus choose probabilities of one-quarter for the high and low rates and one-half for the one in between; or we might judge from the personalities involved that only an extreme outcome was possible, assigning probabilities of one-half to each of these, and zero to the intermediate value. However, in the case where subjective probabilities can be assigned we are arguably moving away from the situation of pure uncertainty.

20. Once probabilities have been chosen we can adopt the criterion of choosing the course of action which has the highest expected value, or possibly rank alternatives in accordance with dispersion as well as expected value, along the lines referred to in section E of the paper. If expected value is taken as the criterion, and each of our three outcomes is assigned a probability of one-third, then E becomes the best choice.

21. It is doubtful whether the case of pure uncertainty is one that need be taken seriously in relation to choosing criteria for

116. Cf. Dorfman in chapter 3 of Maass [31].

165

public investments, since in most situations there will be at any rate some evidence on which to base judgements concerning probabilities. To this extent the problem of choosing criteria is less intractable. On the other hand, the example that we have used to illustrate choice under conditions of uncertainty abstracted in one important respect from the complexities of the real world. While we assumed that nothing at all was known about the probabilities attached to different outcomes, which is admittedly extreme, we also assumed that the results that would ensue from the choice of any particular strategy under each possible outcome were known with certainty – i.e. that the values of the elements in the payoff matrix were single-valued and known with certainty. This of course need not be the case. It may be that these values can be specified only in terms of a probability distribution, the characteristics of which are not known with certainty.

Appendix II

Acknowledgements and Disclaimers

1. An early version of this paper was written in the National Economic Development Office in 1963. Acknowledgements are due to a number of people who were then working in the N.E.D.O. and who commented on this draft. In particular, I would like to thank Sir Robert Shone, who at the time was the Director-General of the Office; Sir Donald MacDougall, who was then its Economic Director; and Messrs E. O. Jones, M. F G. Scott, and P. E. Watts.

2. A much-altered version, on which the present paper is based, was published in the *Bulletin* of the Oxford University Institute of Economics and Statistics in February 1965. In the process of revising the paper, I benefited considerably from the ideas and comments of a number of Oxford colleagues, notably Martin S. Feldstein, C. D. Foster, D. L. Munby, Richard Portes, Paul Streeten, and C. B. Winsten.

3. In preparing the present paper, the opportunity has been taken both to bring up to date the *Bulletin* article, and to amend it in various ways. Substantial additions and deletions have been made. In this second process of revision, I have been greatly

helped by ideas and suggestions from Dr I. M. D. Little and Mr Ralph Turvey.

4. The status of the paper is entirely unofficial. It should not be taken as reflecting the past or present view either of the National Economic Development Office, or of the Government department in which I worked during 1965–6. Further, none of the individuals mentioned bears any responsibility for the views expressed in the paper, or for the deficiencies which remain in spite of what they have contributed.

References

1. WILLIAM J. BAUMOL, *Economic theory and operations analysis*, Prentice Hall, second edn., 1965.
2. M. E. BEESLEY and C. D. FOSTER, 'The Victoria Line: Social benefit and finances', *Journal of the Royal Statistical Society* (Series A), 1965.
3. E. B. BERMAN, 'The normative interest rate', RAND Corporation paper, P-1796, Santa Monica, California, 1959.
4. JAGDISH BHAGWATI, *The economics of underdeveloped countries*, Weidenfeld & Nicolson, 1966.
5. C. D. BUCHANAN *et al.*, *Traffic in towns*, H.M.S.O., 1963.
6. LAUCHLIN CURRIE, *Accelerating development: The necessity and the means*, McGraw-Hill, 1966.
7. ALAN DAY, *Roads*, Mayflower Books, 1963.
8. ROBERT DORFMAN, 'Operations research', published in vol. 3 of *Surveys of economic theory*, Macmillan, 1966.
9. ROBERT DORFMAN (ed.), *Measuring the benefits of government investments*, Brookings Institution, 1965.
10. MYLES M. DRYDEN, 'Capital budgeting: Treatment of uncertainty and investment criteria', *Scottish Journal of Political Economy*, November 1964.
11. OTTO ECKSTEIN, 'A survey of the theory of public expenditure criteria', published in *Public finances: Needs, sources and utilization*, Princeton University Press, 1961.
12. OTTO ECKSTEIN, book review, *American Economic Review*, June 1961.
13. STEPHEN ENKE, 'Using costs to select weapons', *American Economic Review*, May 1965.
14. ALAIN C. ENTHOVEN, 'Economic analysis in the department of defense', *American Economic Review*, May 1963.
15. M. S. FELDSTEIN, 'Net social benefits and the public investment decision', *Oxford Economic Papers*, March 1964.
16. M. S. FELDSTEIN, 'The social time preference discount rate in cost–benefit analysis', *Economic Journal*, June 1964.

17. M. S. FELDSTEIN, 'The derivation of social time preference rates', *Kyklos*, 1965.

18. M. S. FELDSTEIN, 'Opportunity cost calculations in cost-benefit analysis', *Public Finance*, 1964.

19. M. S. FELDSTEIN and J. S. FLEMMING, 'The problem of time-stream evaluation: Present value versus internal rate of return rules', *Bulletin of the Oxford University Institute of Economics and Statistics*, February 1964.

20. C. D. FOSTER and M. E. BEESLEY, 'Estimating the social benefit of constructing an underground railway in London', *Journal of the Royal Statistical Society* (Series A), 1963.

21. EUGENE L. GRANT and W. GRANT IRESON, *Principles of engineering economy*, Ronald Press, fourth edn., 1960.

22. P. D. HENDERSON, 'Political and budgetary constraints: Some characteristics and implications', paper presented to the 1966 Conference of the International Economic Association, to be published in the proceedings of the Conference.

23. JACK HIRSHLEIFER, JAMES C. DE HAVEN, and JEROME W. MILLIMAN, *Water supply*, University of Chicago Press, 1960.

24. CHARLES J. HITCH and ROLAND N. MCKEAN, *The economics of defense in the nuclear age*, Oxford University Press, 1960.

25. HOUSE OF COMMONS, Report from the Select Committee on the Nationalised Industries, *British Railways*, House of Commons Papers, 254–1, July 1960.

26. JOHN G. KEMENY, ARTHUR SCHLEIFER JR, J. LAURIE SNELL, and GERALD L. THOMPSON, *Finite mathematics with business applications*, Prentice-Hall, 1962.

27. J. V. KRUTILLA and OTTO ECKSTEIN, *Multiple purpose river basin development*, Johns Hopkins Press, 1958.

28. G. H. LAWSON and D. W. WINDLE, *Tables for discounted cash flow, etc.*, Oliver and Boyd, 1965.

29. R. G. LIPSEY and KELVIN LANCASTER, 'The general theory of second best', *Review of Economic Studies*, 1956–7.

30. I. M. D. LITTLE, 'Public sector project selection in relation to Indian economic development', to be published in a Nehru memorial volume of essays edited by A. V. Bhuleshkar and published by George Allen & Unwin.

31. ARTHUR MAASS, MAYNARD M. HUFSCHMIDT, ROBERT DORFMAN, HAROLD THOMAS JR, STEPHEN A. MARGLIN, and GORDON MASKEW FAIR, *Design of water resource systems*, Macmillan, 1962.

32. ARTHUR MAASS, 'Benefit–cost analysis: Its relevance to public investment decisions', *Quarterly Journal of Economics*, May 1966.

33. ROLAND N. MCKEAN, *Efficiency in government through systems analysis*, Wiley, 1958.

34. STEPHEN A. MARGLIN, 'The Social rate of discount and the optimum rate of investment', *Quarterly Journal of Economics*, February 1963.

35. STEPHEN A. MARGLIN, 'The opportunity costs of public investment', *Quarterly Journal of Economics*, May 1963.

36. STEPHEN A. MARGLIN, *Dynamic approaches to investment planning*, North–Holland, 1963.

37. R. L. MEEK, 'Ideal and reality in the choice between alternative techniques', *Oxford Economic Papers*, November 1964.

38. A. J. MERRETT and ALAN SYKES, *The finance and analysis of capital projects*, Longmans, 1963.

39. D. L. MUNBY, 'Investing in coal', *Oxford Economic Papers*, vol. 11 (1959), pp. 242–69.

40. National Economic Development Office, *Conditions favourable to faster growth*, H.M.S.O., 1963.

41. National Economic Development Office, *Investment appraisal*, H.M.S.O., 1966.

42. R. R. NEILD, 'Replacement policy', National Institute of Economic and Social Research, *Economic Review*, November 1964.

43. MERTON J. PECK and FREDERIC M. SCHERER, *The weapons acquisition process: An economic analysis*, Harvard University, Graduate School of Business Administration, 1962.

44. A. C. PIGOU, *Economics of Welfare*. Macmillan, fourth edn., 1932.

45. P.E.P., 'French planning: Some lessons for Britain', *Planning*, September, 1963.

46. A. R. PREST and R. TURVEY, 'Cost–benefit analysis: A survey', published in vol. 3 of *Surveys of Economic Theory*, Macmillan, 1966.

47. PETER STEINER, 'Choosing among alternative public investments in the water resource field', *American Economic Review*, December 1959.

48. J. A. STOCKFISCH, 'The interest rate applicable to government investment projects', unpublished paper.

49. RALPH TURVEY, 'Present value versus internal rate of return – an essay in the theory of the third best', *Economic Journal*, March 1963.

50. UNITED KINGDOM GOVERNMENT, White Paper on *Public expenditure: planning and control*, Cmnd 2915, H.M.S.O., 1966.

51. UNITED KINGDOM GOVERNMENT, Report of the committee of inquiry into the future of the aircraft industry (Plowden Report), H.M.S.O., 1965.

52. UNITED STATES BUREAU OF THE BUDGET, *Standards and criteria for formulating and evaluating federal water resources development* (report of a panel of consultants), Washington, D.C., 1961.

53. G. D. N. WORSWICK and P. H. ADY (eds.), *The British economy in the nineteen-fifties*, Oxford University Press, 1962.

54. J. F. WRIGHT, 'Notes on the marginal efficiency of capital', *Oxford Economic Papers*, July 1963.

55. J. F. WRIGHT, 'The marginal efficiency of capital: Corrigendum and addendum', *Oxford Economic Papers*, November 1964.

Part Two Application to Particular Industries

While Berrie's discussion of investment in electricity generation expresses the views of a practitioner, Warford and Hazlewood are concerned to make suggestions. Finally Crew, in his examination of electricity tariffs written to provide material for discussion in courses on management, puts forward conflicting views. All four papers show that considerable knowledge of the institutional and technological characteristics of an industry is required for the application of the general principles considered in Part One of this book.

5 T.W. Berrie

The Economics of System Planning in Bulk Electricity Supply

T. W. Berrie, 'The economics of system planning in bulk electricity supply', *Electrical Review*, vol. 181, 15th, 22nd, and 29th September 1967.

Part One: Margins, Risks and Costs

Planning

1. Planning is basically estimating and evaluating, whether it be for events in the immediate future, the middle distance (five to seven years ahead) or the far future (fifteen to thirty years ahead). It is also a circular process whereby certain estimates require to be made before others can be made; yet the latter often (through further links in the chain) imply, when deduced, rather different values of the first estimates which must, in consequence, be adjusted. The planning loop must be broken into at some point to make a start and this is usually done by regarding certain estimates as basic from which other estimates are derived. When applied to power system planning this procedure normally means regarding estimates of demand for electricity as the basic estimates. This gives these estimates a place of great prominence in the planning process [1].

Demand for electricity

2. Demand[1] estimating is at the heart of power system planning. This article deals mainly with the planning of a large interconnected thermal system with a long-established growth in electricity demand. Such a system will broadly be in an 'equilibrium of growth' (taking one year with another) for which the middle-term estimates (e.g. for five to seven years ahead) of the

1. In these articles, the normal terminology used in electricity supply is adhered to, i.e. 'Demand' or 'Power' (measured in kW) are instantaneous concepts relevant to plant capacity, while 'Consumption' or 'Energy' (measured in kWh), which have a time dimension, relate to plant output.

maximum demand for electricity in kW to be made on the system become those of crucial importance for decision-making on generating and major transmission plant extension programmes. This is because plant must continually be installed to meet the increasing demand for electricity and the most vital year ahead of all is that corresponding to the 'lead-time' required between making the decision and the commissioning of the plant. It would be more convenient if this lead-time were only one or two years (as in most industries) instead of four to six years, as all processes of estimating suffer a marked decrease in accuracy the further ahead of the event being planned the estimates are being made. In arriving at values for the estimates for these crucial years it is well to approach the problem from two or three independent directions rather than to rely on one forecasting 'method'.

3. All power systems also require forecasts to be made of annual consumption of electrical energy but systems containing predominantly hydro-electric plant must, at the planning stage, give equal or greater consideration to these estimates for five to seven years ahead than to those of maximum system demand when making decisions on generating plant. On a thermal system, installing sufficient generating capacity to meet (to a defined risk standard) the expected maximum system demand usually ensures adequacy of generating capacity throughout the rest of the year. An exception may be on a system where there is more than one period of maximum system demand in the year (e.g. the distinct summer air conditioning and winter heating peaks of America) which may prevent adequate time being available for maintenance, unless special provision is made.

4. If the demand for electricity is noticeably sensitive to weather conditions, then it is necessary, for consistency, to refer all estimates of kW demand to a standard weather condition appropriate to the season for which the estimates are being made. Applied to maximum system demands, which, in England and Wales occur in winter, the standard could either be taken as the median condition or the extreme weather condition. Once these conditions have been statistically defined, then it is possible to refer all actual and forecast figures to the standard weather base using past experience of the response of demand to variations in

weather. Figure 1 shows a fitted trend of the historic growth in
maximum system demand in England and Wales between the
winters of 1920–21 and 1966–7. The figures used have been cor-
rected to a standard weather condition (in this case it is the
median weather condition – usually known as average cold spell –
as this is the base found to be the most convenient to use in
practice).

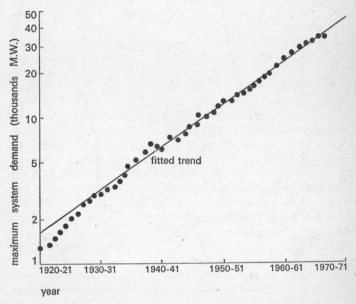

Figure 1 Growth of maximum system demand in England and Wales and fitted
exponential curve

5. For system planning purposes, demand estimates must also
be made for other periods of the year and various hourly periods
in typical days of the year; this must be done both on a national
and a local basis. Figure 2 shows typical present-day system daily
demand curves for summer and winter working days in England
and Wales and also the components, with respect to consumer
types, which make up the curves. These must also be estimated
for the period five to seven years ahead with some degree of

175

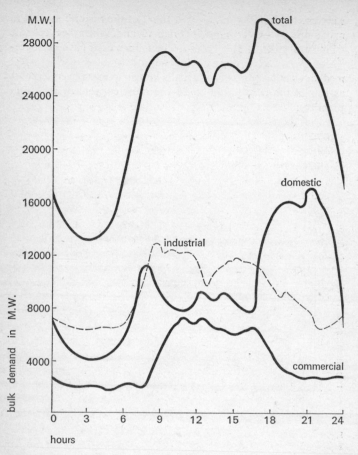

Figure 2(*a*) Illustrative curves for winter weekday in mid-1960s of daily demands in bulk in England and Wales

confidence. Once more it is as well to have several methods of approach.

6. Although not as significant as those for the middle years, estimates must also be made for the longer term as generating plant, once installed, can be expected to have a long life.

7. One difficulty in all estimating of the demand for electricity

176

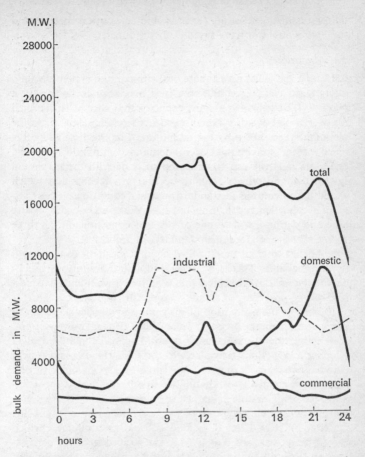

Figure 2(b) Illustrative curves for summer weekday in mid-1960s of daily demands in bulk in England and Wales

is to decide what direct allowance (if any) should be made for attempts to change deliberately the rate of growth in the national economy, e.g. by means of a National Plan. If the Supply Authority plans on the assumption that a National Plan will be fulfilled, then it may be seriously over capitalized and overplanted if the Plan fails. On the other hand, should the Plan succeed, then all the planned generating capacity will certainly be needed and the Plan would not have succeeded without it.

Plant margins

8. Having arrived at an estimate of the maximum system demand in standard weather conditions, it is necessary to decide on a margin [2] of generating plant capacity that should be planned for over and above this level of maximum system demand. At the planning stage, not only the magnitude but the time of occurrence of the maximum system demand is unknown; system operators must indeed be prepared to cope with the maximum system demand which actually occurs rather than that which would have occurred in standard weather conditions. The maximum system demand in England and Wales may occur at any time and within a wide range of weather conditions in the three winter months of December, January, or February.

9. At that time all the installed generating plant capacity will not be available. This is because complete immunity to breakdown is an unattainable ideal that would involve infinite expenditure on the provision of standby generating equipment.

10. Just as the estimation of maximum system demand is the first step taken in the process of planning a thermal power system, then estimating the percentage of total plant capacity installed which is expected to be available at the time of maximum system demand (whenever it might occur) can be regarded as the second step. Once again the estimating of this percentage is most important for the middle years of five to seven ahead. It requires a margin of spare generating plant, expressed in terms of the maximum system demand in standard weather conditions, which can be derived approximately from the reciprocal of the percentage availability. Thus if, at the time of maximum system demand, the expected availability of the total plant installed is taken as 90 per cent then this requires a margin of spare generating plant capacity of $(100/90 - 1) \times 100$ or about 11 per cent. In predominantly hydro-electric systems a margin of spare generating capacity (based on the product of installed capacity and available hours) will also be needed to cater for the possibility of a low rainfall year.

Uncertainties

11. Plant margin allowances of a somewhat different kind must be made for errors in making the basic estimates [3]. Estimates of the total plant capacity expected to be in commission (made up from plant ordering schedules and a scrapping policy) can often be wrong in the event. The estimate of the percentage availability at time of maximum system demand of the total plant capacity installed may be wrong, as may the estimate of the maximum system demand in standard weather conditions itself. Moreover, the weather at time of maximum system demand may be far from 'standard' (the 1962–3 winter is a good example of this). In all cases some guidance on what variance with respect to demand for electricity to take for these uncertainties can be obtained from a statistical analysis of past deviations from their mean expectations. Table 1 illustrates this by showing the errors made in estimating the maximum system demand on the England and Wales system in the period since the war years. Such a table is useful when deciding upon a value to take for the assumed variance of error in estimating the maximum system demand at the planning stage. Guidance on the values to be taken for the other variances can be obtained in a similar manner.

12. In considering the overall planning margin it must be recognized that these variances are unrelated and do not necessarily deviate in one direction at the same time. Indeed, to allow for deviations all in the one direction for each uncertainty would call for a very large plant margin indeed. It is not absolutely necessary to deal with each uncertainty stochastically, i.e. by the process of giving each a mean estimate and a variance. Experience has shown that the uncertainties connected with the new plant capacity expected to be commissioned and the capacity of plant expected to be withdrawn from service can be more conveniently dealt with deterministically by a straight allowance in MW for the first and an obsolescence policy (see later) for the second.

13. Normal probability theory can be of more assistance in dealing with the other uncertainties [4]. Table 2 shows the elements in the risk tableau. Those uncertainties not dealt with deterministically by a straight allowance or a policy can usually

be catered for adequately by a normal distribution about a mean expectation.

14. There must always be a finite risk of failure to meet the maximum system demand for electricity in the event, unless a

Table 1

Errors in Forward Estimates of Maximum System Demand (in Standard Weather Conditions) in England and Wales Expressed as a Percentage of the Estimates

Year of estimate	Number of winters ahead to which estimates relate							
	1	2	3	4	5	6	7	8
1947	−3·4	−3·3	−7·1	−8·8	−5·4	−6·0	−6·4	−8·5
1948	−3·6	−8·0	−9·4	−6·3	−7·3	−8·0	−10·3	−14·5
1949	−6·6	−8·6	−4·8	−4·9	−4·9	−7·5	−11·0	−11·9
1950	−6·3	−1·9	−1·5	−1·2	−2·7	−5·7	−6·8	−8·7
1951	+2·1	+3·2	+3·0	+1·2	−2·2	−2·6	−3·8	−6·6
1952	0	+1·2	+0·6	−2·8	−2·6	−4·4	−6·6	−9·8
1953	−0·6	−2·4	−4·5	−4·8	−6·5	−8·6	−12·3	−16·4
1954	−1·8	−3·9	−4·2	−5·4	−8·1	−11·3	−15·9	−16·1
1955	−2·0	−1·8	−3·5	−4·8	−7·8	−11·3	−14·9	−17·7
1956	+0·8	−0·1	−1·1	−4·2	−7·3	−10·7	−13·3	−12·2
1957	−0·4	−1·0	−3·8	−6·8	−9·9	−12·4	−11·4	−11·2
1958	−1·0	−3·2	−6·2	−8·9	−11·3	−10·2	−9·8	−10·5
1959	−2·4	−5·0	−7·2	−8·8	−6·9	−5·6	−5·1	−1·6
1960	−1·6	−4·2	−6·1	−4·6	−4·0	−3·6	0	
1961	−0·7	−1·4	+0·8	+2·6	+3·4	+7·1		
1962	+0·7	+3·6	+5·8	+7·3	+11·5			
1963	+4·2	+7·8	+10·4	+15·6				
1964	+3·7	+6·8	+12·4					
1965	+1·0	+5·4						
1966	+5·0							
Mean Error	−0·6	−0·9	−1·5	−2·7	−4·5	−6·7	−9·1	−11·2
Standard deviation (%)	3·1	4·7	6·2	6·7	7·2	8·5	10·5	12·5

Note: + Indicates overestimate.
 − Indicates underestimate.

system of infinite capacity is envisaged. The greater the capacity of plant then the smaller the risk of failure to meet the demand but the larger the capital cost that will be required. In order to determine which absolute standard of risk is economic, it is necessary to ensure that all costs are included in the balance sheet. By far the most difficult costs to assess are those that arise to the community at large if the standard of electricity supply is materially changed. Few exercises on this have even been attempted.

Table 2

The Risk Tableau for System Planning

Basic estimates	Uncertainties	Remarks on type of treatment
Total plant capacity installed (previous plant extension programmes and scrapping policy)	Early or late commissioning	Straight allowance in MW capacity
Maximum system demand in average-cold-spell weather	Error in estimating	Variance given from experience of past and judgement for future
	Unstandard weather	As above
Availability of generating plant at time of maximum system demand	Error in estimating	As above

15. In practice, the arguments usually centre round those concerning decreasing or increasing the generating plant planning margin and on differentials rather than absolutes. Before one can argue about this it is necessary to know what standard of reliability of supply has actually been achieved in the event over a reasonable period of time. This is not always easy to put down into simple terms. What is often much easier to specify is the current generating plant planning margin, i.e. the plant margin being built into plant extension programmes. If the current planning plant margin does not appear to be giving satisfactory standards in the event (five years later), then thought must be given to increasing that planning margin.

16. The standard of risk being planned to is often expressed in the form of the number of winters in one hundred in which at least some consumers can be expected to be disconnected because of a shortage of generating plant capacity. As it is usually possible to shed some load by voltage reduction before resorting to

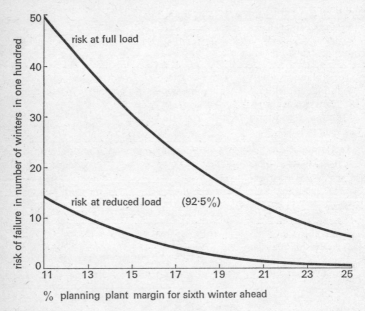

Figure 3 Risk of failure of supply in England and Wales with increasing planning plant margin

disconnexion, then the standard is perhaps better expressed as the numbers of winters in one hundred when at least some voltage reductions will be necessary.

17. Figure 3 shows, for the England and Wales system, a graph of the required generating plant margin against risk, the latter defined in the alternative ways expressed at the end of the last paragraph. The Supply Authority must, in practice, choose a risk standard which enables the good image of electricity with consumers at large to be maintained but without committing those

182

consumers to too heavy a capital burden. Currently this standard in England and Wales has been chosen to be a 24 per cent risk of voltage reduction (i.e. at least some voltage reduction may be expected to take place about twenty-four winters in one hundred). Coupled with this there is a risk of disconnexion of only 3 per cent (i.e. at least some consumers may be expected to be disconnected about three winters in one hundred). The above remarks apply only to risks of failure to meet demands due to shortages of generating plant and not for other reasons, e.g. faults in transmission or distribution plant.

Combined uncertainties

18. Taking the standards of risk being planned to as mentioned in the last paragraph, the combined allowance for the England and Wales system amounts to about 6 per cent of the maximum system demand in standard weather conditions; this, when added to the allowance of 11 per cent required for the mean expectation of the non-availability of generating plant at time of maximum system demand (paragraph 10), gives a total plant planning margin of 17 per cent for the sixth winter ahead.

19. There will probably always be controversy over what the planning plant margin should be. The consequences of underplanning are painfully known. On the other hand, a high plant margin increases the costs borne by the consumers to service the high capital costs involved (see, however, paragraph 25).

Regulators

20. Not all types of plant, in fact, require five years to build. Gas turbine plants of the aircraft-type can be built in about three years. Basic estimates made three winters ahead instead of six can be expected to be more reliable and this reduces the plant margin which is required to allow for uncertainty (paragraphs 11–18). If all generating plant needed only three years to build (rather than five), then the generating plant planning margin required for a given risk would be one to two percentage points smaller. Although, due to their relative economic worth, gas turbines usually form only a small percentage of generating plant programmes, the fact that firm decisions on their ordering

need not normally be taken until two or three years after all other plant has been ordered when all estimates can be made more accurately, provides a flexibility which enables the plant margin to be trimmed nearer the event.

21. A second 'regulator' of the plant margin, which can act in the interval between the normal planning stage six winters ahead and the winter being planned for, is a rephasing of previous generating plant extension programmes (usually possible in only one direction). This, however, is often at a heavy economic penalty in that 'follow-on' units already being manufactured for stations already commenced are involved.

22. A third 'regulator' of plant margins is the average capacity of old generating plant planned to be shut down each year. This can act as a regulator because the decision to shut down old plant need not be taken until about two years before the event, i.e. about three years after the decisions have been taken on the main generating plant programmes. The capacities of old plant thus involved will be very dependent on the actual capacity installed in a twelve months period, about (say) forty years before, and this may vary markedly from year to year. The use of this regulator may mean incurring an economic penalty in that transmission reinforcement may be needed if the generating station is prematurely shut down.

23. However, if the normal procedure when planning for the sixth winter ahead is to count in the planning plant margin all plant which can be described as 'expected to be fit for service', then a change in the scrapping rate is but a one-way regulator which must be used with discretion.

24. In using these regulators on the plant margin it is important to prevent a serious unbalancing of:

(a) the long-term risk of failure to meet the maximum system demand, i.e. the standard of risk of failure over a period of ten or more years;

(b) the plant 'mix' (i.e. the proportions of the different types of generating plant on the system).

The way to prevent (a) is to allow as far as is practical equally free use of the regulators in both directions, i.e. increasing or decreasing the plant margin (increasing it, for example, by installing a 'crash' programme of gas turbines). The unbalancing of the plant mix in (b) needs to be watched under certain conditions, e.g. if several crash programmes of gas turbines have been installed.

Economics of plant margins

25. Additional plant margins incur additional capital costs. As will be seen in a later article, however, the installation of modern, highly efficient generating plant on to the system makes savings in the total system operating cost in that, for the same total electrical energy requirements of consumers, some of the existing plant need not generate so many units. In the case of the nuclear plant to be installed on the England and Wales system in the early 1970s, these operating savings are expected to be about sufficient to offset the annual charges on the capital. Increasing the planning plant margin by installing additional nuclear plant is thus at little (if any) extra nett annual cost. In the case of oil-fired plant, the operating savings (with the present tax) are expected to be only sufficient to offset about two-thirds of the annual charges and the corresponding proportion for the best coal-fired plant is only about one-half.

26. Figure 4 illustrates how, for the early 1970s, the gross and nett capital and annual costs vary with the generating plant planning margin.

27. The other side of the balance sheet is, in practice, impossible to measure, i.e. the incremental cost to the community at large of varying the planning plant margin. The ideal way to proceed would be to determine that planning plant margin at the level at which the incremental benefit to the community of a lower probability of failure to meet demands for electricity just equalled the extra cost in additional generating plant required to secure that reduction in the probability of failure. The loss of revenue from disconnexion of consumers owing to shortage of generating plant is insignificant and not a worth-while measure to include in the balance sheet. What needs to be costed are the social costs to the community at large of loss of supply, e.g. the inconvenience costs of having no electricity, loss of output in factories (especially for export), travel delays, loss in morale, etc. it is doubtful whether meaningful numbers can be put to these

quantities but the shut-down in the North Eastern United States in November 1965 showed the grave consequences of a widespread failure of supply.

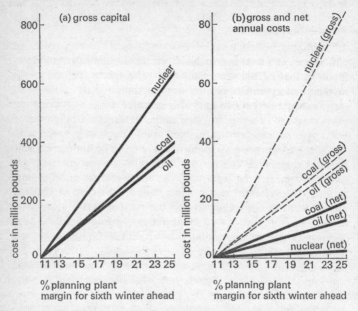

Figure 4 Costs of increasing planning plant margin in England and Wales

Obsolescence policy

28. It has already been described how the generating plant margin can, with certain provisos, be trimmed nearer the event by the greater or lesser capacity of old generating plant which is planned to be scrapped. This must be viewed against a general obsolescence policy applicable over a long period of years which leads to plant being scrapped normally at a certain age spectrum (about forty to fifty years in England and Wales at present). It is only the annual operating cost and the fixed other-works cost which are normally saved by advancing the scrapping of a station. The saving of these annual costs helps to defray the capital cost of replacing old plant by new (paragraph 25).

186

29. The final balance sheet shows that, in the 1970s, it will pay to replace a large quantity of old plant by nuclear plant (or oil plant without tax) but that it will pay, in that period, to replace only a limited amount of old plant by oil plant (with tax) and even less, if any, by coal plant.

Interconnexion between generating stations

30. The most fundamental plant planning margin to be decided upon is that of the generating plant capacity additional to the maximum system demand in standard weather conditions. The process described above of determining this margin assumes that each power station on the system is interconnected with each of the other stations by a transmission system of infinite capacity, i.e. there is complete 'pooling' of generating plant capacity. In reality the transmission will be finite and will be called upon to pool the generating plant in accordance with unbalance in demands for electricity and generating plant capacities between different geographical areas on the system.

31. The existence of a finite, as distinct from an infinite, transmission system increases the risk to consumers somewhat and the planning problem is to estimate just how much the increased risk (i.e. extra to the risk of a possible shortage of generating plant capacity) should be. Once this has been decided upon, then the same type of analysis as that described for generating plant capacity can be carried out to determine the amount of transmission capacity to install. The network can be divided into several geographical areas with local demands for electricity, local weather, local generating plant capacities together with the local mean expectation of generating plant availability. In fact, the same quantities as Table 2 can be said to apply with a local connotation; to these must be added correlations between geographical areas (e.g. with respect to weather) and the probability of outages on transmission plant. All these are amenable to normal probability methods but a further factor needs to be considered, viz. the almost infinite number of permutations covered in the multi-area problem of a large interconnected system. This particular type of approach to the transmission interconnexion problem is being studied at present (using a Monte Carlo approach for the multi-area problem) in substitution of the present

method used in England and Wales, which is empirical and based on past experiences [5].

Part Two: Background to System Planning and Economics

Planning objectives

32. All planning procedures require objectives [6]. These objectives must be spelled out at least in general terms before any real progress can be made. It is important for a Power Supply Authority to specify its objectives clearly, electricity being both

> basic to all sectors of the economy and
> highly capital intensive in its requirements.

33. Electricity Authorities are often monopolistic producers, wholesalers, and distributors; they are usually, therefore, regulated by Government or Local edict. The minimization of total costs to meet a standard of supply is one way of describing their planning objective. Formal objectives are often laid down [7]; these can be broadly paraphrased as:

> to supply each type of consumer with the quality and quantity of supply which he requires and at the same time to meet a financial target defined over a period of years.

Provided the means of meeting the prescribed financial target are taken care of correctly in the sums, then this policy involves charging the consumers the long-run costs which the Supply Authorities incur on behalf of the consumers [8].

34. In some cases, it may be difficult to define in a precise way some of the national objectives, e.g. preservation of amenity. Somewhere in the planning procedure this type of constraint must nevertheless be properly considered, costed (if possible), and provided for.

Planning process

35. Planning may be defined as formulating, evaluating, and choosing between the various courses of action being considered in the light of the planning objectives. This process takes place within a framework of the following major considerations:

(i) Nowhere in the world is there any firm sign that we are approaching saturation in the growth of electricity demand; the latter is still tending to grow at a relatively high and continuous rate.

(ii) Generating plant is relatively expensive and the power supply industries are, therefore, highly capital intensive.

(iii) Although some progress has been made to store energy, storage schemes connected with electricity production are usually indirect and expensive. The bulk of the demand for electricity at any instant must thus still be met from concurrent generation.

(iv) It takes a long time to build generating stations and transmission lines. (In England and Wales it takes about five years for the former and four to five years for the latter from executive decision to commissioning.) The planning must thus be done with 'decision points' four to six years in advance.

36. The planning process may require the exploration of a considerable number of courses of action; the implications of each course must be examined and costed. As the system being examined is that postulated for a future date, simulation techniques must frequently be resorted to as a means of evaluation of consequences. When dealing with a large interconnected power system these explorations are often carried out at suitable intervals to formulate two types of plan, viz:

(a) a long-term plan, looking about fifteen to twenty years ahead and revised infrequently – say every five years; and

(b) an annual development plan, the latter being an annual review in the medium-term future of five to seven years ahead. This latter plan is usually the one used for executive decisions.

37. In a smaller power system this procedure is too cumbersome to be warranted; the problem is then more one of judicious timing of plant and system reinforcement. Much judgement is needed in this case as there are very few precedents to be relied upon.

Simulation and computation

38. Modern facilities, especially the digital computer, enable many more alternative courses of action to be studied than in the

past [9]. As long as a careful check is kept on the usefulness of the studies these can be extremely beneficial to the planning procedure. Moreover, the computed information can be processed and then presented in a more digestible form to the planner, courses of action can be eliminated automatically by criteria built into the digital program by the planner from the start and optimization processes are facilitated.

39. A spectrum of 'models' is needed stretching from those formulated for handling demand type data, through those required for simulating future system operation, to a hybrid type of model for doing project economic worth calculations. These models are now usually mathematical (rather than in any way physical) and may exist on paper for hand calculation or within the store of a digital computer. They must be properly organized and be only as complex as the standard of data available and the problem being solved require.

40. The most important models at present used in a large thermal system such as that in England and Wales are those connected with calculating the broad composition of new generating plant programmes, i.e. the broad proportions of the different types of new generating stations ('plant mix'), and future fuel requirements. Any further production of models must give special attention to the compatibility of data between models and the ability to perform sensitivity analyses and input and output studies.

Loading simulation

41. A power system like that in England and Wales is composed of many generating stations linked by a transmission grid system; the latter also provides the means of taking power to the distributors and thus to the consumers. Not all of the generating stations will be required to run at all times since the pattern of demand for electricity varies continuously. The cheapest way of satisfying the demand is always to run the stations with the lowest operating (or running) cost first. One of the simpler models thus simulates this procedure [10] by arranging generator units in ascending order of operating cost (called the 'merit-order') and loading these successively according to the changing pattern of demand with time.

190

42. In this procedure individual generating units may be 'lumped' together to form a composite unit; similarly demands for electricity may be formed into composite items either by demand–duration histograms or average demands for typical seasonal days and for particular hours of the day [11]. Due attention must be paid to the expected non-availability of generating plant due to either outage or planned overhaul. This can be forecast statistically from past experience for existing plant. Forecasts for future plant need judgement exercised on the basis of past statistics of the performance and reliability of the most recent plant commissioned which is of similar design. It may take as many as six years for a new type of plant to settle down and up to four years for any new plant item to settle down [12].

43. Transmission losses and network limitations may need to be taken into account. The former can be allowed for in the merit-order of generating plant units by dividing the total demand for electricity into geographical areas and applying 'loss' factors to the different generators depending on their location with respect to the location of the demand areas. The merit-order is then made out according to the cost of delivered (instead of source) power. The cost of possible future network limitations can be allowed for by 'operating allowances' based on past experience.

44. The concept of 'spinning reserve' for emergency usage in the event of losing the largest generating unit can also be incorporated into the model by restricting the output of a number of generators to a fixed percentage of their capacity and by stipulating the sum of unused capacities as the spinning reserve which is required to be immediately available.

45. While these and other added refinements can be incorporated into the model it is possible and often adequate to use the model in its simplest form without them.

Coal transportation

46. In England and Wales, as in many other countries, another important aspect in determining the operating cost of a power system still largely dependent on coal is the optimum allocation of this fuel between the numerous collieries to the generating station. This has certainly been of major importance in planning in the past; the factor which is now beginning to make the

difference is the advent of thermal stations burning other fuels and especially nuclear fuels.

47. The coal transportation problem itself can be solved using the criterion of minimum total cost by standard linear programming methods [13]. It is possible, however, to combine loading simulation with the coal transportation problem and to attempt to optimize the combination. This combination of models can be achieved either by extending the scope of the linear programming technique or by sequential sub-optimizing of first one model and then the other model to a general combined optimum.

Output

48. The output from the use of loading simulation models can be very large in volume. It does, however, contain much information of vital importance to system planning and economics. In fact, this information (together with the demand estimates and risk standards described in the previous article) constitute basic data essential to all system economics work (perhaps the only other basic category not yet mentioned is the capital costs of projects). Included in this catalogue of vital information are power station incremental and decremental generating costs, station load factors, station fuel requirements, station operating costs, system thermal efficiency, total operating costs, total system fuel requirements, and the incremental influence on each of these of incrementally changing the plant composition or pattern of demand for electricity.

Plant mix

49. The term 'plant mix' may be used to describe the proportions of the different types of generating plant on the power system at any point in time. These are usually classified by fuel, i.e. nuclear, oil, coal, gas turbine, or hydro. It is important to determine at least guide-lines on the optimum plant mix for the next ten to twenty years ahead in order to be able to make more exactly the crucial decisions for the next five to seven years ahead, upon which the planning of future generating projects will be based.

50. Guide-lines on plant mix may best be looked upon as targets to be aimed at. Different mixes will be obtained for different

optimization criteria (the most common criterion is minimum total system costs) and for different external constraints applied. The determination of mixes for the different constraints enables the overall cost penalty of applying these constraints to be determined. In this matter it is important to have a broad picture of how the system would be developed in the 'free' state, i.e. in the absence of all such constraints.

Global method

51. General determination of the plant mix requirements over a longish period of years is usually done by methods which relate to the power system as a whole, i.e. global methods. One approach is to compare the total (capital plus operating) system costs of alternative mixes of new plant added to the existing plant on the system to give a total mix. The loading simulation models described before can be used to determine the changes in total operating costs due to installing the new plant in any year. When these are added algebraically to the charges on capital for the new plant the total system cost can be determined. A 'trial and error' method can then determine approximately that plant composition which gives the minimum total system costs over a period of years. Since existing generating stations' original capital costs are non-optional and are a common factor to all plant mixes, they need not be included in the above calculations. This procedure gives sufficient general guidance on plant mix for a longish period ahead for many problems.

52. The most difficult assumptions to be made in this type of global method are those concerning future load growth (and hence the rate of plant installation) and future fuel costs per kWh of existing and future generating plant. The best estimate of these must be made in order to make evaluation possible at all. The method should not be abandoned because of the difficulties encountered in making these assumptions; the sensitivity of the answers to changes in these basic assumptions can be evaluated. Furthermore, the modern discounted cash flow techniques (see next paragraph) give most weight to the figures for the early years of a generating plant's life and less and less weight to the later years, when the difficulties of making assumptions are at their worst.

193

53. Discounted cash flow techniques [14] are normally used to relate cash flows occurring at different periods in time to a 'present value'. The relevant cost minimization, in other words, is the minimization of the present value of costs over the period of years taken.

54. The determination of the present value of costs for a large number of postulated developments in plant composition can, however, be a formidable task under any global technique. Also, in any global study, there are dangers in dealing with differences between very large numbers. Fortunately, some degree of simplification is usually possible as is some mechanization [15] (to replace the trial and error) in the optimization process. It is necessary, when considering a limited number of specified generating projects (e.g. for inclusion in a plant extension programme) to develop a simpler approach and one which does not basically depend on the single difference between two very large numbers.

Incremental methods

55. For the given total system energy requirements in any year, the change in total system operating costs resulting from the insertion of an increment of new generating plant capacity can be evaluated, using data from the global study of annual operating conditions and costs. This change, which may be referred to as the 'operating cost saving'[2] can be plotted against the particular operating cost of a particular increment of new plant capacity. The resultant graph allows the operating cost saving per unit increment of any new generating plant capacity to be read off at a glance once its operating cost is known.

56. A useful measure of the economic worth of a specified increment of new generating plant capacity may be obtained by subtracting the present value of the operating cost savings made by that increment of plant over its life from the plant's capital cost. This gives a nett effective cost of that plant.

2. Except in the case of peaking plant, e.g. gas turbine plant of the aircraft-type, increments of new generating plant capacity, owing to technological advance, increase the overall system efficiency and thereby produce a saving in the total system operating cost for given total system energy requirements.

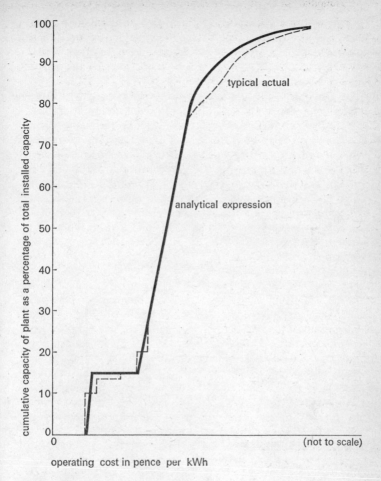

Figure 5(*a*) Generating plant capacity and operating cost

57. The mechanism for finding the incremental operating cost savings can be quite complex using the loading simulation techniques described above. For many purposes, however, this degree of complexity is not warranted; the approach can be simple and analytical [16]. Figure 5 illustrates the representation by

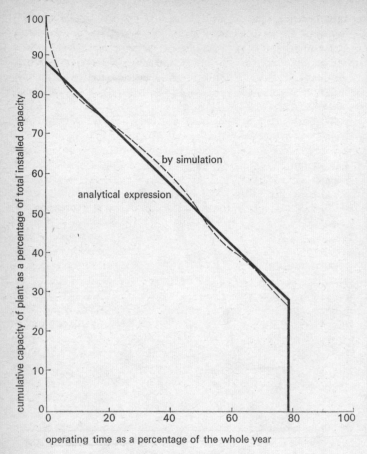

Figure 5(*b*) Generating plant capacity and operating time

analytical expressions both of the generating plant capacity/
operating cost curve and of the generating plant capacity/operat-
ing time curve.

58. The generating plant capacity/operating cost curve shows
for any year the amount of generating plant capacity which has
an operating cost equal to or less than a particular value. The
generating plant capacity/operating time curve shows the amount

of generating plant capacity which operates for a number of hours in any year equal to or more than a particular value. Generating plant is normally operated in a 'merit-order' which utilizes the plant with the cheapest operating cost first, bringing on plant of higher operating cost as the demand for electricity builds up over a daily or annual cycle. The reverse process takes place when the demand is decreasing in the cycle.

59. Once the hourly demands for electricity through the year have been estimated together with the expected availability of generating plant, then the generating plant capacity/operating time curve can be derived directly from the generating plant capacity/operating cost curve. (In practice it is only necessary to deal in 'typical' hours in 'typical' days and 'typical' seasons of the year.) The problem of writing an analytical expression for these two curves is to find the simplest expression which matches reasonably well.

60. The analytical expressions of figure 5 can be integrated by normal mathematics to give the operating cost savings per unit increment of generating plant capacity as a function of the position of the latter in the merit-order. Figure 6 shows results obtained in this way, comparing these with those obtained from the more complex loading simulation approach. Sensitivity analysis of basic system parameters can be done quickly using this simple analytical method by the normal process of differentiation, an advantage when several ranges of sensitivities are to be examined in a study.

Optimization of plant mix

61. Once a rough determination of the best development of plant mix has been made, further trimming can be achieved by calculating the nett effective costs (paragraph 56) of increments of various types of generating plant as measured from within the rough mix. One can then generalize by saying types of plant which have a low nett effective cost are basically 'beneficial' to the mix and should have their share in the mix increased, while those types of plant which give a high nett effective cost are 'detrimental' to the mix and should have their share decreased. These alterations in the mix will throw up different system operating savings (which can be estimated by either the loading simulation

197

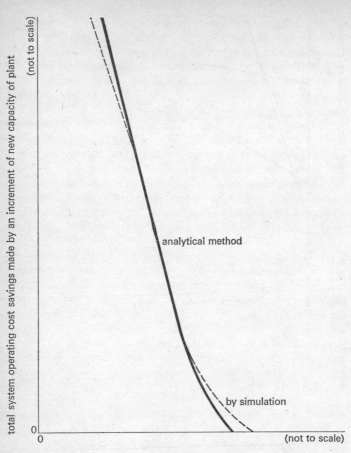

Figure 6 Total system operating savings made by an increment of new plant capacity

method or the simpler analytical one) and the process can be repeated by trial and error until little improvement is being made.

62. The optimization process, however, can be more formally mechanized within certain limits. The total cost for any year of installing and operating an increment of generating plant capacity

198

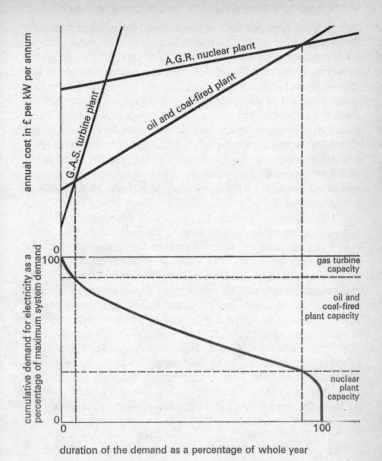

Figure 7 Determination of plant mix

is the sum of its annual capital charges and the product of its operating cost and its operating time, the latter being determined by its position in the merit-order. The cost of each plant item can be represented by a straight line where the total annual cost for the increment of generation capacity $Y = gt + c$, where c is the annual capital charges of the increment of capacity, g is

199

its operating cost per unit of time, and t its operating time in merit-order.

63. A typical construction is shown for a single year in figure 7 with lines illustrating the above equation for increments of gas turbine plant, conventional plant, and nuclear plant. Proceeding in the direction of increasing duration of operation, gas turbine plant is seen to give the lowest total cost until its cost line intersects that of conventional plant; thereafter the latter provides the lowest total costs until the nuclear line is encountered. This gives a rough measure of plant mix for, by referring the intersection points to the demand/duration curve in figure 7, the approximate optimum capacities of the increments of the new plant types can be determined.

64. This simple approach, however, only fits a static system. A dynamic approach is needed. In this, the capacity of plant items in any one year can be regarded as fixed for succeeding years. In each succeeding year this constraint will have some cost penalty to attribute to it, depending upon what is the real optimum plant mix for that year. For each plant item the present value of these constraint costs can be accumulated and the estimated capital costs of the various types of plant can be 'adjusted' by 'shadow costs' to the amount of these accumulated present values.

65. Successive iterations can be made using these shadow costs until further change achieves little reduction in the present value of total system costs. When the optimum mix of plant needs to be looked at in great detail, e.g. in a long-term system development study, this process can be carried out on a computer.

General considerations

66. In general, the detailed comparative economic worth of individual generating units for a plant extension programme relating to a particular year in a development plan cannot be adequately dealt with by any of the above methods, which are mainly applicable to determining the general development of the mix of generating plant, producing general background data for system planning and economics. Methods of comparing in detail the economic worth of specific proposed generating stations put forward in a plant extension programme for approval to construct are dealt with in Part Three.

Part Three: Economic Worth of Projects

Economic appraisals

67. All electricity supply systems are highly capital intensive. It is thus important to ensure that the type of plant chosen for installation at any time and place is the correct choice, so far as can be ascertained, constituting the minimum total cost solution of providing new plant. As shown in the previous article, Electricity Supply Authorities usually plan on the basis of minimizing the present value of the costs of providing a defined facility to their consumers. The decision on any individual project can only be taken after the broader policy decisions, described in the previous Part, have been taken on how the power system as a whole should develop over the next ten to fifteen (possibly more) years, especially with respect to the mix of the different types of generating plant and the likely technological advance.

68. Both prudent investment in new projects and efficient system operation require a carefully chosen overall policy of planting generating stations and of balancing the fuel-burning mix. The selection and siting of a particular new generating plant is usually a compromise between economic, technical, political, and amenity considerations. The object is to deploy plant of different fuel/capital/running cost characteristics in such a way as to meet the growth of demand in kW. for electricity at minimum total cost to the power system.

Simple comparisons

69. The simplest form of economic appraisal of alternative generating projects is a comparison of their total (capital plus operating) costs expressed in the form of pence per kWh. of electricity sent out to the system, and assuming that they operate at a load factor which is the same for all projects and for all years of operation. This approach is quite adequate for comparing many projects, e.g. when assessing tenders for the same plant item [17]. Table 3 shows the application of this simple method to comparing various nuclear (*Magnox*) and nuclear (*Agr*) generating plants.

70. When making economic comparisons between two projects with differing annual load factors (possibly differing one year

with another) it is usually possible to pick an average annual load factor to use for the simple comparison which does not drastically distort the answer. It is often possible to apply this 'juggling' to three projects with different load factors. The method, however,

Table 3

Estimated Costs of Generation at Nuclear Generating Stations at 75 per cent Load Factor

| Type Station | MAGNOX | | | | AGR | |
	Berkeley	Hinkley Point 'A'	Sizewell 'A'	Wylfa	Dungeness 'B'	Hinkley Point 'B'
Year of commissioning	1962	1965	1966	1969	1970	1972
Station output MW.	276	500	580	1,180	1,200	1,320
Construction cost £/kW.	185	155	106	107	81	71
Generation cost d/kWh.						
Capital charges	0·86	0·73	0·49	0·48	0·37	0·33
Running cost	0·37	0·30	0·21	0·17	0·15	0·15
Total generation cost	1·23	1·03	0·70	0·65	0·52	0·48

breaks down for many situations encountered in the planning of a large interconnected system [18]. A method which is more universal is required; if necessary one which can adequately compare plants designed for very low load factors (e.g. peak load gas turbines) with plants designed for base-load (e.g. nuclear plants).

Whole system costs

71. The load factors of the items of new generating plant being considered for a plant extension programme will vary widely. As shown in Part One, the total capacity in kW. of new generating plant required is determined basically by the growth in maximum system demand. The make-up of this total amount, however,

into plants using different fuels has to be determined broadly from the rough patterns of development described in Part Two, and then fitted more precisely from an economic appraisal which takes the whole system, with its complete cross-section of plant items, into account.

72. Whatever combinations of plant items are chosen to make up the plant extension programme, the system as a whole must meet the actual demand for electricity at any instant in time and Part One showed how the system can be planned to a standard of risk to just fail to do this at full voltage at time of maximum system demand one winter in four (say). The cost effect on the whole system of installing each type of plant must therefore be examined.

73. It may be considered best to carry out this detailed study on the global basis described in Part Two. By this method the total (capital plus operating) system costs, present valued, would be computed over the economic life of the new project using various combinations of projects to make up the plant extension programme. This method, however, suffers from the disadvantages of all global methods (see Part Two); in any case, it is much too complex when dealing with a large number of combinations of named power station projects with designated fuel types and ranges of fuel prices, etc.

74. This type of problem clearly calls for a simple incremental method which, although it still deals with whole-system costs, can have the components in its calculation readily calculated separately and discreetly. The end result of such a method must be the economic worth of an increment (say one kW. of capacity) of any generating project which could be installed to help make up a particular plant extension programme.

Life-time comparisons

75. Before describing a method which has been evolved on the principles described in the last paragraph, it is necessary to deal with the question of the time-span over which the comparisons should be made. The first seven to ten years of the life of any plant are probably of the most crucial importance in such a study. Economic lives are usually, however, chosen longer than this; in the range of twenty to thirty years for thermal plant and

203

major transmission works and about fifty years for hydro plant. Economic lives are often chosen shorter than expected operational lives to allow for the uncertainties of the future (amongst other things).

76. Uncertainties of the future are made less important by discounting the various costs to present value. Ideally, the calculations of costs consequent upon installing a particular generating project should be present valued over an infinite period. This is clearly impractical even if it were desirable. The best compromise would seem to be to do the sums over the economic lives of the projects with some mechanism for dealing with projects with different assumed economic lives.

Standardized system costs

77. The power system is in a state of continuous growth. The growth in maximum system demand is accompanied by a growth in the requirements for electrical energy (in England and Wales the overall load factor of the consumers' load is about 50 per cent).

78. Each increment in the growth of maximum system demand requires an increment of additional generating plant capacity, chosen from several possible projects. Each project will involve an initial capital outlay and annual management, insurance and other fixed costs. Each will have an annual position in the merit-order in any year determined by its fuel cost d/kWh. by virtue of which it will incur annual fuel and other operating costs. The discounted total of these three types of cost over the assumed economic life gives the present value of installing and operating, in merit-order, an increment of each type of project.

79. Part Two described methods of varying complexity for determining the best plant-mix development with time of the various types of generating plant, the load factors of individual plant projects operating within this development and the savings in the total system operating bill (operating savings) made by inserting (for the same energy requirements) a new highly efficient plant on to the system whereby older plant need not generate so many units.

80. The reference or zero point for these operating savings,

however, must be carefully chosen in that, as described in paragraph 77, the system is in a state of continuous growth. If the increment of maximum system demand is met by an increment of aircraft-type gas turbine generators which operate but a few hours a year, then the increment of system energy requirements must be met entirely by production from existing plants. The total additional operating cost of this increased production in a year n is E. This is the datum from which to measure fuel cost savings in a dynamic system.

81. The alternative projects under investigation for meeting the increment in maximum system demand can now be assessed against that datum. Each project in year n, besides incurring fuel and other operating costs (O), will make marginal savings (M) in the operating cost of the remaining plant on the system, such that the net production cost of the latter is $(E - M)$.

82. The present value of the nett cost $(E - M)$ over the assumed economic life of the plant project being considered can then be added to the present value of the capital charges plus fixed costs of installing (C) and the present value of the fuel plus other operating costs of the plant in merit-order (O), i.e. $(C + O)$ to give a whole-system cost or a standardized system cost of the project being considered, i.e. $(C + O) + (E - M)$.

83. Although it is quite feasible to work the above costs out in £ million, it has been found to aid judgement more if they are expressed in £/kW. of plant installed.

84. Table 4 shows, for illustration, a condensed version of such a calculation (as described above) to give a standardized system cost which can be used for making comparisons. The table starts with the basic parameters in lines 1 to 6. Line 7 shows the present value of the capital charges and fixed costs (C); line 8 the present value of fuel plus other operating costs in merit-order (O) and line 9, the sum of the two previous lines, the present value of installing and operating the project in merit-order $(C + O)$. The present value of the adjustment term $(E - M)$ to allow for the effect on the operating cost of the remaining plant on the system is shown in line 10 giving a total cost $(C + O) + (E - M)$ to the system in present value terms of line 11. In order to deal with the question of different economic lives the present values have been annuitized (at a rate of interest equal

205

to that used for present valuing) to give equated annual costs which can be directly compared.[3]

85. The purpose of Table 4 is solely to illustrate the methods and the examples chosen should not be taken as necessarily representative. It should also be noted that the differences in the equated annual costs are strictly applicable to relatively small increments of plant. For example, it would not be economic to install gas turbines (although not shown in Table 4 they could have been) in such large proportions that they were obliged to run at an appreciably higher load factor than about 2 per cent. All incremental comparisons of individual projects are done within the broad background of plant mix settled previously for a development of generating plant types over many years ahead. These incremental comparisons themselves cannot, therefore, be used directly to determine the plant mix, i.e. the optimum capacity of the various types of generating plant in a development over a number of years. The incremental comparisons are most valuable when comparing individual actual projects in the year of decision, i.e. about five or six years ahead.

Plant extension programmes

86. As stated briefly above, it is realized that it is the comparative economics of complete alternative plant extension programmes for a number of years ahead, rather than individual projects, which should be studied. This would treat the year of installation of a particular station as a variable thus posing problems of great complexity, the benefits from whose solution may well be second-order. The choice of new generation projects which it is practicable to proceed with at any one time is limited. When considering plant extension programmes at or near the 'decision' stage, broad economic pointers to assist the formulation of policy and to guide the search for new station sites are of more value than complex optimization techniques.

3. There is no absolutely accurate way of directly comparing the economic worth of projects with different economic lives. Theoretically the cash flows should be discounted to infinity. In practice, however, it has been found sufficiently accurate to take either the total present values and compare them directly or the total present values annuitized over the respective economic lives.

Table 4
Life-Time, Whole-System Cost Comparison of Generating
Projects

1	Type	Fossil Fuel		Nuclear
2	Fuel	Coal	Oil (with tax)	Uranium
3	Fuel cost d/therm	4·1	3·8	1·4
4	Thermal efficiency %	37·0	36·5	39·5
5	Economic life years	30	30	20
6	Capital cost * £/kW.	55	53	93
7	Annual capital charges and fixed costs £/kW. p.a. (C)	5·5	5·3	10·4
8	Annual fuel and other operating costs when operating in merit-order £/kW. p.a. (O)	6·9	7·4	3·3
9	Annual cost of installing and operating plant in merit-order £/kW. p.a. ($C + O$)	12·4	12·7	13·7
10	Effect on operating cost of remaining plant on system £/kW. p.a. ($E - M$)	−1·7	−2·6	−4·6
11	Equated average (or standardized) system cost £/kW. p.a. ($C + O$) + ($E - M$)	10·7	10·1	9·1
12	Average life-time load factor %	46	53	75

* Capital costs, as shown above, include capitalized interest during construction and, in the nuclear case, the net cost of the initial fuel loading

Transmission

87. Any particular selection of generating projects must fit the pattern of transmission network structure which has been developed to meet the expected patterns of demand and location of generating stations. The load factors of individual groups of demand for electricity vary considerably geographically and from one year to the next, and this must be carefully allowed for. The

207

overall pattern of development in England and Wales is for a recti-linear grid-iron pattern of 400-kV. transmission circuits to be constructed by the early 1970s to which can be easily connected either new generating stations or new points for supplying electricity in bulk. Once more, after this global picture has been determined, incremental costing should be used.

88. It is possible to split up the incremental transmission costs allocated to an increment of maximum system demand into four broad categories (expressed as £/kW. of extra maximum system demand):

1. Cost of connecting individual generating stations to the grid.
2. Main transmission cost (400 kV.).
3. Cost of secondary transmission (275 kV. and 132 kV.).
4. Cost of bulk supply points.

Item 1 varies with the generating projects being considered as does, to a lesser extent, item 2. These must therefore be assessed separately for each power station project comparison and added to the standardized system cost described before. Items 3 and 4 can either be ignored in the comparison or (perhaps better) a standard blanket item can be put in for each.

Return on capital

89. So long as the demand for electricity continues to increase, a decision whether to build generating stations at all or not, is not a meaningful one. For this non-optional investment the Supply Authority will normally choose, within internally and externally imposed limits, the project which offers the lowest present value of total system costs, i.e. the lowest present value of future income requirements. A suitable return on capital will be used in choosing the interest rate used for discounting.

90. It is not possible or, indeed, conceptionally meaningful within a large interconnected system to estimate the net revenue derived from individual power stations. What can be calculated is the return on the incremental capital investment when one power station project at higher capital cost is chosen instead of another project at a lower capital cost. The minimum capital costs would be incurred if entirely aircraft-type gas turbine plants were chosen to meet the increase in maximum system demand. If

more than the minimum capital costs are to be expended by choosing coal, oil, or nuclear-fired plant instead of gas turbine plant, then the additional operating savings must give an acceptable return on the extra investment.

Table 5

Yield on Extra Capital Investment

	Coal plant	Oil plant (with tax)	Nuclear plant	Aircraft type gas turbines
1 Capital cost* £/kW.	50	49	93	26†
2 Extra investment compared with aircraft gas turbines £/kW.	24	23	67	—
3 Average annual value of operating savings over economic life £/kW.	1·9	2·6	8·9	0
4 Yield on extra investment %	7	12	13	—

* Capital costs include capitalized interest during construction and, in the nuclear case, the net cost of the initial fuel loading

† Credit has been allowed to these gas turbine units on account of their average ability to make transmission savings

91. Table 5 illustrates the method of assessing profitability or yield. Capital costs per kW. are shown in line 1; the extra investment cost per kW. of plant over that required for aircraft-type gas turbines is shown in line 2. The average annual value of the operating savings over the economic life is shown in line 3. The calculation includes the same type of components as Table 4. The operating savings made by the new plant item (against the datum E) are made up of two components, viz. the marginal savings in the operating cost of the remaining plant on the system (M) less the operating cost in merit-order of the new plant (O). The actual values of Table 4 have not been used in Table 5 as no gas turbines are included in the former table. The actual savings will fall from a much higher value than the average to a much lower value over the life of each type of plant. In line 4 the actual annual operating savings over those of gas turbines (which are zero) are expressed

as a yield on the corresponding extra investment, i.e. the discount rate that will equate the present value of operating savings with the extra investment.

92. The results shown in Table 5 are illustrative only. In order to assess the level of adequate profitability, some acceptable value must be put on the yield.

93. Multiple yields can also be determined, e.g. by shifting the base from gas turbines to coal plant and calculating the yield as the discount rate that equates the present value of the *difference* in operating savings between nuclear and coal plant with the difference in extra investment between nuclear and coal plant. (These multiple yields cannot be deduced directly from Table 5.)

Conclusions

94. The comparative economic worth of a power station project is only one factor in the decision-making process on which power stations should be constructed. Nevertheless, it is an important one and one which needs to be determined with as much precision as can be justified. A method for calculating this worth may be very simple but must be capable of a degree of complexity which can adequately compare all types of generating plant, with widely varying capital and operating (running) costs and with differing economic lives.

95. These comparisons can only be made adequately on an incremental basis against a broad background of development of the various types of generating plant or 'plant mix' previously investigated. There should always be some 'feed-back' process one year with another between the incremental comparisons and the plant mix studies by exploring sensitivities of the final answers to changes in the basic estimates.

96. The plant mix development itself can only be investigated once the basic philosophy of system planning has been settled with respect to planning standards for security of supply. The basic elements in this philosophy normally revolve round the estimates for five to seven years ahead of maximum system demand and the availability of generating plant at the time of that maximum system demand. The study of the plant mix development also requires estimates of future fuel and construction costs to be made.

97. The future maximum system demand itself depends (through costs and tariffs) on the investments made in future generating plant projects and their operating costs, i.e. on the decisions taken on assumed estimates of maximum system demand. This loop, however, is not closed when power system planning is carried out. While in principle it should be, system planners would need very much more (and reliable) information on price elasticities than they have in practice before even attempting to close the loop.

References

1. D. Clark and R. S. Edwards, 'Planning for expansion in electricity supply', *British Electrical Power Convention*, 1962, pp. 3–9.
2. As above, pp. 11–14.
3. T. W. Berrie and I, J. Whitting, 'The exploration of alternative plans for an expanding electrical power system', *First Power Systems Computation Conference*, London, 1963, pp. 4–6.
4. As above, pp. 6–7.
5. F. J. Lane and W. Casson, *The economic aspects of high voltage transmission*, figure 8.
6. As [3], p. 1.
7. Electricity Act 1957, chapter 48, section 2, sub-section 5.
8. P. A. Lingard and G. England, 'Electricity supply industry and economic growth', paper presented to the British Electrical Power Convention, 1964; or P. A. Lingard, 'Economics of the domestic space heating load', paper presented to the Space Heating Symposium at the I.E.E., 1964.
9. T. W. Berrie, 'Further Experience with simulation models in system planning', *Second Power Systems Computation Conference*, 1966, p. 1.
10. P. J. Jonas, 'A computer model to determine economic performance characteristics of interconnected generating stations', *British Computer Conference*, Brighton, 1966, p. 1.
11. As [9], p. 2.
12. 'Report of equipment availability for the six year period 1960–65', Edison Electric Institute, October 1966.
13. As [9], p. 3.
14. 'Investment appraisal', National Economic Development Council Report, 1967.
15. As [9], p. 5.
16. As [9], p. 6.
17. 'An appraisal of the technical and economic aspects of Dungeness "B" nuclear power station', *C.E.G.B.*, July 1965, Table 1.
18. Mackenzie Report: one theme of the report.

6 J. J. Warford

Water Supply

J. J. Warford, 'Water requirements: The investment decision in the water supply industry' (with an appendix by W. Peters), *Manchester School*, vol. 34 (1966), pp. 87–112. Amended by the author.

The Projection of Water 'Requirements'

This paper is concerned with the procedures used by the water supply industry for estimating future water 'requirements' or 'demands', and the acceptability of the resulting estimates as a basis for investment decisions. The particular problems of water supply in North-West England, and evidence of the approach of water engineers to these problems will be used for purposes of illustration.

The attitude of the water supply industry is typified by the Jellicoe Conference,[1] which was established to investigate the problems of water 'shortages' in the North-West. A technical committee of this Conference, consisting solely of water engineers, stated that 'Careful consideration has been given to the demands for water that can be expected in the immediate and more distant future. Each water undertaking has been asked to make estimates of requirements and these have been examined to make sure that they have been based on acceptable principles.' It appears that 'acceptable principles' include consideration of expected population changes, improved housing and domestic appliances, and expected industrial development; to this is added an allowance (in this case 5 per cent) to cover abnormal demands in dry years, etc.

The committee followed the conventional procedure in the water supply industry, in which water 'requirements' are calculated statistically by extrapolation of past trends, with adjustments on the basis of the above considerations. This method involves implicit assumptions about the rate of change of all

1. Conference on Water Resources in the North-West (Ministry of Housing and Local Government), S.O. Code No. 75-113, 1963.

variables affecting the level of water consumption; we are here concerned with the fact that one of these variables, price, is ignored in the calculation. The projection in fact approximates to a forecast of the expected consumption of domestic and trade supplies, made on the assumption that the price of water relative to the prices of other goods and services will follow the same trend as in the past. Since in the past there has been little change in the relative price of water, this is equivalent to assuming that present relative prices will continue to rule. If the projection indicates that by a certain date in the future there will be an excess of demand over the supply that can be furnished by existing resources, then the sole concern of the industry is to make good this deficiency.

The projection of 'requirements' on this basis is obviously unsatisfactory as a general rule to be followed in investment decisions,[2] since changes in the relative costs and prices of water supplies may well have an effect on the quantity of water demanded. This aspect of the method has in fact been effectively dealt with by Ciriacy–Wantrup[3] in the case of water supply. It might also be noted here that similar arguments have been levelled against projections of future demand for manpower, such as have appeared in N.E.D.C. and other official reports.[4]

A simple diagram may help to clarify this point. In figure 1, assume that the initial equilibrium position is one in which demand is represented by D_1, price is P_1, and the quantity consumed is OA m.g.d. (million gallons per day). Assume further that the water undertaking concerned follows an average cost pricing policy – an assumption that, in the case of metered supplies, is

2. Extrapolation of past trends is also used to aid the investment decision in the electricity and gas industries, but direct competition between them (as well as with oil and directly consumed coal) means that relative prices must of necessity be of primary importance in any such calculation. In fact, estimates of future consumption of gas and electricity are in several ways subject to more sophisticated techniques than in the case of water. Despite this however recent history has shown that the accuracy of the gas and electricity industries' estimates still leaves much to be desired.

3. S. V. Ciriacy-Wantrup, 'Projections of water requirements', *Journal of Farm Economics*, May 1961.

4. See for example, Alan Peacock, 'Economic growth and the demand for qualified manpower', *District Bank Review*, June 1963.

broadly justified, given British legal and administrative requirements. The water undertaking now calculates, on the evidence of past trends, that the consumption of water x years hence will be OC m.g.d. This implies a shift in the demand curve, here represented by D_2, which reflects an increase in income, changes in the prices of other goods, and a time variable, which includes changes in tastes. To meet these 'requirements', a project capable

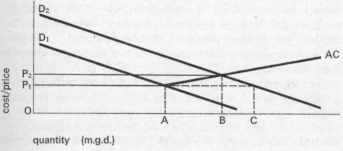

Figure 1

of yielding AC m.g.d. is built. However, this project is more costly per unit of water produced than existing investments, so the price of water will rise. In figure 1 price rises to P_2, and the quantity consumed to OB m.g.d. which is less than the 'requirements' figure by an amount equal to BC m.g.d.[5] This simplified example therefore serves to illustrate the danger of making long-range assessments of future water consumption without taking into account data on costs, and the risk of over-investment thereby entailed.

Although this criticism is valid for all such projections, we will now examine its relevance in a purely British context, in which the most important fact is the distinction to be drawn between metered and unmetered consumption. It is a peculiar feature of the British water supply industry that domestic consumption, which accounts for about 60 per cent of the water supplied by statutory water undertakings, is unmetered.[6] Domestic users

5. In fact, consumption may be even less than OB, since if capacity is under-utilized average costs and therefore price will be somewhat higher than shown above.

6. Malvern U.D.C. water undertaking is an exception to this rule.

merely pay a water rate, based on the net annual value of the premises occupied; thus the price at the margin is zero. Industrial and trade users on the other hand are obliged to pay for water on a quantity basis; these supplies are therefore metered.

To give some idea of the rate of growth in consumption that has been observed in the past, unmetered consumption of water provided by statutory water undertakers in the United Kingdom has increased from about 935 m.g.d. in 1900 to 1,850 m.g.d. in 1964. Total unmetered consumption has thus doubled, while consumption per head has risen from 24·6 to 34·2 gallons per day. Metered consumption has roughly trebled during the period, from 375 to 1,110 m.g.d. These figures must be treated with reserve however; first, the figures for unmetered consumption refer to the quantity of water going into supply less that consumed by metered users; apart therefore from certain non-domestic uses that are not metered (such as water used for municipal purposes), this figure will also include any water that is wasted or leaks from mains, so to identify unmetered with domestic consumption is not strictly accurate. Leakage is particularly important; 10 per cent leakage (of the average daily flow) is considered to represent good water engineering practice.[7] Increased emphasis on waste prevention by water undertakers, particularly since the war, suggests that the above figures understate the rise in actual domestic use. Similarly, the identification of trade and industrial consumption with metered consumption is misleading since (by definition) the figures for metered consumption do not include private supplies. Little accurate information at present exists on the quantity of water privately abstracted from rivers or underground by industrial or agricultural users, although this position should be rectified by the new River Authorities (set up under the 1963 Water Resources Act) who have now to grant licenses for all such abstractions. However, the existing evidence suggests that private supplies are quantitatively of great significance.[8]

7. See A. C. Twort, *A textbook of water supply*, Edward Arnold Ltd, London, 1963.
8. Some idea of the magnitudes involved can be gained from the Central Advisory Water Committee's Sub-Committee on the Growing Demand for Water, First Report (S.O. Code No. 75–65, H.M.S.O., 1959), which, on the

Bearing these reservations in mind, it is still convenient to accept the distinction between metered and unmetered consumption, and to consider water 'requirements' projections for these two components of demand separately.

Metered consumption

The situation depicted in figure 1 could be applicable to metered consumption since this water is paid for on a quantity basis. However, conventional 'requirements' calculations may yield a satisfactory result (assuming that the effects of other variables on future water consumption are correctly forecast) if either or both of the following conditions hold:

(*a*) Constant costs
(*b*) Perfectly inelastic demand

(a) *Constant costs.* Figure 1 shows a situation in which average costs, and therefore price, are rising. However, if long run average costs are constant, our basic criticism is not valid, and forecasts based on the 'requirements' principle will be an approximation to the actual outcome. But how valid is the assumption of constant costs likely to be for future water supplies? Water engineers can, and do, point to the recent history of water charges, which have shown little tendency to change in real terms, at least since the war. However, what is true of the past is not necessarily true also of the future; there are several reasons why we might conceivably expect the price of water to increase.

In the first place, as water consumption increases, undertakings might find it necessary to exploit sources that are less and less accessible (the extent to which this is so being partly determined by the success of 'amenity' organizations in opposing the development of convenient sources of supply on aesthetic and emotional grounds). Large areas of the United Kingdom are now

---

basis of a survey carried out by the Federation of British Industries covering six major water-consuming industries (brewing, chemicals, iron and steel, leather, paper-making, and textiles) estimated that these industries plus the nationalized industries (excluding cooling water used by the latter) consumed 1,688 m.g.d. in 1955 from private sources, while the *total* metered consumption from public suppliers was in that year only 730 m.g.d. (figures refer to England and Wales).

on the verge of exhausting the safe yield[9] of their existing resources, Manchester being but one example – albeit a spectacular one – of a fairly common situation. Manchester's choice may lie, in the long run, between going farther afield for water supplies (for example to Scotland), carrying out highly expensive constructions nearer home (such as the Morecambe Bay Barrage), or resorting to more extensive treatment of polluted water. Desalination, much in the news recently, is a further alternative; given the present state of technical knowledge there is not in the foreseeable future much possibility of this competing on the basis of costs with existing sources of supply; it may not be long, however, before it is used to augment existing supplies.[10]

(b) *Inelastic demand.* It is generally recognized by the industry that the average costs of water will rise[11] as new supplies are made available. Thus the use of the 'requirements' principle contains the implication that the demand for water is totally inelastic, and this would probably be the answer of most water engineers asked to rationalize their approach. Even if costs do rise in the long term, then as long as the increased demand for water is perfectly inelastic, the 'requirements' prediction will be accurate.

The observed (short-run) reactions to price changes under present cost conditions would appear to justify the assumption that the demand for water by metered users is highly inelastic.[12] However, the assumption that this is so over wide price ranges has not been statistically tested; there are in fact reasons for believing that in the event of substantial increases in price, substitutes for (piped) water may be employed. Firms may substitute private supplies of fresh river water, or brackish or saline water for that provided by statutory water undertakers: in addition, capital equipment may be substituted for water, for example

9. The 'safe yield' of a reservoir is that rate of abstraction which in the long run will not alter the quantity of water held in that reservoir.

10. The States of Guernsey Water Board use a desalination plant to augment existing supplies in the summer months.

11. Even if a technological breakthrough meant that average costs actually fell, a similar criticism would of course apply. In this case, 'requirements' would mean an underestimation of future consumption.

12. This view is founded on the evidence supplied by numerous water engineers, based on their weekly or quarterly water consumption records.

if recirculation equipment is installed, or if air cooling is substituted for water cooling. The possibility of substitution of other inputs for water makes it unlikely that the demand for water for industrial use will invariably be inelastic; thus as far as metered supplies are concerned, at least, the 'requirements' principle is likely to lead to over-investment.

Unmetered consumption

Another, even more important, aspect of the water 'requirements' attitude is to be found in the case of unmetered consumption. After having paid the water rate, the domestic consumer is free to consume as much water as he likes without further charge. Given this system, it is technically possible to calculate future water consumption levels in the conventional way, since the unit price of water will not change irrespective of the cost of the additional supplies.[13] However, it is this very fact that should be causing concern to those responsible for decision making in the industry. The present method of charging is an open invitation to wasteful use or at best low-value use of water, since as the price at the margin is zero, the consumer will tend to use water till the value to him of the marginal unit consumed is also zero. The system owes its nature to the original conception of the water supply industry as a social service. As such it has been a tremendous success, particularly in helping to reduce the incidence of water-borne diseases such as typhoid, but whether it should continue to be looked at in this light is open to question.

The Investment Decision

As observed earlier, the only criterion used for investment in additional supplies is that expected future demand should exceed present potential supply (i.e. the quantity of water provided in a given period by existing sources, plus those works already under construction), at present prices. Costs are introduced only to assist in the decision whether to build scheme A or scheme B – or in other words, to find the cheapest method of producing x m.g.d. irrespective of the value of that increment.

13. Even here, however, higher costs could conceivably raise the domestic water rate sufficiently to exert an 'income effect'.

This procedure stems partly from the view that water is some-how special, and that any measures to remedy 'shortages' are justified. However, the attitude that water is a commodity pos-sessing a 'unique importance' has been challenged.[14] It is true that we must have a certain amount of water to live, but we also need food, shelter, and clothing. There is indeed no reason, in principle, why water should be treated any differently from these goods, yet the very possibility that even the cheapest source of water may be too expensive relative to the benefits it provides, is an idea that is alien to the industry. Thus the financial adviser to Manchester Corporation Waterworks stated at the public inquiry into Manchester's Windermere and Ullswater schemes that rela-tive to its importance, water was 'cheap at any price'. However, the unique importance of water used for washing cars or spraying lawns is not readily apparent; the average value of water con-sumed by domestic users may be high, but this is not incom-patible with the possibility that the marginal value may be negligible, and, by definition, provision of new water supplies is relevant (for existing consumers at least), not to average but to marginal values.

Ideally, therefore, a decision to invest in capacity should in-volve an explicit assessment of the value of the additional water made available: we now turn to a discussion of the criteria that should be employed to assist in the decision. We will first con-sider the case in which universal metering exists, i.e. where it is possible to influence consumption by changes in price.

Let us suppose that, as long as capacity is under-utilized, a policy of equating price to marginal running costs is followed. (We assume throughout that marginal costs are defined to take account of technological externalities, and represent true social opportunity costs.) If such a policy were to be introduced in Britain, prices would in most cases be considerably lower than (metered) prices ruling at present. However, as capacity is approached, this may no longer be true, since, as the marginal cost curve becomes vertical, price should be raised to establish a new equilibrium of supply and demand.

14. See for example, J. Hirshleifer, J. C. de Haven, and J. W. Milliman; *Water supply, economics, technology and policy*, University of Chicago Press, Chicago, 1960.

Assuming that demand continues to grow over time, it will now pay to continue to invest in capacity as long as the marginal benefits (represented by the increase in the size of the area under the demand curve), discounted at the social rate of discount exceed the marginal costs associated with the investment, similarly discounted, taking into account any external economies and diseconomies.

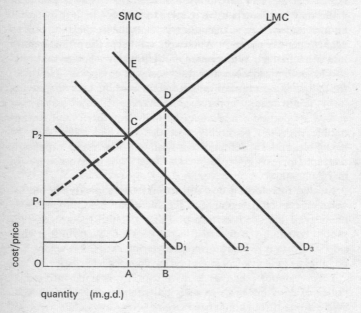

Figure 2

Let us look at this in terms of figure 2. This shows a situation in which demand is increasing (for ease of exposition, by discrete jumps) over time and in which price is set to equal short run marginal costs (*SMC*). The *SMC* schedule is seen to become vertical at level of output *OA*, signifying that existing capacity is being fully utilized. A further schedule, *LMC* is also shown. This represents long run marginal (capacity plus operating) costs, where marginal capacity costs are expressed as a flow at the social rate of discount. The *LMC* schedule is higher than the *SMC* schedule up to *OA* since by definition the latter, referring to a situation in which capacity costs bear no opportunity cost, refers solely to operating costs. The fact that long run marginal costs are rising[15] may therefore be due to the influence of rising capacity or operating costs or both.

If demand is initially represented by curve D_1, existing supply should be rationed among consumers by a price set at P_1. As demand increases, it now pays to raise price along the vertical *SMC* schedule until price equals *LMC*, or in other words until the price consumers are willing to pay for a marginal unit of output equals the sum of the capacity and operating costs incurred in producing that marginal unit. Once this point has been reached (demand curve D_2, price P_2), any further increase in demand will justify investment in capacity. In fact, if demand now shifts to D_3, the appropriate increase in capacity will be that sufficient to provide an additional *AB* m.g.d. Figure 2 clearly shows that any increase in demand over D_2 will justify investment in capacity; in this case the value of the additional output provided by the increment in capacity = *ABDE*, while the cost = *ABDC*. The net benefit is therefore represented by triangle *CDE*.

Assuming a zero gestation period for investment, once capacity has been installed the appropriate price to charge will continue to be that which equals *SMC*. But since this new capacity will be at once fully utilized (i.e. the new *SMC* schedule,[16] SMC_2 is vertical) price should remain at P_3 as shown in figure 3. An optimal situation therefore requires that capacity be used to the full, and that price should equal both short and long run marginal cost.

The theoretical analysis is not substantially affected by the probability that additional capacity can only be supplied in large, indivisible units, in which case the *LMC* schedule may rise in steps from one capacity level of output to another, rather than as a smooth curve. Should the extra capacity supply a further x

15. Although a rising *LMC* schedule is shown, the analysis is equally applicable to a situation in which *LMC* is falling.
16. In this example, SMC_2 is shown to be higher than SMC_1; this is not a necessary condition, even if *LMC* is rising, since higher capacity costs may offset the lower operating costs associated with a new investment.

m.g.d., price should still be raised along *SMC* until the price consumers are willing to pay for the xth unit equals the *LMC* of producing it. The only difference is that as soon as the new capacity has been installed, price should fall, after which it will again require upward adjustment until further investment in

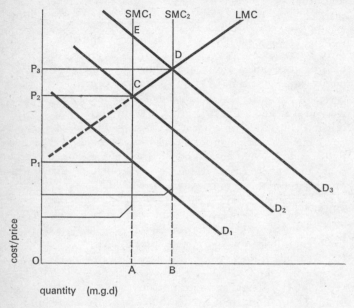

Figure 3

capacity is justified, whereas given infinitely divisible units, there is only one price consistent with long and short run equilibrium for each level of output. A similar situation is created even with divisible factors if, after additional capacity has been installed, demand should fall from D_3 to a lower level. In this case, price should fall to the level at which the new demand curve intersects SMC_2. Subsequent increases in demand will require that price should be raised, as before, until equality of price and *LMC* is again achieved.

J. J. Warford

The 'Metering Decision'

Clearly, the foregoing model represents an ideal solution. In practice, however, strict adherence to it might involve us in all sorts of difficulties, the nature of which has been discussed time and again in the literature. General problems associated with marginal cost pricing are not dealt with here, but attention should be drawn to one particular difficulty involved in applying the above solution to water supply. This is that lumpiness of investment and very low marginal running costs are characteristic of the industry; the consequence of the above pricing rule may therefore be excessive or frequent fluctuations in price, which alone may be considered sufficient to justify its rejection. Nevertheless, the analysis serves to illustrate the fact that neither investment decisions, nor, therefore, projections of future consumption should be dissociated from considerations of price, this conclusion being applicable whatever pricing policy is considered appropriate in the short run.

On the other hand, the analysis is only relevant where the physical means of implementing a pricing system exist, i.e. where all supplies are metered. In Britain, therefore, there would be particular difficulties in the application of the suggested criteria. First of all, as indicated, the value of the benefits provided by a scheme must be known if any logical choice is to be made whether to invest or not. This necessitates a knowledge of the amount consumers would be willing to pay for increments of water; ideally a knowledge of the benefits represented by the increase in the area under the demand curve made possible by the increment would be required. However, such statistical calculations abound with difficulties in the absence of a market for such a large proportion (i.e. the unmetered component) of the commodity concerned.[17] A prolonged large-scale metering

17. Little of this nature has been attempted even in those countries that do meter domestic supplies. However, a study undertaken by M. Gottlieb, 'Urban domestic demand for water: a Kansas case study', *Land Economics*, May 1963), in which a multiple regression of *per capita* domestic water consumption on price and income levels was carried out suggests that the price elasticity of demand for water use (for the United States as a whole) is about 0·4 for large cities and 0·65 for smaller communities, the difference

experiment,[18] covering undertakings with a wide range of costs, and therefore prices, could be of immense worth in terms of improving our knowledge of domestic consumers' evaluation of domestic water supplies.

Secondly, if on the evidence of such an experiment, it were determined that the value of increments of water made available did not justify the construction of a scheme to meet 'requirements', it would be necessary to introduce metering of domestic supplies; otherwise clumsy methods such as reducing pressure, appeals to industry to recirculate, to domestic users to economize, and the cutting off of supplies during certain hours, would have to be employed. (The much-publicized provision for the imposition of fines on New York restaurant proprietors who serve a customer with a glass of water without being requested to do so, is but an extreme example of this sort of thing.) Thus the value of the water supplied by a project must be shown to exceed the costs of the project minus the costs of introducing domestic metering. In other words, although the value of the water may be less than the cost of producing it, the scheme may still be economically justified if the cost of metering that would otherwise be required is sufficient to offset the difference.

At present, due to legal and administrative requirements that insist on an approximation to average cost pricing in the industry, water undertakers are unable to exert adequate control even over metered consumption; hence the resort to the above methods. It need hardly be mentioned that efficiency is more likely to be obtained by conscious use of the price mechanism than by appeals to industry's sense of social responsibility. On the other hand, it may be argued that these 'administrative' methods offer a feasible alternative to metering or investment in additional sources of supply; however, the cutting off of supplies and the reduction of pressure (which in some cases amount to the same thing) would mean a severe disruption of productive processes as well as constituting a threat to public hygiene and health. These

being explained by the notion that the most price-responsive uses (particularly lawn sprinkling) are of greater significance in smaller than in larger cities.

18. Certain individual undertakings have carried out their own experiments (see below, p. 229).

effects could in principle be quantified, but there is a *prima facie* case for supposing that the costs entailed would outweigh those of, for example, the installation of domestic meters.

Our attitude towards domestic water 'requirements' is therefore inescapably bound up with the question of domestic metering. The water supply industry presents a fairly united front on this matter, and is, in general, against it. Briefly, the main argument against it is that the costs of metering – the purchase and installation of meters, and subsequent reading, billing and maintenance costs – are too high relative to the cost of the water presently supplied. The Sub-Committee on Water Charges,[19] which examined this question, found that the capital and running costs of metering, at £2 per household per annum, would be 'more than many householders pay at the present time for their water supply'.[20] In itself, however, this argument is not conclusive; more important than the cost of existing supplies is the likely cost of future supplies. It must be re-emphasized that the relevant costs to be considered are marginal and that the cost of metering and the price to be set should be examined with this in mind.

If demand continues to grow over time, the most valuable result of introducing metering would be, since the price at the margin

19. Central Advisory Water Committee, 'Report of the Sub-Committee on Water Charges', S.O. Code No. 75–110 H.M.S.O., 1963.

20. Information from Malvern indicates that the initial cost of a domestic meter plus installation is £8 10s.; the life of the meter is conservatively estimated at 21 years and it requires changing and servicing every seven years at a cost of £3 10s. a time. Annual costs of extra billing and (twice yearly) meter reading approximate 3s. 10d. per household. Thus over the life of the meter, the present worth of the stream of costs associated with the introduction of domestic metering will only be about £14 per household, if discounted at 7 per cent. (This rate of discount is used since it is the sort of interest rate water undertakings must pay; it is in no way intended to represent a social rate.) The cost of installing meters in Malvern is probably somewhat lower than the cost of doing so in an area in which domestic metering is being introduced for the first time, since in Malvern meters only have to be installed in new houses or for replacement purposes, and suitable sites are thus more likely to be easily accessible; the figures do however suggest that the Sub-Committee's estimate of the annual cost attributable to domestic metering may be rather high. For a discussion of the lessons to be learned from Malvern's experience, see P. A. Bird and C. I. Jackson, 'Water meters, why not?', *New Society*, 17 June 1965.

would now be positive, to encourage economy in water use. This would either defer the need for further investment, or, should the increase in demand eventually tail off, obviate the necessity for some investment altogether. This can be shown by figure 4, in which the growth of consumption in the absence of domestic metering is represented by curve C_1, while C_2 shows the consumption growth path if metering already exists and an optimal pricing policy is being pursued. The difference between the two

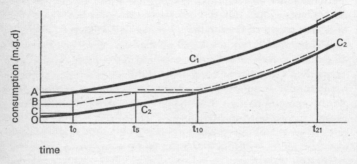

Figure 4

curves will depend upon the relative importance of domestic and industrial consumption in the area concerned as well as the (metered) price actually charged. In fact, if we retain the assumptions of infinite divisibility and zero gestation period for investment, the optimum price would be, as indicated in the previous section, equal to short and long run marginal cost.

We now examine the effect of introducing domestic metering at time t_0, at which time it is assumed that existing capacity can supply no more than OA m.g.d. Price is raised from zero to a level equal to SMC, and consumption initially falls from OA to OB. (Not to OC, it will be observed, since, if metering already existed, price should equal SMC and LMC, but if metering is newly installed and consumption falls, there will temporarily be excess capacity. The only opportunity costs now involved are running costs; price equals SMC, but this is less than LMC. Price will thus be lower, and consumption greater, than if metering had always been in operation.)

226

J. J. Warford

The new consumption path is represented in figure 4 by the dotted line. As demand grows over time, consumption is shown to increase from OB, until at t_5 consumption returns to OA and capacity is again being fully utilized. It is not worth investing in further capacity until the price consumers are willing to pay equals SMC and LMC. This will be at t_{10}, since curve C_2 shows the level of consumption if an optimal pricing policy is being followed; consumption will in fact then continue to follow C_2 until t_{21}, which represents the end of a meter's life. If it is decided that meters should not be replaced at t_{21}, desired consumption will then return to the original (i.e. unmetered) growth path.[21]

At time t_0, existing capacity could supply no more than OA m.g.d., so the effect of metering in this example is to defer the necessity for investment in additional capacity to t_{10}. In fact, a series of investment projects which would have been carried out in the absence of metering will now be delayed a number of years. The value of this deferment is the difference between the present worth of the series in the absence of metering and the (smaller) present worth of the series if delayed by the introduction of meters. In addition, there is a saving due to the exclusion of demands for which consumers are not prepared to pay marginal operating costs.

As counterweight to these benefits, metering involves two sorts of cost: first, installation, maintenance, and running costs of the meters themselves, and secondly, due to the restriction of consumption, the cost imposed on consumers, represented roughly by the diminution of the area under the demand curve. If at time t_0 we must make a choice between the two alternatives, to invest in capacity or to install meters, the decision is straightforward; we have merely to compare the benefits of metering with the costs involved over a period of twenty-one years. If the (discounted) benefits exceed the (discounted) costs, then meters should be installed. If not, further investment in capacity is the correct course of action.

21. Figure 4 perhaps oversimplifies the effect of abandoning metering at t_{21}, since an immediate return to C_1 implies that metering has had no effect on water consumption habits, investment in water-using appliances, etc. In practice, there might well be a time lag before consumption does return to the original growth path.

Twenty-one years, or the life of a meter is the relevant time period to consider in such a calculation[22] since at t_{21} a new decision has to be made; to invest in capacity or to replace existing meters. If meters are replaced, any further benefits and costs are attributable to the new meters. It will be appreciated that if capacity costs continue to rise over time, the replacement of meters is likely to show an even greater net benefit than did the original decision to install domestic metering.

However, the choice at a given moment of time does not lie simply between metering for the next twenty-one years or doing without meters for the next twenty-one years. A decision not to install meters at time t_0 does not preclude doing so at a later date; thus it may be better to defer metering a number of years, while building extra capacity for the intervening period. A formal analysis, embodying a treatment of this complication, is to be found in the Appendix to this paper.

In contrast to the reasoning implicit in the foregoing analysis, the current attitude of the water supply industry is summed up in the view of the Sub-Committee on Water Charges, that '... we should not be justified in recommending universal metering of supplies. This conclusion would merit review if the cost of water were to rise greatly or there were significant increases in water consumption'. Although this is a recognition of the problem, the implication here is that we should wait till costs have risen[23] before thinking about metering, whereas the primary aim, as indicated above, should be to forestall, by means of a price mechanism, construction of high cost schemes if deemed necessary.[24]

22. Theoretically, a new decision can be made at any time over a meter's life; i.e. the annual costs of metering can be avoided by returning to the old charging system even before the meters are due to be scrapped. However, once installed, the annual costs are very low relative to the initial cost, so for all practical purposes the investment in metering involves a commitment for the whole of a meter's useful life.
23. Even if the demand for water does not increase, changes in the opportunity cost of resources at present devoted to water supply (e.g. an increase in the relative price of land at present flooded), could be a justification for introducing domestic metering, or raising prices of metered supplies.
24. I would however agree with the view that the costs of metering are far too high if the aim is merely one of equity – to discriminate more fairly as

Opposition to domestic metering is sometimes based on the grounds that the demand for water is inelastic, and that the installation of meters would not have the deterrent effect noted above. Evidence in support of this is provided by experiments that have been carried out by individual water undertakings; installation of meters has typically shown a temporary fall in consumption, followed by a fairly quick return to the original level. However, although the demand for water at present prices may be inelastic, if prices are set, as indicated above, at a level relevant to future costs, this will not necessarily continue to be true.[25]

In direct contrast to the above argument is the traditional support for our system of water charging; the fear that if water is paid for on a quantity basis, people will be deterred from using it, with adverse effects on their own health and the health of those with whom they come into contact. In fact, the 'externality' argument is the sole possible justification for treating water, in all conceivable circumstances, as a commodity, the consumption of which should not be inhibited by such mundane considerations as price. Even so, this argument is not convincing. For one thing, the fear that individuals will endanger their own health presupposes a degree of irrationality among consumers that is probably unjustified – and in this particular case, this will take

---

between, for example, extravagant and economical users of water living in houses of identical rateable value.

25. Subsequent research into foreign experience clearly indicates that domestic metering reduces recorded consumption, but equally clearly it is shown that once meters have been installed, consumption is unaffected by price changes. This apparent paradox could be explained by two things. First, the facts are consistent with the hypothesis that metering will encourage individuals to reduce the amount of water *wasted* on their premises, but having done this, their demand for water *use* remains inelastic. Secondly, universal metering reveals discrepancies between the quantity of water going into supply and that actually received on consumers' premises. Such discrepancies, which reveal the extent of leakage from the mains, at once facilitate and provide an incentive for the improvement of waste prevention methods by water undertakers, and, as we have noted, waste outside consumers' premises would, prior to metering, have been recorded as domestic consumption. Metering would therefore result in a permanent reduction in annual wastage and this would obviously be unaffected by subsequent price changes.

care of the externality problem as well. Furthermore, there is no evidence from the experiences of Malvern or from overseas, that metered domestic consumers are noticeably dirtier than unmetered. The possibility that rising costs and prices may induce a less than optimum consumption of water could be remedied, if it threatened to become a serious problem, by giving consumers a 'free allowance'; a flat rate could be charged which would entitle consumers to use water free of further charge up to a certain level of consumption, after which they must pay at a positive marginal rate. This is done for example in Belgium.

Conclusion

It must be emphasized that it is the method of arriving at the decision to invest in capacity that is under attack, not necessarily the results themselves. For example, although we might criticize the means by which Manchester Corporation arrived at the recent decision to attempt to abstract further water from the Lake District, if an adequate cost–benefit analysis were to be carried out, it might well be that the value of the water provided would be shown to exceed the costs of providing it. Thus the opponents of the schemes are possibly right in choosing as their main platform the argument that alternative schemes are preferable, rather than to question the wisdom of building any scheme at all. However, this is not inevitably the case; consideration of a scheme such as the Morecambe Bay Barrage, which will yield arge quantities of water (estimates vary from 200 to 400 m.g.d.) and involve a high initial outlay (estimated at £40 million, which does not include the cost of building aqueducts to the consuming areas) requires at least some notion of the value that consumers will place on the water provided. Given present pricing arrangements this information is hardly likely to be forthcoming, but without it, although we are able to choose between alternative investments in water supply, we have no grounds on which to weigh the benefits of investment in water supply against the benefits of any other form of expenditure, be it public or private.

Thus although 'requirements' predictions may have been instrumental in producing correct investment decisions in the past, and could conceivably continue so for some time to come, a reorientation of our attitude towards water is now due. As provision of extra supplies becomes more costly, and as (particularly in the case of domestic consumption), water becomes used for less and less necessary purposes, the 'requirements' concept may no longer be sufficient; more sophisticated techniques of assessing the relative costs and benefits of water supply projects are now appropriate to match scientific and engineering advances in the industry. The assumptions implicit in the engineering or technological approach to investment in water supply, those of perfectly inelastic demand and/or perfectly elastic supply, should no longer be accepted without query; the view, for example, that 'water is cheap at any price' is almost certain to lead to over-investment in water supply projects.

Appendix

Notes on the timing of the introduction of meters

1. This appendix looks at the problem of timing in the context of the criteria used in the article for assessing investment and pricing policy. These criteria rely, roughly, on three assumptions: (i) that the money costs facing water supply undertakings are, for the purposes of the analysis, adjusted where necessary so that they reflect social opportunity costs; (ii) that £1 of expenditure by different persons is given equal weight; and (iii) that the area under the demand curve is an acceptable measure of the value to consumers of additional supply.

2. Given that meters have a limited life, say L years, it is possible to compare the benefits and costs of supplying unmetered demand for the next L years with the benefits and costs of metering and of supplying metered demand for the next L years. This comparison, however, biases the choice in favour of immediate metering if the gains from metering are growing over time relative to the costs of metering. An analogy should make this clear. Suppose an elderly machine is costing more to run each year, and we are thinking of replacing it with a new machine expected to last ten years. A comparison of the costs of the new machine with what it would cost to continue with the old machine for ten years more may indicate that replacement is worth while, because of the high costs of the old machine towards the end of the

ten-year period; but this does not imply that immediate replacement is the best course, since these high costs can also be avoided by replacing in, say, three years time.

3. The expected growth in consumption of water per household and the expected rise in the marginal cost of providing supplies both suggest that gains from metering relative to its costs will rise over time, and that we should recommend the introduction of meters only if we have satisfied ourselves on the question of timing as well as establishing that the benefits of metering, over the life of the meters, outweigh its costs. This appendix therefore is concerned with the conditions which have to be satisfied if it is to be worth while to introduce meters at time t_o (policy 1) rather than at a later time $t_o + \delta t$ (policy 2). Provided that the gains from metering are steadily growing, if policy 1 is preferable to policy 2 for a small δt it will be preferable to *any* policy involving deferment of metering; hence immediate metering will be indicated.

4. The following relationships are used:

(a) *Demand* $D_t = f(p_t, t) \cdot \frac{\partial D}{\partial t} > O$. For diagrammatic purposes the special form $D_t = f(t) \cdot (a - bp_t)$ is used.

(b) *Marginal capital cost* $w = g(K)$, where w is the cost of adding an extra unit to capacity and K is existing capacity. $\frac{\partial w}{\partial K} \geqslant O$.

(c) *Current supply costs*. Supply costs per unit, h, are constant up to existing capacity and over time. Capacity sets an absolute limit on current supply.

(d) *Metering costs*. Metering costs per period, μ, are defined as that level of costs which would, if incurred evenly throughout the life of the meters installed at time t_o, have the same present value as the actual capital and operating costs associated with those meters.

(e) *The rate of discount r* is assumed constant throughout.

(f) *Changes in the general level of prices* are allowed for by treating all prices and costs used in the analysis as having been deflated by a general index of prices, and by assuming the rate of discount to have allowed for this deflation.

5. The basic approach used here to assess whether immediate introduction of meters is justified can be illustrated with reference to figure 5. In the upper part of the diagram, the curve *JABC*

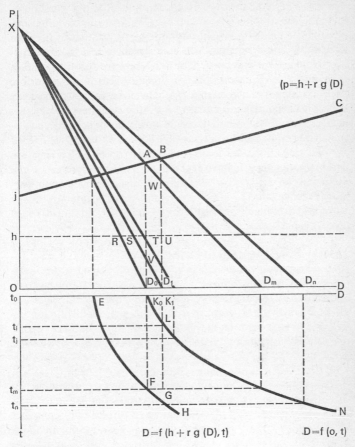

Figure 5

may be called an investment curve: it shows, for different levels of output, the level of price which would make it just worth while to invest in additional capacity. Curves XD_0, XD_1, XD_m, and XD_n are demand curves at times t_o, t_1, t_m, and t_n. In the lower part of the diagram, the curves $K_o N$ and EH show respectively the course of unmetered demand over time and the course of demand if meter charges are imposed on the long-run marginal cost basis described in the article.

The case where current supply costs are zero

6. Consider first the simplified case where there are no current supply costs, i.e. h is zero. If meters are introduced at time t_o, with capacity, based on unmetered demand, at K_o, price will in the succeeding periods rise gradually from zero to $D_o A$, in such a way as to keep demand equal to K_o. After price reaches $D_o A$ (at time t_m) it will become desirable to invest in additional capacity, and price and demand will thereafter both rise along $JABC$. If the introduction of meters is delayed to time t_1, by which time unmetered demand will have reached K_1, price will thereafter rise from zero at time t_1 to $D_1 B$ at time t_n in such a way as to keep demand equal to K_1. After time t_n, price and output will be the same whether meters are introduced at time t_o (policy 1) or at time t_1 (policy 2).

7. The advantage of policy 1 is that costs of increasing capacity from K_o to K_1 are deferred from the period between t_o and t_1 to the period between t_m and t_n. Against this must be set two disadvantages. First, there are metering costs μ incurred between t_o and t_1. Secondly, policy 2 involves the production of a greater output than policy 1, and although the marginal value of this output is not high enough to justify the capital outlay involved it must not be left out of account altogether.

8. Provided that the demand curves XD_o, XD_1, etc., are approximately linear, a consumers' surplus measure of the value, in successive periods, of the output sacrificed under policy 1 is easily obtainable: at t_1, for example, $(K_1 - K_o) \cdot \frac{1}{2} D_o V$, and at t_m, $(K_1 - K_o) \cdot \frac{1}{2} (D_o A + D_1 W)$. However, as the period of delay between t_o and t_1 is shortened, the difference between the price required to hold demand to K_o and the price required to hold demand to K_1 tends to zero, and the consumers' surplus measure, for any time t, tends to $p_t \cdot (K_1 - K_o)$, where p_t is the price required to hold demand to K_o (or K_1).

9. Writing ∂t for $(t_1 - t_o)$ and using the approximation

234

$K_1 - K_o = k_o \, \partial t$, where $k_o = \dfrac{\partial D}{\partial t}$ for $p = o$, $t = t_o$, the gains and losses from following policy 1 rather than policy 2 may be set out as follows (for small ∂t):

Gains due to postponement of capital investment:

$$k_o \, \delta t \, g(K_o) \cdot \left(1 - e^{-r(tm-to)}\right) \text{ or } k_o \delta t \int_{to}^{tm} rg(K_o)e^{-r(t-to)}dt$$

Losses due to metering costs:

$$\mu \cdot \delta t$$

Losses due to sacrificed output:

$$k_o \, \delta t \int_{to}^{tm} p_t e^{-r(t-to)} \, dt, \text{ where } f(p_t, t) = K_o; \; p_{tm} = rg(K_o)$$

Setting these together indicates that immediate metering is justified if

$$k_o \cdot \int_{to}^{tm} \left(rg(K_o) - p_t\right) e^{-r(t-to)}dt > \mu \qquad (1)$$

This confirms certain expectations which would be held on the basis of general reasoning. It can never be profitable to introduce meters at once, in this case without supply costs, if demand is currently static ($k_o = O$); and low elasticity of demand is an unfavourable point, since p_t will then have to rise rapidly to hold demand to K_o and the time interval covered by the integral will be short.

The case with supply costs positive

10. If there are current supply costs, the introduction of meters involves an immediate increase in the price of water and reduction in demand to below existing capacity: in terms of figure 5 demand and price follow a course OD_oRTAC with policy 1 and OD_1SUBC with policy 2. The gains due to postponement of capital investment and the losses due to metering costs remain as in the foregoing paragraph, but output differences need to be handled differently. For this purpose it is convenient to divide the interval between t_o and t_m into three parts. First, between t_o and $t_o + \delta t$, policy 1 involves an output lower by $f(O, t_o) - f(h, t_o)$.

235

This is a gain, since consumers do not value these marginal units highly enough to pay their costs of supply; with a linear approximation to the demand curve we can write the gain for the period as $\frac{1}{2}h \cdot \delta t \cdot (f(O, t_o) - f(h, t_o))$ or $\frac{1}{2}h \cdot \alpha D_o \cdot \delta t$, where α is the proportionate reduction of demand caused by raising the price from O to h. Secondly, between $t_o + \delta t$ and t_j, defined by $f(h, t_j) = K_o$, output and price are the same with the two policies. Thirdly, between t_j and t_m, output with policy 1 is again lower, but in this period the sacrificed output would command a price more than sufficient to pay current supply costs, so that a loss is involved. As δt tends to zero, this loss tends, for any t between t_j and t_m, to $(p_t - h) \cdot (K_1 - K_o)$ or $(p_t - h) \cdot k_o \cdot \delta t$.

11. The gains and losses from introducing metering at once rather than slightly later, in the case where supply costs are significant, can now be set together. This indicates that metering at once is desirable if the following inequality holds:

$$k_o\left[\int_{t_o}^{t_j} rg(K_o)e^{-r(t-t_o)}dt + \int_{t_j}^{t_m}\left(rg(K_o) - (p_t - h)\right)e^{-r(t-t_o)}dt\right]$$
$$> \mu - \tfrac{1}{2}h\alpha D_o \qquad (2)$$

Comparison of this result with condition (1) of paragraph 9 reveals two significant differences. First, if operating costs are large and demand is responsive to price the right-hand side of (2) might be zero or negative, so that metering might be justified even if demand were not rising. Secondly, inspection of condition (1) shows that throughout the period t_o to t_m there was an offset to the postponement gains, which were at the rate of $r \cdot g(K_o)$ per period per unit of capacity, in the form of the value of sacrificed output. In (2), however, a similar offset applies only between t_j and t_m. There is a simple explanation of this difference. Increasing price from O to h in the second case creates surplus capacity at time t_o, and not until time t_j, when this surplus capacity has been absorbed by rising demand, can the extra capacity involved in following policy 2 bring any benefit at all.

7 A. Hazlewood

Telephone Service

A. Hazlewood, 'Optimum pricing as applied to telephone service', *Review of Economic Studies*, vol. 18 (1950–51), pp. 67–78. Amended by the author.

General Principles

The discussion which began in the 1930s on the optimum price policy for public enterprises was carried on mainly in very general terms, without detailed reference to specific industries.[1] By 1950 the analysis and argument had contributed curiously little to the practical problem of determining the proper pricing policy for any particular industry. It would be wrong to imply that nothing useful emerged from the discussion, but the study of pricing policy cannot rest at such a level of abstraction, for it is reasonable to suppose that no single pricing rule, arrived at by general theoretical reasoning, will be readily applicable to industries so different as coal, railways, and electricity, to take three examples. Detailed study of the conditions peculiar to individual industries is necessary before theoretical analysis can safely lead to policy recommendations. Only when optimum pricing policy is viewed from the standpoint of particular applications will the complications come to light. The present article is an attempt to formulate a desirable tariff structure for telephone service, taking into account the complexities which arise from the particular characteristics of the service.

There is no need to reiterate the objections to the marginal cost

1. See Nancy Ruggles, 'The welfare basis of the marginal cost pricing principle' and 'Recent developments in the theory of marginal cost pricing' paper 1 in this edition, *Review of Economic Studies*, 1949–50, and works cited therein. See also I. M. D. Little, *A critique of welfare economics*, 2nd edn, 1957, p. 185, and A. M. Henderson, 'The pricing of public utility undertakings', *Manchester School*, 1947, p. 223, for the main references.

pricing rule. They have been set out in many articles.[2] A consideration of these objections leads to the conclusion that there is no hope of pursuing a policy which will ensure the theoretically ideal allocation of resources, and hence an ideal output, 'even supposing there is such a thing in the real world as an "ideal" output'.[3] In fact, it may well be thought that the concept of an ideal allocation derives from such unrealistic assumptions as to be of purely theoretical interest.[4] Yet this does not mean that there is nothing to choose between one method of pricing and another. If ideal allocation of resources is abandoned as a chimera, there is much to be said for a pricing policy which enables consumers to obtain extra units of the product if they are willing to pay the cost of providing them, on condition that there are no obvious external costs or benefits or social considerations which are deemed to warrant modification of this principle. At least this will prevent undue restriction of output so far as the individual industry is concerned, and it has appeared that we are not in general able to look much beyond the industry with respect to the allocation of resources.

An attempt will be made, then, to construct a telephone tariff

2. See, for example, A. M. Henderson, 'Prices and profits in state enterprise', *Review of Economic Studies*, vol. 16 (1), no. 39. See also Little, *A critique of welfare economics*, chapter 11.

3. Little, *A critique of welfare economics*, p. 193.

4. The impossibility of applying the criteria for general optimum allocation is further illustrated by consideration of the two-part tariff. Assume a product or service the cost of which consists of: (a) costs varying directly with output; (b) costs of fixed equipment, such as a meter, which are directly attributable to the consumer but are invariant with respect to his consumption of the product. Marginal cost pricing would require a two-part tariff in these circumstances, with a fixed component equal to the 'customer costs'. But what exactly are these costs? Presumably they are the capital costs of the fixed equipment turned into an annual cost, which can then be covered by a charge per period. The fixed charge will depend, then, on the rate of interest used for converting to an annual basis. If the current rate at which the enterprise can borrow is used for this purpose, little welfare significance can be claimed for the resulting tariff, for various arbitrary or institutional factors are a predominant influence on that rate. Only if the rate of interest used reflected solely time preference could any general welfare significance be given to a price policy of which it was a constituent.

which adheres as closely as possible to the basis of cost of service, taking this to imply that:

(1) Any existing subscriber to the service should be able to obtain extra units of the service if he is willing to pay an amount equal to the cost of providing those units.

(2) New subscribers should be able to come on to the system so long as they are willing to pay the extra cost involved in having them on the system.

(3) Consumers of the service as a whole should be provided with the service so long as they are willing, and only if they are willing, to pay the whole cost of providing the service.

A tariff conforming to this principle would involve no concealed or open subsidy. The body of consumers would not be subsidized by the general taxpayer; neither would one group of consumers of the service be subsidized at the expense of others. The problems which arise in applying this general principle to telephone service will appear later.

Although the tariff advocated here is neutral with respect to the distribution of income, affecting it neither one way nor the other, we do not fall into the trap of implicitly accepting the existing distribution, while at the same time claiming that we are making no normative statements. A policy in which the norm for a public enterprise is taken to be that it covers its costs, and so involves no redistribution of incomes, need not reflect a hidden preference for the *status quo*. It merely implies the view that it is not the function of the management of individual State enterprises to determine in what way the distribution of income shall be influenced; nor should the cost characteristics of particular industries be the determining factor. Income redistribution is a function of social policy, of which the price policy of the enterprise in question may certainly be an instrument, but only at the instigation of the political authority. We shall assume that there are no social grounds for a general departure from a cost basis in charging for telephone service.[5]

5. Particular cases which are thought to justify such a departure may be taken care of without vitiating the argument. The burden of subsidy in such cases should not be automatically placed on other consumers of the service, so that costs are covered 'overall'. It is equally wrong to suggest

The advantages deriving from a telephone tariff closely related to the cost structure of the service may be expressed in terms of proper exploitation of the intensive and extensive service margins: the greatest desirable traffic between existing subscribers, and the greatest desirable extension of the service among new subscribers. In practice it is impossible to base a tariff structure strictly on cost. Apart from imprecision of cost measurement and the impracticability of too fine a differentiation, and hence too complicated a tariff, the existence of unallocable costs makes deviation from a cost basis inevitable. This is taken into account in the following analysis, the principle of treatment being to allocate to those responsible all those costs which can be allocated, and to distribute the rest in such a way as least to restrict the development of the service. The cost basis provides a norm to which any practicable tariff is a more or a less close approximation. Analysis of the cost structure of the service is necessary to provide a yard-stick against which particular tariffs may be compared.[6]

Lack of adequate cost data makes it impossible to put the following discussion in quantitative terms. General knowledge of the technical conditions of the telephone service enables us to analyse and categorize the various cost items, but little can be said in quantitative terms about the relative importance of the various categories. The analysis can do no more than point to rather broad conclusions as to the appropriate type of telephone tariff.

The Cost Structure of the Service

A telephone exchange system consists essentially of the equipment necessary to connect the telephone of a subscriber, at his

---

that the burden should never be borne in this way. The point is that the subsidy should not be concealed, however it is met. The decision to subsidise should be deliberate and open.

6. For a more recent discussion favouring a cost-based telephone tariff along rather the same lines as the present article, but with an American reference, see C. W. Meyer, 'Marginal cost pricing of local telephone service', *Land Economics*, August 1966.

request, to that of another subscriber, to enable the second subscriber to be notified of the connexion, and to permit the transmission of speech. At the end of the call the subscribers' apparatus must be made ready to receive or originate further calls, and the exchange equipment must be made available for use by other callers. In addition to the telephone instrument required by each subscriber, the necessary equipment includes the wires connecting the telephone to the central exchange,[7] and the switching equipment, whether designed for 'manual' or 'automatic' operation,[8] needed to connect one subscriber's line to another. Where a system consists of more than one exchange, telephone calls may be distinguished according to whether they are completed between subscribers connected to the same exchange or between those connected to different exchanges, so that connexion needs to be set up between one exchange and another. In practice, where a telephone system has developed to a substantial size, a three-fold division is necessary. In a large system more than one exchange is technically needed to cater for subscribers who are situated in an area in which there is essentially a general community of interest, as in the centre of a large city, so that calls between exchanges are just as frequent as calls between subscribers on the same exchange. Calls between such exchanges are routed over 'junction circuits' connecting the exchanges and are known as 'junction calls'. It is different with calls between areas, for these will form only a small proportion of the calls completed within either area, and the use of such 'trunk' service varies very largely between different subscribers. The costs associated with trunk service are also somewhat different from those associated with junction and local exchange service. These differences justify separate treatment of the two types of call.[9]

7. Unlike most other services, e.g. electricity and gas, independent connexion is required by a telephone subscriber the whole way to the central office. It is not a matter of connecting to a nearby 'main'.

8. In manual switching systems the connexion is made by an operator at the exchange. Automatic switching is performed by apparatus located at the exchange but controlled by the calling subscriber by means of the 'dial'.

9. Unlike the subscriber's local line, separate trunk and junction circuits are not, of course, required for each subscriber. Any trunk or junction can be made available for the use of any subscriber, so their provision depends on the expected maximum calling rate.

The cost structure of a telephone system is very complicated. It is much more complex than that of electric power supply which, at first glance, might appear to be a service of a similar type. In electricity supply one can broadly say that part of the equipment, comprising such items as consumers' meters and the cables into their premises, varies in proportion with the number of consumers, while another part, such as the generator and virtually all power station equipment, varies in size with the peak load. In telephone service, however, the greater part of the exchange equipment is a function both of the peak calling rate and of the number of subscribers. Whereas, in the supply of electricity, the size of the generator needed to supply a given peak demand is the same irrespective of whether that demand derives from a few large consumers or from the simultaneous demand of many small users, in a telephone system the equipment needed to handle a given calling rate will vary very much according to whether there are only a few or many subscribers connected to the system.

Perhaps the most readily isolated costs are those directly allocable to the individual subscriber, but which are independent of the number of calls he makes. These 'customer costs' consist of the capital cost, converted to an annual basis, of the subscriber's telephone, the line connecting him to the exchange and the terminating equipment at the exchange, together with the cost of meter reading and of rendering regular accounts. A fixed charge per period of time is the desirable way to cover this cost item. The charge on this count would differ for different subscribers owing, for example, to their varying distances from the exchange, with consequent differences in local line cost. It would be inconvenient to charge each individual the exact cost appropriate to him; a standard charge for all subscribers within a certain radius of the exchange, with a surcharge proportional to distance for those outside the radius, would be the simplest method. Differences in charge according to locality might also be appropriate, for the cost of providing a given length of local circuit will probably not be the same in, say, an urban as in a rural area.

Some costs, while varying with the number of subscribers to be served, are not costs of equipment reserved for the sole use of a particular subscriber. This category includes, for instance, the cost of providing switching equipment to give interconnexion between 10,000 subscribers instead of between 1,000. Much external plant is of the same character. Main duct and pole routes are provided to cater for the existing size and expected future development of the system, but the costs involved are not directly attributable to any particular subscriber, nor do they vary with traffic. There are sufficient indivisibilities in these cost items to make it undesirable to divide them equally between subscribers, for such a charge would exclude from the system some subscribers who would be willing to pay the *extra* cost incurred in connecting them. These indivisible costs should be allocated as a fixed charge proportional to 'consumers' surplus', or on the principle of 'what the traffic will bear'.

This proposal begs the question of how to measure consumers' surplus, and it is clear that, in practice, any allocation on this principle must be of a very rough and ready character, according to a few very broad categories. It seems less impossible of application, however, if it is considered as applying the well-known principle of 'what the traffic will bear' instead of being thought of in terms of the rather esoteric 'surplus' concept. Probably a higher charge for business than for residence subscribers would be justifiable, and perhaps a differentiation according to some rough index of wealth, such as size of house. The differential between the various charges would inevitably be arbitrary, but it is in the nature of the case that accuracy in the allocation of these costs is impossible.[10]

The border line between these indivisible costs and the customer costs is by no means precise. A particular cost item may fall in one category or the other according to circumstances. In rural areas where no very considerable advance provision of line plant

10. It must be recognized that 'willingness to pay' is not an ideal social criterion. The man who crosses Dupuit's bridge to visit his dying father is heavily mulcted. This objection is partly met by our claim that any glaring cases of social need can be subsidized. Also, as far as the telephone service is concerned, the public call-office system provides an outlet for calls of great necessity without heavy mulcting. In any case, our suggestion of certain objective criteria to determine the differential charge may be expected to eliminate many examples of social need, although they do not provide so accurate an index of consumers' surplus as would some less objective, though impracticable, test.

is made, a high proportion of total line costs will be customer costs, for the connexion of a new subscriber will often involve the construction of a new route. The whole problem of indivisibilities is raised here. Just as there is the problem that the carriage of an extra railway passenger may necessitate the cost of an extra coach, yet once that cost is incurred another fifty passengers can be carried virtually for nothing, so there is a similar problem when a new subscriber is to be connected to the telephone system. To connect a subscriber in a so-far-undeveloped part of a rural exchange area will involve the cost of erecting a new pole route, while later subscribers situated along the route can be connected at much lower cost. Should the first subscriber be charged the whole cost of erecting the route? Clearly, there must be some averaging of costs. A route should be erected to cater for the number of subscribers who can reasonably be expected to come on to the system in the not too distant future, the average cost being charged to each subscriber as he is connected. Such a method of charging is not ideal: some people may be excluded by a charge which is greater than the cost of connecting them; and the spare capacity, while it exists, is a charge on the system as a whole. Nevertheless, no better alternative presents itself. There is no logical difference between those indivisible costs to be allocated according to 'what the traffic will bear' and the costs considered here. The difference in treatment is justified by the fact that in the latter case the costs are more directly allocable, if not to an individual, at least to a comparatively small group. If there were no prospect of further subscribers being obtained along the line of a new route, it would be reasonable to charge the whole cost of the route to the one subscriber for whose benefit it was erected.

Part of the cost of buildings also seems to be indivisible, dependent on the number of subscribers, but not directly allocable to individuals. This is so because the size of any exchange building, as well as the number of exchange buildings, is partly dependent on the number of subscribers to be served. A similar argument applies to junctions, because the number of junction groups, though not the number of individual junction circuits, depends on the number of exchanges to be inter-connected. These two groups of cost, then, to the extent that they can be isolated from building and junction costs dependent on other factors, would also be properly allocated on the 'what the traffic will bear' principle. This principle should also be applied to expenses of the character of general administration and research.

Turning now to the costs dependent on traffic we find that many are related not to traffic in general, but to peak traffic. When demand for a product is unevenly distributed over time, so that there are periods of peak and periods of off-peak demand, a problem arises when possibilities of storing the product are limited or impossible, as in the provision of telephone service. Equipment which must be provided to cater for peak demands will be idle at off-peak periods. The problem is how to allocate the cost of this equipment. No capital cost (except 'user cost', which is considered later) is involved in supplying extra units of the service at off-peak times, so that any price charged which is greater than prime cost is unnecessarily restrictive. The cost of all equipment that is required to satisfy the peak demand should be a charge on peak traffic. The relevant costs are those of switching equipment, junctions, and buildings (except that part which has already been discussed as depending on the number of subscribers), and of batteries and other power equipment, the capacity of which must be sufficient to deal with the peak load. These costs should be allocated as a variable charge to each call made at peak periods.

Unless there has been excessive investment in plant, the equipment will be working at full capacity at times of peak load.[11] But the concept of capacity working is one which must be carefully handled when applied to a telephone system. The calling rate a given amount of equipment can deal with depends on the 'grade of service' it has been decided to provide. 'Grade of service' is a concept based on the chance of encountering 'busy' apparatus in setting up a connexion. The higher the calling rate, with a given amount of equipment, the greater is the chance of

11. In reality, equipment will be installed in excess of that needed to cater for current demand so as to allow for growth without expensive piecemeal additions. Pricing policy must ignore this growth margin, otherwise excess capacity will always exist, and the capital cost of all traffic-determined equipment would have to be treated as an 'inescapable' cost which need not be covered by revenue.

failure in setting-up a call, owing to a lack of disengaged apparatus, and hence the lower is the 'grade of service' being offered. Once it has been decided not to tolerate less than a particular 'grade of service', it is necessary to install an amount of equipment which will give this at times of peak load. At such times the equipment may be considered as working at capacity. The calling rate could increase, but the frequency with which engaged conditions of the exchange apparatus[12] were encountered would rise. It follows that the extra money cost imposed on the system by a call is not the relevant marginal cost for determining the correct charge for a call at peak periods. The relevant cost includes the cost of the capital equipment necessary, not to permit the call to be made, but to maintain the predetermined 'grade of service'. This is the 'long-run marginal cost'[13] on which the charge per call at peak periods should be based.

Finally, we come to the costs entailed by a call irrespective of the time at which it is made: the prime cost or 'short-run marginal cost'. In a manual switching system this cost is predominantly that of the time during which the operator is occupied in handling the call, and in addition there is a certain user cost or wear and tear which must be made good, as far as possible, by maintenance expenditure. With automatic working the item of operating cost does not enter for normal, automatically completed calls, but the cost of wear and tear is increased. Although maintenance in an automatic exchange is done on a routine basis, the rate at which equipment components have to be repaired and renewed is largely dependent on the number of calls.

The importance of user cost in the analysis of cost structure warrants a digression at this point. Professor Lewis claims that 'if we are dealing with equipment which wears out proportionately with use, there is no problem (of the peak). The cost of the equipment enters directly into marginal cost, which is therefore the same for all units of output.'[14] In this situation there is,

12. It is essentially the exchange apparatus and not the called subscriber's line that is relevant here. The chance of the subscriber's line being engaged is not a function of the total calling rate at any time.

13. For a discussion of the meaning of 'long-run marginal cost' and 'short-run marginal cost' as used here, see Lewis, 'Fixed costs', *Economica*, 1946, reprinted in *Overhead costs*.

14. *Overhead costs*, p. 45.

he implies, no true off-peak excess capacity and no special problem of peak costing; peak and off-peak costs are the same. This casts doubt on the relevance of our analysis of the peak problem as it applies to telephone service. If the wear and tear of equipment with use is such that we may almost say it 'wears out proportionately with use', there is no basis for discriminating between peak and off-peak traffic. If we fill in the troughs of apparent excess capacity by encouraging off-peak use we are doing so only by sacrificing an equal use of the equipment in the future; extra use now will necessitate proportionately earlier renewal. But there appears to be an error in this argument. Even if equipment 'wears out proportionately with use' it is costlier to provide a given amount of service in the form of a regular peak than in the form of a steady demand, because more capital is required in the former case, so that interest charges are higher. Professor Lewis appears to neglect the factor of interest cost.[15] In addition, although wear and tear is important in telephone service, particularly with automatic working, much of the equipment dependent on peak demand does not wear out proportionately with use, buildings and junctions being notable examples. It may be concluded that the analysis of the costs imposed by peak and by off-peak traffic is not vitiated when user cost is taken into account, though it is true that the larger wear and tear bulks, the smaller must be the differential between peak and off-peak charges correctly to apportion costs.

In summary, the cost structure of the telephone service warrants a tariff having:

(1) A fixed component covering customer costs plus certain items of capital cost (which are invariant with respect to calling rate and are not directly allocable to individual subscribers) apportioned according to a rough index of 'what the traffic will bear'.

(2) A charge per call during peak periods equal to long-run marginal cost, which includes an element of capital cost for that equipment which is a function of traffic.

15. It should be noted that he is also making an implicit assumption about expectations.

(3) A charge per call during off-peak periods equal to short-run marginal cost, user cost being the only part of the cost of fixed equipment included.

Alternative Pricing Policies

The advantages of a tariff based on the cost structure of the service are clearly revealed when the practical consequences are considered of tariffs which diverge markedly from that type. Two limiting cases may be investigated: firstly, where the charge per call is zero, and, secondly, where the fixed charge is zero.

The first of these, or the 'flat rate' has a long history as a method of charging for telephone service. It did not finally disappear from the service of the British Post Office until 1921, when its defects could no longer be tolerated. That it does not correspond to the cost structure of the service is clear; it would do so only if all costs were a function solely of the number of subscribers, and not of the number of calls or of their time pattern. A tariff consisting of a lump-sum payment, for an un-limited number of calls, encourages a wasteful use of the tele-phone, in the sense that calls are made which the caller would not make if he had to bear directly the cost they impose. If the charge is set so as to cover the whole cost of the system, large users pay less, while small users pay more than the cost of giving them service, so that small users subsidize the large. Further, potential small users, who would be prepared to pay the cost of giving them the service they actually require, are kept off the system by the high charge demanded. Since extension of the system must be to an important degree among small users, the flat rate seriously retards growth. But it is an important characteristic of telephone service that its utility depends, to a significant extent, upon the number of persons with whom connexion is available. So anything hindering development limits the value of the service to existing subscribers. The flat rate stands condemned, then, on grounds of economy, equity, and value of service.

The valid arguments against the flat rate method of charging have often been confused with an irrelevant argument about 'overloaded' lines.[16] Because a flat rate subscriber can obtain extra calls without extra charge, while a substantial charge is incurred in renting an additional circuit, subscribers' lines are often made to take more traffic than they can carry, if their efficiency for handling incoming as well as outgoing calls is not to decline seriously. As a result, the proportion of calls which cannot be completed, because the called subscriber's line is engaged, rises substantially. This involves a deterioration in the quality of the service being given. It also involves an increased money cost to the system, for many calls will be completed only after a number of unsuccessful attempts, so that, since 'engaged' calls are as costly to operate as successful ones, the cost per effective call is increased. These conditions of overloading could arise, however, under any system of charging. Moreover, they could arise not only from a large number of calls made over a line, but equally because the calls were of long duration; and they could arise not only from outgoing calls, but equally from an unusual number of incoming calls. The question of overloading needs examination, then, on its merits, and not as an argument against the flat rate tariff.

The fact that a subscriber overloads his line by making numerous or lengthy outgoing calls must be taken to imply that he values those calls more highly than the incoming calls he may be losing. Similarly, a subscriber who loses incoming calls by renting too few lines to handle them must be assumed to value those calls at less than the cost of extra lines. Such valuations cannot be criticized. Yet it is true that the engaged condition of these subscribers' lines imposes costs on the system which are not directly reflected in the charges they pay, whether they are on a flat rate or some form of charge-per-call tariff. Some account should also be taken of the disutility imposed on callers of subscribers who have overloaded lines.[17] Consequently, there

16. Cf. for example, *Report of the Departmental Committee on Telephone Rates*, Cmd 804, 1920 (BPP, 1920, XXV); Hall, 'Differential telephone rates', *Journal of Land and Public Utility Economics*, 1932,

17. There are certain clear cases where this disutility may be important, such as the theatre box-office and the railway inquiry service. But we must take care not to get generally enmeshed in tricky comparisons between the utility of a call to the caller and to the called.

are grounds for arguing that such subscribers are renting too few lines. It would be reasonable to require subscribers to pay a surcharge, or to take extra lines, if observation showed that engaged calls constituted more than a predetermined proportion of their total incoming traffic. Second and subsequent lines could be made available at reduced rental, a discrimination which would be justified on the basis of cost by the saving effected through a reduction in the number of ineffective calls.

This discussion has assumed that the limiting factor is the telephone line and not the person called. Therefore it is applicable to organizations rather than to individual subscribers. Price policy cannot be expected to ensure that individuals are ready, waiting to receive their telephone calls! But, in reality, it is in organizations, where a number of people use the same line, that overloading is likely to be a significant problem.

Returning to a consideration of tariff structures, we find that a system of covering all costs by a charge per call has disadvantages even more serious than those of the flat rate. An almost universal demand for free connexion to the system would arise, although many would be unwilling to pay the cost incurred in connecting them, if they were called upon to do so. At the same time, the charge per call would have to be extremely high if total costs were to be covered, and so the calling rate would be low. In contrast with the flat rate, under this system of charging it would be the small users who were subsidized.

The objections to the tariffs discussed in this section merely amplify the basic objection that they do not take account of the cost structure of the service. However, it is of use to have examined some of the specific results of this.

Some Complications

Before discussing the effect of considerations other than those of cost upon the desirability and practicability of the proposed tariff, there are certain cost items, not previously considered, which must be taken into account.

250

Is the duration of calls irrelevant to the cost structure of the service, or should calls be charged in proportion to the time they last? Since the significant cost of any call is that involved in establishing the connexion, there being only very slight costs incurred in its continuation, there would seem to be little justification for charging according to duration. But, given a peak period, the amount of equipment needed to handle the traffic during that period is directly affected by the duration of the calls being made: the shorter the calls the less is the equipment needed to handle a given calling rate. This provides good reason for charging on a time basis during *peak* periods if a cost basis for the tariff is to be followed at all closely. The duration of off-peak calls is not a significant cost item, and it would be wrong to charge for these according to their duration. In Britain local calls were not timed, nor was there a differentiation between peak and off-peak, until the gradual introduction of Subscriber Trunk Dialling (STD) in the 1960s. Trunk calls were (and arc) charged at all times according to their duration, though at a cheaper rate at off-peak. Our analysis suggests that there should be no limit to the duration of off-peak calls.

We have already noted that engaged calls are a cost to the system. At one time a small charge was put on originators of ineffective trunk calls, but it seems undesirable and impracticable to revive this practice, particularly applying it to local calls. The caller expects to pay for being connected, but not for failing to be connected. This sort of problem is not peculiar to telephone service: the cost to a millinery establishment of serving the woman who tries on twenty hats, and in the end buys none, is greater than that imposed by the rare person who buys the first hat she is shown, but no charge is levied on the first customer. The costs imposed by ineffective calls must be borne by the system as a whole, but the burden should be mitigated by the proposal made in the previous section.

In a multi-exchange area, calls between subscribers connected to the same exchange are cheaper to set up than calls between two different exchanges. Yet it is impracticable in a tariff to distinguish between such calls. Neither is it feasible, nor desirable, to charge more for calls which, on an automatic system, require the assistance of an operator owing to difficulty in

251

obtaining connexion being experienced. Further, it is not practicable to charge differently for calls completed automatically from those operated manually, though the cost may well be different, when the existence of manual and automatic exchanges operating together depends on the fact that the programme of change-over to automatic working is uncompleted.

Most of the things to be said about trunk calls have been mentioned earlier. The number of circuits to be provided in any trunk route depends on the peak calling rate and on the duration of the calls, so that there should be differentiation between peak and off-peak trunk calls both in the charge and in the time allowed. The effect of increased distance is to increase the length of the trunk circuit and hence the capital cost to be covered. This gives reason for peak period charges to increase with distance; to the extent that operating costs increase with distance, as is likely owing to the greater number of operators needed to establish the connexion, the greater also should be the charge both for peak and for off-peak calls. As in the local system, there are certain costs of trunk service which cannot be attributed to traffic. The difference is that the unequal use of trunk service would make it inequitable to allocate these overheads to subscribers in general as a fixed payment, so that all costs of trunk service must be covered by payments per call, whether or not they are directly attributable to traffic.

So far the argument has implicitly assumed conditions of constant cost. But conditions of increasing or decreasing cost may possibly exist with respect either to growth in the number of subscribers or to increase in the number of calls. Some account must be taken of these possibilities.

The effect on cost of a growth in the number of subscribers has received perhaps disproportionate attention in the literature on the telephone tariff. Generally it has been argued that the characteristic of telephone service, that each new subscriber must be given facilities to connect with every existing subscriber, means a rise in equipment costs more than in proportion with the increase in the number of subscribers. Up to a certain point the increased costs arise from the increased complexity of the 'multiple' equipment in the exchange, and beyond that point from the duplication of exchanges and the consequent increase in the

number of junction groups.[18] The significance of this for a
theory of the telephone tariff is not as great as might at first
appear. Although it indicates that the total costs to be covered
are likely to rise more than in proportion with the growth of the
system,[19] it does not alter our analysis of the desirable tariff
structure. The costs which increase with the number of subscribers are those which we have suggested should be apportioned according to 'what the traffic will bear'; they are
indivisible costs. Although telephone equipment is divisible, in the
sense that exchanges can be built to cater for any particular
number of subscribers, an exchange cannot be extended piecemeal. An exchange would originally be constructed for a particular number of subscribers, probably with building space left
for extension, and any extension would have to be carried out in
a fairly large unit, not as every two or three new subscribers came
in. The increased costs cannot, then, be attributed to particular
subscribers: we cannot meaningfully draw a rising marginal cost
curve such that, if a charge is made equal to that cost, a substantial surplus to cover indivisible costs will be available. The
increased costs are themselves essentially indivisible, to be apportioned according to 'what the traffic will bear'.

Some cost items, such as administration, do not rise proportionately with numbers. The greater the number of subscribers
the more fully utilized are pole and duct routes. As the number
of subscribers increases so does their density, and so the average
length of local line falls. These factors tend to offset those leading
to increasing costs as numbers grow. Operating costs, however,
are likely to rise with the growth of the system, due to an increase
in the proportion of junction calls.

18. The 1920 Departmental Committee gave some figures which illustrate
the more than proportional increase in the number of junctions and in
length of external circuit as the number of subscribers increases:

	London	Manchester
Number of subscribers	150,000	20,000
Number of exchanges	81	23
Number of junctions	17,000	1,850
Miles of wire	150,000	8,000

19. Hence refuting the view, which has frequently been voiced in controversy about the British telephone system, that an energetic policy of expansion would, of itself, permit drastic reductions in charges.

An increase in the number of calls at peak periods probably takes place at decreasing cost, since the number of junction circuits needed in a group increases less than in proportion with the traffic: 'a group of five junctions will carry only 0·9 traffic units, but seven junctions will carry 1·8 units, i.e. twice as much'.[20] It is essentially marginal cost which should be charged for a call, though this may often not be easily identified, so that to the extent that decreasing cost per call exists there will be further indivisible costs to be apportioned according to 'what the traffic will bear'.

The above discussion of certain complications in the cost structure of the service emphasizes the principle that it is impossible to differentiate completely in charging according to cost. The most that one can hope or try to achieve is a tariff constructed so as to conform to the broad cost categories of the service. Minor cost differences must be averaged out in the interest of simplicity and practicability.

We have already strayed from the sphere of cost analysis into that of 'practicability'. But before we finally abandon 'science' for 'politics' it is necessary to consider a characteristic of telephone service which is in the nature of an 'external economy', and which may therefore justify a departure in price policy from a strict money-cost basis. When discussing the flat rate tariff it was stated that the value of telephone service resides essentially in the number of potential connexions it offers. A telephone service with one subscriber is useless! Every new subscriber increases the number of possible connexions, and so enhances the value of the service. Although each new subscriber may not, in practice, have connexion with more than a small fraction of the total subscribers, there is no doubt that the general utility of telephone service, or the 'quality of the product', increases with the numbers on the system. This is why particular importance must be placed on the establishment of 'promotional' tariffs, and why a tariff which, by charging more than cost, unnecessarily restricts the number of subscribers is so much to be deplored. The policy we have advocated of levying indivisible costs as a fixed charge on consumers is not liable to criticism on this ground as the principle of charging 'what the traffic will bear'

20. P.O. Engineering Department, *E/P Telephones* 3/1, p. 3.

expressly covers this point, since a charge which keeps out a potential subscriber is clearly one which the traffic will *not* bear. The consideration of external benefits does suggest, however, that a strictly cost basis might with advantage be departed from in some circumstances, less than the full customer cost being charged to some subscribers whose connexion to the system is thought to yield a particular external benefit.[21] A dangerous principle and precedent is being introduced here, however, and one tricky of application, so it must be used sparingly.

In conclusion we must ask how practicable is a tariff based on the principles we have proposed, for practicability must be the final criterion of proposals in this field. Discrimination between persons by a publicly owned monopoly is likely to lead to public outcry: there must be neither discrimination nor appearance of discrimination. It must be admitted that our proposals do not show up well against this standard. Difference in charge when the cost of service is different is not discrimination to the economist, though it may appear to be such to the layman, particularly if he is unacquainted with the cost structure of the service. This difficulty could be overcome, and the price policy defended, by clearly stating the costs involved. It would not be easy, for experience has revealed a deeply rooted idea that differences of treatment are unjust, even where the costs involved are clearly different. How much more difficult, then, would it be to defend the principle of 'what the traffic will bear', which is discrimination in its most obvious form, or the policy of sometimes allocating particular cost items as a direct customer cost and sometimes as an indivisible cost, where the difference of treatment is based on estimates and conjectures of future development? We must expect to have to sacrifice principle to expediency.

21. Such a policy is only reasonable if it is assumed, as is fairly clearly justified, that some subscribers enhance the general utility of the service more than others. If all subscribers were of equal value from this point of view there would be no grounds for departure from a cost basis. There is a difference between this reason for charging less than cost and the case where such a policy is justifiable on general social grounds. Here, some subscribers subsidize others because the existence of the subsidized benefits the subsidy-payers by more than the amount of the subsidy. Here, the benefit is external to the one subscriber, but internal to the subscribers as a whole; in the other case the benefit is external to both.

But there need be no complete abandonment of principle. We certainly do not have to submit to the 'postalization' of the telephone. We can hope to be able fairly accurately to allocate customer costs, charging according to distance from the exchange beyond a certain radius. One general type of discrimination is possible, and has been introduced by telephone administrations: business subscribers can be charged a higher rental than residential subscribers. This form of discrimination is probably in broad conformity with the 'what the traffic will bear' principle and can be defended, though perhaps with a touch of casuistry, with the argument that a wider development of residential service is in the direct interest of business subscribers.

Discrimination between peak and off-peak calls, including charges according to duration at peak times, is an important feature of a tariff related to the cost-structure of the service. Here the problem of public antipathy does not arise, since there is not an obvious discrimination between individuals. At one time the technical difficulties and cost of differentiating peak and off-peak local calls seemed a serious obstacle in the way of a cost-based tariff. In the absence of a direct discrimination according to the originating time of the call, something of the same effect might be obtained by a heavier charge per call, or even a heavier rental, for users likely to contribute to the peak. But this would be a very poor second, for the incidence of the charge would inevitably be inaccurate and it would do nothing to encourage a shift from peak to off-peak use. The introduction of the STD system, in which all calls are timed, made it practicable to differentiate peak from off-peak calls, and to charge according to the duration of calls. The discrimination introduced was not directly in terms of price, but in terms of the time available for a given charge. 'For both local and dialled trunk calls you buy telephone time in twopennyworths, the amount of time bought for 2d. depending upon the distance of the call.'[22] For local calls the 2d. buys six minutes at the full rate and twelve minutes at the cheap rate. Although in some respects this new charging system is nearer than the old to reflecting the cost-structure of the service, it diverges from it by differentiating peak from off-peak according

22. *Subscriber trunk dialling: Dialling instructions and call charges*, GPO, 1966.

to the time allowed for a given charge. It was argued above that the duration of a call does not significantly affect its cost at off-peak times, so that there is no reason on grounds of cost for charging off-peak calls according to their duration.[23]

The aim of studies in the field of pricing policy must surely be to arrive at practical recommendations. But it is prudent to refrain from making them in an analysis not based on detailed quantitative data. Although it is believed that the present analysis does point to practical conclusions of some importance, its purpose should be taken, not primarily as prescriptive, but rather as indicating the problems which arise in attempting to apply optimum pricing criteria to a particular industry.

23. This statement applies to true off-peak periods. In practice trunk lines are sometimes fully occupied at cheap-rate periods, which is a peak, not an off-peak condition.

8 M. Crew

Electricity Tariffs

Abridged from M. Crew, *Pennine electricity board: A study in tariff pricing* (Bradford Exercises in Management, No. 8), Thomas Nelson, 1966.

Supply of Electricity to P.E.B.

The Pennine Electricity Board (P.E.B.) serves some $1\frac{1}{2}$ million consumers with power in an area stretching up the centre of England. Its customers include a large conurbation, many smaller and medium-size towns, and country districts. It has the responsibility of dealing with certain matters of a non-commercial nature such as questions of amenity and the supply of electricity to outlying country districts.

Besides having to undertake certain social obligations it has financial obligations agreed with the Government, along with the rest of the industry, as a result of the 1961 White Paper, 'The financial and economic obligations of nationalized industries'. The agreed gross return on net assets is meant to take into account the extent of P.E.B.'s non-commercial obligations and is fixed at 12·1 per cent per annum for the five-year period 1962–7. It is reviewed annually and has every prospect of being increased in view of the massive demand for capital from the industry and the Government's desire to get its own expenditure under control. This point will arise again in the discussion of the problem of tariffs.

The P.E.B. has a monopoly of power distribution in its area. Put simply, P.E.B. and its fierce competitor, the Gas Board, are the only undertakings apart from the Water Boards with a basic statutory right to dig up the streets. It has no monopoly of electricity generation, however. Some big firms in its area do in fact generate electricity for their own use and sell their surplus to the national grid which is owned by the P.E.B.'s main supplier, the Central Electricity Generating Board (C.E.G.B.).

The bulk of the electricity produced in England and Wales

comes from C.E.G.B. which supplies the P.E.B. under the terms listed in its two-part Bulk Supply Tariff.

Before the provisions of the Bulk Supply Tariff are examined it is necessary to look at certain features of the C.E.G.B.'s operations. The C.E.G.B. operates 233 power stations as an integrated system, in merit order, a basically simple procedure. The underlying principle is that stations are operated according to their efficiency – those with lowest running costs for longest, and those with highest running costs for as short a time as possible. Thus as demand at any moment increases the C.E.G.B. brings in less and less efficient plants. Likewise if demand is falling it cuts out its least efficient plant. Base load will be met with its newest and most efficient plant. This means that the C.E.G.B. produces electricity at the lowest possible cost from its system at any given level of demand. Indeed this is one of the advantages of an integrated system.

Existing C.E.G.B. bulk supply tariff

The terms of the bulk supply tariff, for the year ending 31 March 1967, were announced by the C.E.G.B. on 3 March 1966. Table 1 shows the provisions of the tariff.

Table 1
Current C.E.G.B. Bulk Supply Tariff

Total capacity charge for 1966–67	£370·9m

Unit charges
0·6d. per unit supplied during the 16 hours 07.00 to 23.00.
0·47d. per unit supplied during the 8 hours 23.00 to 07.00.

Fuel cost adjustment 0·000485d. per unit per penny variation in the cost of fuel from 85s. per ton.

The *fuel cost adjustment rate* takes into account any variation in the fuel costs incurred by the C.E.G.B. in generating the electricity it supplies to an area board from a basic 85s. per ton. The *capacity charge* is payable by all area boards in proportion to their contributions to system peaks in the past two tariff-years.

Thus under the terms of the bulk supply tariff each area board contributes to the C.E.G.B.'s capacity charges according to its share of system peak demand. As can be seen from Table 1 the C.E.G.B. determines the amount it requires to meet its anticipated fixed costs, and irrespective of actual system peak demand achieved this amount must be collected. This means that if system peak is smaller than anticipated the area boards pay more per kilowatt, and if it is greater than anticipated they pay less per kilowatt. In either case the C.E.G.B. collects in full! This is a quite reasonable provision since, if the C.E.G.B. were merely to anticipate maximum demand and fix a price per kilowatt, in years of bad weather it would make a great profit – and the area boards would make big losses – while in years of mild weather the reverse would happen. At least under this present arrangement both sides know where they stand in advance.

The bulk supply tariff has evolved over several years and has gradually become more and more sophisticated. Originally it merely charged area boards according to their individual maximum demands between 07.00 and 19.00. Because one area board had its individual peak at week-ends (that is at a time when the C.E.G.B. system was nowhere near peak demand), it was eventually modified to exclude week-ends. Since 1962–3, when the tariff was changed, each area board has paid according to its share of C.E.G.B. system peak. (The actual amount payable in any year is based on the average of an area board's contribution to two system peaks – the first prior to 31 December and the second after 31 December.) At the same time provision was also made for 'special consumers'. These were larger consumers who were prepared to make reductions in their demands at certain times and as a result received appropriate concessions.

However, the current tariff must not be allowed to escape criticism altogether. The C.E.G.B. itself appears to have a critical attitude towards it. In fact, it has announced various changes to come into force on 1 April 1967.

Chairmen of the area boards have themselves expressed concern with certain features of the tariff. For instance, criticisms have been made of the fact that the capacity charge is payable on the average of contributions to system peak over *two* occasions. Although this provision was incorporated into the tariff to protect the individual boards from the worst effects of excessively bad weather, it is argued that this averaging arrangement would in fact result in a gain for certain boards with widely divergent peaks. The day and night differential on the unit charge has also been criticized because some boards, against their better judgement, have had to make a similar reduction to their consumers.

New C.E.G.B. bulk supply tariff

On 12 May 1966 the C.E.G.B. announced its own reforms in the tariff structure, to be effective from April 1967. This new tariff replaces the single capacity charge based on the share of system peak of each area board by two capacity charges; one for peaking kilowatts and the other related to the cost of basic system capacity

Table 2
New C.E.G.B. Bulk Supply Tariff

Capacity charges

Peaking capacity charge: 10 per cent of the forecast system maximum demand sent out for the Area Boards, adopted by the industry for the year of account for which the tariff applies, at about £4 per kilowatt.
Basic capacity charge: The remaining 90 per cent at something over £10 per kilowatt.

Unit charges

A peak-period running rate for each unit supplied between 08.00 and 12.00 and between 16.30 and 18.30 during December and January, excluding Saturdays, Sundays, Christmas Day, and Boxing Day (250 hr. to 260 hr.).
A day running rate for each unit supplied between 07.00 and 23.00 throughout the year, excluding units charged at the above peak period running rate (about 5,600 hr.).
A night-period running rate for each unit supplied between 23.00 and 07.00 at night throughout the year (about 2,900 hr.).

---

used for meeting loads of longer duration. In addition to the day and night unit rates of the present tariff, a *third* unit rate for all units supplied during specified short daytime periods in December and January is to be introduced. The new tariff can be seen in Table 2. The basic capacity charge will be something over £10 per kilowatt; the C.E.G.B. has yet to announce the precise figure.

The aims of the new bulk supply tariff are thus clear: costs are to be more closely reflected. The new unit charges are an attempt to collect the marginal cost of each unit according to the time it is produced. It is getting somewhere near the economist's concept of marginal unit cost being exactly covered by the marginal unit revenue.

One claim for pricing according to marginal cost is that it leads to a more efficient allocation of resources. Under the current tariff there has been a considerable incentive for an area board to install its own peak lopping plant since the C.E.G.B.'s capacity charge has been based on the average costs per kilowatt of capacity. As an average it has hidden the great variation in running costs for the various kinds of plant, and the low capital costs of peak plant have been totally obscured. Under the current tariff area boards have been charged much more than cost for the last units of demand, thus encouraging them to make their own arrangements. However, these might not fit in with the economic supply of electricity, since they would tend to encourage the installation of a more than economic amount of gas turbines since the alternative costs of them (as paid by the Boards to C.E.G.B.) are distorted by the current tariff. The new tariff gets over this difficulty and removes the incentive to an area board to install its own gas turbine plant for peak lopping, and thereby leads to a more efficient allocation of resources.

The other change that will be introduced in the new tariff, although it will take several years to implement, concerns the fuel cost variation between areas which was used previously. This variation has been shrinking as nuclear power has been introduced, and the grid has been used to concentrate generation in cheap fuel areas. The C.E.G.B., in fact, proposes to discontinue the present annual recalculation of the different area fuel factors and will introduce predetermined factors until 1970–71. These will gradually converge although unity may not be achieved for some years.

Sale of Electricity by P.E.B.

As indicated earlier, the P.E.B. has certain obligations to its customers imposed by statute. These obligations affect its freedom in framing its own customer tariff structure. The P.E.B.'s responsibilities are, to quote the 1947 Electricity Act, 'to secure as far as practicable, the . . . cheapening of supplies of electricity; to promote the simplification and standardization of methods of charge for such supplies; and to avoid showing undue preference to any person or class of persons'. In addition the industry accepts the principle in the Report of the Committee on National Policy for the Use of Fuel and Power Resources that tariffs should 'as closely as practicable' reflect the costs of supply. This latter obligation directly conflicts with the statutory aim to simplify and standardize tariffs. Different classes of consumers have differing load characteristics and any resulting tariff structure can hardly be simple and standardized. Each individual tariff is fairly easily understood by the customer but the total tariff structure can become somewhat complex. (Appendix A gives the P.E.B.'s current customer tariff structure.)

Table 3
P.E.B.'s Financial Performance 1962–5

	1962–63 £m	1963–64 £m	1964–65 £m	Average £m
Depreciation and other capital provisions	3·5	4·0	4·5	4·0
Interest	3·4	3·9	4·9	4·0
Balance of revenue	1·3	1·2	3·4	2·0
Total	8·2	9·1	12·8	10·0
Net capital employed (average of amounts at beginning and end of year)	88·1	101·0	119·0	102·7
Gross return	9·3%	9·0%	10·8%	9·8%

The P.E.B. has this structure urgently under review for several reasons, the most important being its failure to meet the financial obligations resulting from the 1961 White Paper. For many years the P.E.B. sold some of the cheapest electricity in the country, yet despite recently increased tariffs, Table 3 shows it has still not managed to achieve the required 12·1 per cent return for the period.

To achieve the 12·1 per cent return required for the period 1962–7, the P.E.B.'s advisers have indicated the targets given in Table 4.

Table 4

P.E.B.'s Financial Targets 1965–7

	1965–66 £m	1966–67 £m	Total 1962–67 £m
Depreciation	6·5	8·1	26·6
Interest	6·4	8·4	27·0
Balance of revenue	5·2	8·5	19·6
Total	18·1	25·0	73·2
Net capital	139·1	157·5	604·7
Gross return	13·0%	15·9%	12·1%

The P.E.B.'s management is divided on the best way to achieve these targets. A recently appointed economist favours a new customer tariff structure which reflects costs more closely. He has in mind a time-of-day tariff. Some senior colleagues support him, including the marketing manager who has charge of statistical analysis and forecasting. All the engineers are against his ideas.

P.E.B.'s present tariff structure[1]

The present rationale of the P.E.B.'s consumer tariff making, in addition to the basic principles already outlined, requires that costs be divided into three categories:

Consumer related costs
Unit related costs
Demand related costs

1. J. L. Leson in his 'Fixing electricity tariffs', *Electrical Power Engineers Journal,*' June, July, August 1963, has explained in some detail the basic principles behind the construction of tariffs by an area electricity board.

The P.E.B.'s tariffs (given as Appendix A) aim to recover all these costs in full for the class of consumer to whom any individual tariff applies. Although an individual consumer may be undercharged or overcharged for his consumption, the class of consumers to which he belongs pays the full cost of its consumption. The only subsidization outside classes is for consumers in outlying districts. Thus, the P.E.B.'s first principle of tariff making is to divide consumers into classes on the basis of load characteristics. The second principle is a division of costs into the categories described above.

Consumer related costs are those which will be incurred no matter how large or how small the number of units consumed – e.g., billing and collection, connexion, consumer service. For domestic consumers these are recovered by a charge for the initial block of 68 units at 6d. less 1·75d. For many domestic users the consumer related charges constitute the major part of their bill. Some, in fact, never fully pay them where their consumption falls below 68 units a quarter – this is one of the social obligations that the P.E.B. undertakes. For the industrial maximum demand tariffs consumer related costs are so small a proportion of total costs that they can be ignored as a separate item in the tariff formula.

Unit related costs are those which vary directly with the number of units consumed. If a consumer needs a given amount of energy this fixes the number of units he requires. As far as the P.E.B. is concerned such costs are made up mainly of the fuel costs of generation, a small part of distribution costs, and certain other works costs of generation and main transmission.

Demand related costs vary with the level at which a user consumes the energy, the cost of which is covered in the unit related charges. Because electricity cannot be stored on any scale demand must be met when it occurs. Consumers who require energy at system peak or contribute to a distribution peak on the P.E.B.'s system are charged through demand related costs.

While we have now described the basic thinking behind the P.E.B.'s tariffs its application to an example requires the introduction of the concept of *diversity*. Consumers do not all make their peak demands at the same time. At the time of the P.E.B.'s peak demand very few individual consumers will also be having their own peak demand for the year. The sum of all individual maxima in the groups, as measured by the relatively simple maximum demand meters, far exceeds the group peak. The diversity factor of a group is described as the ratio of the sum of individual maxima to group maximum.

Table 5 gives the total costs of the board and how they are

Table 5

Analysis of the P.E.B.'s Costs

	Total costs £m	Demand related (X) £m	Unit related (Y) £m	Consumer related (Z) £m
Generation and maintenance	51·0	23·1	27·9	—
Distribution	4·3	3·3	0·7	0·3
Consumer service	2·1	—	—	2·1
Meter reading, billing, etc.	1·4	—	—	1·4
Administration and general	1·5	0·5	—	1·0
Training and welfare	0·7	0·3	—	0·4
Rents, rates, and insurances	1·5	1·1	—	0·4
Contribution to Electricity Council	0·2	0·1	—	0·1
Depreciation	6·5	4·5	—	2·0
Interest and balance of revenue	11·6	10·1	—	1·5
Total	80·8	43·0	28·6	9·2

allocated under the various headings. It is now necessary to see how these work out for the various classes of consumers. It is assumed, for purposes of explanation and simplicity, that there are only three categories of consumer – industrial, domestic, and others (Table 6).

Elements of cost

$$\frac{240Y}{M} = 0·58\text{d. per unit} \qquad \frac{X}{1,000P} = \text{£18 per kilowatt}$$

$$\frac{Z}{Q} = \text{£4·73 per consumer}$$

Thus the following basic cost formula can be arrived at:

Demand cost + unit cost + consumer cost

$$\text{Total cost (£)} = 18K + \frac{0{\cdot}58U}{240} + 4{\cdot}73C$$

where K = demand in kilowatts, U = units, and C = consumers.

Table 6

P.E.B.'s Costs for Tariff Making

Class of consumers	Units (M) Millions	Contribution to P.E.B.'s peak load as defined above (P) Megawatts	Weighted number of consumers (Q)
Other	2,930	590	342,000
Domestic	3,450	990	1,321,000
Industrial	5,420	810	284,000
Total	11,800	2,390	1,947,000

Industrial loads will be examined first. Consumer costs may be ignored for the moment since they are small in relation to total costs. The pence cost per unit can be derived by the following formula:

$$d = \text{pence cost per unit} = \frac{18 \times 240K}{U} + 0{\cdot}58$$

But $\dfrac{100U}{8{,}760K} = L$ = load factor as a percentage

(U is multiplied by 100 to give a percentage. K is multiplied by 8,760 since there are 8,760 hr in a year.)

$$\frac{8{,}760}{100} \times \frac{K}{U} = \frac{1}{L} \qquad \frac{K}{U} = \frac{100}{8{,}760L}$$

Let d = cost per unit in pence. Then

$$d = \frac{18 \times 240 \times 100}{8{,}760L} + 0{\cdot}58$$

$$= \frac{49{\cdot}32}{L} + 0{\cdot}58 = 1{\cdot}0732$$

where L = 100 per cent.

Thus the link between load factor and cost per unit is apparent. In very general terms

$$d = \frac{a}{L} + b$$

where a and b are both constants, b being the unit related costs and a the constant calculated above.

The above formula would give the exact answer. The consumer's charge would be determined by his load factor alone. However, these calculations assume no diversity of individual maxima. They accordingly require modification wherever load factors are less than 100 per cent. Experience and research by the P.E.B.'s engineers have revealed that consumers with a load factor of 10 per cent have a diversity factor of 2; accordingly the correct tariff for these consumers provides for a demand related charge of one half of the £18 calculated. A tariff which recovers the costs of both consumers of 100 per cent load factor and 10 per cent load factor can be achieved by altering the demand charge per kilowatt, and increasing the unit charge. Such a tariff may collect the correct revenue for consumers with 100 per cent and 10 per cent load factors but it does not necessarily collect the correct revenue for the other load factors. Therefore if the load factors and diversities between these points are examined it can be discovered how closely the tariff comes to collecting the correct revenue. The P.E.B.'s way round this difficulty has been to introduce 'steps' into their two-part tariff to get as close as it considers desirable to reflecting the costs of groups at selected load factors over a wide range.

It will be remembered that the current C.E.G.B. bulk supply tariff has a fuel cost adjustment clause. Since fuel price plays an important role in unit related charges it is customary for the maximum demand tariff to include a fuel variation clause which allows for changes in the price of fuel.

With domestic consumers it is assumed that the effective load factor of the group is 38 per cent. It is also apparent that the domestic consumers' load factor does not improve with increased consumption and so their annual consumption is a good measure of their effective demands. Demand related charges are accordingly recovered in the unit rate. Thus the tariff is:

Fixed charge of £4·73 per year. This is recovered quarterly in the initial block of 68 units at 6d.

Unit charge of 1·75d.

    Consisting of: Demand related 1·17d.
               Unit related   0·58d.

Domestic off peak tariffs are fixed on similar principles. Their cheapness comes from the fact that demand related costs are, by the very definition of off-peak, negligible. A small element of demand related distribution costs is normally included plus an insurance element to cover any further reinforcement of the distribution system. For most of the off-peak period the C.E.G.B. operates its most efficient plant and offers the P.E.B. bulk supplies at 0·13d. per unit less than the price in other periods.

Other considerations sometimes have to be taken into account in framing off-peak tariffs. For instance load at one off-peak period may be growing faster than load at other off-peak periods. It will need to be monitored in case the former off-peak period should become a possible peak period and accordingly unsuitable for special treatment in the form of a lower price.

Criticism from the new economist

The new economist criticizes the existing P.E.B. tariffs for several reasons.

1. He argues that while the tariffs recover total cost quite accurately they do not cover costs within classes nearly accurately enough. The division between classes, based on experience of load characteristics, is neither detailed nor accurate enough, especially for domestic consumers. Within this class there is extensive cross subsidization. The domestic consumer who uses electricity for intermittent space heating which occurs mainly during peak periods, but gas for cooking and water heating, almost certainly pays less than it costs the industry to supply him. The probability is great that his maximum demand is at or near the system peak. His summer consumption is negligible. The loss in supplying him has to be made up by consumers with a more even consumption all the year round, e.g. those using electric cooking but not electric space heating.

2. He argues that the present structure gives consumers no

incentive to bring their interest into line with those of the industry. Consumers do not realize the extra costs involved when they consume electricity at 18.00 on a cold winter's evening. They pay the same price as they pay for electricity on a warm summer's evening. Mere exhortations to economize during a cold spell are not enough.

3. He claims that the present tariff structure is far too complicated and suggests that a tariff which would apply to all classes of consumers, with variations only in the standing charges, is far simpler.

Alternatives considered

In his review the economist has considered several alternatives to the present structure:

Installed load rate. This consists of a unit rate plus a standing charge related to the number of kilowatts of load installed on the premises. He rejected this on the grounds that it would be administratively expensive and would do nothing to discourage switching on at system peak. It might also discourage the purchase of appliances.

Subscribed demand tariff. Here there is a unit charge and a standing charge for an agreed or subscribed demand. A current breaker has to be installed to stop him taking more. He rejected this because he felt that it would discourage activities like electric cooking and water heating, and because the load limiters required would add extra consumer costs. In addition, since the majority of domestic consumers have their maximum demands outside system peak times the gains from them at system peak would be small but the losses at other times great.

Seasonal tariff. He rejected this as a basis of charging by itself since a high winter rate would discourage sales at times when there is spare capacity.

Load-rate tariff. This is used extensively in Norway where there is extensive hydroelectric power available. It might also be useful in a system with a substantial proportion of nuclear power. It is a development of the subscribed demand tariff. The consumer pays a standing charge, related to his estimated annual demand. When his load is below the maximum of his subscribed demand he pays at a low rate. When it rises above this he pays a surcharge for the excess units. This tariff involves installing a meter costing about £10 with two dials, one for high rate and one for low rate. An indicator is also desirable to show the consumer what his demand is at any given time. He is then able to switch off appliances to cut down demand. This, however, could have the disadvantage of limiting consumption at times when plenty of spare capacity was available, and of reducing diversity.

In its simple form the economist rejected it, but he considered that, with an arrangement which relaxed the subscribed demand restriction during off-peak periods, it might be worthy of consideration.

Time-of-day tariff. Examination of both the P.E.B.'s and the C.E.G.B.'s load curves reveals the way such a tariff would operate. It would charge a high price when the system was fully loaded and a low price when lightly loaded. For intermediate loads it would charge intermediate prices depending on whether load was growing more quickly or less quickly than average. Thus the aim of such a tariff would be to reduce the peak and transfer some of the consumption to other periods as well as trying to attract entirely new loads.

Tariff recommended for P.E.B.

The tariff which the new economist recommends incorporates features of both seasonal and time-of-day alternatives (see Table 7). It attempts to take into account the price elasticity of various loads, e.g., individual peak loads regarded as fairly inelastic bear a large charge. Individual off-peak loads, however, are judged not only on their price elasticity but also on the extent to which they are growing. An afternoon off-peak load which was growing quickly would not be priced far below the peak load charge. (See both C.E.G.B. and the P.E.B.'s load curves in figures 1 and 2.) During the night, on the other hand, there is plenty of spare capacity and rapid growth here would be a useful way of increasing sales.

Fixed charges. All block tariffs would be abolished and replaced by tariffs comprising a fixed charge and a unit charge. Domestic

271

consumers would pay an additional £4 10s. fixed charge a year to cover the extra metering costs over and above the existing block charge which amounts to £4 15s. a year. The other classes of consumer would pay according to size with a minimum extra payment of £4 10s.

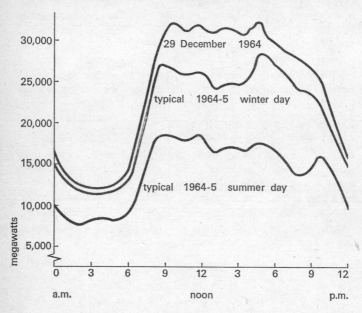

Figure 1 Summer and winter demands on C.E.G.B. system 1964-5

High voltage. The preceding charges are for low voltage supplies. High voltage consumers get a reduction of 0·036d. per unit.

Debate on the economist's tariff

The economist arrived at the structure shown after taking into account the C.E.G.B.'s new bulk supply tariff. His aim is to make consumers pay according to the strength of their demands. Thus the peak users would have to absorb most of the capacity costs at 4·95d. per unit for the months mid-November to mid-February. The aim of this charge is to reduce the amount payable under the

272

bulk supply tariff through reductions in the peak. The charge of
1·85d. per unit aims at giving mild discouragement to demands
which make up the winter plateau, and which are therefore

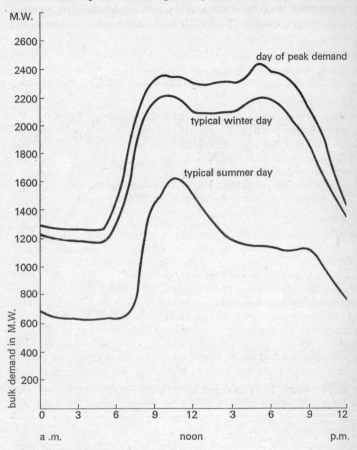

Figure 2

chargeable under the C.E.G.B.'s basic capacity charge. He is
particularly dissatisfied with the P.E.B.'s present off-peak tariffs
which give demand a boost in the afternoon. He argues that the
P.E.B. has no afternoon 'slack' worth taking up and neither has

the system much to spare. He is also concerned that this demand seems to be growing quickly in the P.E.B.'s area through the sale of storage heaters requiring a three-hour afternoon boost. He argues that these consumers now ought to pay the costs involved in supplying them but should be allowed the alternative of reduc-

Table 7

P.E.B. Economist's Proposed Tariff

Winter rates

All units supplied from 20.30 to 08.00 0·64d. per unit

All units supplied from 12.00 to 16.30 ⎫
All units supplied from 18.30 to 20.30 ⎬ 1·85d. per unit

All units supplied from 08.00 to 12.00 ⎫
All units supplied from 16.30 to 18.30 ⎬ 4·95d. per unit

At week-ends, Christmas Day, and Boxing Day the above does not apply. All units are charged at 0·64d. at these times.

Summer rates

Winter rates only apply in the months of November, December, January, and February. At other times the following summer rates apply:

All units supplied from 12.00 to 16.30 ⎫
All units supplied from 18.30 to 08.00 ⎬ 0·64d. per unit

All units supplied from 08.00 to 12.00 ⎫
All units supplied from 16.30 to 18.30 ⎬ 1·15d. per unit

---

ing their consumption in the afternoon as a means of saving. With cheap units available at night, the sale of appliances with greater heat storage qualities should be encouraged in this way. He also argues that water heated by electricity can be made very attractive in this way even for consumers with gas central heating!

His plan for the revision of the P.E.B.'s tariffs involves an entirely new approach for a British nationalized industry. Partly because of this he realizes the need for a large advertising campaign aimed at educating the consumer. He aims to show consumers, including industrial consumers, how they can benefit most from the new tariff. Two kinds of load are to be encouraged

– storage heating with the emphasis on appliances that do not need an afternoon boost, and water heating by consumers presently using another fuel for both central and water heating in the winter. These are just the types of load that the P.E.B. can supply easily and the summer rate distinctly encourages this.

He claims that his tariff brings the interests of consumers into line with those of the P.E.B. The consumer under the tariff now realizes that it does not cost the P.E.B. a uniform amount to supply him irrespective of the time of day or time of year. Whilst claiming to ensure that the price a consumer pays never falls below marginal cost to the P.E.B. his basic formula is arrived at by pricing according to demand. Marginal costs merely provide a reference point below which the P.E.B. would refuse to sell. To this extent the tariff is discriminatory – it attempts to charge what the traffic will bear – and as such perhaps goes against the obligations outlined earlier. However, the P.E.B.'s present tariff structure is already discriminatory – it discriminates against all-year-round, or mainly off-peak, consumers.

The economist contends that his proposed tariff will bring considerable savings although under the C.E.G.B.'s bulk supply tariff they will not be as substantial as those accruing under the bulk supply tariff which remains in force until 31 March 1967. By March 1967 only some 50,000 of the largest consumers will have been equipped with time-of-day meters. This should yield an initial saving in the P.E.B.'s share of system peak demand of $1\frac{1}{2}$ per cent. The saving in later years could reach a 10 per cent cut in peak demand by the time all time-of-day meters had been installed. Under the C.E.G.B.'s new bulk supply tariff the gain will, however, be more than halved. This explains why the winter midday/early evening unit charge is relatively high at 1·85d. pe unit in the hope of reducing the winter plateau, or at worst slowing down its rate of growth. Although savings here are likely to be fairly small, about 2 per cent, it is suggested that they can be increased by increasing this rate. In any event savings at such times should increase as those loads which are currently attracted by off-peak tariffs will no longer be attracted. Instead, the consumer will get very cheap electricity at the week-ends, at night, and in the summer, when there is virtually no chance that such consumption will incur any of the bulk supply tariff's basic capacity charge. The economist hopes for a growth of demand in these periods of around 15 per cent per year when his tariff is fully operational. He expects the P.E.B.'s load factor to rise to nearer 70 per cent.

It is readily admitted that the metering costs will be very high (approximately £25 per consumer); a little less when existing metering and time switches can be adapted. None the less these may well fall with an increase in the scale of meter production. The new system will also provide the opportunity for the introduction of mechanized billing (as with G.P.O.'s S.T.D. telephone accounts), thereby saving the costs of meter reading.

Finally the economist argues that this tariff will be acceptable (again citing the G.P.O. tariff which varies according to time-of-day and distance). The P.E.B. will be given the chance of selling those loads which it has an advantage in selling, thereby utilizing its capacity more fully.

The engineers argue strongly against the tariff for many reasons:

1. They argue that the cost of the metering equipment involved will be very high. Their estimates vary from anything between £30 and £60 capital cost, plus maintenance.

2. They suggest that although the assumption behind the prices of the tariff takes into account present and future demand it is almost impossible to make such estimates with the forecasting techniques available.

3. They would rather the industry spent the money involved on new plant to enable it to supply the consumers with more power rather than spend a lot of money on restricting them.

4. They feel that the proposals would exacerbate an already severe manpower problem. The P.E.B. is currently 50 electricians below its establishment and this proposal would require many more men to fit the new metering equipment. They feel that the P.E.B. must either recruit many more men, or cut down on its other activities such as its trade in fittings and appliances. Alternatively, the installations could be simplified and the P.E.B. could recruit and train labour for this specific purpose. However, this would need the co-operation of the trade union. Such a task could not be performed quickly. The waiting list, or a limit on

size of consumer who was to be connected, would make for bad public relations.

5. They argue that the extra consumer related costs would be high and that the consumer would have no incentive to incur them.

6. They argue that the new tariff is discriminatory and not as fair as the present tariff which collects costs exactly for the class of consumers concerned. They argue that the economist is trying to make the P.E.B. act like a private discriminating monopolist.

7. Finally they will not accept that the failings the economist attributes to their tariffs are as significant as he makes out.

The marketing manager also has his reservations. He feels that the engineers' point 5 is particularly valid, especially at a time when the local Anglian Gas Board is pushing its sales of gas very hard with the great finds of natural gas just off the coast. The Gas Board now offers a very attractive tariff especially for space heating (see Table 8), and is also holding out the prospect of even cheaper gas as more natural gas is pumped ashore.

Table 8
Anglian Gas Board's Tariffs

Quarterly standing charges	Price per therm
£1 10s. 0d.	1s. 3d.
£2 5s. 0d.	1s. 1½d.
£7 0s. 0d.	1s. 0d.
£45 0s. 0d.	11d.

He believes that the time-of-day tariff may be too complicated to be communicated effectively to the consumer in the face of cheap gas and a simple gas tariff.

However, the competitive position of the P.E.B.'s product is most worrying. At present prices it is nowhere near competitive with the Anglian Gas Board for unrestricted heating. For storage heating it is only just about competitive, taking into account the lower installation costs of storage heaters. He feels that the new tariff could give the P.E.B. the competitive edge on the Anglian Gas Board for storage heating especially since it can now be supplemented at certain times by low cost electricity. Around eight in the evening storage heaters often need supplementing from other room heaters and under the new tariff they could be used with advantage. He also feels, along with the economist, that water heating by electricity can now be sold very much more easily.

The marketing manager is therefore prepared to co-operate and try using the proposed tariff to sell the P.E.B.'s products. He gives a simple calculation to show its competitive position with regard to the Anglian Gas Board on central heating. He wants to sell on the basis of this claim.

Electricity at 0·64d. per unit consumed at 95 per cent efficiency in storage heaters: cost per useful therm   19.75d.

Gas at 1s. 1½d. per therm consumed at 70 per cent efficiency in gas boiler/warm air unit: cost per useful therm   19·29d.

Electricity at 0·64d. for other uses at 100 per cent efficiency: cost per useful therm   18·76d.

Taking into account the higher initial capital cost of gas and the gas standing charges which are avoided with an all-electric house, he feels that electricity is now demonstrably competitive.

In the not far distant future when gas will undoubtedly secure a further cheapening of its supply, the electricity supply industry will have a hard job to compete. The marketing manager believes the new tariff may be a powerful weapon in the domestic market. The new tariff may also prove more suitable for the industrial consumer, by abolishing the high kilowatt demand charge about which many industrialists have complained and by giving industry the choice of economizing at certain times and making appropriate savings.

Thus the economist faces some significant opposition. His replies to the various points made by the engineers are as follows:

1. He can get a firm tender for metering of £30.

2. He admits the inaccuracies that may occur in forecasting but claims his forecasts are very pessimistic.

3. Compared to the capital cost of new plant, the cost of metering is low. The national industry at present invests about £700m. per year. If half the consumers were given meters for a time-of-day tariff it might eventually cost about £225m. to £250m., as the very numerous small consumers would never be equipped with them.

4. He thinks that manpower is the greatest difficulty.

5. On the contrary, the consumer will have every incentive when he has understood that he can benefit greatly from the proposed tariff.

6. The higher priced units are not thought to be sufficiently high to make industrial consumers think it worth installing gas turbines.

7. The old tariff structure is discriminatory along the lines already explained. Both his proposals and the present tariff have a problem of overhead allocation. He regards his proposals as providing a more efficient allocation, and casts doubts on the justice of charging a consumer with a very high load factor (say 100 per cent) the demand related cost of a system working at 50 per cent load factor. Finally, he says that the industry is being exposed to increasing competition which his tariff acknowledges.

Appendix A: P.E.B. tariffs

For convenience a distinction is made between the block and two-part tariffs although the former is only another version of the latter unless consumption is very low. Where consumption is low the block tariff involves payment of less than the full standing charges. The block tariff then has the feature of putting an upper limit on the rate per unit at which electricity is purchased.

Except where otherwise stated the charges are on a quarterly basis. Overseas readers should note that P.E.B. is imaginary.

Block Tariffs

Domestic tariff

6d. per unit for first 68 units
1·75d. per unit for the remainder

There is a surcharge of 8s. per quarter for those consumers using a prepayment meter.

Farm tariff

The same as domestic except 180 units are added to the first block at 6d.

Commercial tariff

6d. per unit for the first 150 units
3d. per unit for the next 700 units
1·85d. per unit for the remainder

Industrial tariff

(This requires that the load does not exceed 50 kVA)
6d. per unit for first 600 units
1·85d. per unit for the remainder

Churches, public halls, and meeting houses tariff

6d. per unit for the first 150 units
3d. per unit for the next 200 units
The remainder at 0·95d. if taken during the hours 18.45 to 08.00 during week-days, or at any time during the week-end, or 2d. per unit if taken at any other time.

Public lighting tariff

4d. per unit for the first 1,000 units
1d. per unit for the remainder

Commercial catering

1·65d. per unit for all units

Two-part tariffs and maximum demand tariffs

Industrial maximum tariffs

Annual demand charge	High voltage	Low voltage
For each of the first 300 kVA. of max. demand	£7 4s. 0d.	£7 10s. 0d.
For each of the next 200 kVA. of max. demand	£6 18s. 0d.	£7 4s. 0d.
For each of the next 400 kVA. of max. demand	£6 11s. 0d.	£6 18s. 0d.
For each of the next 900 kVA. of max. demand	£6 3s. 0d.	£6 11s. 0d.
Unit charge		
For each of the first 1,752 units supplied per kVA of maximum demand in that year	1·0d.	1·03d.
For the next 1,752	0·882d.	0·912d.
Remainder	0·846d.	0·876d.

Fuel adjustment

The payment in respect of each month shall be subject to an addition or reduction of 0·0005d. for high voltage supplies, and 0·00053d. for low voltage supplies, per unit supplied in that month. It is computed on each penny by which the invoiced cost per ton of fuel used for the supply of electricity in bulk by the C.E.G.B. to the P.E.B. in the previous month exceeds or falls below 85s. per ton.

Night units

A reduction of 0·13d. will be allowed for each unit supplied in the period 23.00 to 07.00 provided the consumer pays the P.E.B. a rental sufficient to cover the extra costs it incurs with metering, and for the time switches necessary to enable the reduction to be calculated.

The Industrial Maximum Demand Tariff applies to all but the P.E.B.'s smaller industrial consumers, and justifies more expensive metering. (A maximum demand in kilovolt-amperes, because certain industrial loads place a demand on the system which is not registered on a meter recording kilowatt hours.) Area boards which use a demand tariff in terms of kilowatts have to specify some power factor.

Restricted Hour Tariffs

It is important to note that these are tariffs which are available by arrangement with the P.E.B. with regard to satisfactory wiring and with regard to use which they are put. Normally they are only available for storage heating, water storage heating, and battery charging. Charges vary inversely with amount of restriction accepted.

In all three cases standing charges of 8s. 6d. per quarter apply:

1. A charge of 0·65d. per unit with supply restricted to the period 23.00 to 07.00 and unrestricted at week-ends.
2. A charge of 0·7d. per unit with supply restricted to the period 19.00 to 07.00, and unrestricted at week-ends.
3. A charge of 0·8d. per unit with supply restricted to the period 19.00 to 07.00 and 13.00 to 16.00, and unrestricted at week-ends.

Appendix B: Glossary of technical and economic terms

Discrimination. When the relative prices charged for various units of product are disproportionate to the relative cost of these units.

Diversity. The concept that all individual demand maxima will not coincide. Total simultaneous maximum demand or system peak is therefore less than the sum of individual demand maxima.

Load factor. This is a means of measuring the extent of the use of capacity by a consumer. The system load factor is the ratio, expressed as a percentage of (i) units of electricity supplied through the system in a year to (ii) the number which would have been supplied if maximum demand had been maintained for all the 8,760 hours of the year.

Peak. Maximum demand in kilowatts measured over half an hour. System peak is the maximum simultaneous demand on the C.E.G.B.'s system in any year. Distribution peak is the maximum demand on an area board's distribution network. Any given distribution system has to be made big enough to meet the peak demand on it. Thus where a lot of storage heaters are installed the distribution peak may be intensified and reinforcement may be needed.

$$Power\ factor = \frac{useful\ power\ in\ kilowatts\ absorbed\ by\ a\ load}{kilovolt\text{-}amperes}$$

Price elasticity. The relationship between quantity demanded and price. Where price is reduced and quantity demanded increases in greater proportion than the cut in the price, demand is said to be elastic.

Unit. Equivalent to a kilowatt of load of one hour's duration (kWh.).

Volt-ampere. Measures the apparent power (VA.).

Watt. The unit of electric power. The rate at which 'work' is done when current flows in an electrical circuit is measured in watts (W.).

The prefixes *kilo* or *mega* mean one thousand and one million respectively.

Part Three Case Studies of Performance

These four studies have been chosen to show how economists can analyse the performance of public enterprises. The first three provide some incidental information about the cost structure and pricing problems of postal services, coal-mining, and telephones. The final paper by Simon is one of the very few systematic comparisons between state and public enterprise and offers a stimulating reminder that public enterprises are not confined to the fields dealt with in the rest of the book.

9 J. Keith Horsefield

British and American Postal Services

J. Keith Horsefield, 'Some notes on postal finance', *Bulletin of the Oxford University Institute of Economics and Statistics*, vol. 26 (1964), pp. 39–58.

I

Recent public discussions of the problems of the postal services in the United States and in this country suggest some reflections on the similarities and differences between the American postal services and our own. The similarities are perhaps less apparent than the differences, but they are no less significant. That there are large differences is obvious. In the United Kingdom, as in most of Europe, the postal service is administered by a department which is also responsible for telegraphs and telephones, whereas in the United States the two latter are run by private enterprise. Again, as the United States is so much larger a country than the United Kingdom, it is natural that the volume of mail handled by the U.S. Post Office should also be larger – though, in fact, with a population three and a half times that of the United Kingdom, the United States sends more than six times as much through the mails, the figures for 1961–2 being respectively 10,833 million and 65,987 million 'pieces'.

A third difference is that the United Kingdom has nearly always made a profit on its postal services, whereas for many years the United States has made a large loss.[1] Ignoring the remittance and agency services, as we shall throughout, the results for 1961–2 were a profit of £0·3 million in the United Kingdom, and a loss equivalent to about £280 million in the United States.

---

1. Since this article was written the United Kingdom record has been blemished by three years of heavy postal losses – 1962–3 (£8·1 million), 1963–4 (£7·8 million) and 1964–5 (£19·6 million). The contrast with the United States, however, is still sharp: since 1925 the U.S. Post Office has made a profit only in the three war years 1943–5.

For 1960–61 the corresponding figures were £5.3 million profit and £300 million loss.

In what follows, an attempt will be made to compare the experience of the two postal services, to seek to examine some of the special problems of each, and to see how far economic standards can be applied to their operations. We shall consider first the resemblances between them, and then their differences. For detailed comparisons we shall generally use the data for 1960–61, which is a year in which there were no tariff increases to complicate the exposition, and which happens also to be the year studied (for the United States) in a recent book by Professor Baratz.[2]

II

We may begin by examining one aspect of the organization of postal services in which there is necessarily a close resemblance between the two countries: their cost-structure. We shall attempt to discover to what extent their costs are capable of varying with the work-load, and what proportion of them represents payments for personal services. The right hand side of Table 1 is suggested by an analysis in Professor Baratz's book, but has been recalculated from the original United States data to conform more closely to an analysis of British costs supplied to me *ad hoc* by the British Post Office.

There are certain peculiarities about the classification in Table 1, resulting from the organization of the British Post Office, on the one hand, and that of the United States on the other. The most disparate items are, in the United Kingdom the remuneration of sub-postmasters (who are paid mainly on a commission basis), and in the United States 'substitutes and temporaries'. It will be seen that these account for 2·6 per cent of British costs and 17·5 per cent of U.S. costs, respectively.

It is understood that some small part of the British total for salaries and wages is attributable to auxiliary postmen and casual working (e.g. at Christmas), and should therefore strictly be classed as variable costs. On the other hand, much of the British

2. Morton S. Baratz, *The economics of the postal service*, Public Affairs Press, Washington, D.C., 1962.

entry for night pay represents night duty allowances to regular staff, and is therefore more of a fixed cost. As regards the U.S. figures, it appears from a footnote to Professor Baratz's table[3] that some of the U.S. 'substitutes and temporaries' are gradually acquiring at least semi-permanent status, so that some part of the

Table 1

Analysis of Costs in United Kingdom and United States Postal Services, Fiscal Year 1960–61 (in percentages)

United Kingdom Fixed costs		United States Fixed costs	
Salaries and wages	52·6	Compensation of regulars	53·9
Pension liability	8·3	Pension liability	3·5
Transport services	1·5	Transportation services	2·7
Accommodation	2·0	Accommodation	3·9
Interest and depreciation	2·4	Depreciation of buildings	1·0
	66·8		65·0
Variable costs		Variable costs	
Sub-postmasters remuneration	2·6	Substitutes and temporaries	17·5
Overtime and night pay	8·3	Overtime and night pay	3·6
Hire of transport	19·4	Hire of transportation	10·8
Supplies and maintenance	2·9	Supplies and maintenance	3·1
	100·0		100·0

17·5 per cent representing their cost should be regarded as fixed rather than as variable costs. If adjustments are made for these several factors, it would appear that in both countries fixed costs closely approximate to 70 per cent of the whole.

It will be seen that in most of the other categories of expenditure there is a fair similarity between the structure of costs in the two services. The two major differences are in pension liability and hired transport. As regards the former, U.S. Government Departments and their employees each contribute 6½ per cent of salaries and wages to the Government pension fund, but only the

3. M. S. Baratz, *The economics of the postal service*, p. 86, n. 7.

governmental contribution appears in Table 1. If the employees' contributions are added, pension liability works out at 7 per cent of total expenditure, compared with 8·3 per cent in the United Kingdom, where the Post Office provides the whole contribution. The divergence between these two figures is in fact a percentage point or so greater than appears, because the pay of full-time (pensionable) staff has about one per cent greater weight in the United States than in the United Kingdom. While, however, current pension contributions total 13 per cent of pay in the United States, they are only 10·3 per cent of pay in the United Kingdom. The difference between the latter figure and the overall pension contribution – 14·1 per cent of pay – in the United Kingdom, derives from the special provisions to make good deficiencies in the pension fund, as discussed below; there is no equivalent to these in the U.S. accounts.

Two partial explanations of the differences in the cost of hired transport are apparent from the data. One is that a slightly larger proportion of the transport usage in the United States is undertaken with transport which is the property of the Post Office. Another is that the United Kingdom makes more use of air transport for domestic and overseas mails; it sends by air 4 per cent of all mails and spends on them about 5 per cent of total costs, compared with 2½ per cent and 2 per cent, respectively, in the United States. Moreover, as these percentages suggest, the proportion of airborne letters carried on the cheaper domestic routes is substantially greater in the United States than in the United Kingdom.

In contrast to these minor differences there stands out from Table 1 a major similarity – the preponderance in both countries of the cost of personal services in total expenditure. This reinforces the inference to be drawn from the smallness of the cost of interest and depreciation (depreciation alone in the United States) – that neither country has yet been able to economize substantially in its postal services by capital expenditure. It is true that in both countries some advances have been made in the development of machines which 'face' and sort, as well as cancel, letters, thus reducing the amount of manpower required in sorting offices. But except for straightforward cancelling machines, which have been in use for many years, the advance so far has made little visible impression on costs. In any event, no machine is ever likely to supersede the postman on his walk. This is a particularly important fact for the U.S. Post Office, since personal services are relatively expensive in that country. Factory-made products, clothing, and food in Washington cost little more than in London; but a U.S. postman gets about $5,300 a year, equivalent to £36 odd a week, whereas the average British postman receives £10 8s. a week. This differentiation explains why, despite a basic similarity in organization, and despite the greater flexibility possible in the United States because of the high proportion of temporary and substitute employees, the cost of current salaries and wages there (i.e. excluding pension liability) is 75 per cent of total expenditure, compared with 63·5 per cent in Britain. It is noteworthy, however, that the difference between postmen's salaries is much greater than the difference in average income. National income in the United States in 1962, divided by the total population, is equivalent to £876 a year per head whereas the comparable figure for the United Kingdom is £426.

III

We turn next to the relationships between the volume of correspondence, revenue, and costs. Pursuing our study of the resemblances between the two countries, we shall consider for both postal services firstly how costs are linked to the volume of correspondence and wage rates; and secondly how increases in GNP and in postal charges affect the volume of correspondence. For this purpose it will be convenient to confine our analysis to the relatively homogeneous category of inland correspondence, which covers 90–95 per cent of all mail handled in each country. The inclusion of parcels (other than books) and of overseas mail would add little to the coverage, while introducing two categories with characteristics different from the remainder. Table 2 summarizes the data which we shall seek to explore.

The most obvious feature of this Table is, of course, the steady rise in numbers of pieces and in costs. The volume of correspondence has risen in the United States every year and in the United Kingdom in five out of the eight years. Costs have risen in every year except one in both countries. An equally obvious point is that British revenues have always exceeded costs, while American costs have continued to exceed revenue. In both countries 1957–8 was the worst year, and since then there has been some improvement in the net position.

Table 2

Inland Correspondence: Number of Pieces, and Revenue and Costs per Piece, Fiscal Years, 1953–4 to 1961–2

	United Kingdom				United States		
	Pieces (1953–4 =100)	Revenue per piece d.	Cost per piece d.		Pieces (1953–4 =100)	Revenue per piece d.	Costs per piece d.
1953–54	100·0	2·10	1·71		100·0	2·29	2·91
1954–55	104·3	2·10	1·76		106·1	2·29	2·91
1955–56	106·5	2·14	1·87		108·4	2·31	3·05
1956–57	105·9	2·40	2·18		113·5	2·31	3·11
1957–58	104·9	2·61	2·41		115·7	2·31	3·52
1958–59	106·3	2·78	2·51		118·1	2·94	3·72
1959–60	110·9	2·80	2·47		122·9	3·02	3·82
1960–61	116·2	2·88	2·51		125·5	3·12	4·11
1961–62	116·2	3·03	2·73		130·5	3·33	4·17

The Table suggests two lines of inquiry: (1) Why have costs risen in general, and why did they fall in the United Kingdom in 1959–60? (2) How can we account for the spasmodic variations in the volume of correspondence, particularly in the United Kingdom? The first of these will be dealt with in this section, and the second in section IV.

Remembering the high proportion of costs which represents the remuneration of personal services, we should expect to find a fair correlation between the increases in costs and the increases in wage-levels. On the other hand, the high proportion of fixed costs should make for an inverse correlation between costs and traffic. We may check the former relationship by studying the increases in wage-rates in the two postal sectors. We have to assume that the proportion by which the costs of handling inland correspondence rose because of wage increases is the same as that by which all costs in the postal sector rose (including remittance and agency services). The discrepancy is, however, likely to be marginal only. Given this assumption, we can illuminate the increases in costs in the postal services as follows:

Table 3

Factors explaining the Increases in Unit Costs of Carrying Inland Correspondence: Fiscal Years 1953–4 to 1961–2

	United Kingdom % Increments of			United States % Increments of		
	P.O. wage rates[1]	Number of pieces[2]	Unit costs[3]	P.O. wage rates[1]	Number of pieces[2]	Unit costs[3]
1953–54	2·8	3·4	−1·2	—	2·6	−1·0
1954–55	3·6	4·3	2·9	2·2	6·1	—
1955–56	5·1	2·1	6·3	4·3	2·1	4·8
1956–57	8·9	−0·6	16·6	—	4·8	2·0
1957–58	6·2	−0·9	10·6	3·9	1·9	13·2
1958–59	4·3	1·3	4·1	3·9	2·1	2·7
1959–60	2·0	5·3	−1·6	—	4·1	2·7
1960–61	2·7	3·8	1·6	6·5	2·1	7·6
1961–62	3·8	—	5·2	—	4·0	1·4

[1] As percentage of previous year's aggregate postal costs.

[2] As percentage of previous year's number of pieces of mail.

[3] As percentage of previous year's average costs per piece.

These figures are revealing. It is true that they do not yield any close mathematical correlation between the increases in postal costs on the one hand and the increases in wage-rates and in the volume of correspondence on the other. In any event, part of the explanation of the former lies in increases in other costs. Nevertheless, there is reasonably clear confirmation that handling costs rise directly with increases in pay-rates, and inversely with increases in correspondence. For the United Kingdom this is particularly striking between 1958–9 and 1959–60, and is partly explained by the fact that in the latter year 104 million pieces of election literature were handled over a short period in addition to the normal flow of mail. (There was also an election in 1955–6, but there the benefit was lost because of increases in wage-rates and a falling off of the normal growth of correspondence.) For the United States, the correlation of costs with wage-rates and volume is less close, and the influence of other cost factors is more apparent.

Professor Baratz has attempted to use data similar to those given above to calculate for the U.S. Post Office the marginal cost of each class of mail (including parcels and overseas mail) for the period 1953–4 to 1959–60. His method yields marginal costs for first-class mail (letters and postcards) equivalent in 1953 dollars to 2·27d. (compared with average costs in 1959 of 3·60d.), and for third-class mail (printed papers) of 2·71d. (compared with an average of 3·40d.). For second-class (newspapers) and fourth-class mail (parcels) his method yielded no useful results. A possible reason for that was that his data did not enable him to allocate pay awards separately to the four classes of correspondence, and it is doubtful whether the cost structures appropriate to the four classes are sufficiently similar to enable the assumption to be safely made that each class attracts pay increases in proportion to total costs. (For instance, the cost of fourth-class mail naturally includes a substantially larger element of transport costs than do the other three categories.) But, in addition, Professor Baratz's method fails to allow for the shifting of fixed costs between categories as their relative volume grows. During the period which he studied, third-class mail grew appreciably more than first-class mail, and accordingly was allocated, by the cost apportionment method, an increased proportion of the Post Office's fixed costs. It appears probable, therefore, that the true marginal cost of third-class mail was smaller than that calculated by Professor Baratz, and that of first-class mail larger.

While therefore the attempt to calculate these costs is an interesting one, and it would undoubtedly be helpful to know what they were, I have not tried to apply the process to the United Kingdom data, which are equally inadequate for the attempt. The large proportion of fixed costs suggests that marginal costs will be appreciably lower than average costs, and we may be content with that conclusion.

IV

The second question prompted by Table 2 was why the volume of correspondence varies as it does. It we assume that the habits of the average man in the matter of correspondence are not lightly altered, it would seem that the most likely factors to be considered in seeking this explanation are increases in economic activity (including those due to increases in population), and increases in postal charges – the former tending to expand postings, and the latter to deter them. Changes in economic activity are perhaps best measured in terms of real GNP, and for this purpose the index of wages may be considered a better deflator than an index of prices, although unfortunately the available wage-index, being given to the nearest whole number, produces only a relatively crude indication of year-to-year changes in real GNP. For a measure of increases in postal charges we may take the increase in unit revenue from year to year, most of which will be due to higher tariffs, though some small part of any change may be due to fluctuations in the proportion between letters, printed papers, etc.

In the following Table, therefore, the percentage increase in the volume of correspondence from year to year is compared with the concurrent changes in GNP and increases in postal charges, both measured as above, and both expressed as percentages of the corresponding totals for the preceding year.

For the United Kingdom, the figures in Table 4 appear fairly well to account for the variations in correspondence, even though (once more) no precise correlation can be calculated. At least, the three largest increases in the volume of correspondence took place in the years when the increase in charges was smallest, except for 1955–6, which seems to have been a depressed year for correspondence on both sides of the Atlantic. In the remaining years, the volume of correspondence in the United Kingdom varied directly with real GNP. Experience shows that the announcement of increases in tariffs tends to have an immediate effect in reducing the volume of correspondence, even before the increase has taken effect. As the large increase shown for 1956–7 was in fact announced in autumn 1955, some part of the falling off in correspondence in 1955–6 may be attributed to this effect; another part was undoubtedly due to the railway strike. Again, the mails compete with the telephone as a means of communication, and therefore the availability and cost of telephone calls also have an influence on the volume of letters. Finally, the practical

Table 4

Factors Explaining Changes in the Volume of Inland Correspondence (Fiscal Years, 1954–5 to 1961–2)

	United Kingdom % Increments of			United States % Increments of		
	Real GNP.[1]	P.O. charges[2]	No. of pieces[3]	Real GNP.[4]	P.O. charges[2]	No. of pieces[3]
1954–55	0·5	0·0	4·3	0·7	0·0	6·1
1955–56	0·6	1·9	1·1[5]	2·5	0·1	2·1
1956–57	0·5	12·1	0·5	0·5	0·0	4·8
1957–58	−0·1	9·0	0·9	−1·2	0·0	1·9
1958–59	1·4	6·3	1·3	0·8	27·3	2·1
1959–60	1·4	0·6	4·2[5]	2·9	2·7	4·1
1960–61	3·6	2·9	4·9	0·8	3·3	2·1
1961–62	0·9	5·9	0·0	2·1	6·7	4·0

[1] Increase in GNP for calendar year in which the fiscal year begins, deflated by the index of wages, as percentage of corresponding GNP for the preceding year.

[2] Increase in revenue per piece, as percentage of unit revenue in the previous year.

[3] Increase in number of pieces of inland correspondence, as percentage of the number in the preceding year.

[4] Increase in the average GNP for the two calendar years in which the fiscal year begins and ends, deflated by the index of wages, as percentage of the corresponding GNP for the preceding twelve months.

[5] About 100 million election items posted in 1955–6, and again in 1959–60, have been disregarded, since these may be considered not to have been influenced by real GNP or Post Office charges. (These items cost the candidates nothing to post, although the Post Office takes credit for the equivalent postage.)

discontinuance in recent years of the dispatch of receipts has reduced substantially the volume of printed papers.

In the United States the relationships are again not so easy to trace. Certainly in three of the four years in which the increase in the number of pieces was small, the increase in real GNP was also small; the fourth year, 1955–6, has already been commented on. But increases in Post Office charges seem to have little effect – perhaps because these charges are too low to be significant to the ordinary user of the mails.

While it would be rash to draw any sweeping conclusions from the figures for the few years studied, one is tempted to form the hypothesis that in the United States – perhaps even in both countries – correspondence tends to increase at a rate of about 4 per cent a year unless there is some markedly adverse influence, such as an actual decline in real GNP or a sharp increase in charges, in which case the rate of growth tends to be halved in the United States and in the United Kingdom to disappear altogether. This latter difference may in turn be attributable to the fact that the population of the United States rises at a rate of 1·8 per cent a year, whereas in the United Kingdom the rate is 0·5 per cent a year.

V

We turn now to those aspects of the finances of the two postal services which emphasize the differences between them. The most obvious is the relationship between costs and revenues earned, and it will be convenient first to identify the classes of mail in which profits and losses have been made. Table 5 shows the revenue, costs, and profit or loss on each major category of mail in 1960–61, the U.S. figures being converted, for convenience, into millions of pounds sterling.

There is little difficulty, from this analysis, in locating the cause of the large deficits incurred by the U.S. Post Office; it lies in the inadequacy of tariffs to cover costs in the reduced-rate classes of mails. We can take the discussion a little further by turning these aggregates into revenues and costs per unit of mail. These figures are readily derivable from the U.S. data, and for the United Kingdom they have been calculated from information about the number of pieces of mail in each category, which has been supplied to me *ad hoc* by the Post Office. Table 6 gives the figures for prepaid mail, in pence.

We note straight away from Tables 5 and 6 that in both countries the large proportion of total mails consisting of printed papers (36 per cent in the United Kingdom, 28 per cent in the United States) was carried at a loss, amounting to about $\frac{1}{8}$d. apiece in the United Kingdom and the equivalent of $1\frac{1}{2}$d. apiece in the United States. The sheer volume of this mail (over 3,900

Table 5

Revenue, Costs and Profit or Loss by Category of Mail, 1960–61 (in millions of pounds)

| | United Kingdom | | | United States | | |
	Revenue	Costs	Profit/ Loss	Revenue	Costs	Profit/ Loss
Letters and packages[1]	81·9	62·9	+19·0	574	561	+13
Postcards	2·5	2·4	+0·1	26	36	−10
Printed Papers	35·1	37·1	−2·0	192[2]	307[2]	−115[2]
Newspapers	2·0	3·4	−1·4	32[3]	158[3]	−126[3]
Overseas Letters	20·3	20·5	−0·2	36	42	−6
Parcels[4]	31·1	38·2	−7·1	232[5]	268[5]	−36[5]
Miscellaneous[6]	6·2	9·3	−3·1	67	94[7]	−27[7]
Total[8]	179·1	173·8	+5·3	1,159	1,466	−307

[1] Including domestic airmail letters.

[2] Third-class mail plus books and 'controlled circulation'.

[3] Second-class mail.

[4] Including airmail parcels and overseas parcels.

[5] Fourth-class mail excluding books.

[6] Registration and other postal services.

[7] Including also Penalty, Franked, and Free for Blind.

[8] Excluding remittance and agency services.

million pieces in the United Kingdom, and nearly 18,000 million in the United States) turned these adverse margins into aggregate losses of £2 million in the United Kingdom and the equivalent of £115 million in the United States.

The cost calculations reflected in Table 6 make allowance for the fact that postcards and printed papers may be deferred in the mails (except, in practice, at Christmas) if by so doing overtime working can be avoided; whereas letters and newspapers are not so deferred. In the United States the effect of such deferment can only be trifling – certainly in relation to the very large loss sustained – because the availability of part-time and temporary workers enables man-hours to be adjusted to load without much recourse to overtime pay. In the United Kingdom, however, the effect of such deferment must be slightly to reduce the impact of a rush of work on the amount of overtime undertaken.

Table 6

Percentage of each Category in total Prepaid Mail, and Revenues and Costs per Piece of Mail, Fiscal Year, 1960–61

| | United Kingdom | | | United States[1] | | |
	Percentage of total %	Revenue per piece of mail d	Costs per piece of mail d	Percentage of total %	Revenue per piece of mail d	Costs per piece of mail d
Letters and packages	53·9	3·36	2·58	52·8	4·15	4·05
Postcards	2·2	2·50	2·37	4·0	2·58	3·46
Printed Papers	36·0	2·16	2·28	28·3	2·58	4·13
Newspapers	1·3	3·50	5·92	12·6	0·93	4·76
Overseas Letters	4·4	10·96	11·06	0·9	15·02	17·64
Parcels	2·2[2]	29·43	36·44	1·4	61·81	71·36

[1] Categories as in Table 5.   [2] Inland and outward overseas.

In contrast to printed papers, the proportion of the mail occupied by newspapers in the United States was much greater – indeed, ten times greater – than in the United Kingdom. In 1960–61 they totalled nearly 8,000 million pieces in the United States (12·6 per cent of the whole number carried), whereas in the United Kingdom they numbered only 137 million (1·3 per cent). The fact that the United States incurred a loss equivalent to 3·8d. on carrying each piece accounts for another 43 per cent of its total adverse result. This loss per piece is the less surprising when it is found that 53 per cent of all items in the second-class category paid no more than one-half cent per copy, and 40 per cent of these paid $\frac{1}{8}$ cent or less.

The relatively small losses sustained by the British Post Office in these two categories of mail prompted increases in the charges made for them in January 1956, October 1957, and October 1961. The U.S. Post Office has long been pressing the Congress to authorize increases in the corresponding rates. An average increase of one-half cent per piece on second-class and third-class

299

mails was introduced in 1958–9, and some further small increases in certain categories are now coming gradually into effect. But the publishers' lobby is strong, and is supported by the tradition, which dies hard in the United States, that newspapers and magazines render a public service by bringing information to the backwoods. The Post Office itself argues for concessionary rates for second-class matter on the ground that 'low postage rates for these media have reflected the belief of Congress that wide distribution of reading matter should be encouraged for the public good'.[4]

It is curious how this argument persists, despite the practical elimination of the backwoods, the nearly universal diffusion of radio and television, and the fact that a large proportion of the material sent at second-class rates can by no stretch of the imagination be regarded as educational. This is, indeed, partially recognized by the tariff itself, which distinguishes between reading matter, for which a flat rate of $2\frac{1}{2}$ cents a pound is charged, and advertising matter, which is charged on a tariff varying with distance, from 3 cents a pound for the nearest zone to 14 cents a pound for the most distant zone. However, publishers contrive in practice to overcome this differential by shipping magazines in bulk to distributing points within the cheapest zone from the point of destination, and putting them into the mails there.

But there is a second feature of the American scene which is also partly responsible for the persistence of these very low rates of postage – the non-existence of newsagents. Daily newspapers in U.S. cities are delivered by boys employed by the newspapers themselves, in the outer suburbs by newspaper vans, and in country districts by mail. The only retail outlet for magazines is the ubiquitous drugstore, and in fact 67 per cent of all American magazines are delivered through the post. A vicious circle has thus been created. The newsagent cannot exist because his delivery costs would exceed the postage charges; postage charges cannot be raised to economic levels because the absence of a cheap alternative method of distribution enables publishers to claim that such an increase would ruin them.

4. *Survey of postal rates*, p. 17.

VI

It will be useful next to identify some of the separate elements in the cost of the various categories of mails. This is done in Table 7.

The U.S. categories do not correspond completely with the British ones, but for purposes of comparison first-class may be equated with letters and postcards, second class with newspapers, and third class with printed papers.

Table 7

Analysis by Function of Costs of Postal Operations (in per cent. Fiscal Year, 1960–61)

	Collection and delivery	Mail handling	Transport	Other
United Kingdom				
Letters	49·4	36·2	6·9	7·5
Postcards	50·9	37·3	1·3	10·5
Printed papers	52·7	34·1	6·4	6·8
Newspapers	41·0	33·4	18·5	7·1
United States				
First class	31·4	44·3	4·3	20·0
Third class	46·2	28·7	6·0	19·1
Second class[1]	45·8	22·6	14·0	17·6

[1] Including controlled circulation publications.

The most striking feature of this table is the lack of variation in the United Kingdom in the cost of handling the various classes of mail, compared with the wide range in the United States – from 44·3 per cent to 22·6 per cent of costs. The reduced proportion of total costs incurred in mail handling in the second-class and third-class categories, compared with the first-class, is attributed by the U.S. Post Office to the obligation placed upon those using second-class mail, and those sending third-class items by bulk mail rates (75 per cent of the whole) to presort the mail by major city or State, and hand it in at a Post Office. The increased proportion of total costs comprised in collection and delivery in these categories is said to be a reflection partly of the lower aggregate costs connected with them, and partly of the large size of the average item in these categories, which greatly increases the cost of delivering them.

The only feature of importance in British Post Office practice corresponding to the obligation to presort, placed on senders of second-class and third-class mails, relates to the printed papers emanating from the Football Pools Promoters, (about 10 per cent of the whole of printed papers) which are presorted before being collected by the Post Office. No estimate of the saving arising from this to the United Kingdom Post Office is available. However, the U.S. Post Office has estimated that the saving to it of presorting and delivery to the Post Office of an item of third-class mail is about 14 per cent.[5] Of this, not more than 10 per cent can be saving through presorting. If we use this figure for the United Kingdom (and it is likely to be a maximum) the overall saving represents 1 per cent of the total cost of printed papers, i.e. about 0·02d. per piece. The recently introduced bulk mail facility is far too little used for the accompanying obligation to presort to have any visible effect on costs.

Disregarding for the moment such economies as these, we can classify letters, postcards, printed papers, and newspapers according to the volume of work which they create in the sorting-office. One part of the flow of letters and printed papers will be meter-franked, which means that they do not require cancellation; the mail handling of such items is confined to sorting. A second, and preponderant, part of all classes except newspapers will be items of minimum size and weight, amenable to machine cancellation. The remainder (including all newspapers) will be too bulky for mechanical handling. These will have to be cancelled by hand, and sorted into the so-called 'drop-bag fittings', which occupy more space and are slower in use than the standard sorting racks. These items will also take up more room in the bags; and more bags means more documentation, more handling, and more transport costs. Broadly speaking, the different costs of handling the various categories of mails reflect the differing proportions in

5. *Survey of postal rates*, p. 79.

which the flow of items in these categories divides between these three sorting-office procedures.

For the United Kingdom the proportions of letters and printed papers dealt with in these different ways is as follows:

Table 8
United Kingdom: Analysis of Mails by Method of Cancellation

	Meter-franked	Machine-stamped	Hand-stamped
Letters	20·5	63·6	15·9
Printed Papers	40·5	51·8	7·7

The data in Tables 6, 7, and 8 enable us to analyse costs in the sorting office somewhat further. The average cost of carrying a newspaper (Table 6) in the United Kingdom is 5·92d., of this, 33·4 per cent represents mail handling (Table 7), which therefore costs 1·98d. Most newspapers are hand-stamped, but a few are sent in meter-franked wrappers, requiring no cancellation, so that the average cost of handling a hand-stamped item must be at least 2d. Simultaneous equations based on the three Tables enable us to calculate the corresponding costs of meter-franked and machine-stamped items. For this purpose we take the total cost of a letter as 2·58d. (Table 6); Table 7 gives its handling cost as 36·2 per cent of this, i.e. 0·93d. The comparable total cost of a printed paper is 2·30d. (Table 6, adjusted for presorting), and Table 7 shows its handling cost is 34·1 per cent of this, i.e. 0·78d.

Putting x as the cost of a meter-franked item and y as the cost of a machine-stamped item, and taking the cost of a hand-stamped item as 2d., we have from Table 8 equations as follows:

$$0·205x + 0·636y + 2(0·159) = 0·93$$
$$0·405x + 0·518y + 2(0·077) = 0·78$$

Solving for x and y gives us approximately 0·5d. and 0·8d. respectively. It is obvious that in these equations the values of x and y depend very greatly on the value given to the cost of handling hand-stamped items, and the solution here given is therefore only correct if we are right in estimating the latter cost at 2d.

However, the emerging values for x and y are themselves plausible. They result in the following schedule:

Cost of sorting by racks	0·5d.
Cost of machine-stamping	0·3d.
	——
Cost of handling machine-stamped item	0·8d.
Added cost of hand-stamping and sorting by drop-bag-fittings, with consequential costs for documentation	1·2d.
	——
Cost of handling hand-stamped items	2·0d.

If we turn to the American figures we can deduce from the data for postcards (nearly all of which are machine-stamped) that the cost of sorting and machine-stamping an item of minimum size and weight is something like 44·3 per cent of 3·46d., i.e. 1·53d. (We cannot be more precise, as we do not have a breakdown of first-class costs between letters and postcards in Table 7.) This is about double the British figure. More comprehensive comparisons are not feasible because nothing is known of the proportion of U.S. mails which is meter-franked, and because of the greater degree of presorting required of the users of second-class and third-class mails in the United States. Comparison of second-class mail costs with those of British newspaper is also vitiated because much of the former are paid for in bulk, and we have no information about the saving in cost which this represents.

If we turn to the costs of collection and delivery, it is possible to make comparisons of the costs for a letter, but they yield somewhat surprising results. In the United Kingdom to collect and deliver a letter costs 49·4 per cent of 2·58d., i.e. 1·27d. In the United States the corresponding figures are 31·4 per cent of 4·05d., which is also 1·27d. Thus while mail-handling of a minimum-sized letter costs the U.S. Post Office something like twice what it costs the British Post Office, it appears that collection and delivery costs are the same in the two countries. It seems highly probable that to some extent this discrepancy reflects different methods of cost apportionment – compare, for example, the very different proportions of costs classified as 'other' in the two countries. The difference may also reflect the fact that more letters are written per person per annum in the United States than in Britain; we shall return to this possibility later. But the coincidence of costs is noteworthy.

Here we need only add that the relatively high cost in the United States of the one category of mails not mentioned above – parcels – is fully understandable. Parcels are the single type of domestic mail for which transport costs are a sizeable proportion of the whole, and the average distance travelled by parcels in the mails in the United States is, naturally, much greater than in the United Kingdom. In addition, of course, parcels require special handling at the counter as well as in the sorting office.

VII

The next question to which we may turn is one to which Professor Baratz chiefly addresses himself: what should be the relationship between charges and costs? He treats two aspects of this problem, the first being whether the basis for charges should be the average cost of each service or something else, and the second whether some part of Post Office costs should be met from sources other than Post Office revenue. Discussion of this second question may be postponed for the moment. On the first, Professor Baratz shows some hankering after a two-part tariff, or even for a system by which charges would cover only marginal costs, but regretfully reaches the conclusion that the only practicable method of charging is to relate tariffs to average costs. This has been the basis enunciated by successive British Postmasters-General, and it seems unnecessary to argue for it here.

The British Post Office was indeed regarded until comparatively recently as an agent for making profits for the Chancellor of the Exchequer, and its obligation to cover the whole of its costs was explicitly accepted in the White Paper (Cmd 9576) initiating the transition stage in 1956. Since then, successive Postmasters General have reaffirmed the principle that aggregate prices should cover aggregate costs (and therefore average prices cover average costs), and moreover that as far as possible each separate category of mail should be self-supporting.

We may pause for a minute to consider one of the minor difficulties of this aim. The public has been conditioned to expect cheaper tariffs for printed papers than for letters, but the main element in the difference in the cost of handling the two categories of mail is that which arises from the differing proportions of meter-franked, machine-stamped, and hand-stamped mail among letters on the one hand and printed papers on the other. Actually, except for a possible small saving arising from the ability to defer the handling of printed papers in rush times, the cost of handling an individual item of either class of mail is the same. Even if it were plausible (as it is certainly not logical) to differentiate the tariffs for the two classes on the basis of the difference of 'mix', the overall difference in cost, 0·3d. (Table 6), cannot accurately be reflected in the tariff because the minimum fraction of a penny available for tariff purposes is a halfpenny, except in so far as the rebate scheme for bulk posting allows in effect adjustments within small fractions of a penny for the relatively few users of that scheme. In fact, in a logical tariff, the principal distinction drawn would not be between letters, postcards, printed papers, and newspapers, but between items capable of being machine-stamped and those requiring hand-stamping, with metered items in a third category, divided between those of normal size, which can be sorted into racks, and those (such as newspapers) which have to be sorted into drop-bag fittings. It would be an interesting, if hardly politically sensible, exercise to draw up a tariff along these lines.

In practice, given the limitation to halfpence in the tariff, the existing charges for inland correspondence are adequately fair, except for the under-charging of newspapers. So, on the whole, are those for overseas mail, although there letters subsidize printed papers to a considerably greater extent. Parcels, however, continue to constitute a drain on the postal finances, and this is true also in the United States; in both countries, revenues cover only some three-quarters of costs. As there is some evidence that the demand for the services of the parcel mail has a downward elasticity greater than unity, there is no obvious way to remedy this. In the United States the Postmaster-General has recently had to obtain Congressional relief from a statutory obligation to cover parcel costs within 4 per cent, his argument being that any further rise in the tariff would be futile as the volume of traffic would fall off more than in proportion.

This problem, though perplexing, is minor compared with

certain philosophical questions about postal rates which exercise public opinion in the United States. These correspond closely to Professor Baratz's problems, the first being whether average revenue should be matched to average costs *for each category of mails separately*, and the second whether the Post Office should be expected to cover from revenue the whole of its costs.

On the first problem, the position of the U.S. Post Office is that first-class mail, as a premium service, should cover substantially more than its costs, allowing second-class and third-class mails, viewed as of less 'value' to users, to earn less than their own costs. Yet, as the Post Office itself recognizes, the economies derived from not treating second-class and third-class mails as premium services are fully reflected in their average costs, through the mechanism of cost apportionment. Objectively, therefore, there can be no case for relieving these services of the obligation to cover their costs. The only justification for doing so would be that the 'value' of these services includes some kind of negative subjective element, and that of first-class mail a conveniently equal positive subjective element; in economic terms the greater 'value' attributed to first-class mail must mean something more than the equivalent of the greater costs incurred in giving a premium service. But there seems to be no criterion by which to measure such subjective value. And since the Post Office is a monopoly there can be no economic check on any estimate which it (or indeed anyone else) may make of this subjective value. This is a difficulty which we shall encounter with even more force in considering the second problem.

Discussing this latter, Professor Baratz's conclusion is that some part of Post Office costs should be regarded as a public service, to be paid for out of taxation.[6] This is the position adopted in the 1958 legislation laying down the policy for the U.S. Post Office. Public Law 85–426 declared that 'Postal rates and fees shall be adjusted from time to time as may be required to produce the amount of revenue approximately equal to the total cost of

6. The arguments for this view, together with arguments for adding to U.S. Post Office costs some items previously omitted, are set out in detail in an article by Jane Kennedy, 'Structure and policy in postal rates', *Journal of Political Economy*, June 1957, which also has much useful information about U.S. postal rates and regulations at that time. Subsequent developments in the U.S. cost ascertainment methods have, however, overtaken to some extent the analysis in this article.

operating the postal establishment less the amount deemed to be attributable to the performance of public services. . . .' (This obligation was superimposed on the separate requirement, mentioned above, to cover the costs of the parcel service.)

The 'public services' referred to fell into three groups. The first was the loss sustained on performing non-postal activities, such as the remittance services and also various functions for other Departments: this was estimated by the U.S. Post Office at a total equivalent to £22 million in 1960–61. The second group was the loss sustained on the transmission of mails by certain persons or bodies having the privilege of paying reduced rates. The largest element in this group consisted of three special classes of second-class mails wholly or partly exempt from postage, and the next largest a loss on the transmission of books. Altogether, this group is estimated to have caused in 1960–61 a loss equivalent to £66 million. The third group was defined as 'the loss resulting from the operation of such prime and necessary public services as the star route system and third- and fourth-class post offices'. (Star routes are routes on which mails are carried by contract otherwise than by railway or steamboat.) The loss on this third group proved impossible to identify, and no estimate has been made of it for 1960–61.

If we compare these categories with British practice, we see that the first group matches the Savings Bank, remittance services, and agency services, of which the costs have been omitted from our Tables. The only British item corresponding to the second group is a concessional postage rate to the blind, of which the cost is charged to other users of the mails, not to the general public; for a purely marginal amount, such as this, the procedure amounts to very much the same thing. I know of no public attempt in this country to argue that postal costs equivalent to the third group should be reimbursed to the Post Office out of taxation. Somewhat comparable suggestions have been made by the Committee on Nationalized Industries in connexion with uneconomic railway[7] and air[8] services, but these have not been accepted by the

7. *Report from the Committee on Nationalized Industries – British Railways*, 11 July, 1960, para. 424.

8. *Report from the Committee on Nationalized Industries – The Air Corporations*, 14 May 1959, para. 117.

Government, and the losses continue to be carried by the industries concerned. In the United States, however, the issue is sharply defined; for on the justification for this concept of 'public services' depends the legality of the present tariff, which so signally fails to comply with the direction that revenues should cover costs.

In the light of this, it is interesting to see that Professor Baratz accepts the validity of the 'public service' concept, and justifies it by reference to the educational, cultural, and business-fostering aspects of the Post Office's work. It is not, however, clear why these benefits should be regarded as stemming only from Post Offices. It would seem to be equally arguable that the Western Union Telegraph Company, or for that matter the village store which constitutes the local civic focus (to say nothing of booksellers) should not also be able to claim to be supported partly by taxation. Professor Baratz's argument is rendered even more difficult to accept precisely because he is unable to quantify the alleged benefits. This drives him to argue that the appropriate amount to be allowed is 'the sum decided upon by a majority of Congressmen, each acting upon his personal preference'. This is surely a counsel of despair. Quite apart from Sergeant Willis's apprehensions about a lot of M.P.s all thinking for themselves, the annual cerebration would make it impossible for the Post Office to know in advance what were the costs which it would be expected to cover.

Possibly realizing this double hazard, the Congress in October 1962 changed the law. P.L. 87–793 now requires the Post Office to estimate (and subsequently calculate) by accounting methods, the value of the public services which it renders. The sum so derived is in future not to be specifically appropriated, but is to be treated as a notional deduction from costs for the purpose of adjusting postal charges. Moreover a new definition of 'public services' was provided, which included the losses on the first two groups mentioned above, and added 10 per cent of the cost of operation of third-class post offices and the star-route system, plus 20 per cent of the cost of operation of fourth-class post offices and rural routes. In 1960–61, third-class post offices numbered 13,071 and fourth-class ones 11,116, out of a total of 44,764. There were 11,149 star routes, and 31,341 rural routes.

No estimate of the value of 'public services' so defined for 1960–61 has been made, but for 1961–2 the Post Office estimates them at the equivalent of £151 million, made up of non-postal services, £26 million; concession rates, £92 million; and the appropriate proportions of costs for third-class and fourth-class post offices, etc., £33 million.

VIII

That the British Post Office has not been faced with philosophical problems of the kinds just discussed does not mean that there have been no questions about the kind of costs that the Post Office here should be required to cover. On the contrary; there have in recent years been three specific doctrinal developments, all associated with the five years of transition from the wartime and post-war system (by which the whole Post Office surplus was surrendered to the Treasury) to the autonomy which the Department acquired in April 1961 under the Post Office Act of that year. Arising out of these developments, the British Post Office has accepted obligations to cover depreciation on capital at current replacement cost; to cover increases in the cost of providing for pensions caused by increases in rates of pay; and to earn a minimum return on capital employed.

Both the first and the second of these obligations were explicitly recognized in the White Paper of 1955 (Cmd 9576). They flow, of course, from increases in costs, and are important only in and after periods in which costs have risen significantly, as they have done since the war. The arguments for them are similar: the economic cost of the wearing-out of plant in rendering services at any given time must be measured by the current cost of replacing that piece of plant, not by its historical cost; and the provision of pensions for Post Office employees necessitates setting aside each year sums sufficient to build up an adequate fund for that purpose. There is, however, a minor difference in the extent to which these additional costs are covered. Depreciation provisions, while including an element, known as 'supplementary depreciation', to relate the whole to current instead of historical cost, do not go so far as to make good the short fall in past instalments of depreciation, provided when costs were lower. When, therefore, a

J. Keith Horsefield

piece of plant comes to be replaced, the depreciation provisions made for it are not wholly adequate, and part of the cost of the new plant has to be charged to new capital. This is reasonable, since on the one hand users of the plant have consistently been charged depreciation on its current value at the time they used it, and on the other the few funds invested are represented by a tangible asset. In the telephone service the obligation to provide supplementary depreciation is an onerous one, representing some 7 per cent of total costs. In the postal service the amount involved is so far almost negligible because so little plant (as distinct from buildings) has been installed; but it may assume importance later.

In contrast to the limited provision for depreciation, there is considered to be no logical escape from the necessity to ensure that the hypothetical pension fund, by the time that an employee retires, is wholly adequate to ensure his pension for life. The additional contributions to the notional pension fund, made whenever pay is increased (and therefore the prospective pension, to be based on final years of salary, is increased) are therefore calculated to be sufficient to eliminate altogether the deficiency which such increases create in the fund. This is done by making good the actuarially ascertained deficiency for each year over the ensuing twenty years (that being the average length of future service of the staff at any one moment).

By contrast to the foregoing, it does not appear that in the United States supplementary provisions are made either for depreciation or for pension liability. Until 1959–60 the U.S. Post Office wrote off capital expenditure out of revenue. In 1960–61, in the course of an adjustment of the accounts from a cash to an accrual basis, an allowance for depreciation at original cost was substituted for the entry for capital expenditure. Supplementary depreciation in the British sense is not included in the U.S. accounts. Again, the small amount of plant involved would mean that such supplementary depreciation, if provided, would be of negligible amount. As regards pensions, it has been noted above that equal contributions by the Post Office and its employees provide 13 per cent of pay to the pension fund. This is sufficient in normal times, but since pensions are based on an average of the five years' highest pay earned, recent general pay increases have made the pension fund no longer adequate. If contributions were

311

henceforward to be made on the United Kingdom pattern, and were shared equally between the Post Office and its employees, the additional cost to each might be of the order of the equivalent of £4½ million a year – about ⅓ per cent of total costs.

The third element which revenue is expected to cover in the United Kingdom, the 'return on capital', has no parallel in the United States. In this country it made its appearance for the first time in the *Report* for 1959–60. The 'return' is calculated as the percentage on capital employed represented by gross profits, struck before the payment of interest and 'supplementary depreciation'. In the postal service, unlike the telephone service, the amount of capital is very small in relation to turnover; in 1960–61 it was only about one-quarter of revenue, whereas in the telecommunications services it was about three and a half times revenue. Accordingly, in the postal service, interest and supplementary depreciation are relatively small elements in gross profits, and the 'return' tends to fluctuate sharply with revenue and costs. (£1 million profit represents 2½ per cent return on capital.) For example, in the three years 1957–8, 1958–9, and 1959–60, the return was respectively 3·7 per cent, 7·4 per cent, and 11·1 per cent; in 1961–2 it was back to 3·8 per cent.

The rationale of this preoccupation with the return on capital employed is, of course, the Government's wish to control investments in public enterprises by some economic criterion. As such, it is obviously commendable. But the postal service is unique among such enterprises in the low ratio of capital to turnover, and it may be questioned whether the obligation to earn 8 per cent on this capital is as sensible as it sounds. It might be better, as would be more normal for what is essentially a retail business, to aim at a ratio of profit to turnover. The fact that the postal services are tied to the telecommunications services, wherein the obligation to earn a return on capital employed is clearly fully appropriate, probably makes such a separate standard impossible. But if the day ever comes when the Post Office is seen to be too large for any one man to manage, a separate earnings standard for the postal services might well be appropriate.

IX

We are now ready to tackle the crucial question of the relative efficiency of the two services. We are faced at once with a highly significant fact, that for a total expenditure eight times that of the United Kingdom Post Office, the United States postal services carry six times as much mail under the handicap of a wage-level about $3\frac{1}{2}$ times as high as in England. Since over 75 per cent of U.S. Post Office costs represent salaries and wages, one might have expected prima facie that its aggregate expenditure would be nearer 16 times than eight times the British total.

The comparison, however, ignores a number of other relevant factors. One important one is the greater intensity of traffic per head of population in the United States; in 1958 the Post Office there carried 323 pieces per person, compared with 189 pieces per person in the United Kingdom.[9] This in itself tends to economy, since collection and delivery costs are proportional rather to the number of points visited than to the number of letters carried. If conditions in the two countries were otherwise equal, the relation of U.S. to United Kingdom manpower costs per item for this part of Post Office work should therefore be $3\frac{1}{2} \times 189/323$, or approximately double. In practice, two other factors enter: addresses in the United States tend to be more widely scattered than in the much more densely populated United Kingdom; and there is a limit, set by the maximum permissible bag-weight, to the extent to which intensive correspondence in a limited area enables manpower to be economized. United States labour costs for collection and delivery per unit of correspondence might for these two reasons be expected to be more than double United Kingdom costs – whereas in fact they are apparently no greater, as we saw above.

Let us, however, assume for present purposes that labour employed in collection and delivery does cost twice as much in the United States as in the United Kingdom; what then should be the relationship of total costs? Collection and delivery represent (Table 7) about 45 per cent of total U.S. Post Office costs. We may assume without being far wrong that this includes 2·5 per cent of total costs for transport (Table 1), leaving 42·5 per cent of

9. Universal Postal Union, *Statistique complète des services postaux*, 1958.

total costs for the labour cost of collection and delivery, out of cost for labour for all purposes of 78·5 per cent (including pension contribution) of total costs. If we further make the extreme assumption that all other costs are no greater in the United States than in the United Kingdom, we reach an overall ratio for the costs in the two countries of 2·32 : 1.[10] That is, the volume of mail carried by the U.S. Post Office should cost it about fourteen times the cost to the United Kingdom Post Office of the mail which it carries; whereas in fact it costs only eight times as much.

There are, of course, a number of modifying circumstances. In the first place, while baiting the Post Office is a popular pastime on both sides of the Atlantic, the average travelled American tends to regard the services received from the British Post Office as appreciably more efficient than those which he is given at home – particularly in two respects, the rapidity of transit through the mails, and the early hour at which letters are delivered. (On the other hand, the U.S. Post Office is at present engaged in speeding up deliveries, and undertakes, for example, that any letter posted before 11 a.m. in a business area will be delivered to any address in the same business area on the same day.) Secondly, the obligation placed on U.S. mail-users to presort and hand in at the Post Office all second-class mail and three-quarters of third-class mail (representing between them over a third of all mail handled) affords the U.S. Post Office a saving estimated by it at 14 per cent of the cost of carrying that mail – i.e. about 5 per cen, of the cost of carrying mail in total. Moreover, as we have seent the British Post Office covers costs, in some relatively minor respects, which the U.S. Post Office ignores. Finally, the fact that the U.S. postman is paid more than twice the average American national income per head, whereas the British postman receives only one and a quarter times the corresponding British figure, may suggest that the capacity of the average American postman is somewhat higher, so that more can be expected of him. Yet, when all is said and done, the gap between eight and fourteen is a wide one, and the factors mentioned in this paragraph do not seem adequate to do much to close it. It would seem at least possible that the greater reliance of the U.S. Post Office on part-time and temporary help may enable it to keep costs down. The

10. $(2 \times 42 \cdot 5 + 3 \cdot 5 \times 36 + 21 \cdot 5)/100 = 2 \cdot 32$.

United States has also tackled the question of maximum bag-weight by providing postmen with light foldable wheeled carriers to hold their bags, and with a large number of light mechanized carriers for long distances. And finally there is the possibility that the better service given by the British Post Office costs more than its benefits are worth. But whatever the reason, it would seem that the U.S. Post Office can rightly claim to be relatively economically run.

10 William G. Shepherd

Cross-subsidization in Coal

Abridged from William G. Shepherd, 'Cross-subsidizing and allocation in public firms', *Oxford Economic Papers*, vol. 16 (1964), pp. 132–60.

The phenomenon of cross-subsidizing has attracted increasing attention in recent British discussions of resource allocation in publicly owned enterprises.[1] Most of the commentary has been distinctly critical, linking cross-subsidizing with distortions of the pricing mechanism and misallocation of resources, especially of investment resources. Concurrently, discussions both of theory and of practical policy for public firms have shifted toward solutions which would, as one main objective, eliminate cross-subsidizing.

Much of the discussion has centred on the National Coal Board, and so the empirical work in the present study also centres on the Coal Board's actual patterns of cross-subsidizing and allocation during the years 1948–61. But official policies for all of the main public corporations in Britain have been influenced by the criticisms to be reviewed in this paper, and these 'lessons' about public-firm policies have been widely accepted, both in Britain and abroad.

For all the discussion and its near-consensus, the concept of cross-subsidizing and its possible relations with resource allocation – and with efficiency criteria – have not been thoroughly

1. For the present discussion, cross-subsidizing is defined as the covering of financial losses on individual services and production units (according to allocable costs and revenues) by profits accruing elsewhere in the same enterprise. This formulation begs some important problems of definition and workability of the concept. For example, the allocation of joint costs may pose insuperable difficulties in defining and measuring cross-subsidizing. Because of this, the previous discussions of cross-subsidizing have focused on instances where joint costs are not important. The coal-industry cross-subsidizing treated in the present study is largely free of such joint-cost problems. Some other problems of definition are taken up in section 1 below.

analysed.[2] Nor has there been much empirical work on the amounts and patterns of cross-subsidizing and on their actual connexions with trends of output and investment in public firms. The present paper first offers (in section 1) some analysis of cross-subsidizing and allocation, in relation to certain private-market criteria which have recently been proposed for public firms. Then (in section 2) it presents some factual evidence about cross-subsidizing and post-war trends of output and investment within the National Coal Board. Section 3 suggests that a shift is needed from the present direction of analysis and policy concerning cross-subsidizing in public firms.[3]

Background

An historical summary will help place the issues in perspective. The British coal industry has undergone a secular decline in output, employment, and number of pits, since the peak reached around the time of World War I; this is indicated in Table 1. But basic reorganization was largely postponed by the Coal Mines Act of 1930, and the adjustment problems were intensified by the further capital depletion of most of the mines during

2. The one rigorous treatment of some aspects of cross-subsidizing has been almost wholly neglected; see R. H. Coase, 'The economics of uniform pricing systems', *Manchester School*, 1947, pp. 139–56.

3. The present paper is drawn from a larger study which also dealt with inter-industry patterns of prices, interest rates, and investment in the public fuel and power firms; and also (though less extensively) with cross-subsidizing and allocations within the Scottish Gas Board. To a large degree the study of micro allocation patterns, such as in the present paper, is helpful, if not actually necessary, in evaluating the broader charges of misallocation *among* industries.

This paper is deliberately confined to some relatively technical questions of allocation within certain types of public firms. Such problems, however, comprise only one area of public-firm performance and not, perhaps, even the most important area. For example, other areas and criteria include: technical progress and innovation, effects on other industries, foreign exchange repercussions, working conditions, stabilization of employment, income distribution, broadening of individual opportunity, freedom of individual choice, and others. Because the narrower allocation problems present interesting technical issues, economists may be prone to overrate their importance. But in thorough evaluations of public-firm performance, the problems of allocation discussed in this paper may not be of primary importance.

World War II. The National Coal Board inherited, in 1947, both a basic reorganization problem and an array of existing patterns of users and suppliers (including labour) which lay at the heart

Table 1
British Coal Production, Employment, Productivity, and Prices, 1913–61

	1913	1923	1938	1946	1951	1957	1961
Total output (tons million)	287	276	227	181	212	210	182
Total wage-earners (1,000)	1,075	1,151	776	693	695	710	575
Number of mines: Total U.K.*	3,024	2,607	1,860	1·564	1,314	1,355	1,090
National Coal Board	—	—	—	—	845	833	662
Output per man-shift (tons)	n.a.	n.a.	n.a.	1·05	1·24	1·25	1·45
Average pithead price (shillings/ ton)	n.a.	20	17	39	51	82	91
Coal as a percentage of all domestic energy consumption	n.a.	97·2	93·0	92·8	89·0	84·3	71·9
Gross fixed capital formation by the National Coal Board, as a percentage of the U.K. total	n.a.	n.a.	n.a.	n.a.	1·5	2·7	1·9

SOURCE: Ministry of Power *Statistical digest*, 1961; and Central Statistical Office *National income and expenditure*, 1962.

* Several hundred very small mines have remained in private hands, under the Federation of Small Mines of Great Britain. Their output has been about 1 per cent of the national total.

of British industry and society. Almost every major post-war action has involved divergences, often substantial, between private and social costs and benefits. As is well known, government influence and control over industry policies has been extensive and continuing during the post-war years; average coal prices have been directly controlled, investment totals and wage agreements have been closely influenced, and investment patterns have been affected.[4]

During its first ten years, the Coal Board was under intense pressure to increase and maintain total coal output. In doing this, the Board reversed the long-run declines in coal output and employment, but it also delayed some of the basic reorganization of the industry, which was detailed in 1950 in the Board's *Plan for Coal*.[5] The coal shortages and the pressures to maximize coal output, which were essentially the outcome of governmental restraints on coal prices, continued until about 1957. Then the abrupt post-Suez shift in European fuel conditions, reinforced by the current recession, caused substantial coal surpluses to accumulate in Britain during 1957–9. The sharp reduction in total demand for coal now permitted the reorganization programme – which had been proceeding since 1948 – to bear fruit relatively rapidly, through pit closures and spatial shifts in output and employment. The peak in coal-industry investment was passed in 1959; by 1962 all major projects had been completed or begun, and the new shape of the coal industry was becoming clear.

4. These controls, the strength of which has generally increased further in recent years, have been copiously discussed before the Select Committee on the Nationalized Industries; see, for example, the *Reports* on the coal industry (H. of C. 187–I, 1958), the railways (H. of C. 254, 1960), and the gas industry (H. of C. 280, 1961). Many writers, in apparent ignorance of the actual state of governmental controls, have been quick to attribute all policies and behaviour to the public firms themselves. Many of the resulting 'lessons of nationalized industry experience' are therefore at least dubious. See for example, S. R. Dennison, 'Investment in the nationalized industries', *Transactions* of the Manchester Statistical Society, 1958–9; M. F. Long, 'The marginal-cost price of coal, 1956–1957', *Economica*, 1962, pp. 395–409; or, as an extreme example, R. Kelf-Cohen, *Nationalisation in Britain*, 2nd edn, Macmillan, 1962. By contrast, a recent study has laid heavy stress on governmental interventions as the putative cause of most difficulties and apparent inadequacies of the public firms. See Michael Shanks (ed.), *Lessons of public enterprise*, Cape, 1963.

5. Hobart House, October 1950. This delay was deplored by A. Beacham in a prescient article, 'The present position of the coal industry', *Economic Journal*, 1950, pp. 9–18.

We may now review briefly the Coal Board's basically revised price structure. Established in 1951, it represented a complete departure from the old pricing procedures, although it did not break sharply with the pre-existing patterns of prices themselves. The new structure, which has undergone some further adjustments since 1951, sets out standard relative prices for coals of different physical qualities.[6] There are seven such 'quality' grades for household coals (presently 17 per cent of total coal use) and several *thousand* grades for all other types of coals. These nation-wide standard prices are adjusted for different regions, to allow for differing costs of producing and transporting identical quality coals. There are sixty-four pricing zones for domestic coals, which are sold at delivered prices. The overall result of this system is that coal prices differ substantially by location and types, although within certain limited areas and coal grades there are price uniformities. It bears noting that since 1950 the Coal Board has compiled extensive, standardized yearly data on prices, costs, revenues, and other technical conditions at individual pits. These are used in the present study.

1. The Issues

As far back as 1925 the Royal Commission on the Coal Industry had argued that financial pooling among mines would lead to a retardation of the proper reorganization of the coal industry. The Commission's broad endorsement of a private-market solution was, however, combined with proposals for direct action to promote structural adjustments.[7]

Coal industry cross-subsidizing arose during World War II

6. See National Coal Board, *Report*, vol. 1, 1956, pp. 39–42.

7. Thus, concerning financial pooling: 'The closing of uneconomic mines, always a matter of difficulty, would become far more difficult under nationalisation. There would be a strong temptation to draw upon the profits of the better mines rather than to inflict the hardships and incur the resentment involved by such an operation' (p. 71). But, as for private-market solutions: 'If nothing were done than to leave economic forces to work themselves out, it would probably be found twenty years from now that over a large proportion of the area the same conditions as those of today would still be prevailing', (pp. 59–60). Royal Commission on the Coal Industry, 1925, *Report*, vol. 1 Cmd 2600 1926.

under the Coal Charges Account, which pooled profits and losses among the 25 producing districts.[8] The Coal Board's revised price structure of 1951 preserved some of this averaging, as has been noted. In 1952 Dennison argued that the resulting cross-subsidizing, together with an extension of delivered pricing to all coals, would prevent efficient allocation of production and investment among pits, areas, and regions.[9] The Herbert Committee in 1956 criticized cross-subsidizing in electricity supply, and favoured a detailed relating of prices to costs on individual services as the fair and efficient method.[10] On similar general grounds, cross-subsidizing was condemned by Edwards and Townsend in 1958.[11] Cross-subsidizing within the North of Scotland Hydro-electricity Board was deplored in 1956 by Munby for its alleged distorting effects on the marginal conditions determining allocation. However, in 1959 Munby carefully avoided attributing possible inefficiency of coal industry investment to cross-subsidizing, and confined his remarks mainly to rate-of-return considerations.[12]

Ramanadham discussed cross-subsidizing critically at some length in 1959, mainly in general terms. He attempted to distinguish between cross-subsidizing and price discrimination, arguing that discrimination may provide unambiguous welfare gains, whereas cross-subsidizing also involves relative losses for some consumers which may offset the gains for others. Ramanadham also noted that cross-subsidizing may lead to a *reduction* in the

8. See chapter 18, 'The finance of the coal industry', pp. 333–51 in W. H. B. Court, *Coal*, History of the second World War, United Kingdom Civil Series, H.M.S.O., 1951; also the White Paper, *The coal charges account*, Cmd 6617, 1945.

9. For example: 'To put the matter bluntly, the Board announces its intention of being guided in the main by market criteria, and then goes out of its way to destroy such criteria as are available to it. . . . This static quality is a common feature of centrally-administered price systems; not only is there no guide to change, but the mechanism by which it would normally be brought about is stultified.' See S. R. Dennison, 'The price policy of the National Coal Board', *Lloyds Bank Review*, 1952, pp. 17–34.

10. *Report of the Committee of Inquiry into the Electricity Supply Industry*, Cmd 9672, January 1956.

11. R. S. Edwards and H. Townsend, *Business enterprise*, Macmillan, 1958, pp. 515–20.

12. D. L. Munby, 'Electricity in the north of Scotland', *Scottish Journal of Political Economy* 1956, pp. 19–43; and Munby, 'Investing in coal', *Oxford Economic Papers*, 1959 pp. 242–69.

unprofitable service relative to efficient levels, rather than to an *expansion* of it.[13] More importantly, Ramanadham held that cross-subsidizing would cause investment misallocation, by dissolving what he termed the usual profitability basis for investment decisions.[14] Cross-subsidizing therefore being unjustifiable, probably inequitable, and a cause of investment misallocation as well, Ramanadham argued that it should be ruled out for public firms.

More recently Long has criticized the Coal Board's pricing system for being 'divorced from underlying market conditions', because of its averaging of costs in setting prices. Long also offered the second empirical study of any consequence which has appeared in the entire post-war debate over nationalized industry performance.[15] Using a modified linear programming analysis,

13. V. V. Ramanadham, *Public enterprise in Britain*, Cass, 1959 (American title, *Problems of public enterprise*, Quadrangle Books), pp. 77–8, 109–11. With the exception of Coase's analysis (op. cit.) and a passing comment by Munby (op. cit., 1959), all other writers have assumed that a loss-earning service will be *over-expanded* relative to supposed efficient levels. But the outcome may go either way, depending on the circumstances in the market and within the public firm.

14. Ramanadham, *ibid.*, pp. 77–8, 109–10, 142–71. Thus (p. 146): 'If the nationalized industry makes a profit from a region, product or plant, the *prima facie* indication is that further outlays in that direction are justified. Larger outputs may go with lower prices and, in the process, we may reach a stage where high profits cease to repeat themselves.' After discussing some problems, Ramanadham squarely favours the profitability criterion for investment, where social-private cost divergences, and government interventions which affect prices and costs, are not involved.

This 'normal' basis is also propounded by I. M. D. Little, in his important theoretical discussion of public-firm price-output policies; see his chapter 11, 'Output and price policy in public enterprise', in *Critique of welfare economics*, 2nd edn, Oxford, 1957. The criterion seems to hark back to such earlier theoretical treatments as those by Lerner, Meade, Lewis, and Crosland. See in particular N. Ruggles, 'The welfare basis of the marginal cost pricing principle', *Review of Economic Studies*, 1949–50, pp. 29–46; and 'Recent developments in the theory of marginal cost pricing' [paper 1 in this edition], for a review of the earlier discussions. See also C. A. R. Crosland, 'Prices and costs in nationalized undertakings', *Oxford Economic Papers*, 1950, pp. 51–68, which, as Little notes, has influenced his own proposal.

15. The first was I. M. D. Little's *The price of fuel*, Oxford, 1953. Applying a judicious blend of marginal-cost and other criteria, Little proposed higher average coal prices and time-of-day tariffs for electricity. His findings do not bear on the intra-industry questions chiefly at stake in this paper.

Long presented estimates of improved allocation which a marginal-cost pricing system – without cross-subsidizing – would assertedly have prescribed for the industry in 1956–7. There are, as Long admits in part, some serious weaknesses in the methods underlying these estimates.[16] More interestingly, actual adjustments in the coal industry since have followed Long's prescriptions (published in 1962) with astonishing exactitude.[17] Apparently either Long's own estimates are invalid, or the Coal Board's allocation decisions are not 'divorced from underlying market conditions'; or both. In any event, as criticisms of long-run allocation patterns, Long's strictures were clearly premature.

Further statements linking cross-subsidizing and misallocation can be found in the more recent literature.[18] Moreover, such

16. M. F. Long, op. cit.; this paper is drawn from Long's dissertation, 'The price of coal: A study of the policies of the National Coal Board', University of Chicago, 1961. The chief methodological problems concern the cost and demand functions hypothesized for the 51 separate producing areas, each of which is treated like a single market. Long assumed that the highest-cost pit is the 'marginal' output in each area, but this is dubious in view of the variety of coals produced at each pit and within areas, and for other reasons discussed by Little in 1953; see I. M. D. Little, *The price of fuel*, op. cit., chapter 1. Also, this method forced Long to assume constant costs at each pit in the range up to 'capacity', and then vertical cost functions *at* 'capacity' *as measured by actual output in 1956–7*. Long also assumed that the industry and each of its parts was in equilibrium in 1956–7. Both of the foregoing two points are highly dubious.

Long also uses hypothesized demand elasticities which are based on pre-war demand conditions. Perhaps most seriously of all, Long assumes that factors at 'extra-marginal' pits are mobile, whereas they are typically, and in some cases notoriously, immobile. This is compounded by his assumption that transport costs per ton mile are constant, but this is far from true whether accounting costs or genuine social opportunity costs of rail and road transport are used. A proper evaluation of the opportunity costs of transport would tend to weaken the direction of his conclusions by a possibly significant amount.

17. In fact the concentration of production in profitable regions rather than unprofitable regions had by 1961 even gone beyond Long's prescriptions; see Long, op. cit., pp. 404–5.

18. For example, R. L. Gordon, 'Coal price regulation in the European Community, 1946–1961', *Journal of Industrial Economics*, 1962, pp. 188–203; and A. J. Merrett and A. Sykes, 'Financial policy for the nationalised industries', I and II, *The Banker*, March and April, 1962.

criticisms have been assimilated at the textbook level, and they are current in popular discussion.[19] From a policy standpoint, the most important discussions have been those on the Select Committee on the Nationalized Industries, in successive reports.[20] The Committee has become increasingly hostile to cross-subsidizing, until recently the elimination of cross-subsidizing has become a major objective. By contrast, there has been one recent defence of certain instances of cross-subsidizing, mainly on equity grounds but also as a device to ease some problems of transition. But in the same discussion some other instances of cross-subsidizing come in for sharp criticism.[21]

The policy proposals emerging from these discussions have been based on competitive private-market trends, as the criterion for evaluating and for guiding public-firm behaviour. In many respects this constitutes a regression from marginal-cost pricing, which has in turn recently undergone two damaging attacks.[22] It

19. For sample textbook attitudes, see G. C. Allen, *The structure of industry in Britain*, Longman's 1961, pp. 135–8; and C. Wilcox, W. D. Weatherford, Jr, and H. Hunter, *Economics of the world today*, Harcourt, Brace, 1963, pp. 54–61. Prime examples of popular discussions include F. Cassell, 'The pricing policies of the nationalised industries', *Lloyds Bank Review*, 1956, pp. 1–18; and R. Kelf-Cohen, op. cit.

20. Select Committee, op. cit., concerning coal, the railroads, and the gas industry. However, significantly, its evaluation of the coal industry on this score in 1958 was far less critical than were such observers as Dennison and Long.

21. See Shanks, op. cit.

22. The first of these attacks is based on the theory of 'second best'. The *locus classicus* is R. G. Lipsey and K. Lancaster, 'The general theory of second best', *Review of Economic Studies*, 1956–7, pp. 11–32; further analysis is given in A. Fishlow and P. A. David, 'Optimal resource allocation in an imperfect market setting', *Journal of Political Economy*, 1961, pp. 529–46. For a more cautious approach to the importance and insolubility of second-best problems, see E. J. Mishan, 'Second thoughts on second best', *Oxford Economic Papers*, 1962, pp. 205–17.

The second attack, based on the alleged emptiness of the marginal-cost pricing 'rule' – because the definition of marginal cost is unavoidably arbitrary – is by J. Wiseman, in 'The theory of public utility price – an empty box', *Oxford Economic Papers*, 1957, pp. 56–74. In a subsequent exchange Wiseman demonstrated further that marginal-cost pricing 'rules' are necessarily *ad hoc* in character, despite Farrell's argument that the 'rule' is valid except for certain unusual situations. See M. J. Farrell, 'In defence of public-utility price theory', *Oxford Economic Papers*, 1958, pp.

also represents in the main a reversion to pre-Pigovian analysis, with a de-emphasis or – in some cases – an outright exclusion of social-cost considerations.

In any case the two main discussions of price–output policy have been by Little and Ramanadham, and the gist of the private-market proposals appears to be as follows. Price–output decisions should be decentralized to the smallest producing units which can still realize economies of scale. These units will then operate as commercial units, according to pure or modified profit-maximizing. This, it is contended, will provide (1) an approximation to the purely competitive solution; thereby (2) an approximation of a marginal-cost pricing solution; and consequently, (3) an approximation of genuinely efficient allocation. Investment allocation will be determined by the 'normal profitability criterion'; profitable units will be expanded and loss-earning units will be contracted.

It has also been proposed to supplant cross-subsidizing by direct subsidies from general tax revenues. This would involve separating out the 'social service' activities of the public firms for Exchequer subsidies, leaving all other allocation decisions to be determined by purely 'commercial' calculations. Such an approach has gained wide and influential support.[23] But direct subsidies, though adopted in principle by the government, have not yet been provided in practice, nor are they likely to be. Instead, as testimony before the Select Committee has made clear,

---

109–23 [paper 2 in this edition]; and Wiseman, 'A further note', ibid., 1959, pp. 88–97.

For an extended analysis of the main problems connected with the classical 'problem of the deficit' in marginal-cost pricing, written by a proponent of marginal-cost pricing, see G. J. Oort, *Decreasing costs as a problem of welfare economics*, Drukkerij, Holland, 1958.

The applicability of 'second-best' analysis will be touched on later in this section.

23. Proponents include the Herbert Committee, Edwards and Townsend, Ramanadham, Merrett and Sykes, and, most enthusiastically of all, the Select Committee on the Nationalized Industries. Further bipartisan endorsement has recently appeared in the Fabian Society Study edited by Shanks, op. cit., and the approach was adopted as a matter of principle by the government in its important 1961 White Paper, *Financial and economic obligations of the nationalized industries*, 1961, Cmd 1337.

official and unofficial pressure is mainly directed simply at closing down loss-incurring operations, in order to have the public firms conform to 'commercial' patterns.

The first point to be made in evaluating the foregoing criticisms and proposals is that the urgency of adopting the proposals hinges directly on the actual extent and effects of cross-subsidizing. Some evidence on actual patterns will be given in section 2, but first it can be readily shown that cross-subsidizing within multi-unit public firms is not necessarily associated with misallocation. To put it more generally, a variety of financial patterns can be associated with any number of allocational patterns, without any indication of the relative efficiency of those allocation patterns.

In several types of situations, cross-section patterns of profits and losses within public firms may be wholly consistent with efficient allocation. To take some principal examples, there may be:

1. Stochastic disequilibria (for example, year-to-year fluctuations in financial results at individual coal pits and areas).

2. Transitional disequilibria (for example, if demand is shifting inward or outward more rapidly than the feasible rate of capacity depletion or expansion).

3. Demand fluctuations (for example, if off-peak production levels are below the optimum scale of given plant and/or if peak production levels are above the optimum scale).

4. Sunk costs or other rental elements in cost. Thus in a depleting-resource industry such as coal, total accounting costs at any producing plant may include an element of rent, which is entirely irrelevant to efficient price-output policy.

5. Externalities and other divergences of market costs from true social opportunity costs. In textbook terms, the economic and social costs of a particular decision may greatly exceed the plant's own incremental profit from taking that decision, so that 'commercial' decisions would directly violate the Pigovian marginal net social productivity conditions. Such divergences over both the short and medium run may be prominent in industries undergoing basic transitions and technical change.

These points simply reflect some of the obvious qualifications which have to be made for any conclusions based on purely static equilibrium analysis under perfectly competitive assumptions. Some of these conditions have undoubtedly been important in the coal industry during the post-war period. Therefore the existence of cross-subsidizing provides no *a priori* proof of genuine misallocation; it may show just the opposite. Undeniably accounting profits and losses are useful indicators for allocation decisions, at least for preliminary purposes, and under static pure-competitive conditions they would assume prescriptive importance for allocation decisions over both the short and long run. But actual misallocation in the post-war coal industry can only be demonstrated by direct evidence, including information on marginal social productivity conditions. No such demonstration has yet been made; the existence and extent of misallocation within the National Coal Board remain largely unproven and unknown.

The practical urgency of adopting private-market patterns, or any other new criterion, is therefore less certain than has been thought. In any case, private-market criteria themselves usually have limited validity in prescribing specific allocation patterns, except for the cases in which static perfectly competitive conditions are satisfied, with no private-social cost divergences. In such model textbook situations, identical efficient solutions would result from (1) private-market simulation, from (2) marginal-cost pricing, and (3) from case-by-case determination according to all relevant social costs and benefits. But under real-world conditions, the private-firm and marginal-cost pricing approaches will almost certainly yield different, and possibly markedly inefficient, solutions. In particular, private-market rules break down precisely in those situations – involving externalities and other private-social divergences – which comprise the really difficult allocation problems of the National Coal Board.

This is no more than simple Pigovian economics, but it appears to have been overlooked in much of the recent discussion of cross-subsidizing and of private-market criteria and policy rules. It also bears mentioning that the mere fact of large numbers of plants (i.e. 700 coal pits) in an industry-wide public firm does not ensure competitive conditions for each plant. In fact, many public-firm plants and products are involved in highly imperfect market conditions, on both the buying and the selling sides.

Therefore, decentralization on a private-market model would yield an efficient allocation solution at each unit only by a very remote chance. Nor is this point affected by 'second-best' considerations. Departures from Pareto or pure-competitive conditions in private industry do *not* establish the need for similar departures in public firms. Instead they establish the need for case-by-case consideration of specific intermarket conditions, and the resulting second-best prescriptions for public firms may diverge sharply from private-market simulation.[24]

Practical difficulties of the proposals are also formidable, especially regarding the instructions and the information to be provided to the decentralized decision-makers. The rules for individual units have not been adequately defined, nor can it be assumed that clear and valid general rules could be formulated. The present state of knowledge about economies of scale – in production and at other levels – gives faint hope that the 'optimum' unit of decentralization can be clearly defined. In fact a major gain from public ownership has been to internalize various economies external to the individual plant. These factors may not permit much decentralization at all; in any case the problems are complex and require detailed treatment. Not surprisingly, most writers have found it necessary to discuss individual problems in extended detail, and it is to be expected that the important allocational decisions would continue to require such specific attention, even if a private-market approach were formally adopted.

In view of the foregoing points, the vague private-market criteria and policy rules which have recently been proposed can be said to comprise essentially an empty economic box. Even if cross-subsidizing has been associated with demonstrable misallocation, this cannot be deduced from financial patterns alone, least of all by a mere citing of divergences from 'commercial' financial criteria and patterns. Nor would an alteration of the financial patterns alone necessarily provide efficient allocation, as has been suggested. The extent of possible misallocation, and the need for revising allocation criteria, are therefore primarily empirical questions at this point.

24. This conclusion emerges clearly in the discussions by Lipsey and Lancaster, Fishlow and David, and Mishan mentioned earlier.

2. Evidence on Cross-Subsidizing and Allocation Trends

Instances of cross-subsidizing can be found in most of the British public corporations.[25] But cross-subsidizing and its effects can be studied most systematically in the case of the coal industry. This is in large part because of the excellent data which are available from 1951 on, and also because the coal industry's outputs are relatively standardized – spatially and intertemporally – and its producing units are very numerous. Unpublished data on costs, profits, production, productivity, and investment at individual pits were made available for this study by the Coal Board, or were drawn from published sources.[26] The actual extent of cross-subsidizing, and its relations to changing patterns of output and investment, are indicated by the following evidence.

The extent of cross-subsidizing

There are as yet no standard procedures for measuring cross-subsidizing. In the present study, cross-subsidizing is computed for each year as the sum of financial losses incurred at unremunerative individual plants, areas, or regions. This sum, expressed as a percentage of a standard magnitude – total costs – is the 'degree of cross-subsidizing'.[27]

25. This has been brought out in Select Committee hearings; see its reports on gas, op. cit.; the air corporations, H. of C. 276, 1959; and British Railways, H. of C. 254, 1960.

26. Because data for all pits were made available, the following material represents complete coverage rather than samples. Individual-pit data were used only for the years 1951–3 and 1959–61, in order to show longer-run trends. The investment data, as will be seen, present the main problems of concept and accuracy. The published sources are chiefly the industry's yearly *Accounts*, and the Ministry of Power *Statistical Digest*, also yearly.

27. Adjustments were also made to allow for the moderate yearly fluctuations in the Coal Board's overall profit or loss. Luckily, the coal pit costs do not include rent elements held over from compensation payments to the private owners, since these payments have not been imputed as such to the pits. Therefore the costs are relatively free of sunk cost elements. Interest charges are also not imputed separately to pits in these data, but this does not pose a serious problem: first, because the amounts involved in interest payments are small in most years (about 2 per cent of total costs) and second, because the variations in capital-intensity of pits are in directions which would tend to make the present estimates *overstate* the true amount of cross-subsidizing rather than understate it. All in all, the present

As shown in figure 1, the coal industry contained substantial cross-subsidizing before public ownership was established, under the war-time coal charges account. Since nationalization, and especially since the new price system was applied, cross-subsidizing has been reduced though by no means eliminated. During the

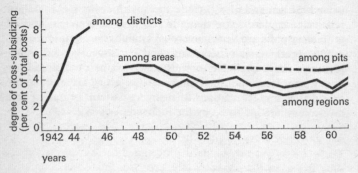

Figure 1

1950s it has been of moderate extent and declining, while the anxiety about it has been growing.[28] The table appended to this paper shows that by 1961 the losses were located mainly in the Scottish and South-Western Divisions, and profits were mainly in the North-Eastern and East Midlands Divisions.

Cross-subsidizing and changing output patterns

For an industry-wide survey of output trends, it would be desirable but impossible to construct meaningful marginal cost and demand schedules – allowing for social costs and benefits – for individual producing units. Instead, intertemporal tests of output and profit changes at individual pits were made in this

---

measures probably do not understate cross-subsidizing at all. This is not to deny, however, that a better measure of cross-subsidization would be the saving that could be achieved by closing down pits with current losses.

28. The apparent increase during 1960 and 1961 reflects in part the increased profits earned by the Coal Board as a whole in order to cover its rapidly increasing interest costs. This is essentially a technical factor; if it were allowed for, the degree of cross-subsidizing would show a continual decline.

study. The results of these tests, though tentative, bear directly on the issues which have been raised in the literature; they show the emerging outlines of long-run reorganization of the coal industry; and they provide an initial step toward an adequate assessment of allocation patterns.

The tests inquire: Have the producing units which have been incurring significant losses been either restored to profitability, contracted substantially, or closed altogether? This would correspond approximately to the treatment which the private market would *in theory* prescribe, as was noted in section 1 above. In the present work a 'substantial contraction' is arbitrarily defined as 30 per cent or more of the initial output level; in view of natural rates of depletion at pits, this is not an unreasonable benchmark. If a given pit's conditions in 1961 or 1960–61 did not satisfy the three-part criterion, it was classed as 'deviant'. Two tests were made for coal pits: one covered all pits showing more than negligible losses in 1950–51, and the other covered pits which in 1951 did not cover their *variable costs*.[29] These tests provide minimum and maximum estimates of the extent of deviance of output patterns from theoretical private-market prescriptions.

The *maximum* estimates of deviance are given in Table 2; the minimum estimates will also be discussed. The 259 separate pits which showed average losses in 1951–2 of at least 5 shillings per ton comprised the statistical population in which 'deviant' pits might occur. These 259 pits produced 34·0 million tons of coal in 1951, which was 16·2 per cent of total industry output; and their

29. Since interest costs are not allowed for in computing losses, the present estimates may slightly understate the true amount of deviance.

There are some yearly variations in pits results, but a study of these indicated that they are not substantial except for a small number of large-loss, small pits which would be classed as deviant in any case. The use of 1951–2 and 1960–61 average figures takes care of all but a small amount of this stochastic variation; for most purposes single-year data are fairly reliable.

The total time span of ten years is possibly too short to reflect long-run trends at some pits. To this extent, the present estimates of deviance are *overstated*. This depends on the natural rate of depletion of capital and labour at declining pits, which may be slow in many cases. The estimates were somewhat sensitive to the cut-off point used. If a 20 per cent criterion for shrinkage had been used, only 54 pits – with 4 per cent of total 1951 output – would have been classed as deviant.

summed financial losses were 20·5 million, which was 3·4 per cent of total industry costs.

Of these pits, 81 were classed as 'deviant' on the basis of their 1960–61 results. As shown in Table 2 these 81 pits accounted in 1951 for about 10 per cent of the industry by number of pits;

Table 2

National Coal Board: Data on 'Deviant' Pits

	Scotland, Northern, Durham, and South Western	All other regions	Totals for all regions
Number of 'deviant' pits	74	7	81
As a % of total in 1951	9·5	0·9	10·4
Output of 'deviant' pits in 1951 (millions of tons)	10·5	1·9	12·4
As a % of total	4·98	0·91	5·89
Employment at 'deviant' pits in 1951 (thousands)	46·88	7·85	54·73
As a % of total	6·74	1·13	7·87
Annual output per worker at 'deviant' pits (tons)	223	245	226
As a % of industry average	73·4	80·6	74·4
Average size of 'deviant' pits (1,000 tons per year)	141	276	153
As a % of industry average	52·5	102·7	56·9
Total reported losses at 'deviant' pits; average 1951–2 in millions of pounds	6·80	1·31	8·01
As a % of all reported losses	19·0	3·4	22·4
As a % of total industry costs	1·12	0·19	1·31

5·9 per cent by output; and 7·9 per cent by employment. The average size of the deviant pits was only about half the industry-wide average size. The total reported losses at the deviant pits during 1951–2 comprised only 1·31 per cent of total industry costs in those years. These are significant but not large proportions. More than nine-tenths of the deviant pits were clustered in the Scottish, Northern, Durham, and South Western regions. In fact, 45 per cent of the total 1961 employment at deviant pits is concentrated in only 6 of the 51 producing areas. Despite this clustering, the deviant pits comprise only about one-eighth of the output and employment in the four regions in question.

The *minimum* estimate of deviance involved only 27 pits out of more than 800 total pits in 1951, and these 27 accounted for only 0·7 per cent of total industry output. This variable costs test – which has the more direct normative implications of the two tests – therefore indicates a very small amount of deviation. Again, regional clustering was evident; the four regions accounted for 25 of the 27 deviant pits. Henderson's linear programming estimate of 'inefficiency' in the American soft-coal industry, though not directly comparable, suggests departures from efficiency at least as great as those which may be suggested here.[30] Moreover, the problems are common to most European coal industries, and the Coal Board's activities toward reorganization do not compare unfavourably with those in continental, and American, coalfields.[31] In any case, the present tentative estimates of deviation are lower than one would expect on the basis of previous writings.

In view of the continued long-run concentration of the industry, the present estimates are only preliminary, but they do indicate that some previous commentaries have been decidedly premature. They further suggest that long-run production-allocation decisions

30. See J. M. Henderson, *The efficiency of the bituminous coal industry*, Cambridge, Harvard University Press, 1958. Significantly, Henderson concludes: 'The high cost capacities have not been reduced through the automatic working of the market, and their reduction would not be easy. The relocation of the displaced workers would be a difficult task, for which the government would have to assume at least partial responsibility.' And against Henderson's finding of approximately 19 per cent of transport costs as 'inefficiency' in American coal mining may be set Ailsa Land's linear programming estimate for transport costs of coking coals in 1953 in the National Coal Board; the estimated 'inefficiency' was no more than 10 per cent. See A. H. Land, 'An application of linear programming to the transport of coking coal', *Journal of the Royal Statistical Society*, Series A (General), 1957, pp. 308–19.

31. Some indication of this can be found in Gordon, op. cit.; *The Coal Industry in Europe*, A Study by the Coal Committee, Organization for Economic Co-operation and Development, Paris, 1961, pp. 37–44; W. Baum, *The French Economy and the State*, a RAND study, Princeton, 1958; and in the yearly *Reports and accounts* of the National Coal Board.

by the Coal Board have not been largely 'divorced from under-lying market conditions'.

The spatial clustering of deviant pits indicates that deviance is probably involved in localized problems of industrial contraction, labour immobility, and other related departures from the assumptions for smoothly functioning competitive markets. Since, as is well known, this is very much the case, an evaluation of allocation based on marginal social opportunity costs would probably show even less 'deviation' than the present results.

Delays in closing uneconomic pits may stem not only from considerations of social welfare, but may also make commercial sense. If the rate of closures exceeds what the workers consider to be fair (regardless whether their criteria are economically sound, and they often are not), there follow repercussions on labour co-operation and productivity throughout the industry. In turn, other factors – including rates of unemployment in alternative occupations and the introduction of new establishments in declining coalfields – condition the coal-miners' responses to closures. Therefore the commercially appropriate rate of closures (as well as the socially appropriate rate) depends partly on government policies toward full employment, retraining, and the location of industry.

Cross-subsidizing and long-run investment patterns

The present investigation of investment patterns focuses on two questions. First, is there evidence that the profitability of individual coal pits has influenced the allocation of investment among them? Second, and more important, is there evidence that investment has, in turn, improved profitability in accordance with criteria of efficient allocation? Within the limits of the data, some fairly definite evidence on these points was unearthed. Before we consider these results, it should be noted that most investment by the coal industry undergoes detailed reviews and financial tests, including rate-of-return criteria, similar to those putatively applied in private firms.[32] Whether these reviews yield

32. This may be seen in the evidence given in the Select Committee's hearings on the coal industry in 1957; see also Shanks (ed.), op. cit., chapter 2, for a useful, though not necessarily disinterested, discussion of investment evaluation problems.

efficient patterns is of course an open question, which the following evidence may help to answer. A number of tests are used, including both regressions and comparisons among groupings of investment totals. The data have a number of serious defects: yet some fairly clear results were obtained.[33]

There have been two major types of investment in the coal industry: (1) the major reconstruction projects, which comprise the industry's 1950 *Plan for coal*, as subsequently adjusted; and (2) the various smaller projects to increase the power loading of coal at the coal face. Major projects have absorbed half of all fixed investment in the coal industry; but of the nearly 300 projects only about 110 had been completed by 1961. Investment in power-loading equipment, most of it since 1954, has taken about one-third of fixed investment. The power-loading projects have been largely supplementary and interstitial to the major reconstruction programme. Since the major projects are the heart of the long-run investment programme, they are of primary interest here.

First, have the broad trends of investment allocation among coal pits been influenced by profitability at those pits during the early post-war years? This would accord with the private-market prescriptions noted in section 1, which treat producing-unit projects as the normal basis for allocating investment. It should be noted, however, that studies of actual private investment have shown at most only a weak lagged statistical association of investment with profitability.[34] In the present case the available

33. The chief defects are:
   1. No individual-pit data at all are available for the years before 1951.
   2. Cost breakdowns for individual pits included only two categories, 'Wage costs' and 'Other'. This precluded a good measurement of variable costs.
   3. Investment data are very incomplete.
      (a) The only indicator of power-loading investment is the per cent of output power-loaded: this is a very crude measure of investment, owing to different conditions at different mines.
      (b) The reconstruction investment totals are grossed over the entire project, thereby including investment at changing prices. Moreover, reconstruction affected only some operations and faces at some pits, whereas profit data are for entire pits.

34. See, for example, R. Eisner, *The determinants of investment demand*, Urbana, University of Illinois Press, 1956, and J. J. Diamond, 'Further

data permit some testing, using simple lagged profitability-investment hypotheses, but the results are so tentative that they will only be summarized briefly here. [...]

Concerning individual pits, a comparison was first made between mechanization at 'deviant' pits and at all other pits. By 1961 some 48·4 per cent of total national coal output was power-loaded. Of the 74 deviant pits in the Scottish, Northern, Durham, and South-Western Divisions, 34 had been allocated no power-loading machinery at all by 1961. The average proportion of output power-loaded in the 74 deviant pits was only 25·4 per cent. Statistically this mean is significantly different from the average increase in power-loading at all other pits, at the 1 per cent level. The deviant pits have formed a distinct group in terms of the allocation of investment for power-loading.

The only available single indicator of investment at all pits is the increase in per cent of output power-loaded during the period. This proxy variable for investment is of limited relevance, since power-loading investment, though substantial, has been only a supplementary part of the total.[35] Multiple and simple regressions were run nevertheless, to see if any pattern emerged. Data were available for 621 pits altogether; regressions were repeated for 309 larger pits, to remove most of the stochastic elements connected with the smaller pits.

As expected the results, in Table 3, suggest very little association between 1951 profitability and subsequent power-loading investment.[36] At the larger and more important pits, power-loading investment appears to have been positively associated with profitability. But evidently other influences, including those associated with the size of pits, have been predominant. In view of the supplementary role of power-loading investment, and the defects of the variables, these results are not inconsistent with

---

development of a distributed lag investment function', *Econometrica*, 1962, pp. 788–800, and references therein.

35. The profitability variable (in shillings per ton of output) is also weak, since it is only an estimator of profitability on investment, and it is available no earlier than 1951.

36. Similar regressions using 1951–2 average profitability data showed no clearer association than did the regressions based on 1951 profitability only, which are reported in Table 3.

Table 3 National Coal Board: Results of Regressions of Increased Power-Loading as a Function of Profitability and Size of Pit, 1951 to 1961

Regressions involving all 621 pits

	F Ratio	R^2
% Increase in power-loading = $11\cdot35 - 0\cdot235$ [Profitability in 1951] $+ 0\cdot08$ [Output in 1961]	125·7	0·289
$\qquad\qquad\qquad\qquad\quad(1\cdot78)\;(0\cdot081)\qquad\qquad\qquad\qquad(0\cdot01)$		
T values $\qquad\qquad\qquad\;\;6\cdot37\quad\;\;2\cdot94\qquad\qquad\qquad\quad\;15\cdot83$		
% Increase in powe -loading = $33\cdot14 + 0\cdot066$ [Profitability in 1951]		0·001
$\qquad\qquad\qquad\qquad\quad(1\cdot34)\;(0\cdot092)$		
T values $\qquad\qquad\qquad24\cdot77\quad0\cdot71$		
% Increase in power-loading = $12\cdot36 + 0\cdot077$ [Output in 1961]		0·279
$\qquad\qquad\qquad\qquad\quad(1\cdot76)\;(0\cdot005)$		
T values $\qquad\qquad\qquad\;7\cdot04\quad15\cdot49$		

Regressions involving the 309 larger pits

	F Ratio	R^2
% Increase in power-loading = $26\cdot85 + 0\cdot163$ [Profitability in 1951] $+ 0\cdot049$ [Output in 1961]	19·5	0·113
$\qquad\qquad\qquad\qquad\quad(3\cdot91)\;(0\cdot268)\qquad\qquad\qquad\qquad(0\cdot008)$		
T values $\qquad\qquad\qquad\;\;6\cdot87\quad0\cdot608\qquad\qquad\qquad\quad5\cdot94$		
% Increase in power-loading = $47\cdot13 + 0\cdot502$ [Profitability in 1951]		0·011
$\qquad\qquad\qquad\qquad\quad(2\cdot01)\;(0\cdot276)$		
T values $\qquad\qquad\qquad23\cdot51\quad1\cdot822$		

The critical values for T are 1·96 at the 5 per cent and 2·58 at the 1 per cent significance level. The critical values for the F ratios at the 1 per cent level are as follows: 621 observations and 3 variables, F is 4·66. With 309 observations and 3 variables, the critical F is 4·70.

The power-loading variable ranged from zero to 100, with an average of 48 and a standard deviation of about 26. Profitability in 1951 ranged from −63 to +29, with a standard deviation of about 7. Output in 1961, which was used to represent the actual or expected long-run level of output, ranged from 4 to 1,126 thousand tons, with a mean of 306 and a standard deviation of about 170.

the other indications that there has been some influence of profitability on investment allocation decisions. Conversely, the evidence does not confirm the hypothesis that investment has been channelled relatively heavily into loss-earning units.

The weak association between actual profits and subsequent investment has little economic meaning because it is prospective rather than past returns which should form the basis of investment decisions. But it has been argued accusingly that investment has been channelled to unprofitable pits. It has therefore seemed worth while to discover that the data do not in fact suggest any broad such weighing of investment.

We now turn to the possible influences of investment *on profits*. The most damaging criticisms of public-firm investment patterns have been that much public-firm investment has not provided returns as high as were available in comparable alternative uses. These criticisms have relied almost entirely on deductions that 'low' rate-of-return criteria will lead to over-investment (presumably as judged by marginal social opportunity costs, although this latter point is rarely explicitly stated). We have already seen that this reasoning wrongly assumes an identity between private and social costs and benefits; that it ignores the problems of defining and allowing for relevant risk conditions; and that it assumes that the rate of interest on loans has closely controlled investment decisions, whereas there is evidence that other long-run considerations have strongly influenced investment programming. Therefore the actual productivity of the investment is not known and is a matter for factual study. The findings given herein are only exploratory and tentative, but no other direct evidence presently exists for judging the actual relations of investment to generally efficient patterns.

The basic hypothesis treated here is that increases in profits at individual producing units have been directly associated with earlier investment expenditure. The nature and strength of the actual associations are indicated both by comparisons among groups, and by regression analysis. The data cover investment levels at individual units, and changes in profits at those units from pre-investment to post-investment levels. As before, data limitations precluded ideal tests. For example, in 1961, the latest available year, many investment projects were still incomplete, and investment and profitability data would, for this reason alone, not show long-run equilibrium patterns with full accuracy. Also, coal production was below capacity in 1958–61, and the continued basic reorganization of the industry caused unusual transitional results at many pits. Moreover, the limitation on overall profits has restricted the improvement which individual projects can show. And if one type of investment (such as reconstruction projects) shows profit improvement, then some other type of investment (such as power-loading) must *a fortiori* show zero or negative effects on profits. This, in broad terms, is what actually happened in the coal industry, as will be shortly seen.

For these and other reasons, one would not expect the empirical tests to show strong investment–profits relationships. And, as before, there is little likelihood that strong associations would be found in actual private industries, even though they have not been subject to constraints of the same sort and severity [. . .].

We will focus on the reconstruction programme. The figures for reconstruction investment (which are published in full in the industry's yearly *Accounts*) do not include all genuine 'net' investment by the Coal Board. Virtually everything they do include, however, is explicitly treated as net investment by the Board, and the programme represents the main outlines of investment allocation in the industry under public ownership and investment control.

Of the total of 296 projects begun by 1961, 111 were wholly completed by the beginning of 1961; most of these were of medium or small size. There were over 60 large schemes for which at least £2 million apiece had been spent or authorized by 1961. But of these only 17 had been completed. Actual spending on all of the large schemes during 1947–61 totalled 57 per cent of all reconstruction investment.

In a crude preliminary test the completed schemes can be plotted according to their 1951–2 and 1960–61 profitability in shillings per ton; this is illustrated in figure 2. On such a chart would also have to be laid an 'equivalent profits line'. This is the *locus* of pits whose profits or losses in 1960–61 were equal as a proportion of costs to profits or losses in 1951–2.[37] Each of the

37. The line's slope of less than one (0·615) reflects the increase in average unit costs during the period; a profit of 6·15 shillings per ton in 1951–2 was equivalent to a profit of 10·00 shillings per ton in 1960–61.

resulting six zones in figure 2 represents a different permutation of profit results for the two periods. Using these zones, one can apply alternative criteria to the patterns of investment. An 'absolute' profits criterion requires only that a pit be profitable in the long run (represented in this case by 1960–61 for pits with completed schemes). Such an evaluation may well be premature; but in any case, pits falling in zones 1, 5, and 6 meet this criterion.

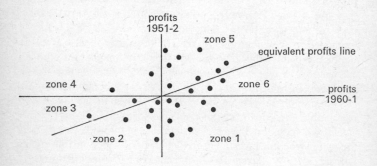

Figure 2

A 'relative' profits criterion requires that profitability be improved at pits undergoing projects. Roughly speaking, pits in zones 1, 2, and 6 qualify on this test. A stricter joint criterion might include only zones 1 and 6. By contrast, zones 3 and 4 would include pits which do not meet either criterion. For all their evident limitations, such tests do suggest the orders of magnitude involved in the trends of profitability and investment.

The results are grouped in Tables 4 and 5. The proportions were first tested statistically to see if they differed from the entire population of pits. In this test, the proportions of output at pits in Table 4 were compared with the output proportions for all pits. This chi-square test is plainly indirect, but it did show the proportions of reconstructed pits to be highly significantly different in the directions prescribed by private-market criteria. The financial status of the reconstructed pits is clearly more in conformity with the criteria than it would have been in the absence of the projects.

Perhaps more interesting are the proportions themselves in Tables 4 and 5. Of all reconstruction investment, some 75 per cent was in pits that met at least one criterion, and 55 per cent of investment was in pits which met both criteria. Three large projects did not meet either criterion, mainly because of unexpected geological difficulties. Also, all small pits suffered a ten-

Table 4

National Coal Board: Profitability 1951–2 and 1960–61 at Pits with Completed Major Reconstruction Projects

Criteria	For all projects, proportions:		Excluding the 3 deviant large projects:		All 17 large projects:	
	by number of pits	by amount of investment	by amount of investment	and all small pits by amount of investment	by number of pits	by amount of investment
	(1) (%)	(2) (%)	(3) (%)	(4) (%)	(5) (%)	(6) (%)
Profitability in 1960–61 (Zones 1, 5, and 6)	66·4	66·9	77·8	87·6	82·3	70·6
Improved profitability (Zones 1, 2, and 6)	65·5	63·2	73·5	79·3	70·6	60·4
One criterion or the other (Zones 1, 2, 5, and 6)	80·8	74·8	87·0	94·5	82·3	70·6
Both criteria (Zones 1 and 6)	51·1	55·3	64·3	72·4	70·6	60·4

dency toward losses during 1951–61 regardless of the intensity of investment. If these two sets of pits are held out, the proportions which meet the criteria are impressively higher, as shown in column 4. The amount of investment in pits which met *neither* criterion was only 5 per cent, and the amount which met both criteria was 72 per cent. This suggests that wide departures from private-market patterns occurred mainly when the Board invested in small pits or made geological errors of prediction at large pits.

The special position of the Scottish and South-Western regions is once more apparent, in Table 5. Considering all projects, investment in these two regions substantially failed both criteria. By contrast, investment in all other regions taken together met the criteria in proportions greatly exceeding the benchmark

Table 5

National Coal Board: Regional Differences in Results from Major Reconstruction Projects

| Criteria | Proportion of investment which satisfies the stated criteria | | |
| | Scottish division | South Western division | All other divisions |
	(%)	(%)	(%)
Profitability in 1960–61; groups 1, 5, and 6	21·4	29·1	81·9
Improved profitability; groups 1, 2, and 6	23·8	22·2	77·3
One criterion or the other; groups 1, 2, 5, and 6	31·4	32·4	90·0
Both criteria; groups 1 and 6	13·8	18·9	69·2

values. Only 10 per cent failed both criteria in these regions, and 69 per cent met both criteria. In general, then, there is a marked conformity with private-market patterns for reconstruction investment.

A more direct attempt to assess the effect of this investment on profits was then made. This involved the following regression for the 111 completed pits:

$$\begin{bmatrix} \text{Change in} \\ \text{total profits} \\ \text{1951 to 1961} \end{bmatrix}_i = \alpha + \beta \begin{bmatrix} \text{Total} \\ \text{reconstruction} \\ \text{investment} \end{bmatrix}_i + \epsilon$$

with the notation as before. The β coefficient gives a direct estimate of the financial 'return' on reconstruction investment, as shown by improved profits at these pits in relation to total reconstruction investment. For example, a coefficient of $+0·05$

342

would indicate that £100 of investment was associated with a £5 improvement in yearly profits. This estimated financial return is, moreover, probably an understatement of the net *social* return.

However, the likelihood of significant regressions was even less in the present case than in previous regressions. The investment totals unfortunately do not allow for changes in investment goods prices over the period. In many cases not all of the coal

Table 6

National Coal Board: Results of Regressions for Changes in Profits at Pits with Major Reconstruction Projects, 1951 to 1961

All 111 completed projects

$$\begin{bmatrix} \text{Change in total profit,} \\ \text{1951 to 1961} \end{bmatrix} = \underset{(46 \cdot 45)}{72 \cdot 23} + \underset{(0 \cdot 029)}{0 \cdot 081} \begin{bmatrix} \text{Total} \\ \text{investment} \end{bmatrix} \qquad R^2 \; 0 \cdot 065$$

T values $\qquad\qquad 1 \cdot 56 \qquad 2 \cdot 76$

All 84 projects in divisions other than Scottish or South Western

$$\begin{bmatrix} \text{Change in total profit,} \\ \text{1951 to 1961} \end{bmatrix} = \underset{(49 \cdot 50)}{108 \cdot 97} + \underset{(0 \cdot 030)}{0 \cdot 122} \begin{bmatrix} \text{Total} \\ \text{investment} \end{bmatrix} \qquad 0 \cdot 166$$

T values $\qquad\qquad 2 \cdot 20 \qquad 4 \cdot 04$

faces at a reconstructed pit were affected by reconstruction projects. Other randomizing factors have also been important. Also, the hypothesis of a linear relation may be incorrect, and the relation may differ among regions.[38]

Nevertheless, the regression coefficient was positive and statistically significant at the 1 per cent level as shown in Table 6. The hypothesis that reconstruction investment has been associated with zero or negative changes in profits can be rejected. Although reconstruction investment 'explains' only 6·5 per cent

38. The linear hypothesis, for instance, implies that the marginal return on investment has been constant, not declining. Under ordinary circumstances such a formulation could be questioned. In the present case, results from a great variety of pit conditions (large and small; difficult and favourable conditions) are taken together, so that a simple hypothesis of linearity may not be an unreasonable first approximation. An exploration of these points is presently in course, including separate tests by regions, restatements of the model, and newer data. The results in this paper are at best exploratory, although they are clearer than data problems would have permitted one to expect.

of the changes in profits, this result is roughly comparable to findings in studies of private-industry profits and investment.

The regression coefficient suggests that there has been an 8 per cent net financial return on reconstruction investment. For reasons already noted above, this estimated return is probably well below the long-run social marginal productivity of the investment. This 8 per cent return, although it is downward biased as a measure of net social return, is higher than has been suggested elsewhere. And for what the comparison is worth, it is at least comparable to average returns prevailing in approximately comparable alternative uses of investment.

To test this further, the regression was re-run excluding the projects in the Scottish and South-Western Divisions. Projects in these two regions did not generally meet the profitability criteria, partly because of more basic economic adjustment problems. In this second regression, 84 pits were included, accounting for 85·5 per cent of total reconstruction investment at projects which had been completed by 1961. Although the regression is somewhat selective, it still covers the great majority of all completed reconstruction projects in the entire National Coal Board.

The results, also in Table 6, show a still stronger association of investment with increased profits. The statistical association is highly significant, and it 'explains' over 16 per cent of the changes in profits. The regression coefficient indicates a net financial return of at least 12 per cent of investment. This is to some degree an understatement of *social* net return. It may be doubted that comparable returns, and closeness of association, could be shown on the average by similar studies of private-industry investment in Britain, if all risk and social cost considerations were allowed for. In view of other factors listed above which have influenced the profitability of individual pits, and in view of the criticisms in the literature, the observed association of reconstruction investment with increased profits is remarkable.[39]

39. Whether or not the Coal Board achieved an *optimum* allocation of reconstruction investment is not shown by this evidence. It is possible that a higher return could have been achieved by a different Plan for Coal (as revised). The data do suggest, however, that the return has not been generally lower than returns supposedly available in private industry, and it may have been higher; and this was despite the outside constraint on the coal industry's overall profits.

William G. Shepherd

My use of the regression estimates of the association of investment with changes in profits should be hedged with further qualifications since the regression coefficients are not rates of return in the economist's sense of the term. It is not unreasonable to assume as a first approximation (though there will be exceptions) that 1951 and 1961 represent 'before' and 'after' equilibrium levels of profitability at the reconstructed pits. To this extent, the change in profitability represents a permanent shift, one which is reaped each year in perpetuity. The productive life of these investments is generally quite long, in many cases exceeding forty years. Suppose also that the stream of net gains is discounted by an appropriate factor (such as 4 to 7 per cent). If so, the estimates in my paper understate the actual discounted investment returns, the amount of understatement depending on the assumptions made about project life and discounting factor. Also, in fact, profitability has further improved at most of these pits since 1961.

All of the foregoing tests are tentative, but they do suggest a fairly general consistency of various investment patterns with private-market hypotheses, and with probable efficiency patterns. Conditions and results in the Scottish and South-Western Divisions have been somewhat singular, but this does not provide direct evidence of inconsistency with efficient patterns according to basic social costs and benefits. Reconstruction investment shows a general, though not complete, consistency with some private-market criteria. In terms of marginal social returns, the consistency with efficiency criteria was probably substantially greater.

For all their limitations, the patterns observed here are clear enough to foreclose further claims that investment allocation has been mainly divorced from, or directly counter to, profitability and efficiency considerations. The patterns appear to be quite similar to those in European countries and in the United States coal industry, regardless of public or private ownership. And as the rate of operations approaches full capacity for more of the major pits, it is to be expected that the appearance of conformity with allocational criteria will become even stronger. Further discussion would be most effectively confined to the role of investment in specific areas, where social cost problems are important

345

and where 'private-market' prescriptions are particularly inapt. There may have been more efficient methods for allowing for the special conditions at small Scottish and South-Western pits, rather than through some adjustments in the types and patterns of investment. This will be considered in the next section.

3. Implications for Policy

This study has found that private-market simulation by public firms would be neither necessary nor sufficient as a means of reaching efficient allocation, although it possesses a kernel of validity and might not be inappropriate for certain trivial cases. Nor is such an approach likely to be workable, even if it could be framed with some precision. Therefore this approach cannot be considered to offer a 'rule' or basis for efficient price-output or investment policy for public firms.

Evidence has also been presented indicating that the National Coal Board's long-run allocation decisions – whatever their bases and procedures may actually have been – have not been generally distorted by the presence of some cross-subsidizing at each point in time. Broadly speaking, the Coal Board has been able to determine which pits and areas need expanding or closing in conformance with probable long-run efficiency.

Instead the really difficult problems and debatable decisions appear to have arisen in the *execution* of the long-run plans, in those areas (Scotland, Durham, South-Western, and others) where pit closures often have social impacts far exceeding the gains to the Coal Board. In this classic sort of Pigovian situation, the Board has not surprisingly attempted to make some allowances for the net social effects of its actions. Prevented from offering direct compensation to the miners and others who would be adversely affected by its reorganization,[40] the Coal Board has to some degree adjusted the character and amounts of its production and investment in certain areas. This was indicated in part in Tables 4 and 5.

Undoubtedly this approach has in some cases been more

40. The reader should note that this paper was written some years ago. [Ed.]

costly in net social terms than other conceivable methods, although the absolute amounts involved have not been large (compared with other instances in other markets in post-war Britain) and their benefits have been substantial in many cases. But what has been chiefly needed is further analysis and framing of more efficient methods for absorbing the social repercussions of reorganization.[41] Proposals for private-market simulation are quite inappropriate in this respect; they explicitly exclude any provision for the really important problems of structural and social adjustment.

Under present conditions, the primary need is not to debate in deductive terms the decision-making of the public firms, but instead to develop alternative government measures to promote the industries' reorganization by compensating for its effects. Up to now the emphasis has been overwhelmingly in the opposite direction, and accordingly much of the discussion has contributed little to understanding or solving the real problems. These problems, to repeat, inhere in the imperfections and externalities of existing markets and social processes.

One possible measure for promoting adjustment in coal, as well as in the railways and rural gas production, would provide lump-sum compensation payments tied to shifts by the individuals or firms affected by the more drastic changes. In the case of disemployed miners or railway operators, such payments would need to be substantial, in order to compensate for the capital losses and other costs incurred in personal relocation and retraining, and in order to induce sufficient voluntary shifts by those who are capable of re-employment.[42] The payments might

41. Thus the structure of coal prices has distinct ramifications for regional economic development, beyond the obvious welfare problems associated with miner redundancy. This is especially clear in the case of Scotland, where in 1961 an increase in the price of coal by more than 10 per cent would have been required to eliminate cross-subsidizing. The impact of such a coal price increase on final goods prices, and on industrial location, could be substantial, and it is evidently a matter of concern to the government.

42. A lump-sum payments method was suggested by Long in the dissertation from which his published essay is drawn, op. cit. No other proposal of this sort has appeared in the literature, nor any study of the main issues and problems associated with the social impact of reorganization in the coal industry and the railways. There are some instructive parallels between the coal industry and post-war agricultural problems in the United

also require the worker to take a retraining course, or be tied in some other way. Payments of the order of £500 to £1,000, perhaps graduated by age, seniority, and other considerations, would be appropriate, in contrast to the nugatory payments – not tied to relocation or retraining – currently being discussed. In the case of the coal industry the once-for-all cost to public revenues of such a scheme would be modest, and probably much less than alternative approaches.[43] This approach would be in addition to the policies for full employment, retraining, and regional location of industry which are obviously needed in any case.

The proposals for direct subsidies for certain 'social' activities of the public corporations (see section 1) are attractive, but they would involve several difficult problems. First, there is little practical likelihood of government acceptance of such continuing direct subsidies.[44] Second, the method would be *more* likely to encourage public-firm inefficiency than would cross-subsidizing. Third, past experience gives little hope that such subsidies would be 'openly and rationally discussed', as is claimed. Fourth, serious problems would arise in specifying which activities are 'social' and which are 'commercial'. In any case, the basis upon which such subsidies would be calculated and reconciled with public-firm accounts is as yet wholly unclear. Perhaps most seriously, such direct subsidies might tend to preserve existing patterns rather than promote adjustment, as properly designed

States, both in the types of market imperfections and the kinds of structural adjustments which are needed. Proposals for lump-sum relocation payments for 'extra-marginal' farmers have been numerous, but have made little practical headway. But the main reasons for this lack of practical action do not appear to be present in the case of British coal and railways.

43. For example, consider a scheme which would have provided in 1961 a £500 terminal payment to miners aged 15–24, £700 for ages 25–34, and so on in £200 and 10-year stages. All miners at the 'deviant' pits (by the maximum test) would receive this payment. There were about 52,000 miners at these pits in 1961. The age structure of miners at these pits is approximately the same as for all pits. Accordingly the once-for-all total cost of this scheme would work out at £49·5 million, which would have been only 5·6 per cent of total coal industry costs in 1961.

44. This has been stressed by J. R. Sargent (in chapter 15 of Shanks (ed.), op. cit.) as one reason for relying on cross-subsidizing to finance certain 'social' activities.

lump-sum payments might be able to do fairly effectively and equitably. Nevertheless it may be possible to make out a good economic case for some such direct treatment for certain types of 'social' services.

The problems, and the possibilities for social policy, are subject to change, and what is needed is research and experimentation on a number of alternative methods rather than an attempt to discover a single all-embracing solution. The important point is that this area – public policies to compensate and promote public-firm adjustment – is perhaps the main area where economists' advice is needed. In recent years, public discussions and official policy on British public firms have been moving away from this sort of problem, toward an insistence on private-market behaviour patterns for the public firms, as though this in itself would solve the difficult problems which remain. For the reasons outlined in this paper, such an attempt must be viewed for the most part with misgivings.

Appendix

Table 1

National Coal Board: Regional Data, 1948–61

Year	Scottish	North-ern	Durham	North-Eastern	North-Western	East Mid-lands	West Mid-lands	S.-East and S.-Western	Total all regions
					Name of Regions				
	Output (millions of tons)								
1948	22·8	11·8	24·3	38·2	13·4	35·1	17·0	24·0	186·5
1951	23·6	13·4	27·2	44·4	15·3	43·0	18·0	26·4	211·3
1955	22·0	13·5	25·6	43·9	15·6	46·1	17·7	25·8	210·2
1959	18·5	12·7	23·3	41·9	14·0	44·6	15·4	22·1	192·5
1961	17·2	11·8	22·3	39·4	11·7	44·1	13·8	19·3	179·7
	Average number of wage-earners (thousands)								
1948	79·3	46·8	106·4	138·4	58·3	96·3	58·2	117·8	701·5
1951	81·2	48·3	105·6	136·3	57·0	96·3	55·5	114·4	694·6
1955	83·7	47·1	102·1	139·3	58·9	101·8	57·4	113·8	704·1
1959	79·9	43·7	95·6	132·1	51·9	100·1	53·1	101·8	658·2
1961	69·4	37·1	85·3	116·5	41·8	91·3	41·8	87·3	570·5
	Output per man-shift (tons)								
1948	1·11	1·05	0·94	1·22	0·97	1·60	1·22	0·83	1·11
1951	1·12	1·12	1·03	1·34	1·08	1·79	1·33	0·95	1·22
1955	1·04	1·19	1·01	1·34	1·10	1·83	1·29	0·93	1·23
1959	1·07	1·30	1·08	1·50	1·26	2·03	1·38	1·03	1·35
1961	1·15	1·41	1·16	1·60	1·31	2·18	1·53	1·05	1·45
	Average cost (in shillings per ton)[1]								
1948	44·6	48·8	52·2	42·6	50·2	36·1	41·8	56·8	45·7
1951	51·5	54·0	55·8	45·7	54·8	38·6	45·8	60·4	49·2
1955	75·5	70·3	77·5	62·0	77·5	50·8	63·3	83·9	67·3
1959	100·3	86·0	96·4	74·9	91·8	62·2	82·1	99·8	82·4
1961	107·9	88·1	100·0	80·5	103·4	65·9	88·0	116·3	88·4
	Operating profit or loss (in shillings per ton)[1]								
1948	+2·8	−2·3	−4·0	−3·4	+0·1	+7·8	+4·5	−4·5	+1·7
1951	−0·5	−2·6	−2·8	+4·5	−0·3	+8·0	+4·5	−2·7	+2·1
1955	−6·5	−1·3	−1·7	+3·9	−5·5	+7·4	+2·4	−4·3	+0·8
1959	−14·2	−3·9	−2·0	+6·7	−3·5	+7·9	+0·2	−1·2	+1·0
1961	−15·3	+0·4	+0·2	+9·2	−6·0	+11·5	+4·5	−8·8	+2·5
	Capital expenditure (millions of current pounds)								
1948	2·8	1·4	2·6	2·9	2·2	4·9	1·8	2·2	20·7
1951	3·2	2·0	3·0	4·6	3·2	5·4	2·0	4·2	27·6
1955	11·6	3·9	9·5	13·7	7·6	12·6	5·6	12·8	77·3
1959	16·7	6·1	10·7	19·1	8·1	16·3	12·5	15·6	105·1
1961	9·3	3·6	8·2	16·5	7·3	15·9	10·1	14·5	85·6

[1] Average cost is exclusive of interest charges, which are not subtracted in computing profits and losses. Interest charges were about 3 per cent of total costs during the period.

SOURCE: Ministry of Fuel and Power, *Statistical Digest*, op. cit.

11 William G. Shepherd

Residential Telephone Service in Britain

William G. Shepherd, 'Residence expansion in the British telephone system', *The Journal of Industrial Economics*, vol. 14 (1966), pp. 263-74.

As a utility system develops toward widespread use, the relative growth-rates of its individual services are influenced in part by tariff policy. Departures from correct price-cost differentials over the array of services may contribute to an uneven development in the structure of the system.

This paper presents the thesis that in Great Britain residence telephone service is over-priced, relative to its cost, as compared with business service. This presumably results in a misallocation of resources, in the form of a bias in the growth pattern of services. In support of this view, the paper surveys the system's evolving structure (in section 1) and analyses tariff policies and patterns in relation to costs (in section 2). A concluding section summarizes the findings.

Two general points concerning tariff policy do need brief mention at the outset.[1] The first concerns rate *structure*. Ordinary telephone service requires a connected instrument for the caller, an open line and instrument for the person being called, and central exchange equipment with capacity to make and hold the connexion. The real cost of this service varies directly with the fluctuations in the system's total traffic; this applies to local service as well as long-distance calling (where rates have always allowed for at least some of the cost differences).

As is well known, an optimum rate structure in principle aligns prices for individual services with their marginal costs, subject to

---

1. Two broad reviews of optimum pricing criteria for telephone service are in Arthur Hazlewood, 'Optimum pricing as applied to telephone service', *Review of Economic Studies*, 1950-51, pp. 67-78 [reading 7 this edition]; and T. A. Morgan, *Telecommunications economics*, MacDonald, 1958.

certain provisos.[2] Accordingly, fluctuating telephone traffic loads justify a temporal differentiation of rates, to reflect the higher real costs of peak-load use. Since much of the total cost of telephone service is equipment cost, a non-differentiated tariff structure is likely to induce excessive, and wasteful, use at peak times. Both in concept and in accounting practice, cost allocation has always posed large problems. Yet accurate price-cost alignment is essential for efficient pricing, with an importance in direct relation to the amplitude of traffic fluctuations, the reserve capacity at peak times, and the relative share of common costs in total costs.

Apart from time-of-day pricing, the main rate-structure problem for local service is in setting local service area boundaries and prices per call unit within those boundaries to correspond with cost patterns. Especially in metropolitan areas, this is difficult as well as important, because (1) the technology is complicated and changing, and (2) the complex, shifting spatial mix of calling patterns usually precludes a clear-cut optimum charging grid.

The second general point concerns the general *level* of rates, and the size of the aggregate revenue surplus. It has become customary for utilities, under public regulation in America and public ownership in Britain, to be assigned overall rate-of-return limits,

2. Among the main qualifications are: (1) It may not be possible to specify marginal costs unambiguously (see J. Wiseman, 'The theory of public utility price: An empty box', *Oxford Economic Papers*, 1957, pp. 56–74; and 'A further note', ibid., 1959, pp. 88–97). (2) In industries with decreasing costs in most types of output, the possibility of an overall financial deficit for the industry may make it necessary to seek some optimum ratio (not equality) of price to marginal costs (see C. J. Oort, *Decreasing costs as a problem of welfare economics*, Drukkerij, Holland, 1958; and J. R. Nelson, *Marginal cost pricing in practice*, Prentice-Hall, 1964). (3) The 'second-best' problem (of non-marginalist patterns in adjacent markets) may require *ad hoc* price policy adjustments. Although the magnitude of needed second-best adjustments is currently thought to be small in most cases, they may in specific cases be large. In the present instance, postal services are the closest substitute, and their pricing is known to be less than ideal. (4) Finally, marginal costs must be at least workably measurable, and the 'cost of marginal-cost pricing' (measuring costs and framing rates) will usually set a limit to the exactitude of the price-cost structure. Among general discussions, see J. C. Bonbright, *Principles of public utility rates*, Columbia University Press, 1961, chapter 3, 16, 17, and 20.

usually about 6 to 8 per cent on existing utility capital.[3] The appropriate limit depends on genuine risk-return conditions faced by the utility, as one claimant among many for investible funds. The economic case for such a limit lies in rationing present use and screening prospective investment, rather than in recording some 'return' on the cumulative frozen array of past investments.[4] A rate-of-return target based on (1) incomplete risk evaluation and (2) a conventional evaluation of the existing capital rate base may deviate widely from the target rate of return consistent with efficient allocation of current and capital resources. And it may in any case have little connection with financial criteria for individual services *within* the system. This point applies with added force if the allocation of major overhead costs among individual services is unavoidably arbitrary, as it is to some extent in a telephone system.

1. Structure of the System

The British case is of interest both in its own right and as one of many partially developed national systems, among which there are widely differing expansion patterns.[5] As Table 1 shows, Britain's early telephone growth was concentrated in business service; only since about 1940 have total residence connexions outnumbered business subscribers. Since 1950, business connexions have increased at an average annual rate of about 2·4 per

3. The American rates are of course mainly ceilings, while the British rates are mainly floors. On American patterns, see, for example, W. G. Shepherd and T. G. Gies (eds.), *Utility regulation: New directions in theory and policy*, Random House, 1966. The British rates date from the White Paper, *The financial and economic obligations of the nationalized industries*, Cmnd 1337, 1961. For comments on them, see M. V. Posner, 'Old Problems and new policies in nationalized industries', *District Bank Review*, December 1962, pp. 3–18; and W. G. Shepherd, *Economic performance under public ownership*, Yale University Press, 1965.

4. See Bonbright, op. cit., esp. chapters 10–15; also Shepherd and Gies, ed. cit., chapters 2 and 7; and the discussion by M. J. Peck and J. R. Meyer in *Transportation economics*, Columbia University Press, 1965.

5. Residence telephones were 43 per cent of all telephones in Britain in 1963; in other major systems the share ranges from 13 per cent in Japan, 18 in Czechoslovakia and 28 in Poland up to about 70 per cent in Canada, Norway, Sweden and the United States; see American Telephone and Telegraph Company, *The world's telephones, 1963*, New York.

cent, and residence connexions at about 5·6 per cent. Yet the expansion of residence connexions has declined from 7·2 per cent yearly in 1950–57 to 4·4 per cent during 1957–64.

Table 1

United Kingdom: Growth in Telephone Service, 1921–64

Year	Business (1,000)	Total connexions (1,000) Residence (1,000)	Total* (1,000)	Size of waiting list (1,000)	Per cent of telephones on automatic exchanges (%)
1921	n.a.	n.a.	n.a.	n.a.	2·9
1925	n.a.	n.a.	799	n.a.	4·1
1930	717	439	1,196	n.a.	21·9
1935	· 837	603	1,507	n.a.	40·9
1940	963	1,016	2,061	n.a.	60·3
1945	1,044	1,096	2,231	250	65·3
1950	1,455	1,588	3,140	552	70·6
1955	1,690	2,198	4,007	372	76·2
1956	1,739	2,403	4,265	344	77·2
1957	1,775	2,573	4,474	246	78·4
1958	1,786	2,584	4,500	171	79·2
1959	1,804	2,668	4,606	145	79·8
1960	1,855	2,792	4,784	144	81·5
1961	1,914	2,985	5,037	170	83·5
1962	1,956	3,112	5,210	147	84·9
1963	1,986	3,223	5,354	161	86·9
1964	2,044	3,429	5,620	171	88·0

* Includes other minor categories.

n.a. = not available.

SOURCE: Post Office, *Telecommunications statistics*, 1963, and Post Office, *Report and accounts*, 1963–4.

The enormous post-war backlog of unfilled orders for connexions reached its peak in 1949 at 560,000, which was 18 per cent of the total of connexions in service. This was reduced to 143,717 in 1960, but there has been an irregular rise since then. The backlog in 1964 was 3·2 per cent of total connexions, which is intermediate by current international standards.[6] Although an early elimination of the backlog (by 1966) is a declared objective of the Post Office,[7] it bears noting that of the world's major telephone systems, Britain's has had the lowest proportional growth in the number of telephones in the years since 1950.[8]

Along with the early emphasis on business service, there was a relatively early conversion toward automatic service. By 1940 the share of dial telephones in Britain (61 per cent) had passed that in the United States (54 per cent). In 1950, the share in Britain (71 per cent) exceeded that in West Germany (50 per cent), France (60 per cent), Norway (58 per cent), and Sweden (62 per cent), among others, though Italy (91 per cent), and some others were higher. Though Britain's relative position subsequently has slipped slightly, by 1964, 88 per cent of British telephones were dial-operated.

The evolving business–residence division of service is shown in Table 2, with comparative figures for the United States, where telephone development has gone generally further. A business–residence contrast is readily apparent. Although Britain has actually led the United States in business telephone development

6. Waiting lists as a per cent of total connexions at the beginning of 1964 were for a number of countries as follows:

Country	Per cent	Country	Per cent
Australia	2·4	New Zealand	4·1
Denmark	0	Norway	0
Finland	0	Sweden	0
France	8·7	Switzerland	2·8
West Germany	8·3	United Kingdom	3·2
Netherlands	8·0	United States	0

Regrettably, the Post Office does not publish the division of the backlog between residence and business applicants. The data are from reports provided by each country to the British Post Office, which kindly made them available. Within certain limits, the ratios may not be precisely comparable, and there are undoubtedly some normal frictional service delays in the five countries reporting zero wait-listing. None of this, however, would appreciably affect the points drawn here.

7. A five-year plan with this objective was announced by the Postmaster-General in November 1963; *The inland telephone service in an expanding economy*, Cmnd 2211, 1963.

8. See American Telephone and Telegraph Co., *The world's telephones, 1963*, New York, 1963, Table 2, pp. 2–3, and *Telephone statistics of the world, 1950*, New York, 1950.

since 1935, British residential expansion has always been much less than that in the United States, and the proportional gap has widened in recent years. For example, British residential connexions per 100 persons have just reached the level attained in the

Table 2
United Kingdom and United States: Business and Residence Connexions, 1921–63

Year	Business connexions per 100 population		Residence connexions per 100 population		Residence connexions per 100 households	
	United States	United Kingdom	United States	United Kingdom	United States	United Kingdom
1921	1·46	n.a.	4·3	n.a.	35·3	0·9
1925	1·77	n.a.	5·7	n.a.	38·7	1·7
1930	1·93	1·60	6·8	0·96	40·9	3·3
1935	1·76	1·78	5·7	1·28	31·8	4·4
1940	1·98	2·00	7·4	2·12	36·9	7·3
1945	2·18	2·13	9·5	2·24	46·2	7·7
1950	2·73	2·91	14·3	3·17	61·9	11·0
1955	2·94	3·32	16·7	4·31	71·7	15·0
1956	3·00	3·40	17·2	4·69	74·0	16·3
1957	3·04	3·45	17·6	4·98	75·7	17·4
1958	3·08	3·46	17·7	5·01	76·7	17·4
1959	3·15	3·47	18·1	5·13	78·3	17·9
1960	3·20	3·54	18·2	5·32	78·5	18·5
1961	3·24	3·63	18·4	5·66	79·2	19·7
1962	3·29	3·67	18·6	5·83	80·3	20·3
1963	3·33	3·69	18·8	5·98	81·4	20·7

SOURCES: Post Office, *Telecommunications statistics*, and American Telephone and Telegraph, *Statistical manual*.

United States in 1927. In the share of households served, the British system is even further back, despite its extensive business service development. Only about one household in five now has a connexion, after more than three generations of telephone growth.[9]

9. The United States figures include a variety of regions, some of them not comparable to the United Kingdom. A comparison using only northern and north-eastern states (more comparable to Britain) would draw the contrast even more sharply.

The impression of relatively slow and limited residence-service expansion is lent further plausibility by an international comparison of the extent of residence service in countries of varying income *per capita* (in Figure 1).[10] The loose apparent covariation of income and residence telephones *per capita* is in fact treated by Post Office officials as indicating the appropriate extent of telephone use.[11] Actually, there is no prescriptive value in such a statistical association; what matters are the marginal allocation conditions and opportunity costs in each country. Yet the comparison is worth noting. If it *were* prescriptive, it would suggest that Britain is below (perhaps substantially below) the appropriate levels. The fitted line would suggest (it is no more than a suggestion in itself) that the existing residence telephones per 100 population in Britain should be approximately doubled.[12]

These comparisons do suggest a relative lag in the development of British residential service. The analysis of tariff policies in the next section provides more specific evidence on that possibility.

2. Tariff Patterns

Since 1961, the overall profit criteria for the Post Office have been the same as for other public corporations; the return on capital is

10. It is based on data in American Telephone and Telegraph Company, *The world's telephones, 1963*, New York and P. Rosenstein-Rodan, 'International aid for under-developed countries', *Review of Economics and Statistics*, 1961, pp. 107–38. The exclusion of some countries, because data are not available, does not affect the conclusions drawn in the text.

11. Family income of £500 yearly is (in 1964) considered the threshold at which households will elect service. Yet that threshold depends on the service charges set by the Post Office (which are argued below to be too high); lower charges, lower threshold. Moreover, disposable income exceeds £500 in probably more than 50 per cent of households, compared to the 21 per cent with telephone connexions: see Central Statistical Office, *National income and expenditure*, H.M.S.O., 1964, Table 22.

12. Also West Germany and France (which lie near Britain well below the fitted line) both have much longer backlogs of demand, and both have higher per-call charges. If they were adjusted upward enough to allow for this, Britain would appear to deviate even further. Certainly no clear interpretation can be assigned to figure 1. At least several causes (incomes, tariffs, expansion capacity, social habits, etc.) are at work. Also some countries may have been lagging behind their long-run trends or relationships in 1961–2.

to be at a level not less than one 'comparable' (with allowance for risk) to that prevailing in industry generally.[13] The tariff's internal structure is, as in most telephone systems, a 'message

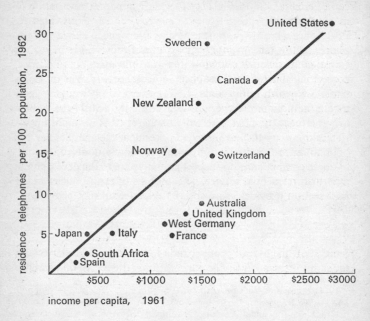

Figure 1 Residence telephones and income *per capita* in various countries

rate' system, in which users pay a quarterly rental plus a charge for each call completed. The tariff has been uniform nationally since 1957.

The residential rental is £2 lower than the business rental, but

13. *Financial and economic obligations*, op. cit.; see also Post Office, *Annual report and accounts*, 1963–4, pp. 7–8. The target rate of return (8 per cent) is 'about half the rate which private enterprise generally expects to earn' (ibid., p. 7) and ostensibly reflects (1) the lesser commercial risks and (2) substantial unprofitable services carried by these public corporations. The target applies to the entire Post Office (postal, telephone, telegraph, overseas, and other various services) and is officially supposed to be based on assets valued at current (replacement) cost.

call charges are nearly uniform for all users.[14] The rental differential has been narrowing in recent years, from 23 per cent of the exclusive-line business rental in 1951 to 12 per cent in 1964.[15] The differential between shared and exclusive residence service has also narrowed, from 21 per cent in 1952 to 14 per cent in 1964.

There is now (since 1961) some effort towards off-peak pricing of local calls, through allowing double (12 minutes) the holding time per call charge for cheap-rate calls as for full-rate calls (6 minutes). Possible refinements of the differential, though only by varying the holding time, are also under consideration.

Several features of the tariff will now be considered, particularly the rate-of-return targets, and the extent of peak-load pricing.

1. The allocational emptiness of the overall rate-of-return targets (based on existing assets, however valued) for the public corporations has been aired at some length.[16] The Government's estimate for the private-industry profit benchmark (16 per cent), based as it is on widely varying accounting practices and investment criteria, is of limited reliability. The average prospective returns throughout industries competitive to the public firms – which is what counts, rather than the rates of return ostensibly sought or attained by a variety of large firms, some of them

14. The charges are as follows:

Category	Rental per year £
Business	
Exclusive line	16
Shared line	14
Residence	
Exclusive line	14
Shared line	12

Local call charges	Full-rate period	Cheap-rate period
Dialled call in areas with Subscriber Trunk Dialling	2d. per 6 minutes	2d. per 12 minutes
Manual calls and dialled calls in areas without Subscriber Trunk Dialling:		
Business	3d. untimed	3d. untimed
Residence	2½d. untimed	2½d. untimed

15. *Telecommunications statistics*, op. cit.
16. Shepherd, op. cit., and Posner, op. cit.

possessing substantial market power – may differ sharply from the 16 per cent benchmark.[17]

Of course, the telephone system's closest substitute is its labour-intensive Post Office sister, the postal service (not to mention the telegraph, also part of the Post Office). The rate of return on postal capital (see Table 3 for the Post Office's reported estimates) has recently been negative. Indeed, the telephone system has had to aim above 8·0 per cent in order to balance the postal (and telegraph) shortfall. In principle, the targets should move in parallel, not inversely.

Moreover, the allowance for differential risk conditions and unprofitable services has been so approximate (a factor of one-half) as to suggest that it has little exact conceptual or factual basis. In view of the system's low apparent risks (attested in part by the waiting lists), its obligation to carry certain unremunerative services and the possible external effects of telephone use, the appropriate rate-of-return target is unlikely to be more than 8 per cent and probably is less. Finally, the attempt to value the capital base at replacement cost has run afoul of all the classic problems raised by changing prices and technology.[18] Calculated using historical cost depreciation, telephone net income in recent years has been approximately 12 per cent of net assets.[19] Although conceptual difficulties and incomplete data make generalization hazardous, one tentatively concludes that the overall profit

17. The actual benchmarks are based on several hundred of the larger firms (using a variety of depreciation methods) in a wide range of industries. Since in addition the highest profit rates are in such 'industries' as Entertainment (46 per cent in 1963) and Shops and Stores (25 per cent), it seems probable that the appropriate benchmark rates are lower. The relationships between firm size (and market power) have been subject to dispute (see H. O. Stekler, *Profitability and size of firm*, Berkeley, 1963; and G. S. Stigler, *Capital and rates of return in manufacturing industries*, Princeton University Press, 1963). Without attempting to canvass the issues or evidence, one may doubt that American patterns apply fully in Britain.

18. To illustrate the mixture of accounting methods, technical advances in trunk circuits have lowered replacement cost *below* historical cost. So the Post Office uses historical cost in this area. The use of whichever method gives higher valuations must bias upward the total. On general problems of replacement accounting, see Bonbright, op. cit., chapter 14.

19. In the official accounts, a supplementary depreciation provision is made, in addition to historical cost depreciation (*Report and accounts*, 1963–4).

targets have been dubious in concept and probably too high in practice.

The objections apply also to the rate-of-return calculations for individual services, shown in Table 3. The cost-accounting basis for these rates of return is unavoidably arbitrary in certain respects. And, as will be seen, revisions of rate structure may alter the apparent profitability of individual services.

2. Peak-load pricing. Telephone traffic has a daily peak during office hours (9.00–12.30, 2.00–5.00), consisting mainly of business-originated calls.[20] This poses a classic peak-load pricing problem, focusing mainly on the allocation of central equipment costs. The holding-time differential, noted above, is a step in this direction, but it provides only a moderate differential (and none at all to calls of less than 6 minutes' duration). Moreover, it mainly encourages longer holding times rather than additional calls.

The following estimates, based on unpublished Post Office accounting and traffic data, indicate the actual time-of-day differential in costs.[21] The disaggregation of total 1962–3 costs ascribed to 'subscribers' local calls' included 69 per cent (36·4 million) classifiable as overhead costs (mainly administrative, engineering, interest, and depreciation). The peak period is taken to be the entire 9.00 to 5.00 period, during which approximately 80 per cent of all calls occur. Of the total 4,750 million local calls in 1962–3, 3,800 million were therefore peak calls, broadly speaking. Overhead (capacity) costs were assigned to peak-load calls, while variable costs were pro-rated equally to all calls.[22]

20. Shown by several Post Office traffic studies, most of them based on London. The 'peak' is (apart from the mid-day drop) relatively flat and wide, and stems almost entirely from business use. Residence-originating use is relatively constant throughout the day and evening.

21. I am grateful to various people in the Post Office for providing the accounting data and discussing problems of interpretation. The reader is warned that the concepts involved in the estimates here have had to be applied with some arbitrariness; also, the actual patterns in the system are far more complex (especially in metropolitan areas) than these overall totals imply. These reservations apply also to the Post Office estimates shown in Table 3. Yet in the present estimates the assumptions and data were chosen deliberately to avoid biasing the results in the direction of the findings.

22. This places peak responsibility at a maximum, but most alternative peak-responsibility assumptions would not markedly alter the results.

Table 3

Financial Patterns on Service Categories, 1961–4 (millions of pounds unless otherwise noted)

	Profits or losses*						1961–2			1962–3			1963–4		
	1955–6	1956–7	1957–8	1958–9	1959–60	1960–61	Revenue	Profit or loss	Profit as a % of net assets	Revenue	Profit or loss	Profit as a % of net assets	Revenue	Profit or loss	Profit as a % of net assets
Inland telephone															
Rentals															
Business	—	—	—	3·2	3·8	3·4	29·1	3·3	8·6	33·1	3·8	8·8	34·0	2·7	7·8
Residence	—	—	—	-3·6	-2·5	-3·0	38·2	-3·8	3·5	45·4	1·9	7·0	48·4	0·7	6·3
Apparatus	—	—	—	-0·7	-0·2	-0·1	22·2	0·1	5·5	27·5	3·7	8·1	29·2	3·3	7·5
Total	-9·2	-12·9	-8·9	-1·1	1·1	0·3	89·5	-0·4	5·5	106·0	9·4	7·8	111·6	6·7	7·1
Subscribers' trunk calls	16·2	13·4	12·6	10·8	14·9	16·9	64·1	16·0	12·9	63·6	14·3	10·7	90·3	36·5	20·4
Subscribers' local calls	-3·7	-0·1	1·2	-1·0	0·4	2·5	46·3	-2·7	4·2	47·8	-4·6	3·6	45·6	-9·6	1·7
Call office receipts	-1·4	-2·4	-1·5	-2·5	-2·2	-1·9	14·0	-2·8	-0·8	14·7	-3·4	-1·7	16·3	-4·5	-2·9
Telephone private circuits	2·6	1·5	1·1	1·0	1·0	1·0	11·9	1·9	7·4	13·5	2·9	8·4	15·8	4·6	10·3
Telegraph and overseas telephone	-0·7	-0·9	-1·4	-1·5	-0·7	-0·4	36·5	0·6	n.a.	53·6	1·6	n.a.	63·1	4·8	n.a.
Total telecommunications	3·8	-1·4	3·1	5·7	14·5	18·5	262·3	12·6	6·6	300·7	20·2	7·2	342·7	38·5	8·8
Postal	-1·5	-1·7	-0·5	3·0	6·4	5·9	233·0	1·0	4·8	241·5	-8·1	-13·2	262·0	-7·8	-10·3

* Profits and losses are calculated *after* deducting interest charges from revenues; but returns on capital are calculated with interest payments counted as part of profit.

SOURCES: Post Office, *Report and accounts*, 1961–2, 1962–3, and 1963–4.

The results of these approximations were average costs of 3·12d. per peak-load call, and 0·78d. per off-peak call. This would confirm the expectation that off-peak costs are substantially below peak costs, and it would suggest that an off-peak per-call charge of 1d. or less might be appropriate.[23]

A tariff alteration in line with these estimated costs might not greatly alter revenues from the various subscriber classes. If calling patterns were unchanged, average business exclusive-line revenues would rise slightly, while average residence exclusive-line rentals would decline from £18·5 to £17·6 (by 1962–3 conditions). Even if residence users rearranged their calls substantially, the revenue change would be moderate. In any case, the refinements in accounts and tariff could markedly alter the profitability calculations; for example, the rate of return now realized on off-peak calls is probably very high. Tariff revision would, at any rate, promote a more efficient temporal calling pattern, and would make service available more cheaply (in line with costs) at off-peak times.

Two other possible influences on the expansion of residential service may be noted. The continuing backlog of service orders, and its recent upward drift, suggest that demand for service (even with the present tariff) may be greater and more rapidly growing than the Post Office anticipates. The tariff revisions indicated above would add to the lists.

The revision of local call areas in 1957 (from 'crow-flight distance' to 'community of interest') greatly expanded most of the areas.[24] Some of the larger areas, especially London, so far exceed the largest sizes of local call areas found in other systems as to suggest that they may exceed the size in which per-call costs are as low as the per-call charge. This possibility is strengthened by the higher rates of return (20·4 per cent in 1963–4) reported for trunk service compared to local service (1·7 per cent in 1963–4) (see Table 3). The possible excess size may be only temporary,

23. A more feasible method, given existing metering apparatus, would be a short time unit (such as 30 seconds rather than 6 minutes) with a smaller per-unit charge. This would affect nearly all calls, not just longer ones.

24. Post Office, *Full automation of the telephone system*, Cmnd 303, H.M.S.O., 1957; in some cases area was enlarged as much as ten times over (p. 3).

but while it lasts it would adversely affect the apparent average profitability of basic local service. Accordingly, under profits guidelines, the size of calling areas may on balance pose a disincentive for promoting and expanding the system's capacity for local (perhaps especially residence) service.

Post Office officials do profess to adhere to profit guidelines in most allocational decisions. One further reflection of the disincentives from low profits on residence services is the Post Office's slight promotion of residence basic services, compared to its vigour in developing various innovations and optional services, mainly for business users.[25]

3. Summary

The foregoing points are tentative, owing partly to gaps in the available information, but the policy implications are reasonably consistent and clear. The overall profit targets need to be derived with more caution and detail, and they need to be applied to individual services with particular care. The present targets are probably (though not certainly) significantly too high.

Cost patterns suggest that further differentiation in time-of-day local call charges would be appropriate. Certain local call areas may also be (at least temporarily) larger than cost patterns would prescribe. Both of these departures would indicate a need for either tariff revisions or shadow re-allocations of revenue between the categories of services.

These time-of-day and calling area allowances would probably raise the calculated profitability of residence service at present prices. This rise, together with (probably) lower overall profits targets and the likelihood (shown by the rising backlog of orders) that demand is rising faster than anticipated, suggests that a more rapid expansion of basic residence service would be appropriate on economic grounds. This accords with indications in section 1 that residential service is – by international comparison and in relation to business service – relatively undeveloped. Revisions both in tariffs and in investment patterns appear to be in order.

25. For indications of these items, see Post Office, *Report and accounts*, 1961–2 (pp. 19–21), 1962–3 (pp. 15–17), and 1963–4 (pp. 16–17).

12 Julian L. Simon

State Liquor Monopolies

Julian L. Simon, 'The economic effects of state monopoly of packaged-liquor retailing', *Journal of Political Economy*, vol. 74 (1966), pp. 188–94.

Introduction

The analysis of governmental experiments with the control and management of economic enterprise can yield information that is of general economic interest, besides being useful for the political assessment of the experiment itself. Yet such experiments have been little studied.[1] State monopoly of packaged-liquor retailing has special advantages for research of this kind. Sixteen states have state monopoly systems, and they may be compared to the states that have completely privately owned retail distribution systems.[2] Throughout the analysis we shall consider each state as a separate observation, and we shall not weight by size of state. Calculated means will be means of state means. This presents no problems in interpretation because we do not seek to generalize to the United States as a single universe.

1. A remark of Professor G. J. Stigler to that effect in a talk at the University of Illinois, 1964, stimulated this research. His presidential address to the American Economic Association made the same point (Stigler, 1965). Jevons (1883, p. 267), referred to in the above, called for Parliament to experiment with economic policies in a cross-section of localities. And he noted: 'What little insight we can gain into the operation of the liquor Licensing Laws is mainly due to the considerable differences with which they have been administered in different places.'

2. Mississippi is officially dry. Several counties in Maryland are monopolized. Wyoming has a state monopoly at the wholesale level only. We shall treat both Maryland and Wyoming along with the private–retail-ownership states in some analyses, and drop them – and other irregular states – from other analyses, as indicated where appropriate. The state monopolies control package-liquor sales, which typically account for 70–75 per cent of total consumption, but our data are for total liquor consumption in the various states, a factor that works to reduce the apparent effect of state monopoly.

The *monopoly* systems differ from state to state on such matters as:

1. Number of off-premise retail-sale outlets (package stores) *per capita*, attractiveness of outlets, and hours of sale.

2. Number of private on-premise sale outlets (bars) allowed, ranging upward from none.

3. Amount of markup above cost, and method of calculating markup.

4. Administrative systems.

Despite these differences in style, the monopoly systems all have the general characteristics of socialized economic subsystems. They may or may not sell a given brand of whisky at their discretion. They set uniform service rules for all outlets throughout a given state at their discretion. They are operated for the profit of the states instead of for individual owners. The monopoly states have also combined to extract an agreement from national liquor suppliers to supply the monopoly states at a common, low price, exclusive of freight (the 'Des Moines Agreement').

Differences among the states having privately licensed ownership are much greater, however:

1. Three states have no fair-trade laws, while the others have price-fixing systems that vary in severity of sanction and source of established prices.

2. Restrictions on number and type of licenses issued for package sales differ. There is freedom of entry in none of the states, and licenses sell at substantial premiums in most states. Some states prohibit multiple ownership of licenses.

3. Restrictions on advertising, hours of sale, and type of other products that package stores may sell differ widely.

The types and variation of regulations affecting package-liquor retailing under both the monopoly and private-ownership systems mean that a comparison of the systems is *not* a comparison of socialism and private enterprise. Rather, it is a comparison of state-monopolized packaged-liquor retailing in an American political context, against privately owned but heavily regulated and restricted retail systems. The latter bear little resemblance to systems of really free retail enterprise such as are found in food, hardware, or other types of unregulated retailing.

We shall not consider the political or social ramifications of the two systems. Rather, we shall consider a few economic variables that we can handle quantitatively: prices, public revenues, and consumption.

The literature on this subject is sparse. State monopoly has been discussed only by special pleaders, applying no rigorous analysis. Serious economic study has been limited to the federal excise tax on liquor (see Hu, 1961; Niskanen, 1961).

Effect on Retail Prices

Two indexes of price were used: (1) the pre-sales-tax price of a fifth of Seagram's Seven Crown blended whisky, by far the largest selling U.S. liquor brand. This is a 'middle-range' price, and a price standard of the liquor industry;[3] and (2) the average of a state's rank order of price for eight medium-priced and high-priced nationally sold brands of liquor.

There are several obvious flaws in this technique:

1. Liquor is sold in many forms and qualities. Even brands among which there is no demonstrated variation in quality are sold at many different prices. This makes for difficulty in comparing 'the price' of liquor between groups of states.

2. Low-priced private-label liquors offer stronger competition to our index brands in private-license states than in monopoly states, and the *average* relative price paid for liquor may consequently be overstated by the index.[4]

3. In the three non-fair-trade private-license states, the price of a brand differs within the states, and in fair-trade states illegal sales and discounts must occur. However, a survey by the

3. Price data for Seagram's Seven Crown and other brands were taken from *Liquor handbook*, which obtains its data from the firms that distribute the brands. A fuller discussion of prices and price indexes may be found in Simon (1966). A major point is that the price of major brands is remarkably constant from year to year.

4. However, market research surveys quoted in the annual *Liquor handbook* indicate that the lowest-price and private-label brands account for a very small proportion of total consumption.

California State Board of Equalization (1952) showed that in all states except two of the three fair-trade states brand-owners' prices closely agreed with comparison-shopping prices.

4. Freight costs vary from state to state and affect retail prices.

Table 1
Prices of Seagram's Seven Crown Fifths, 1961

	No.	Mean	S.D.	Median
Monopoly states	16	$4.35	$0.34	$4.20
Private-license states	27	4.84	0.26	4.85
	$t = 5.36$			

Despite these failings, our comparison can at least compare the prices paid for one given brand (and for a composite of brands) of liquor in the various states. And that has *some* meaning.

The mean and median prices of Seagram's Seven Crown fifths in 1961, in monopoly as compared with private-license states, were as shown in Table 1.[5]

5. In a note in the *Journal of Political Economy* in April 1967, T. J. Whalen adduced new data from a survey of state liquor boards that bear upon this matter. The data confirm the finding of a much lower price for Seagram's Seven Crown fifths in 1963 in monopoly states than in fair-trade free-enterprise states (medians $4.13 to $4.84). Whalen's main point, however, is that non-fair-trade states have *even lower* prices than the monopoly states (medians $3.99 to $4.13). This conclusion is quite plausible, but Whalen's evidence is unfortunately weak. There are only three states in the non-fair-trade category, and the difference between them and the monopoly states ($0·14) is less than half their standard deviations (and only one fifth of the difference between the monopoly and fair-trade states, incidentally). Furthermore, the very nature of non-fair-trade prices is that there is surely diversity within the states, and Whalen's estimates are based on a single informed guess by a liquor-control-board functionary about 'typical or average prices' in his state. (This paragraph refers to median prices, but the results for mean values are much the same for the purposes of this discussion.)

Whalen also makes the point that there is a welfare benefit of greater choice of brands in free-enterprise states, but this seems rather unimportant to me in view of the physical homogeneity of various brands of the same type of liquor (vide *Consumers' reports*; Harold Wattell, *The whisky industry: An economic analysis*, Ph.D. Thesis, New School of Social Research, 1954). [Ed.]

Ranking 43 states[6] from highest price to lowest price, the 16 monopoly states had these ranks: 6, $22\frac{1}{2}$, 25–6, 28 (2 cases), $31\frac{1}{2}$, and 35–43. The 27 private-license states had ranks 1–5, 7–20, $27\frac{1}{2}$ (3 cases), 28, 30, $31\frac{1}{2}$, and 33–4. The Kruskal–Wallis H statistic is a highly significant 17·8, and this is probably a more sensible test than the t-test shown above because there is not much reason for assuming normality in the price distributions.

For the composite index of 8 brands,[7] the 16 retail-monopoly states had an average rank of 33·2, and the 31 private-license states[8] had an average rank of 19·3. The monopoly states accounted for ranks 5, 18, $20\frac{1}{2}$, 24–5, 27, $31\frac{1}{2}$, 37, 39–42, and 44–7. The private-license states had ranks 1–4, 6–17, 19, $20\frac{1}{2}$, 22–3, 26, 28–30, $31\frac{1}{2}$, 33–6, 38, and 43. The Kruskal–Wallis H statistic was 36·6. Among the private-license states, fair-trade states had ranks 1, $27\frac{1}{2}$, and $44\frac{1}{2}$, though these ranks are probably too high because the data are company estimates rather than actual price observations.

The simple correlation between the price of Seagram's Seven Crown and a shift variable for monopoly as compared with private license was 0·64 (43 states). The correlation for the composite-index was 0·49 (47 states).

Since we are interested in the effect of monopoly systems compared to private-license systems, we want to know whether it is 'really' other variables that explain the Seagram's Seven Crown price differential that is apparently caused by the difference in governmental systems. A stepwise multiple regression was

6. Excludes dry Mississippi; 'partial monopoly' Maryland and Wyoming; three non-fair-trade states, Alaska, Missouri, and Texas; and Louisiana, for which data were also not available. These omissions are almost surely a bias against the private-licence group.

7. The composite index is a rank order of forty-nine of the fifty states. Price data were available in the *Liquor handbook* for nine leading brands (including Seagram's Seven Crown – thus this section is therefore not completely independent of the prior section), one from each of the largest selling types of liquors (e.g. gin, scotch). Data for rum were missing for a great many states, whereas data for each of the other brands were missing for only a few states. A mean rank was generated for each of the forty-four states for which data on all eight brands were available. The data which did exist for the other five states were then interpolated to obtain rank estimates for them. Only 'dry' Mississippi offered no basis for estimation.

8. Excludes Mississippi, Maryland, and Wyoming.

therefore run (43 states), with price as its dependent variable. The independent variables were: income *per capita*; number of off-premise outlets *per capita*; number of on-premise outlets *per capita*; monopoly (0) or private license (1); total liquor outlets *per capita*; population per square mile; proportion of population in 'dry' counties; and stills captured *per capita*.[9] A stepwise linear regression indicated that the shift variable for monopoly or private ownership came into the regression first, accounting for 0·412 of the variance ($r = 0·64$). The next variable that came into the stepwise regression, off-premise outlets *per capita*, only increased the proportion of the variance explained from $r^2 = 0·412$ to $R^2 = 0·446$ and the F-test for the second variable is not significant, so we may disregard it and the other variables as influences on price. Regressing the composite price index on the same variables resulted in lower correlations than the Seagram's Seven price regression.

Effect on State Revenues

In this section we shall examine the effects of the two governmental systems on the state treasuries.

The revenue effect of the private-license system is fairly easy to reckon: state and local tax revenues and license fees attributable to hard liquor, less costs of administration.

Local tax revenues[10] in private-license states are included on the grounds that we want to compare the total flow of funds into non-federal public hands under the two systems, and it makes no

9. Sources not otherwise specified were: state populations, population per square mile, total income, and *per capita* income (*Statistical Abstract*); state consumption (Distilled Spirits Institute [D.S.I.], 1961); numbers of off-premise, on-premise, and off-and-on-premise retail outlets (among which we included all licences not limited to beer and/or wine), and percentage of the population of each state living in 'dry' counties (Distilled Spirits Institute, 1961); number of stills captured in each state (Licensed Beverage Industries' [1961] questionnaire survey reported in the 1961 edition of its annual report on bootlegging).

10. It may be helpful to indicate the orders of magnitude of the quantities we are dealing with. *Including* beer and wine revenues, which are perhaps ¼ of the total and which are *excluded* elsewhere in this paper, DSI estimates total U.S. 1961 collections at $4,688,000,000–$124,000,000 local, $1,225,000,000 state, and $3,339,000,000 federal.

conceptual difference whether the collection is local or state-wide. The form of the monopoly-state system makes most local collections impossible, which strengthens the view that state-wide and local coffers are interrelated, as does the common practice in monopoly states of ear-marking parts of the state liquor revenues for local uses. Revenues from beer and wine, and costs of their administration, were not included, though in some cases the job of separating them out required estimation and crude guesses.[11]

Monopoly-state revenues from liquor sales were harder to reckon. Special problems included subtraction of the wholesale cost of wine goods sold and the appropriate allocation of overhead costs. Interest on the inventory investment was reckoned at 4 per cent per year, and turnover estimated at four times per year[12] in calculating the cost of inventory holding.

Revenues from sales taxes were *not* included, and an appropriate subtraction was made for those monopoly states that have general sales taxes. The rationale is that the proper frame of reference is that of the public policy-maker who asks: How much more or less revenue would this state obtain if it had the other system? The sales tax is invariant in this mental experiment, and hence it is properly excluded from the reckoning.[13]

The decision not to include the sales tax had the important side benefit of avoiding the necessity of arbitrarily allocating sales taxes between liquor and beer.

Liquor-production taxes also were excluded on the grounds that our interest is in revenues from consumption and the systems of selling to consumers.

The most obvious comparative measure of the benefits from a

11. Data on revenues come from DSI (1961), and were obtained by a canvass of state agencies and officials, plus some occasional estimation by the trade association. The form in which the data are reported and the degree of disaggregation are different for each state.

12. 'Control inventories generally average around three months' supply' (*Liquor handbook*, 1962, p. 72).

13. We might proceed differently if the public issue were one of prohibition, say, and if the question were asked: How much less revenue would the state get if there were no liquor tariff? To the extent that purchases would be shifted from liquor to other taxable goods the sales-tax revenue would not be lost to the state. However, to the extent that dollars would go into bootleg liquor or into savings, sales-tax revenue would be lost, and hence it might be appropriate to include the sales tax in the reckoning.

state's liquor revenues is revenue *per capita*. The mean of this measure for the sixteen monopoly states is $6.55 per year (S.D. = $2.16); for thirty-one private-license states the mean is $3.22 per year (S.D. = $1.52).[14] Monopoly-state ranks are 1–2, 4–12, 15, 18, 22, 25, and 33. License-state ranks are 3, 13–14, 16–17, 19–21, 23–24, 26–32, and 34–47. The simple correlation of revenue per capita with monopoly versus private license is 0·67.

The appropriate measure of the revenue-extractive *efficiency* of a state is revenue per gallon consumed. The mean of the monopoly states is $5.93 (S.D. = $1.57); for private-license states the mean is $2.35 (S.D. = $1.00). This difference in favour of the monopoly states is despite the lower prices in the monopoly states.[15] Our previous analysis showed that the mean price of a 'medium-price blend', Seagram's Seven Crown, is $0.49 a fifth cheaper in monopoly states. If monopoly states raised their prices to capture $0.49 more revenue per fifth, their mean revenues per gallon would be $11.81 (even higher if we reckoned with the median rather than the mean) rather than $5.93, compared to $2.16 in private-license states. However, a price rise of 11 per cent would be expected to cause a gallonage decline of 9 per cent (Simon, 1966), so that the change in revenue *per capita* would be perhaps an 82 per cent gain instead of almost doubling, as would revenue per gallon.

If sales-tax revenues had been included, the difference between license and monopoly states would be smaller, but the absolute and proportional pictures would not change very much.

That monopoly states obtain greater revenues despite lower prices to consumers is a phenomenon which calls for explanation:

1. Monopoly states have combined to maximize their monopsonistic power in buying liquor for sale through the Des Moines Agreement. But cost is unlikely to account for the entire difference in revenues, because the Agreement only guarantees states a price no higher than the lowest price to wholesalers in private-license states.

14. States omitted were Mississippi (dry) and Maryland (partly monopoly). Wyoming was treated as a private-license state in this analysis despite the state monopoly of liquor wholesaling.

15. And even though the quantities sold per capita in monopoly states are smaller, for reasons that we shall explain in the next section.

2. Consumers in monopoly states may be prevented from obtaining some spatial and temporal utility that is supplied with liquor in private-license states, at a cost to the suppliers. Monopoly states operate many fewer off-premise outlets[16] *per capita* than exist in private-license states – 0·096 per thousand population versus 0·687 – and the monopoly states may thereby achieve lower operating costs. Monopoly states may also operate their outlets fewer hours a day than do private owners.

3. Private profit in the license states at wholesale and/or retail evels may account for some of the difference. (The overwhelming proportion of the profit is at the retail level.) We have attributed interest on inventory investment as a monopoly-state cost, and interest on the entrepreneur's investment must similarly be considered a cost rather than profit. Nevertheless, there is surely some return to the average entrepreneur over and above the returns to his own sales-clerkly and managerial labors and the bank-rate cost of his investment. The increase in the value of the liquor license (which may now sell for $100,000 for a small store in New York State) during the period of ownership must be counted as part of this profit. This accounting difference, small or large, is replaced by state revenue in the monopoly states.

4. If the above factors do not account for the whole of the revenue differences between monopoly and private-license states, there are no further categories in the analysis of pure competition to help us explain these differences. We must therefore look to deviations from competition. In those states in which at least price competition is free, there may be no difference at all to explain, but our lack of price data for those few states prevents further discussion. The other license states, however, may well keep inefficient operators in business by fixing prices, restricting licenses, outlawing price display or price advertising, and employing other practices that make it difficult for more efficient operators to force the less efficient out. For example, some customers might prefer lower prices to geographic convenience. But if the prices everywhere are the same, customers will shop at the nearest store, so there may be more outlets under fair trade than there would be

16. In some states an outlet may sell liquor for off-premise *and* on-premise consumption. These outlets were counted separately in both categories, but were counted only once in the variable 'total outlets'.

with free pricing. All this means that private-license systems may pay for unneeded and/or poor-quality service, that is, store owners may sit on their hands in private-license states who could not do so if liquor were sold as groceries are. And monopoly states may run their systems without such forced inefficiency.

We have no way of guessing how much of the 'excess' revenues in monopoly states stems from the particular factors discussed above.

Effect on Liquor Consumption

Supporters of the monopoly system have argued that under state monopoly consumers would not be 'overstimulated' or 'over-enticed' to drink hard liquor.

For *per capita* consumption, the mean of the sixteen monopoly states was indeed lower: 1·13 gallons as compared with 1·39 for thirty-one private-license states.[17] In increasing order of consumption *per capita*, the ranks of monopoly states were 2, 4, 6, 8, 11, 14, 18, 20, 22–23, 25, 27–28, 30, 35, and 45; and the ranks of license states were 1, 3, 5, 7, 9–10, 12–13, 15–17, 19, 21, 24, 26, 29, 31–34, 36–44, and 46. But the simple correlation between consumption and monopoly or private license was only 0·18.

More revealing, however, is a stepwise multiple regression that included as variables monopoly or private-license, *per capita* ('*per capita* income' is a variable) income, price of Seagram's Seven, composite-index price, stills captured *per capita*, percentage of population in 'dry' counties, and population per square mile. In an earlier regression, the variables included *per capita* measures of off-premise outlets, on-premise outlets, and total outlets. Total outlets *per capita* was a significant variable, and entered the regression second. But it was dropped from the final regression in the belief that the number of outlets is more likely to respond to consumption, rather than be a cause of con-

17. Omits Hawaii (no consumption data), Mississippi, and Wyoming (monopoly at wholesale only). Maryland *is* included in this analysis, with 'proportion of population in monopoly counties', which renders the monopoly-license variable 'continuous' rather than a dummy variable. However, Maryland is not included in the rank ordering, which explains why there are only forty-six ranks.

sumption. The grounds for this belief are largely that it was total outlets rather than off-premise outlets that was significant, despite the fact that it is the latter which is most clearly an exogenous variable and which shows an enormous difference between monopoly and license states. Furthermore, the simple correlation between off-premise outlets per *gallon* and consumption *per capita* is only 0·12.

Per capita income explained 0·50 of the variance ($r = 0·69$) in the first-step simple regression. No other variable comes into the stepwise regression significantly.[18] And the monopoly or private-license variable is three variables down the list. It is also surprising that percentage of population in 'dry' counties was not significant, even though there must be *some* sociological relationship between prohibition and consumption.

We may conclude that the effect of the form of governmental control system on consumption is negligible.

Conclusions

1. The price of advertised liquor brands tends to be lower where the state monopolizes liquor retailing. The explanation is institutional, with a vengeance. Monopoly states have complete power over their prices, and apparently set the prices (or margins) largely with reference to other monopoly states. As a group, they apparently believe (judging by the trade literature) that their present revenues are 'fair' and 'what is necessary'.

It may be pertinent that the cross-sectional differences in prices in private-enterprise states relate closely to excise-tax levels, except in the three states that do not control prices. In the latter, prices are lower than they would otherwise be.

2. By any measure, the treasuries of monopoly states net much more money from the liquor trade carried on within their borders than do private-license states. This is true *despite* lower prices in the monopoly states. The likely sources of this increased revenue are: (a) diversion of profit to the state, (b) monopsonistic operation, (c) efficiencies of operation and/or the consumer bearing the

18. Entine (1963) concluded that 'there is little evidence that states which limit the number of package stores have succeeded in reducing off premise consumption'.

cost of decreased service. It is not possible to determine the relative importance of these factors.

3. Whether liquor is sold by the state or by private enterprises does not affect the *per capita* consumption, after we remove the influence of income.

4. The stills-captured variable did not enter significantly into the regression with *per capita* consumption as the dependent variable. Nevertheless, moonshine production must affect legal consumption in states where a significant quantity of moonshine is made. The extent of this influence can best be gauged by estimates that total yearly moonshine production is approximately 10 per cent of legal and illegal consumption combined.[19] The influence in particular states can be estimated by data on number of stills captured.[20]

5. *Per capita* consumption is related to number of outlets *per capita*, but we cannot establish the extent to which causation runs in one direction or the other.

6. If we consider only the consumer's out-of-pocket welfare – including both prices and taxes – the consumer is better off under a monopoly system. However, over-all welfare judgements must depend on many other important economic and non-economic factors.

References

CALIFORNIA STATE BOARD OF EQUALIZATION (1952), 'Alcoholic beverage prices and taxes in the several states', Sacramento, Calif.: State Board of Equalization.

DISTILLED SPIRITS INSTITUTE (1961), *Annual statistical review*, Washington: the Institute.

DISTILLED SPIRITS INSTITUTE 'Public revenues from alcoholic beverages, 1961', Washington: the Institute.

ENTINE, ALAN D. (1963) 'The relationship between the number of sales outlets and the consumption of alcoholic beverages in New York and

19. Estimate based on recalculation of raw data in Licensed Beverage Industries (1961).

20. Some, but not much, moonshine may be exported from producer states, according to the Alcohol and Tobacco Tax Division of the Internal Revenue Service. Licensed Beverage Industries' (1961, p. 18) estimate is that 9 per cent of total moonshine is exported from states in which it is produced and some of this is also imported by other producer states.

other states'. (Study Paper No. 2, 21 October 1963), Albany: New York State Moreland Commission of the Alcoholic Beverage Control Law.

GAVIN-JOBSON ASSOCIATES, *Liquor handbook*. New York: Gavin-Jobson Associates, Inc. (annual).

HU, TUN-YUAN, (1961), *The liquor tax in the United States, 1791–1947*, New York: Columbia University Press.

JEVONS, STANLEY (1883), 'Experimental legislation and the drink traffic', in *Methods of social reform*, London: Macmillan & Co.

LICENSED BEVERAGE INDUSTRIES (1961), *Moonshine, murder, money*, New York: L.B.I.

NISKANEN, WILLIAM A. (1961), 'The demand for alcoholic beverages', unpublished Ph.D. thesis, University of Chicago.

SIMON, JULIAN L. (1966), 'The demand for liquor in the US and a simple method of determination', *Econometrica*.

STIGLER, GEORGE J. (1965), 'The economist and the state', *A.E.R.* (March), pp. 1–17.

Further Reading

Anyone studying the problems of a particular industry in a particular country will usually find that two kinds of periodical are available. Firstly, there are generally several commercially published weekly or monthly trade journals which provide a news service for those engaged in the industry, together with advertising by suppliers. Secondly, the industry's national association or the professional association of its engineers publishes a journal, transactions or proceedings, containing papers by people who work in the industry. Both kinds of periodical are well worth looking at, if only to get a flavour of the attitudes prevalent in the industry and the problems which preoccupy it. In addition, the student will frequently find papers and articles which, though not written by economists, deal directly with problems of interest to the economist.

The following suggestions for further reading are directed towards students rather than research workers and are intended largely to avoid duplicate treatment of topics covered in this volume.

H. AVERCH and L. L. JOHNSON, 'Behaviour of the firm under regulatory constraint', *American Economic Review*, vol. 52 (1962), no. 5 (December), pp. 1052–69.

   A theoretical analysis which suggests that regulation of the rate of return earned by public utilities may bias them towards an excessive use of capital.

I. C. R. BYATT, 'The genesis of the present pricing system in electricity supply', *Oxford Economic Papers*, vol. 15 (1963), no. 1 (March), pp. 8–18.

K. W. DAM, 'Oil and gas licensing and the North Sea', *Journal of Law and Economics*, vol. 8 (1965), pp. 51–75.

   Examines the virtues of using the price mechanism in allocating drilling licenses.

J. H. DRÈZE, 'Some postwar contributions of French economists to theory and public policy', *American Economic Review*, vol. 54 (1964), no. 4, part 2 (June), pp. 1–64.

   Part I surveys French writings on marginal cost pricing.

A. H. Hanson, *Nationalization: A book of readings*, published for the Royal Institute of Public Administration by George Allen & Unwin, London and Toronto University Press, 1963.

A useful collection covering organization, industrial relations, and many other aspects of nationalization not dealt with in this book.

I. M. D. Little, 'Output and price policy in public enterprises', in *A critique of welfare economics*, Oxford University Press, 2nd edn, 1957, chapter 11.

A powerful criticism of the general case for marginal cost pricing.

P. W. Macavoy, *Price formation in natural gas fields: a study of competition, monopsony and regulation*, Yale University Press, 1962.

The first part analyses the cost structure of natural gas supply.

S. A. Marglin, *Public investment criteria*, George Allen & Unwin and M.I.T. Press, 1967.

A synthesis of recent writings on cost-benefit analysis of investment.

A. J. Merrett, 'A reconsideration of investment and pricing criteria in the Nationalised Industries', *Manchester School of Economics and Social Studies*, vol. 32 (1964), no. 4 (September), pp. 261–89.

Examines alternative criteria, bearing in mind the difficulty of obtaining relevant information and relevant financial constraints.

J. R. Nelson, *Marginal cost pricing in practice*, Prentice-Hall, 1964.

A collection of translated papers on pricing and investment by French economists associated with *Electricité de France*.

Political and Economic Planning, *A fuel policy for Britain*, George Allen & Unwin, and Committee for Economic Development, New York, 1966.

A survey of the fuel industries and discussion of policy problems.

L. C. Rosenberg, 'Natural-gas-pipeline rate regulation: Marginal-cost pricing and the zone-allocation problem', *Journal of Political Economy*, vol. 75 (1967), no. 2 (April), pp. 159–68.

Criticizes a cost formula employed by a regulatory agency in the light of an analysis of cost structure, applying the theory of peak-load pricing.

Select Committee on Nationalised Industries. Over the years this committee has presented a stream of reports and minutes of evidence to the House of Commons on one nationalized industry after another. They are all published by Her Majesty's Stationery Office, London.

W. G. Shepherd, *Economic performance under public ownership*, Yale University Press, 1965.

A study of the British fuel and power industries.

W. G. Shepherd and T. G. Gies, *Utility regulation: New directions in theory and policy*, Random House 1966. Eight papers on American utility regulation.

Acknowledgements

Permission to reproduce the readings in this volume is acknowledged from the following sources:

Reading 1 Nancy D. Ruggles and the *Review of Economic Studies*

Reading 2 Michael Farrell, *Oxford Economic Papers* and the Clarendon Press, Oxford

Reading 3 Oliver E. Williamson and the American Economic Association

Reading 4 P. D. Henderson and Basil Blackwell & Mott Ltd

Reading 5 T. W. Berrie and *Electrical Review*

Reading 6 J. J. Warford and *The Manchester School*

Reading 7 Arthur D. Hazlewood and the *Review of Economic Studies*

Reading 8 Thomas Nelson & Sons Ltd

Reading 9 J. Keith Horsefield and Basil Blackwell & Mott Ltd

Reading 10 William G. Shepherd and the Clarendon Press, Oxford

Reading 11 William G. Shepherd, the *Journal of Industrial Economics* and Basil Blackwell & Mott Ltd

Reading 12 The *Journal of Political Economy* and the University of Chicago Press

Author Index

381

Subject Index

387

Penguin Modern Economics

Other titles available in this series are:

Economics of Education 1
Ed. M. Blaug

The quality of the labour force and the methods of training it
have recently attracted the attention of economists. The
education system is an important factor in economic growth, the
degree of mobility of labour and the distribution of income. These
important issues are considered in this volume of articles. A
second volume, also edited by Professor Blaug, will examine the
internal efficiency of schools and the relations between the costs
of education and methods of financing these costs. These Readings
will be widely welcomed by educationists, sociologists and
political scientists as well as economists. X56

The Labour Market
Ed. B. J. McCormick and E. Owen Smith

'Workers cannot be bought and sold, and people cannot be
disassociated from their services.' This is the starting-point for
an analysis of the workings of the labour market. Wages are a
means of allocating labour and a source of income, and
considerations of efficiency frequently clash with equity criteria.
This volume of Readings throws light on the efficiency of the
wage system as an allocator of labour, the effects of trade unions
and the role of the labour market in the problem of inflation. X55

Managerial Economics
Ed. G. P. E. Clarkson

The growth, range and complexity of problems facing the modern
corporation mean that many managers must acquire new skills.
Managerial economics deals with the process of decision-making
within the firm. It uses the economist's concepts of utility and
maximizing of profit to analyse with mathematical and
statistical techniques a wide range of problems of finance,
marketing and production. X57

Regional Analysis
Ed. L. Needleman

Appalachia, Northern Ireland, and Mezzogiorno are witnesses to the uneven geography of economic development. Indeed they may seem part of an 'underdeveloped' world. The application of the tools of economic analysis to regional problems has only just begun: the editor offers here a full range of regional work on one of the most interesting and exciting areas of economic inquiry. X60

Transport
Ed. Denys Munby

'There is no escape from transport.' 'Almost every transport decision is a public issue.' These two challenging statements form the prelude to a collection of articles devoted to the economics of transport. The quality of the analysis and prescriptions is dictated by Dupuit's article and proceeds through Lewis, Vickrey, Walters, Meyer, and Foster. All demonstrate the important contribution economists can make to the analysis of transport problems and the formulation of appropriate policies. X58

Economic Philosophy

Joan Robinson

This exceptionally stimulating book begins by showing how the
basic human need for a morality on which the conscience can
work has led to the necessity for a philosophy of economics
in any society. It is stressed that economic values and money
values are not identical and it is the task of the economist to
justify the image of Mammon to man – 'not to tell us what to
do, but show why what we are doing anyway is in accord with
proper principles'. The relations between science and ideology
over the last two hundred years are traced from Adam Smith,
through Marx and Keynes, to the dichotomy that exists in
current economic thinking and the pressing fundamental problems
which must now be faced.

'It would be difficult to think of a better book than this to
place in the hands of the reader who thinks that economics is
simply a matter of statistics, and who needs to be convinced of
its intellectual interest and excitement.' Samuel Brittan in the
Observer   A 653/3s. 6d.

Traffic in Towns

The specially shortened edition of the Buchanan Report

'We are nourishing a monster of great potential
destructiveness.' The motor-car is the menace that prompted
Professor Colin Buchanan's famous report, *Traffic in Towns*.
This is the most comprehensive, objective, and radical
examination of urban traffic and its effect on the conditions of
urban living that has ever been made. Because of its profuse
illustrations, the H.M.S.O. edition of *Traffic in Towns* had
necessarily to be published at £2 10s. This Penguin edition is a
condensation which has been approved by Professor Buchanan
and which omits none of the main arguments or conclusions of
the report. It permits this important document to appear at a
price at which a very much wider public can comprehend the
gigantic and terrifyingly urgent task with which Britain is now
faced. S228/10s. 6d.